Muslims in Global Politics

Pennsylvania Studies in Human Rights

Bert B. Lockwood, Jr., Series Editor

A complete list of books in the series is available from the publisher.

Muslims in Global Politics

Identities, Interests, and Human Rights

Mahmood Monshipouri

PENN

University of Pennsylvania Press
Philadelphia

Published by
University of Pennsylvania Press
Philadelphia, Pennsylvania 19104-4112

Printed in the United States of America on acid-free paper

10   9   8   7   6   5   4   3   2   1

Library of Congress Cataloging-in-Publication Data

Monshipouri, Mahmood, 1952–
   Muslims in global politics : identities, interests, and human rights / Mahmood Monshipouri.
     p. cm. — (Pennsylvania studies in human rights)
   Includes bibliographical references and index.
   ISBN 978-0-8122-4181-5 (alk. paper)
    1. Islamic countries—Politics and government—21st century. 2. Muslims—Europe—Political activity. 3. Islam and politics. 4. Human rights—Religious aspects—Islam. I. Title.
JQ1852.A58M66 2009
323.3—dc22

                                        2009005891

Contents

Preface: Muslims' Struggles for Identities, Interests, and Human Rights   vii

1.   Muslims' Quest for Identities, Interests, and Human Rights   1

2.   International Human Rights Norms and Muslim Experiences   25

3.   Gender, Identity, and Negotiating Rights   47

4.   Searching for a Modern Islamic Identity in Egypt   73

5.   Occupation, Sectarianism, and Identity Politics in Iraq   100

6.   The Melding of the Old and New in the United Arab Emirates   121

7.   Secularism, Turkish Islam, and Identity   139

8.   The Reemergence of Populism in Iranian Politics: Constructing New Identities   165

9.   Negotiating Modernity and Tradition in Indonesia   192

10.   Construction of Muslims in Europe: The Politics of Immigration   217

Conclusion: Identities, Interests, and Human Rights   243

Notes   263

Glossary   315

Index   321

Acknowledgments   327

Muslims' Struggles for Identities, Interests, and Human Rights

The concerns that led to this book were both academic and personal. My academic interests and involvement in trying to understand the ways in which human rights can be enhanced in the Muslim world date back to the 1980s, when a wave of Islamic revivalism throughout the Muslim world resulted in a profound transformation in perceptions, attitudes, and behaviors of many Muslims, living in both the homeland and the diaspora. My earlier research involved aspects of continuity and change, modernity and tradition, the emergence of civil society, and the discourse surrounding secular versus Islamic movements. In my subsequent research, I became interested in the impacts of globalization on Muslims' attempt to accommodate shifting identities and their search for new interests and sources of power while raising dissenting voices against their inept and abusive governments. Not surprisingly, resistance to both national governments and external powers in the Muslim world has found deep resonance with human rights campaigns. My personal curiosity about and deep commitment to the study of human rights and democratization in the Muslim world are both emotional and rational.

As globalization permeates different societies, the debate intensifies over how to develop self-assertion, recognition, and new meanings in life. Integral to the definition of culture in a globalizing world is the desire for recognition and determining how to coexist with those of different cultures. Arguably, recognition rather than self-assertion constitutes the culture's most hopeful posture. The quest for authenticity in the pursuit of solutions to socioeconomic, political, and cultural problems (in this volume, most often referred to as cultural politics) has become inseparable from power politics. Muslims' cultures, identities, and interests are dynamic and evolving. Reform-minded Islamists have proven capable of creating hybrids potent enough to challenge existing regimes.

Militant Islamists, in contrast, have either rejected or confronted any intermingling with and exposure to outside cultures. U.S. policies in pursuing the war on terrorism since 2001 have played a key role in elevating resistance and defiance. The rise of Shiism, with its emphasis on the power of beliefs, jihad, and sacrifice, has created a pan-Islamic identity of resistance that is fast spreading throughout the Middle East. Cultural dialogues and exchanges, as well as transnational ties and interests, are likely to empower Muslims and change the way they construct images of the self and the other. When combined with the absorption of new ideas and norms, such exchanges could change domestic structures within which identities, interests, and capabilities are formed.

Globalization has created both limitations and opportunities for cultural politics. A new transnational identity in the form of religiosity—with no attachment to a particular culture—has emerged in the Muslim diaspora in the West and elsewhere. Gender issues, by contrast, have renewed the debate over cultural politics in many Muslim countries. Both reformists and militants have used international law and internationally recognized human rights to promote their ideological and strategic goals. The upshot has been a world of multiple identities, each staking out a claim to authenticity and legitimacy.

This book argues that the task of winning the "hearts and minds" of Muslims throughout the world must be based on certain corrective measures. To offer an alternative to the agenda of Islamic militants (jihadis), who are in fact a tiny minority of the world's 1.2 billion Muslims, the United States and Europe must recognize several realities. The corrective to militant Islamism is to integrate mainstream (moderate) Islamists into the political process of their respective countries. In the cases of Jordan, Turkey, and Yemen, political integration has been the key to reducing violence caused by militant Islamic groups. Islamists themselves are increasingly outspoken about the need for democracy and human rights. The opening of previously closed societies to freedom of the press, civic activism, and electoral competition has served to moderate Islamist political movements—as the 2003 elections in Turkey demonstrated. Without inclusionary politics, the radicals in Islamist movements can often prevail in rationalizing their own exclusionary version of politics.

Finally, effective democratic reforms and state building—that is, establishing strong, legitimate, and successful states—in the Muslim world are likely to diminish the possibilities of growth for the radical Islamic groups. The Western world can help in this endeavor by not imposing its vision.

Pushing for its preferences is likely to lead to a nationalist backlash, which could further intensify the link between religion, culture, and politics. Local politics and attitudes will play an important role in the place Islam will have in Muslim countries' laws. Islamic law is applied in broadly different ways, as we will see in the following chapters, across the Muslim world. Identity-based politics, both locally and globally, are the key to understanding why this is the case. The surest way to advance stability and progress toward democracy in the Muslim world is to incorporate Islamic reformists into the political and legal systems. No longer can identity politics be separated from the articulation of social justice and human rights issues in the Muslim world.

This volume is a comparative examination of similarities and differences between Egypt, Indonesia, Iran, Iraq, Turkey, and the United Arab Emirates, whose people seek new identities and interests. In Egypt, Islamists and secularists have conflicting religious and national identities. Such tensions have significantly subsided in Turkey, as the ruling elites have opted for coexistence between these groups in the name of democracy and national reconciliation. In Iran, the tensions between Islamic groups—that is, traditionalists, reformists, and militants—have come to a head, with a great majority of people supporting reformists' notions of identities, interests, and human rights.

The conservatives and modernists in the United Arab Emirates (UAE), in contrast, have reached a broadly based consensus on promoting economic growth. To achieve this, people's civil liberties and basic rights have been marginalized. The UAE government has pursued this policy without having to provide democratic freedoms for its citizens. In Iraq, the presence of occupying forces and the fear of instability after the U.S. invasion of that country have intensified national, ethnic, and sectarian identities. In such circumstances, the Iraqi people's aspirations have been shaped largely along national and sectarian lines rather than by democratic forces. It is not difficult to understand why the Bush administration's project of democracy promotion has encountered serious setbacks.

In the post-Suharto era, most Indonesian Muslims do not appear to be in favor of implementing a formalist and legalistic conception of the shari'a, preferring to stress its ethical and social justice aspects. Given the country's ethnic, religious, and cultural diversity, the vast majority of Indonesian Muslims are steadily moderate in their political views. This moderation renders negotiating between modern and traditional praxis not only feasible but sustainable in the long run.

The Muslim diasporas in Europe find assimilation problematic in some cases while at the same time hoping for political and cultural liberation in the land of the "other." In the face of globalizing forces, they struggle to strike a balance between maintaining the integrity of their culture, faith, and language and adjusting to the forces of change. The younger generations of Muslim immigrants seek new identities and rights. Born and raised in Europe, these second- and third-generation Muslims have reactions to living in Europe that are contradictory: they are both hopeful and skeptical. While some deny the legitimacy of both European values and the values of their parents, others attempt to solve the tension between their newly acquired citizenship and their faith. The latter group tends to emphasize *ijtihad* (independent reasoning) by questioning the dichotomy between reason and revelation.

The issues of identity and interests are worth closer scrutiny, especially in the face of the apparent contradictions of globalization (e.g., the simultaneous fragmentation and interconnectedness of cultures) and the mind-boggling pace with which change is unfolding on the global scene. Given that Islam is the fastest-growing religion in the world, this book addresses an often-asked question: How will the Muslims living in both the homeland and diasporic communities in Europe and North America come to grips with shifting identities and interests? The study of identity construction, which is a more complex feature of globalization, rightfully is concerned with the extent to which social structures and cultural politics determine dominant interests. There is a complex but consistent view of how identity formation can be used to advance our understanding of international relations. It is important that we not stop at merely understanding identity as one's self-definition, in-group membership, or recognition, but that we place identity in a larger context and explore it in relation to power relations/dynamics, nationalism, developmentalism, human rights, and social justice. Viewed from this perspective, identity is relevant to and an integral part of international relations.

Equally critical to this volume's main thrust is Muslims' growing demands for democratic rights and internationally recognized human rights. To the extent that Muslims' demands relate to human rights, their ruling elites have yet to solve the issue of what is properly "universal" and what is properly "cultural." Moreover, globalization has further intensified the struggle over who is to define modernity, authenticity, legitimacy, and rationality. Muslim experts as well as laymen will find this volume helpful in gaining a better understanding of how globalization works and/or affects their society. The book will also appeal to scholars with interests in international and area studies. Likewise, the implications of this study will be of particular interest to policy makers who have seen the dramatic changes of the post–Cold War era—a period of extraordinary change in the world, especially since 1991. Never before have scholarship and policy-making been so closely tied to each other as well as to the real world. We live in a highly complex and evolving world that requires a fuller and deeper understanding of how modern ideas, rules, and institutions interact and, better yet, how different societies adjust themselves to emerging realities. I have tried in this book to convey such a new understanding in a clear and systematic way.

Structure of the Book

The book's theoretical parts (Chapters 1–3) broaden and sharpen our analytical view of culture and identity as factors that help define the interests of Muslims on the global scene. Chapter 1 introduces conceptual and theoretical frameworks. Different constructions of identity (ethnicity, religion, language, and nation) have become the cornerstone of debate. What is identity? How is it constructed and reconstructed within the context of globalization? And why is it important? These are among the central questions in the contemporary Muslim world. Chapter 2 examines Muslims' reactions to emerging and evolving international norms. In this chapter, I present a fourfold typology of Muslims (conservatives, neofundamentalists, reformists, and secularists) to show how they construct their identities as agents, what sites they use, and what strategies they adopt.

Special attention is paid to Muslim women's struggle for identity and human rights in Chapter 3. Here I argue that "borderless solidarity" has led to the promotion of women's rights across and within cultures. Having contextualized gender analysis in the cultural, economic, and political domains, this section then examines why Muslim women have become the agents of change, reform, and democratization in a globalizing world.

The case studies are presented in the chapters that follow. The countries examined in Chapters 4 through 9 were selected for geographic representation and relevance. Three cases—Egypt, Iraq, and the UAE—were chosen to represent the Arab Middle East and North Africa. One country (Egypt) represents the oldest Muslim civilization, another (Iraq) is a country under occupation, and the last (UAE) is a young and culturally conservative country that has become the hub of the world's growing international trade and foreign investment. Chapter 4 examines the struggles between secularist and Islamist movements in Egypt, which vie over constructing identity and gaining power in that country. Although cultural Islam has become a symbol of resistance to globalization, political Islam is searching for a middle ground in national politics. At the same time, mainstream Islamic forces have increasingly transformed themselves into a more accommodating force at the national level.

In Chapter 5, I explain how the U.S. occupation of Iraq has succeeded in destroying a sense of nation and nation-based identity. While some Iraqis continue to see their future in terms of their religion and a larger Arab identity, others rely on cultural traditions, family nexus, and tribal associations. The resurgence of Islamic culture and identity is bound to shape the future of Iraqi Shia politics whereas Sunni resistance will most likely be directed at both the surge of Shiite power and U.S. occupying forces. In the Kurdish north, Kurdish clans and their leaders appear unlikely to merge with other Sunni Arab Islamist movements in the foreseeable future as long as Kurdish aspirations are not met and a distinct nationalist cause remains among the Kurds.

Chapter 6, on the United Arab Emirates, is designed to unveil the unique character of state and society while revealing the formation of new but contradictory identities among the people of this country. The process of social change in UAE society has been paradoxical. Just as the country's oil revenues and economic development have initially undermined the traditional life of the indigenous people, they have also strengthened the position of the advocates of local cultural traditions.

The discussions on Iran and Turkey are of particular relevance largely because these are two Muslim countries in which Islamists hold sway, even as they pursue different paths to globalization and identity politics. Chapter 7 deals with the way Turkey is struggling to carve out a new national identity for itself. Turkey's pragmatic desire to become a member of the European Union (EU) could redefine the meaning and values associated with the country's Islamic and Western identities. Islamists in Turkey are constructively engaged with the EU in order to advance their modernization project.

Chapter 8 highlights the revival of populism in Iranian politics and the process by which it has generated new forms of identities and agencies. I attribute the cyclical rise and fall of Islamic populism to economic decay following the growth of social freedoms, political reforms, and civil society during Khatami's two-term presidency. The above case studies represent a mix of both the oldest civilizations and cultural entities in the Muslim world (e.g., Egypt, Iran, and Turkey) and the youngest nation-states (Iraq and the United Arab Emirates), which gained their independence after the British Mandate ended or when Britain withdrew from the Persian Gulf region.

In Chapter 9, I turn to Indonesia as a multiethnic state that has had serious concerns about the uneven impact of globalization on its populace, with its ethnic Chinese minority benefiting most from it. This chapter demonstrates how the issue of globalization has weakened the government and undermined the country's national identity and social cohesion. The last case study, Chapter 10, deals with transnational identities and their impact on Muslim migrants in Europe. In this chapter, I examine different types of identity formation (separate but equal, different but equal, respect and recognition, and resistance and protest) as well as different European models (assimilation and multiculturalism) to deal with the immigration issue.

The Conclusion provides a comparative commentary on the relationship between political context, identity formation, and promotion of universal rights. Here I return to the fourfold typology of Muslims' accommodation of and resistance to evolving international standards introduced in Chapter 2 with a view toward providing a general framework for understanding identity politics in the Muslim world. The chapter ends by arguing that Muslim identities are multiple, fluid, and contentious and that the construction of identity is influenced by the various and complex ways in which local cultures and globalization interact.

The book's intent is not to provide an exhaustive study of the Muslim world. Rather, at the heart of this volume lies the desire to contribute to our understanding of identity politics and the way in which engagement in culture-based politics could affect human rights. The exclusion of the Maghreb countries (Tunisia, Morocco, and Algeria) and other Asian countries, such as Bangladesh and Malaysia, had much to do with practical choices that had to be made in relation to space, priority, and the lack of financial support to travel to these countries. The exclusion of these cases was by no means intended to slight their importance.

Let us briefly acknowledge what would be gained if additional countries were considered. Although Islamists have made considerable adjustment to modernizing pressures in some Muslim countries, they have leaned toward militancy in others. Islamists, for example, have assumed top positions in countries like Pakistan and Tunisia and have played an active part in secular political processes in Malaysia. In Tanzania, Islamists have pushed to expand radical versions of Islamic law by attacking bars and beating women they thought inadequately dressed. Similarly, the rise of radical Islamism in Moroccan politics and society has posed a serious challenge to the nation's democratic reform. Diversity, tolerance, and a relatively liberal brand of Islam, which have for decades characterized Morocco, now face a looming threat from the surging Salafist and radical Islamists. These groups' activities will surely have negative consequences for the country's politics of moderation and inclusion, with moderate Islamists and their party (Justice and Development Party—PJD) having much to lose in the process.

Similarly, in Bangladesh, a country generally known for its democratic politics and democratic notions of citizenship, cultural pluralism, tolerance of political dissent, and the great strides it has made toward economic and human development, we have recently seen the rise of Islamist militants. This surge in militancy has exacerbated the problems stemming from ideology-based politics. This development, along with deterioration in the rule of law and human rights conditions caused by two predominant nationalist parties, has led to a deepening crisis in governance. Together, these tensions have undermined the democratic atmosphere that the vast majority of Bangladeshis have enjoyed in recent decades. The study of all these diverse political contexts and how they affect people's identities and their struggles toward gaining freedom is beyond the scope of this book.

It should be noted that the information regarding all case studies in this book is current as of the spring of 2009. The situation in Iraq is evolving, and the outcome of the upcoming Iranian presidential elections remains entirely unpredictable.

Chapter 1

Muslims' Quest for Identities, Interests, and Human Rights

The interplay between market forces, transnational flows, and social relations is a complex and evolving process that is fraught with paradoxes. Nowhere are such complexities and contradictions more apparent today than in the construction of diverse and multiple identities in the imagination of people. Indeed, globalization has precipitated global solidarity on the one hand while facilitating fractionalizing, identity-based politics on the other.

Western powers have typically equated the notion of globalization with the attempt to extensively penetrate and reform non-Western cultures.[1] Globalization is seen by some in non-Western societies as a form of domination and by others as an emancipatory process. While globalization has led to the emergence of new structures and dynamics of cooperation between nation-states, the same cannot be said about its impact in the intrastate contexts, where globalization has empowered the individual vis-à-vis the state, the market, and third parties. Whereas globalization is perceived by the West as a dominant set of ideas and a policy framework, many in non-Western societies contest it as a false universalism.[2] That explains why globalization has often evoked a reaction in individuals in some non-Western societies to define themselves as part of an identified group, such as a nation or a religious community. Despite the profound sociocultural transformations brought about by globalization, religious identity has had an enormous metaphoric value, resilience, and staying power. "Religious symbols and languages may become invested with new meanings," writes Peter Mandaville, "but they still function to provide a framework of familiarity and a sense of identity."[3]

By the close of the twentieth century, the quest for identity had become integral to understanding the global dynamics of power politics, cultural politics, gender politics, and ethnic politics in the Muslim world. With more than one billion adherents throughout the world, Islam is the largest and the most forceful of the cultural rivals to the Western-centric values of globalization. As a religion, Islam is not immutable and travels well across time and borders. Islam provides an alternative moral and political vision to that presented by the globally dominant West.[4]

Although identity process is purposely constructed in some cases, it is a response to situational pressures in other cases. It is not the same for elite actors as for the common individual. The process is very dynamic and constantly in flux. This chapter offers an overview of trends of identity-based politics in the postwar period. It then examines the connection between modernization programs and legitimacy crises in the Muslim world. In the following section, we explore the role of Islam in identity construction utilizing three levels of analysis: Islam as a religious identity (individual level); Islam as a political force (national level); and Islam as a transnational force or space (global level).

In the following section, we analyze the implications for the Muslim world of the post–September 11 era and the U.S.-led invasion of Iraq. Special attention will be given to the nongeographic nature of identity formation as well as the postcolonial context. The chapter concludes by providing alternatives in view of Muslims' search for identities and interests. Lack of attention to the link between identity, interests, and human rights drives the need for rethinking the notion of identity—that is, the desire for belonging and recognition.

Identity Defined

To define concepts such as self-image, beliefs, values, group affiliations, and competing identities has become crucial to an in-depth understanding of the highly complex and evolving politics of the Muslim world. The analysis of different ways in which identities are constructed also helps us make sense of any given situation. This chapter represents an effort to contextualize the components of identity in order to answer three questions: What is identity? How is it constructed? And why is it important?

Identity may simply be defined as the extent to which an individual is aware of herself or himself. This self-understanding, which relates to self-esteem, self-image, and self-reflection, consists generally of those properties that render an individual unique and different from others. How a person defines herself or himself may, therefore, be viewed in relation to certain core values and convictions that broadly structure the individual's life. While psychologists use the term "identity" to describe personal individuality, sociologists tend to use the term to describe the group memberships that define the individual.

Political scientists, in contrast, emphasize social identity as the way that individuals portray and situate themselves as members of particular groups. The social identity can be based on class, language, race, ethnicity, religion, gender, and subnational/subcultural, national, and transnational status. The collectively formed identity as such is shaped and transformed not only through interaction and negotiation with others within that group but also in relation to outsiders and the outside world more generally. Throughout history, the development and dynamics of competing national identities (Palestinians and Israelis) and competing subnational identities (e.g., the Kurds) have affected how people define themselves. The Kurds in northern Iraq, as a minority ethnic group, have stressed an ethnic identity to distinguish themselves from both the Sunni Arab minority and the Shiite Arab majority. The Kurds' separate linguistic-cultural identity on the one hand and political identity on the other have overshadowed their religious identity.

Since the disintegration of the Ottoman Empire, the Kurds have intensified their struggle for self-determination. A combination of internal and external factors, including their socioeconomic marginalization and unequal center-periphery relations in Iran, Iraq, and Turkey, has dashed their hopes. Unlike Iran and Iraq, where the Kurds received official recognition, in Turkey they were for a long time the subject of officially sanctioned discrimination and neglect.[5] Clearly, the construction of Kurdish identity has been affected by such factors as socioeconomic and political exclusion. Despite worldwide support for the principle of self-determination, Iran, Iraq, and Turkey have resisted separatist claims and instead supported the territorial status quo.[6]

Although most Kurds are Sunni Muslims, they are not generally overly religious. There is, however, an enormous religious diversity among the Kurds. Sheikhs continue to play a key role in both religious and political domains in rural areas. As in the rest of the Muslim world, Islamist forces have been gaining prominence among a minority of Kurds.[7] Some Kurdish intellectuals have argued that Kurdish ethnicity is a constant factor that predated Islam and will outlast all religions. Furthermore, they have insisted that the Islamic religion was imposed on the Kurds by violence and that Arabs used Islam to wipe out the Kurds.[8]

Since the U.S. invasion of Iraq, public opinion for Kurdish independence has continued to grow throughout northern Iraq, in large part because order has collapsed in the face of increased armed resistance from Sunni Arabs. In the meantime, U.S. policies have contributed to the processes of state formation among the Kurds, even as the United States has pursued policies to recreate a multiethnic and multireligious state within the *unified* polity.[9]

In other contexts, religion has proven to be a much more significant marker of identity than ethnicity. Today's Shia-Sunni rift in Iraq and resultant sectarian conflict are typical.[10] This conflict, Vali Nasr points out, has been built around two things: (1) it is a struggle between competing theologies and conceptions of the sacred history of Islam and (2) it is also a manifestation of tribal wars of ethnicities and identities—wars with both historical and contemporary roots that are emblematic of clashes of identities. Theological and historical dispute intensify it, but so do today's claims to power and concerns with subjugation, freedom, social justice, and equality—not to mention regional conflicts and foreign plots. In short, faith and identity converge in this paradoxical conflict, which is very old, yet very modern.[11] Historical, theological, and religious differences between the two, like race or language, define what makes each identity unique and determine who belongs to it and who does not.[12]

The broader discourse about the concept of identity in contemporary international relations has traditionally focused on the nation-state as a predominant frame of reference, ideology, and site of identity.[13] The independence and sovereignty of the nation-state is a matter of degree[14] and has been in decline in the post–Cold War era. Group identities other than nation have increasingly asserted themselves as protagonists for the acquisition and accumulation of political power in the global arena. Consequently, it has become imperative to adapt to the increasing salience of cleavages in ethnicity, gender, civilization, development, and religion that are increasingly recognized as sources of social and political power.[15]

Identity is socially constructed. The principles, norms, and practices of international human rights regimes are internalized and implemented domestically through a process of *socialization*. Networks of national and transnational actors alter domestic structures within which identities are constructed. As Thomas Risse and Kathryn Sikkink argue, identities create a measure of inclusion and exclusion by defining a social "we" and delineating the boundaries against the "others." Norms become operative during the process by which actors define and modify their collective identities and interests.[16]

In thinking about identity construction, we need to bear in mind that agency and environment are mutually constitutive. Identities affect the domestic and international environments, and these environments in turn affect the *behavior* of actors, the contingent *properties* of actors (identities, interests, and capabilities), and the *existence* of actors altogether.[17] Cultural and institutional elements—that is, norms—shape identity as well as the national security interests or policies of states. Put succinctly, states' properties are significantly constructed by these environments.[18] To better illustrate this point, Nicholas Onuf grants ontological parity to such an interaction: "neither agents as members of society, nor society as the totality of agents and their relations, come first."[19]

Identities are contextual and relational—the product of their own times and circumstances. They must always be understood in relation to sociocultural and political settings. Identities are dynamic and constantly in flux. And identities are about difference. They constantly acquire new meanings and are subject to reinterpretation. They are situated, as one analyst suggests, in unequal and invariably renegotiated contexts: "it is the relationship—if not the interpenetration—of groups that permits the blossoming and evolution of cultural diversity."[20]

For a nuanced understanding of identity formation in the Muslim world, one must appreciate that a myriad of actors and relationships are implicated in the construction of identity, including state and nonstate actors as well as agents inside and outside the identity community.[21] As a result of broader access to higher education and mass communication, larger numbers of Muslims have participated in the reconstruction of religion, community, and society. Nongovernmental organizations (NGOs) and globalization from below have also provided a major impetus for change.

The unprecedented rise in human consciousness and interconnectedness brought by globalization has resulted in more links and broader contacts with other groups and cultures and has often resulted in the evolution of multiple and overlapping identities. This process has linked individual identity to global cultural and institutional elements. Gone are the days when parochial and localized religious institutions and leaders could control what their adherents know and what they think.[22]

And finally, identity is an important concept because it allows us to analyze how individuals' personal, social, institutional beliefs, values, and affiliations affect their views and the way in which they respond to different situations (crisis and conflict). In situations where minorities face adversity, identity can be an empowering tool. In the case of socioeconomic exclusion and political, racial, and ethnic discrimination, identity may provide solidarity and longevity. For some Muslim women who reside in the West, wearing the *hijab* (headscarf) can be an empowering statement of individual and collective Islamic identity. For Muslim migrants who have a lower social status in a class-divided society such as that of France, Islamic revival provides a point of opposition. Some studies demonstrate that young French women perceive the *hijab* "as an autonomous expression of their identity and not as a form of domination."[23] European Muslims define identity as an aspect of their self-definition and self-determination. That explains why they use the concepts of human rights and minority rights to advance their values and consequently express those in a Western legal and constitutional manner. Muslim women who are not allowed to wear the *hijab* in schools or at work go to court claiming discrimination. Therein lies the significance of the notion of identity, especially when or if it is linked to human rights.

Trends of Identity-Based Politics

Contemporary Muslim states developed in the shadow of European colonialism that fundamentally shaped their ruling elites' attitude toward politics, society, and governance. Anticolonial thinkers and activists throughout the Muslim world have since invoked Islam in their struggle for liberation. Following World War II, there has been an inexorable trend in Muslim societies toward reasserting their identity and defining their own space. In the last quarter of the twentieth century, however, this search for political representation has led Islamic movements to push for control of the state. This persistent political activism by Islamists, articulated largely within the context of the struggle against colonialism, has precluded secular nationalists from retaining the dominant role in the politics of the Muslim world.[24]

At the same time that globalization has helped spread norms and values (albeit of Western origin) throughout the world, it has also given local and regional cultures an opportunity to express themselves. The result has been the simultaneous fragmentation and interconnectedness of cultures.[25] This new interconnectedness of a geographically dispersed community has given rise to Islamic revivalism in the Muslim world and has reawakened the notion of discovering oneself and the consciousness of the Muslim self. To survive the paradoxes of globalization, Islamic groups have offered their followers an opportunity to reconstruct their identity by reassuring them of the global breadth of their feeling for belonging.[26]

To better understand the contemporary trends of identity-based and cultural politics in the Muslim world, we must place the evolution of postwar politics into context. The Muslims' struggles in the postcolonial era, as in many parts of the developing world, have taken several different forms and phases. The first phase began in the late 1940s and marked an era when Muslim ruling elites stressed nationalism and the role of the state in national development. To enter the global power equation, Muslims turned to modernity and became preoccupied with building modern infrastructure.

In the 1970s, the collapse of modernization programs in the Muslim world more generally but in the Middle Eastern and North African countries more particularly marked the second phase. This was the period when Muslims attempted to upgrade their own political, cultural, and ideological assets by Islamizing their societies. The resurgent Islam became the most influential aspect of sociocultural and political change across the Muslim world. Mass media were in place and operating for the 1979 Islamic Revolution in Iran, leading to a solid encounter of globalization and Muslim identity. The revolution provided a spark for cultural resurgence that attempted to create a genuine parity of cultures with the West on the global scene. Cultural revivalism and resistance to Western cultures were the principal message of the Iranian revolution, introducing a new context to the conventional study of world politics.

With the end of the Cold War, globalization became the distinguishing feature of world politics, including its opposite face of broadening the scope of formerly localized and isolated cultures, particularly those of nationalism and religion.[27] Although globalization appeared to have solidified the myth of cultural homogeneity, it also unleashed less foreseen facets of intercultural exchange.[28] It was under such circumstances that the Muslim world entered its third phase of adjustment by underscoring the importance of its cultural traditions and its distinctiveness.

As the processes of globalization intensify, the question arises: How will these trends and transformations affect Muslim societies' views of authenticity, modernity, and legitimacy in the years to come? To answer this question, we must revisit the failures of modernizing and secularizing programs as pursued by the Muslim world's ruling elites in the twentieth century. It is important to realize, however, that the growth of Islamic tendencies is a modern version of resistance or hybridity—not a rejection of modernity per se. While the resistance reflects the tenacity of the Islamic militants, hybridity suggests the efforts of reformists and transnational forces to blend diverse cultural and social milieus.

Secularization, Modernization, and Legitimation Crises

Secularization is often perceived as the process by which the Christian West split religion from politics. The origins of this process are traced to Christ's oft-quoted words "Render therefore unto Caesar the things which are Caesar's and unto God the things that are God's." Muslims, in contrast, have fused religion and politics in an attempt to maintain their unique cultural identity worldwide. This approach has endured a checkered history: a period of decline and external domination followed by the recent reassertion. Muslim leaders and ruling elites have been preoccupied with the nature of state- and nation-building, the absorption of social change, and the adjustment to, or backlash against, the processes of secularization by which property, power, and prestige are passed from religious to lay control. Today, the term "secularization" refers to the process by which religious institutions have been relieved of their economic, political, and social influence in the state context.[29]

Recently, the secularization process has led to a religious revivalist backlash in the Christian as well as the Muslim world. In the Western tradition, religious revivalist movements did not necessarily confront secular orientations and traditions. In the Muslim world, by contrast, there has been an upsurge in antisecular movements even in those societies long exposed to modernization (for example, Turkey). Although modernization has not resulted in secularization throughout the Muslim world, it is viewed as a universal concept over which no single civilization or culture has monopoly. The assumption that Muslim countries will ineluctably grow more secular as they are exposed to Western notions of rationality and progress has proven unfounded. The secularization process has failed to deepen in the Muslim world and in fact has instead contributed to the resurgence of Islam. While a small group of leaders has adopted a Western secular worldview, the vast majority of Muslims have not embraced a secular perspective.[30]

Islam has not experienced a reformation analogous to that of Protestantism in Western Christianity. Islamic movements have sought to purify

Islam of worldly and heretical influences by reinforcing Islamic authority over society and law. Whereas in Europe the secularization process was gradual and proceeded alongside steady socioeconomic growth, in the Muslim world it was often viewed as an externally imposed agenda emblematic of European strategic interests. While in the Muslim world secularization preceded religious reformation, in the European case it resulted more or less from such reformation.

In the Muslim world, secularism resulted entirely from European contact and influence. Many Middle Eastern countries adopted secular legislation, inspired mostly by European models, on a wide range of civil and criminal matters. The modernizing experiences of many Middle Eastern cities were typified by urban sprawl, decaying sociocultural fabric, high unemployment rates, poverty, poor services, and frustrated expectations.[31] Economic failures of assorted kinds undermined modernizing secular states and culminated in the emergence of the countervailing force in Muslim societies: Islamic revivalism.

Resurging Islam captured the imagination of the alienated, the poor, disgruntled groups, the young, and even the educated classes, including engineers, doctors, teachers, and lawyers. "Islam," as one observer noted, "offered a return to the equality and self-worth of the believer community."[32] Islamists questioned those values and practices associated with modernization, including materialism, consumerism, individualism, and moral laxity. The Islamization of social life in Muslim societies was evident in the extent to which Islamic groups influenced and shaped such matters as law, education, welfare provision, and moral standards.[33]

Recent calls for democratic participation (in Algeria and among Shiites and the Kurds in Iraq since the U.S. occupation) by Islamic groups show that Islamism is not antithetical to democratization and modernity. Mustapha Kamal Pasha puts it aptly: "Islamicists are modern, but without the baggage of secularism."[34] In a world of Western hegemony and globalization, as one expert reminds us, we should not underestimate the diffuse counterhegemony of Islamic grassroots and social values. "The battle for culture," Simon W. Murden writes, "was being fought in the homes, streets, shops, mosques, and workplaces of the Muslim world, and it was on these battlefields that Islam was at its most powerful."[35]

Although Muslim societies became increasingly Islamized, Muslim politics remained mostly secularized. The latter was caught between bargaining with Islamic demands and maintaining its secular nature. The bargain precluded social upheavals, but it was so contradictory that it brought

Muslim societies to a standstill. In sum, Muslim politics became "the politics of paralysis."[36] Today, genuine democratic change appears to be the only real option for a resolution of such paralysis. Since the 1970s and Iran's Islamic Revolution, a key question has been whether the struggle between Islamic reformists and Islamic conservatives is legal or political. Arguably the struggle between the two is both political and legal. Both reformists and conservatives have governed most Muslim countries since they gained independence from Western colonial rule.

Emphasizing the separation of religion and politics, these leaders extensively secularized their legal and educational systems. Some nationalists, such as Atatürk, Nasser, and both the Reza Shah and Mohammad Reza Shah, adopted aggressive secularization methods and programs. Others, such as Sadat and Zulfaqar Ali Bhutto, manipulated Islamic symbols and pursued a more subtle and circumspect approach to secularization. Current secular leaders of the Middle East, including King Abdullah, King Hussein II, Qaddafi, Mubarak, and Musharraf, have taken different approaches to secularize their legal and educational institutions.

A variety of governments—including monarchies, military dictatorships, and liberal authoritarian regimes—ruled Egypt for most of the twentieth century. They faced occasional challenges and threats from the Muslim Brotherhood and other Islamic organizations. In both Iran and Turkey, the imposition of a laic state from the top has backfired, resulting in the 1979 Islamic Revolution in Iran and the takeover of political power by Necmettin Erbakan, an Islamist prime minister, in Turkey in 1996. In Algeria, nationalist rule since independence in 1962 has resulted in a bifurcated society like Egypt's. Secular society and culture for the urban bourgeoisie and intellectuals exist alongside an Islamic culture in the countryside and the urban slums. The abrogation of the 1992 electoral process, which prevented Front Islamique du Salut (Islamic Salvation Party—FIS) from controlling parliament, has plunged Algeria into a civil war. Secularism was violently challenged by Islamists.

Since Pakistan's creation in 1947, that country's leaders have faced different forces vying with each other for political power. In Muslim countries where Islamists have ruled (e.g., Iran, Sudan, and Afghanistan), they too have failed to find long-term stability and prosperity. In Afghanistan, the Wahhabist Taliban regime led the country into a civil war as well as into a foreign war as a result of the terrorist attacks of September 11, 2001, on New York and Washington, D.C.

Recent trends throughout the Muslim world point to the emergence of an intense debate over reforming Islam. Women in the Muslim world are beginning to demand greater freedom and to question the restrictive status that cultural traditions have imposed on them. Some Muslim leaders have demanded an Islamic constitution and resistance to Westernization. Others have called for an inward-looking and more humanistic approach that considers Muslims free and responsible individuals, capable of using their independent judgment. The Muslim world has increasingly become the site of an emerging cultural conflict over who controls the process of social change as well as over whose interests are really served by change or resistance to it.

Islam: A Religious Identity

In today's globally interactive world, the issues of self and modernity have intensified the evolution and construction of identity. The dialectic of the local and global, as Anthony Giddens notes, has produced divergent or even paradoxical effects. Similarly, the fragmentation and pluralistic nature of modern experiences have disrupted the security of the stable self.[37]

Internally, the Muslim world today is best characterized by competing visions of Islam and modernity. The dominant discourse in the Muslim world surrounds the debate over who defines rationality, authenticity, and legitimacy. That is, who controls modernity? Although Muslims believe that the Qur'an is the word of God as revealed to the Prophet Mohammad, they disagree on how to interpret it. While conservatives insist on obedience to that revealed truth, modernists argue that reason enables human beings to interpret revealed truth in view of modern conditions.[38]

Islamic reformists see Islamic piety as an alternative construction of modernity, one that is cognizant of ethical and moral dimensions of progress and development.[39] They seek to situate the role of Islamic piety in global politics through an intercivilizational dialogue. Islam's appeal as a faith, covenant, and social movement, they argue, lies in its ability to "produce powerful resistance to foreign intrusion."[40] The upsurge of religious identities, like nationalist movements, has to some extent been a defensive response to globalization.[41] Revivalist movements have also exploited globalization to advance their own cause.[42]

Reform-minded Muslims resist the revivalist antirationalist tendencies, arguing that Islam's appeal rests on its synthesizing capacity for engaging other modern human and civilizational experiences. Mindful of the

"other," they note that pragmatic Islam "does not propose an antirational-
ism but emphasizes taming rationalism to serve human need and dignity."[43]
This vision of modernity, as James H. Mittelman argues, fuses its paradigm
with a struggle for empowerment. Resurgent Islamic groups thus strive to
"construct an identity denied to them in a globalizing world."[44]

Historically, *ulama* (religious leaders) have been greatly fearful of multiple interpretations of Islam, which they have seen as provoking dissension
in the community.[45] But their greatest fear has emanated from the penetration of the Muslim world by Western culture and technology. The influence
of culture and technology has been accompanied by the desire for political
power and empire. Conservative thinkers have pushed for an Islamicization
of all knowledge, espousing the notion that Muslim youth be immunized
against the corrosive influence of secularized scientism and sciences.[46]

The unprecedented access that ordinary Muslims have to sources of
information and knowledge about cultural and religious aspects of their societies has had a transformative impact on the evolving construction of
their identity. In France, Dale F. Eickelman notes, this has meant an identity shift from being Muslim in France to being French Muslim. In Turkey,
the younger generation of Turks see themselves simultaneously as European
and Muslim. And a new generation of Iranians, who were not even born at
the time of 1979 Islamic Revolution, seek a greater autonomy from the formal, conservative religious/political establishment. These young people are
demanding a public sphere in which they can freely participate and advocate religious and political tolerance and pluralism.[47]

Islam: A Political Force

The upsurge of Islam as a political force has both historical and contemporary roots. However diverse its political expressions, political Islam has
taken root basically in the old dynamic of decolonization.[48] In some respects, the rise of political Islam can also be traced back to the 1967 Arab-
Israeli war, in which Arabs were left with an overwhelming sense of disap-
pointment and humiliation. Arab nationalist and secular leaders were discredited in the eyes of their populace in the aftermath of this calamitous
defeat.

Just as important, the establishment of an Islamic state in Iran in 1979
gave political Islam a fresh momentum, highlighting an era in which Islam
became a political vehicle for addressing many issues, including expression

of Muslim grievances, aspirations, and calls for reforms. Long before these developments, however, religion had played a key role in the process of state formation and nation building in the Middle East, largely because it was closely intertwined with central questions of identity and communal values. Today, states and religious organizations compete for power and influence within modern states as well as for the creation of a just and ethical society.[49] This chapter focuses on the recent causes of Islamic resurgence.

Some Western scholars of the Muslim world, such as John E. Esposito, note that, ironically, the resurgence of Islam as a potent political force has occurred in those Muslim societies regarded as the most modern or modernizing—that is, those with a well-trained, Western-oriented, and secular elite. These include, among others, Algeria, Egypt, Iran, Lebanon, Tunisia, and Turkey.[50] Political Islam is a postcolonial or anticolonial phenomenon to the extent that it is a response to the incursions of Western ideas into Muslim lands. It is also part of the drive to restore the identity and dignity of Muslims.

For many Muslims, state-led secularization has resulted in social alienation and exclusion from power. Political Islam has come to represent a reassertion of what is widely regarded as authentic or indigenous. "This reassertion," writes Beverley Milton-Edwards, "often takes place in the face of political rule that is understood as alien, foreign and not of the making of Muslim peoples."[51] The current occupation of Iraq by the United States, the unconditional U.S. support for Israel, and the U.S. military presence in the Persian Gulf are perceived by many Muslims as neocolonialism. This dominant perception in turn feeds widespread anti-Americanism in the Muslim world.

Political repression has also forced political Islam underground. Likewise, mass economic dislocation, as in Afghanistan, Lebanon, and the West Bank and Gaza Strip, has fed fundamentalism. Graham Fuller argues that "extreme conditions generally produce extremist results."[52] Negative sociopolitical conditions in the Arab world—namely, oppressive regimes, incompetent and illegitimate governments, and authoritarian and violent governance—have produced frustration and anger that ultimately push people toward political Islam as a preferred alternative.[53]

Although political Islam has also developed in some part in response to economic and political crises of Muslim societies, it is incorrect to completely link the emergence of the Islamic groups to the collapse of Muslim countries' economies in an effort to explain "a process that is essentially a question of identity."[54] To assume that economic crisis or poverty alone is the cause of Islamist opposition is to overlook the key features of this socio-political movement. It would be a major error to suppose that in the absence of poverty, Muslims would become not only law abiding but also secular.[55]

Islamists are highly organized, enjoy a broad social base, and are seen by some Muslims as offering an alternative to socialism, Arab-nationalism, military dictatorships, and monarchies. The social message of the Qur'an, some Muslims stress, is a lot easier to understand than Marxist dialectics. Many Islamic organizations started as community-based self-help projects. Consider, for example, the Muslim Brotherhood in Egypt. It runs medical clinics, hospitals, day care centers, youth clubs, legal aid societies, and job-training programs; it subsidizes inexpensive food, banks, schools, publishing houses, and drug and rehabilitation programs; and it collects garbage. All these activities are grass roots oriented and far less expensive than similar government programs. The fact remains that many secular governments of the Muslim world have failed to provide such social services effectively.[56]

Perhaps more relevant for the purposes of this chapter is the discussion of the recent roots of political Islam with a view toward questioning the reductionist assumption held by culturalists and Orientalists that Muslims are antimodern and antirational and that they are prone to violence and hostile to progress. This assumption will be explored in the chapters that follow; but in the next paragraphs we will examine the cases of Palestine, Afghanistan, and Iran as part of a broader conceptual backdrop to the study of Islamic resurgence as a whole.

There can be no doubt that the humiliation of the 1967 war strengthened the hands of Islamic groups vis-à-vis secular leaders of the Palestinian community. This was vividly demonstrated in the 1987 Intifadah (social uprisings) and the growth of the Islamic Resistance Movement, popularly known as Hamas. This new movement displaced the older generation's more secular Palestinian Liberation Organization (PLO) fighters. After the Oslo accords of 1993, the PLO rose in power. During 1994–2000, the Palestinian Authority (PA) failed to liberate the lands occupied by Israel. The prestige and authority of the PA among the Palestinians diminished considerably while that of the Islamic movements grew. Since late 2000 and the al-Aqsa Mosque incident in Jerusalem when Ariel Sharon's visit there incited widespread violence, Islamic factions have grown further in influence and regional support.

The rise of the Muslim militia in Afghanistan is also instructive. The Soviet invasion of Afghanistan in 1979 evoked several politicocultural backlashes. Internally, the *mujahideen* (Muslim militia) movement was initially formed to resist Soviet occupying forces—but also subsequently resisted Western powers—chiefly, the United States, which supported the *mujahideen* by giving them advanced tactical and weapon training, and sophisticated arms including mines and antitank and antiaircraft weapons. Regional countries, including Saudi Arabia, the United Arab Emirates, and Pakistan, also nudged along the Afghan resistance movement by providing financial and logistical support.

The 1989 Soviet withdrawal from Afghanistan was followed by a period of uncertainty and a vacuum of power, especially during 1989–94, when the warlords of Afghanistan took over. In 1994, several Islamic groups, under Mullah Omar, led a movement called the Taliban that by 1998 controlled 90 percent of the country. Under the Taliban, Afghanistan became not merely a new national state but also home to an international movement aiming to restore Muslim power by overturning secular governments and Western influence throughout the world.

With the Taliban in control of much of the country, Afghanistan thus became the site of sophisticated training operations and communications for a complex network of Islamic warriors with a global agenda. Al-Qaeda grew in such an environment to be a transnational terror network. One observer notes that America created violent and radical political Islam inadvertently as part of its Cold War strategy. The U.S. support for *mujahideen* to dislodge Soviet forces from Afghanistan proved to have long-term implications for the spread of Islamic militancy in that part of the world.

The so-called jihadi *madrasas* (religious schools) in Pakistan trained both the Afghan refugee children, who later helped form the Taliban regime, and the Arab Afghans, who were later networked by al-Qaeda. U.S. policy makers turned this ideological tendency (Islamism) into a political organization. The Afghan war gave it organization, numbers, skills, resources, and a coherent strategy. In short, as Mahmood Mamdani rightfully argues, "America created an infrastructure of terror but heralded it as an infrastructure of liberation."[57]

Similarly, the 1979 Islamic Revolution of Iran marked a crucial turning point in Islamic revivalism, ending a secular modernizing regime and replacing it with a clergy-led Islamist regime. This revolution, spearheaded by Ayatollah Ruhollah Khomeini, spurred an intense Islamic discourse throughout the Muslim world over the future of cultural politics and power. In many respects, the Islamic Revolution gave rise to Islamic militancy, as evidenced by the increased support for Islamic movements around the world, including those in Lebanon, Palestine, Sudan, Afghanistan, and the former Soviet republics of Central Asia, among others. Consequently, the 1980s saw the resurgence of Islamic influences and their new quest for political power throughout the Muslim world.

Islam: A Transnational and Global Space

The debate over identity construction in a globalizing world moves between two extremes. At one end, globalization has encountered rejectionist and sometimes isolationist narratives within the Muslim world, confronting modern, Western-inspired forms of identity. At the other end of the continuum is cosmopolitanism, whose advocates tend to utilize universalistic ideals to bring about global values and solidarity. In between these extremes one can situate two other types of identities: the hybridity narrative, involving multiple loyalties and identifications, and a so-called third space, especially among the younger generation of diasporic and immigrant communities, as these individuals participate in neither the host country's politics nor the homeland political community.

Explorations of transnational Islam demonstrate that Muslims throughout the world have consciously adopted some global, albeit largely Western, ideas, practices, and institutions. Media and migration have helped transmit to the Muslim world such norms as human rights, gender equality, and democratic reforms. In short, globalization has de-territorialized culture and politics, expanding the choices that can be made by the individual.

A new variant of global Muslim identity has emerged that relates to identifying with Muslim resistance movements in different parts of the world. Diasporic Muslim communities no longer feel an allegiance to a particular national state.[58] In fact, many young diasporic Muslims have attempted to critically reread the founding texts directly into contemporary contexts without the mediation of classical dogmatic theology. This public space has led to the emergence of new translocal communities (the Tablighis Jama'at), spurring a debate over who is authorized to undertake this critical renewal of Islam. Translocal spaces provide fertile grounds for the reformulation of religious traditions and the construction of an Islam for posterity. Such transnational forces are certain to encourage the articulation of a new critical Islam.[59]

Within the spaces of diasporic Islam, Peter Mandaville notes, a new form of interstitial identity—or a "third space"—has emerged in which neither the politics of the majority society nor that of the homeland is embraced. This has created, especially among the younger generation, forms of hybridized political identity that could be situated and conceptualized as somehow in-between. When such identities travel in the context of translocality, a new mode of relating internationally is enacted in which the boundaries of political community are regularly open to negotiation and rearticulation.[60]

With diasporic life reimagined in this way, various processes of cultural translation are set in motion. The resulting syncretisms will consequently give rise to new interpretations of sacred texts, bringing them in line with global sociocultural change and contingencies.[61] Whether Muslims identify themselves as Wahhabis or Salafis, fundamentalists or neofundamentalists, Tablighis or Sufis, militants or reformists, they all are part of a process to recast Muslim identity in a different light, one that is not attached necessarily to a particular culture or territory. Since this form of religiosity is no longer embedded in a given culture or society, it is intrinsically subject to change.

Note, however, that a reassertion of a global Muslim identity may be simply a backlash to the existing social discriminations, racism, and rampant unemployment that Muslims have experienced in their adopted countries. It is equally important to bear in mind that some Western countries have adopted multiculturalism and assimilation policies but have failed to effectively pursue either. The Turkish minority in the Netherlands has frequently turned against the policy of cultural homogenization and assimilation, despite the fact that they consider themselves European Turks.

Since the September 11, 2001, terrorist attacks in New York and Washington, according to one study, Muslim immigrants living in the United States have become targets of indiscriminate attacks and media bias. As a result, they have shown a clear lack of political confidence in the country's mainstream political institutions compared to those of their own ethnic organizations. To address their problems, Arab Americans have increasingly turned to local networks, community associations, and mechanisms of solidarity, sometimes even at the expense of integration. Among both Muslim and Christian Arabs, the sense of reducing one's vulnerability has become highly linked to greater attachment to and confidence in ethnic organizations rather than mainstream institutions.[62] Media bias, which has had a direct impact on the spread of social stigmatization and discrimination against Muslims in the United States, has in fact bolstered the strength of religious identity. Hence the perseverance of Muslims' local networks and local identity in the United States.

In South Africa, where Muslims constitute only 2 percent of a population of forty-two million, many Muslims have identified secular democracy as key to preserving their identity in an ethnically, linguistically, and culturally diverse society.[63] The question hangs pungently in the air: how does globalization affect the interplay of national, cultural, and religious identity?

Globalization has spawned debates within the Muslim world over how to define identities and interests. The emergence of contestations and negotiations between different groups and factions within the Muslim world has created a new opportunity to critically examine and reconstruct new identities. The search for self and faith has boosted Islamic principles, cultural values, and religious/cultural identity not just among those living in the Muslim world but also among those living as minorities in the West.

The emergence of Islamism and neofundamentalism—assumed to be a product of the diaspora—is, in this view, a manifestation of modernity. Olivier Roy approvingly argues that "we should take Islamization as a contemporary phenomenon that expresses the globalization and westernization of the Muslim world."[64] Western experts on the Muslim world view Al-Qaeda as a resolutely modern and innovative organization. As an intangible and shadowy enemy, Gilles Kepel notes, "Al-Qaeda was less a military base of operations than a data-base that connected jihadists all over the world via the Internet."[65]

A third of the world's Muslims now live as members of a national minority.[66] For them, globalization offers a unique opportunity to dissociate Islam from any given territory and culture as well as to provide a model that could work beyond any culture or territory. This growing delinking of religion and traditional and national cultures has led to the reconstruction of a new Muslim identity. Today, Olivier Roy contends, Muslim identity is recast largely according to religious beliefs and ethics, not on the basis of a given culture.[67] Where Islamists have ruled (Afghanistan under the Taliban, Iran since the 1979 Islamic Revolution, Sudan under the Bashir-Turabi alliance, and Pakistan under Zia), their governments have failed to generate— much less deepen—another culture or value system.[68]

Neofundamentalists in the Muslim world pursue an overriding goal: "to reconstruct a true Muslim community by starting from the individual."[69] This reconstruction of the "culture of the self" has generated a form of the privatization of religion that privileges Islamic symbols and norms over political power. In this sense, globalization has advanced the ideological causes of the neofundamentalists. Similarly, Roy argues, "the culture-blind approach of neofundamentalists explains why, in Christianity as well as in Islam, only fundamentalists are winning more converts in an era of globalization and uprootedness."[70] This does not mean, however, that globalization necessarily implies self-restraint and tolerance.

Some studies echo a similar logic, suggesting that Islamic reformists absorb globalization only on their own cultural terms while cultivating a hybrid identity. Militant Islamists, by contrast, pointedly attack local and corrupt authorities, not globalization. They may single out particular Western allies of the repressive regimes, but they are more likely to use globalization to their own advantage, hoping that international markets, international law, or human rights instruments or regimes will undermine local authoritarianism. Because of their anti-autocracy campaign, the identity of these militants is often described as rejectionist.[71]

Muslims in the West have become a permanent feature of these societies. They are no longer foreigners. Their integration into Western societies has been achieved neither through assimilation nor through the construction of a multicultural society. Rather, it has been achieved through the reconstruction of new identities with evolving social circumstances and emerging overlapping identities.[72] Many Muslim organizations, Roy argues, see in the European Union (EU) "an opportunity to bypass their own ethnic and national cleavages and to create something closer to what an *ummah* [community] should be."[73] This perceived rather than real community demonstrates that global Muslim identity has meant delinking Islam from any given culture in favor of a transnational and universal set of specific patterns. This means, in part, that we are witnessing an evolving religiosity—not religion—in the face of the sociological changes of the modern world. Muslims in the West tend to think in Western ways, even when they oppose Western values.[74]

Roy correctly draws our attention to a contradiction here: "The paradox is that the more religions are decoupled from cultures, the more we tend to identify religion and culture. Islamic fundamentalists and many conservative Muslims lobby for Islam to be recognized as a culture in the West, using the common idiom of multiculturalism."[75] Moreover, religion tends to become a sort of neo-ethnicity in certain circumstances. Many Muslims sympathized deeply with Iraqis after the U.S. invasion of Iraq. Likewise, the fear of a possible U.S. attack on Iran brought together, however briefly, that country's nationalists and Islamists.

One empirical study of Lebanese immigrants in New York, Montreal, and Paris shows that the Lebanese diaspora increasingly is engaged in global communities and pursue a form of global solidarity that is not predicated on shared nationality and ethnicity as the basis of cosmopolitan experience or identity. This Lebanese diaspora, which is primarily concerned with the larger issues of injustice and inequality, environmental degradation, and human rights violations, challenges traditional forms of belonging to a particular culture or country and maintains a robust sense of membership simultaneously in the local community in which they reside and the global community that they imagine.[76]

The Shocks of September 11

The relationship between shocks and norm construction merits discussion. Some experts have argued that dramatic shocks to the international system tend to shake existing identities and behavioral norms. Some shocks, however, at least initially reinforce rather than challenge existing collective beliefs. The Japanese attack on Pearl Harbor, for instance, vigorously reinforced American identity while weakening the norm of isolationism that previously had been strongly upheld.[77] Following the tragic and shocking September 11, 2001, terrorist attacks in New York and Washington, D.C., the United States has taken the role of setting new international standards, determining threats, using force to contain global terror, and meting out justice.[78] The continued American hegemony and imperial behavior have generated various forms of opposition, none more extensive and intense than its unilateral foreign policy vis-à-vis Iraq.

The "war on terrorism," declared on September 20, 2001, has renewed discourses over U.S. exceptionalism and imperialistic impulses. In this rhetorical strategy, the relevant actor is no longer the United States but the "civilization."[79] The new enemy—Islamic terrorism—is supposed to occupy the rhetorical place once occupied by communism. The United States has now assumed the role of guardian of human civilization in the war against terrorism. Others will join this struggle against evil or suffer the consequences.

With Islam and Islamic terror taking the place of communism, attention is focused on civilization to the detriment of alternative logics of identity. Attempts to depict Islamism as a threat to Western civilization are dangerously distorted and counterproductive. Some Western scholars have employed core notions of binary oppositions that contrast the "other" with "us," thus painting a picture of an uncultured Islam with a predilection for conflict with the West.[80]

Such commonplace rhetoric was evident in the national security strategy document of the Bush administration: "America will hold to account nations that are compromised by terror, including those who harbor terrorists—because the allies of terror are the enemies of civilization."[81] Reiterating the importance of multilateralism as well as the "coalition of the willing" from time to time has become empty rhetoric, in view of the fact that the United States has already reserved the right to determine who is civilized and who is not, and thus who has to be supported and who has to be vehemently opposed in the name of civilization.[82]

Gruesome images of the abused Abu Ghraib prisoners in Iraq added yet another twist to U.S. exceptionalism. Pictures of American soldiers forcing naked prisoners into compromising positions did enormous damage to U.S. credibility and its stated objective of democratizing the region. Emerging details demonstrated the growing but unregulated role of private contractors and military intelligence officers in the interrogation of detainees in American military activities. These acts of private contractors, who were arguably under no legally binding law or jurisdiction and thus were not accountable to anyone, have substantially undermined the U.S image in the Muslim world. Many Muslims around the world, regardless of their level or intensity of religious practice, citizenship, or political activity, reacted as Muslims against the U.S.-led invasion of Iraq, even if they would not call themselves true believers.[83] This reaction reflects a view of Muslim self-definition as *other*. Many Muslims expressed deep sympathy when they saw the deaths of innocents, Muslims included, on September 11.

Conclusion: Toward a New Conceptual Understanding

As globalization permeates different societies, the debate intensifies over how to develop cultural self-assertion, recognition, and new meanings in life. Integral to the definition of culture in a globalizing world is being recognized and learning how to coexist with those of different cultures. Arguably, recognition rather than self-assertion constitutes the culture's most hopeful posture. As one observer notes, "culture can be a useful corrective in the relationship between religion and politics that, today, is advancing so many insoluble questions."[84]

The quest for authenticity in the pursuit of solutions to socioeconomic, political, and cultural problems (in this volume, most often referred to as cultural politics) has become inseparable from power politics. Muslims' cultures, identities, and interests are dynamic and evolving. Reform-minded Islamists have proven capable of creating hybrids potent enough to challenge existing regimes. Militant Islamists have either rejected or confronted any intermingling with and exposure to outside cultures. Cultural dialogues and exchanges, as well as transnational ties and interests, are likely to empower Muslims and change the way they construct images of the self and the other. When combined with the absorption of new ideas and norms, such exchanges could potentially change domestic structures within which identities, interests, and capabilities are formed.

Globalization has created both limitations and opportunities for cultural politics. A new transnational identity in the form of religiosity—with no attachment to a particular culture—has emerged in the Muslim diaspora in the West and elsewhere. The emergence of a basic awareness of religious diversity and pluralism should bring about a recognition that "all need toleration."[85] The continuing high value with which Americans—unlike their European counterparts—view religious faith "makes possible a broad if not universal view that even minority faiths may possess personal and societal value, as well as legal rights that must be honored."[86]

Gender issues, however, have renewed the debate over cultural politics in many Muslim countries. In some situations, Islamic feminists and secular feminists have converged in their goals in a hopeful attempt to bring about change in old laws. Likewise, both reformists and militants have used international law and internationally recognized human rights to promote their ideological and strategic goals. The upshot has been a world of multiple identities, each staking out a claim to authenticity and legitimacy.

This book offers an alternative to the agenda of Islamic militants (jihadis), who are in fact a tiny minority of the world's 1.2 billion Muslims. The United States and Europe must recognize several realities. The corrective to militant Islamism is to integrate mainstream Islamists into the political process of their respective countries. In the cases of Jordan, Turkey, and Yemen, political integration has been the key to reducing violence caused by militant Islamic groups.

Islamists themselves are increasingly outspoken about the need for democracy and human rights.[87] The opening of previously closed societies to the freedom of the press, civic activism, and electoral competition has served to moderate Islamist political movements—as the 2003 elections in Turkey demonstrated.[88] Absent inclusionary politics, the radicals in Islamicist movements can often prevail in rationalizing their own exclusionary version of politics.[89] Moreover, a just and even-handed resolution of the Palestinian issue could decrease, if not end, the appeal of Islamic militancy in the Muslim world. The perception of injustice toward the Palestinians has motivated political violence in the Middle East and the rest of the Muslim world. Much depends upon progress made in the coming years.

Finally, effective democratic reforms and state building—that is, establishing strong, legitimate, and successful states—in the Muslim world are likely to diminish the possibilities of growth for the radical Islamic groups. The Western world can help in this endeavor by not imposing its vision. Pushing for its preferences is likely to lead to a nationalist backlash, which could further intensify the link between religion, culture, and politics. Local politics, leadership, cultural traditions, and attitudes will play an important role in Muslim countries' laws. Islamic law is applied in broadly different ways in the Muslim world, although it is used in tandem with civil law in some Muslim countries. Understanding identity-based politics, both locally and globally, is the key to discovering why this is the case.

The surest way to advance stability and progress toward democracy in the Muslim world is to incorporate Islamists into the political and legal systems. The exclusion of Islamists is bound to lead to greater political instability and creeping Talibanization of politics in the Muslim world. Change, as one expert reminds us, will be negotiated only if and when the Western world is prepared to sit down and talk directly with Islamists, as well as with liberal politicians and human rights activists. Refusing to acknowledge Islamists' existence and their sociopolitical legitimacy is a policy for failure and for maintaining a nonworking status quo.[90]

Democracies today, however, cannot escape identity politics entirely. By reaffirming ethnicity and communalism, democracies paradoxically intensify identity and sectarian politics. The question of whether democracies will work in deeply divided societies will be tightly bound up with their practical and contextual relevance. Under such circumstances, the success of democracies will be heavily influenced by the extent to which democratic processes are preceded or accompanied by reformulating politics, institutions, and attitudes and behaviors. Without social justice and respect for human rights, identity politics is certain to lead to political repression and division.

Muslim societies must come to grips with the massive changes in world politics that are associated with globalization. This means that they must a find a way to reconcile their interests and values with modern moral orders and legal principles that are based on accountability, transparency, and participatory politics. Islamic feminists and secular feminists will, in the context of globalization, reassert their identity and interests as they become further concerned with being in control of their own lifestyle as well as politics. Muslim leaders should avoid dwelling on historically disputed European colonialism and imperialism because such attempts are unlikely to positively influence and meld with the perspective of human rights justice. Rather, they must insist on a human rights framework that is legally and morally compelling in the present.[91] The Muslim world's social realities, including identities and interests, can be consciously constructed by committed leaders and conscientious individuals—making it a vibrant forum for positive change.

Chapter 2

International Human Rights Norms and Muslim Experiences

Flaws in overly optimistic theories of globalization demonstrate that aside from its pure economic implications, globalization has generated profound social disruption and cultural resistance. The critics of globalization, who see it as a juggernaut of untrammeled capitalism, fear a world ruled by profit-seeking multinational and global corporations. They also question the imposition of cultural standards of one region of the world, namely the West, on all other regions. No issue is more acute in the global debate than the devaluation of local identities. Moreover, the same ethical questions apply to both human rights and globalization: Whom does the process of globalization serve? And who should shape its development?

Some Western scholars, such as Richard Falk, have noted that universalism has been used as a cover to obscure Western hegemony and that any genuine and universal attempt at constructing human rights must be based not on uniformity but on the coexistence of different cultures;[1] and Enlightenment values must be reexamined in the context of both time and space. Others, such as Michael Ignatieff, argue that the moral consensus, which sustained the United Nations' (UN) Universal Declaration of Human Rights (UDHR) in 1948, has increasingly splintered and there is no evidence that economic globalization entails moral globalization.[2]

Some scholars see that as economies have integrated, a countervailing movement has developed to maintain the integrity of national cultures, communities, religions, and indigenous ways of life. Others have noted that the growth of supraterritorial spaces and interests has facilitated the development of many nonterritorial communities based on class, gender, racial, and religious identities.[3] This rise in cosmopolitan bonds, however, should not mask the right to cultural preservation and continuity.

The issue of constructing identity (contextual or relational) in an evolving world of mass education and communications merits particular attention. The right of Muslims to cultural specificity must arguably become an indispensable feature of universality. Claims of universality of human rights need to be negotiated and challenged within the internal discourse of contemporary Muslim societies. To create common values and norms through dialogue and debate appears to be the most sustainable form of enhancing human rights.

In many Muslim countries revolution is highly unlikely and outside intervention is widely regarded as illegitimate. The patriarchal structure of some Muslim societies—not Islam—accounts for some of the fundamental barriers to women's rights. Noting the convergence of certain Islamic and internationally recognized norms in some Muslim countries (e.g., Iran) on matters related to negotiating culture and human rights has gained more public appeal than focusing on distinct or profound differences between Western and Muslim worlds. This chapter argues that without denying the value of universal rights, we must rethink *universalism* in an attempt to reach a common ground with other civilizations and cultures on what constitutes universality. In this basic sense, both Enlightenment laws and Islamic laws deserve close scrutiny and respect.

Before assessing the validity of the proposition of moral equivalency, two general questions need to be raised. First, how is identity shaped and reconstructed within the context of globalization? Second, how would the Muslim world's cultural and epistemological pluralism affect the identity of Muslims?

Islamic Identities and Paradigms

Asserting and reconstructing one's identity in today's global community need not be construed as denying common or shared values; rather, identity must be seen as a form of recognition through difference. This recognition is based on respect and concern for diversity and tolerance. The global era has presented both individuals and communities with new challenges. The individual members of national communities increasingly find themselves "living in an age of both harmonization and dissonance."[4] Under such circumstances, the real question is how to balance the need for identity with the desire for universality. The latter relates to the basic notion of what it means to be human in our modern times. There is the need to belong to a community that accepts and recognizes the individual and within which he or she may be easily understood.[5]

The dynamics of globalization and its impact on religious faith revolve around the issues of legitimacy, identity, cultural integrity, and psychocultural influences and disorientation. Arguably, the main threat to religious faith in a globalizing world is the commodification of everyday life.[6] What renders faith or religious commitment problematic in such a context is that everyday life has become part of a global system of exchange of commodities, one not easily influenced by political leaders, intellectuals, or religious leaders.[7] In fact, the impacts of globalization on the daily life of people have become entirely unpredictable and uncertain.

Islamic resurgence has indeed become an issue of the reconstruction of the Muslim self in the context of globalization. This development has spurred a lively debate in the Muslim world over the relationship of Islam, human rights, and democracy. Pluralism and religious freedom are integral to Islamic values and lie at the heart of Muslim societies. The basis of this religious freedom in Islam is the categorical Qur'anic assertion (Sura 2:256), "there is no compulsion in religion" (*la ikraha fi al-din*).[8] Islam has accommodated in its worldview the religious values and traditions that came before it. Viewing Islam as a universal attitude, Mahmoud M. Ayoub writes that "Islam applies to any human beings or human communities that profess faith in the one God and seek to obey God in all they do and say. It is in this sense that the Qur'an speaks of Noah, Abraham, Moses and Jesus and his disciples as Muslims."[9]

Islam as such has inherited social justice, monotheism, and community from indigenous faiths such as Judaism, Christianity, and Zoroastrianism.[10] Islam has established equality before the law with absolute right to access to courts for all people regardless of their race, gender, religion, or creed. It has also recognized the right of local communities of different cultures to maintain their own courts and laws, thus safeguarding the rights of non-Muslims (*dhimmis*) living in Muslim countries. This policy, known as the "Millet System," has been practiced for many centuries in the Muslim world.[11] Additionally, non-Muslims have the right of access to Islamic courts.

As a source of ethical teachings and moral codes of conduct, the shari'a law has always been regarded as a comprehensive code of life. Yet the shari'a-based legal system has evolved into dynamic patterns of jurisprudence and governance, largely because of the emergence of several equally credible schools of law within it. Under the repressive ruling elites, however, some of the shari'a schools have been used to construct a legal system supportive of the totalitarian political regimes.[12]

Today, some Muslim societies increasingly manifest pluralistic features, both ideologically and culturally. This pluralism has opened their communities to a noticeable degree of criticism and self-evaluation—a condition essential to any meaningful cross-cultural dialogue.

The internal debate over the relationship between Islam, the state, democracy, and human rights gets to the core of the identity issue within the Muslim world. Some Muslim scholars have noted that shari'a is not the whole of Islam but instead it is an interpretation of its fundamental sources.[13] Others, such as Fatima Mernissi, a feminist and founding member of the Moroccan Organization for Human Rights, points out that Islamic ideas and traditions provide rich foundations for ideas of gender equality and the human rights of women.[14] Still others have written of the pragmatic humanitarianism of Islam, arguing that some reconciliation between the traditional shari'a and the modern idea of human rights could be conceivably achieved based on such well-established Islamic pragmatism.[15]

Since the Muslim world represents a multipolar universe of Islamic as well as intellectual thinking and since no one center of Islamic thought dominates the entire Muslim world, it is essential to refer to several schools of thought. The democratization of information has generated as much interest in the issue of legitimacy and human rights as in local identities, values, and traditions. Demographic and social dynamics, as illustrated by the rise of youth and women's movements, have expanded political participation and the demand for democracy. The growth of Islamism at the same time has led to the revival of traditional values and institutions. An examination of the internal power struggle among four groups (conservatives, neoconservatives, reformists, and secular Muslims) helps illuminate the prospects for adoption of human rights in the Muslim world.[16] In the following section, we will examine the reactions of these four groups to emerging global norms by explaining forms, agents, sites, and strategies of resistance and accommodation.[17]

Islamic Conservatives

Islamic conservatives look to both the classical and medieval periods of Islam for their worldviews. They see Islam as an immutable religion that transcends time and space. Conservatives adopt a communitarian outlook that regards the individual as part of the community or a group, to which he or she owes certain obligations. The conservatives' emphasis on drawing boundaries around the community is expressed not only in dress code and veiling (*hijab*) and the repression of women's sexuality, but also in the proclamation of a different way of life and of a transformation of mind by bringing the faithful back to the proper practice of the faith and tradition. For Islamic conservatives, *hijab* is a symbol for the defense of the faith, family integrity, Islamic and communal identity, and solidarity.

They view the Western world's advocacy of human rights as a modern agenda by which the West hopes to establish its complete hegemony over the Muslim world. They have vehemently objected to several articles of the UDHR, including Articles 16 and 18, which deal with equality of marriage rights and freedom to change one's religion or belief, respectively. Conservatives object to the provisions on women's rights, questioning the equality of gender roles, obligations, and judgments. Islam, they argue, prohibits the marriage of a Muslim woman to a non-Muslim man. Apostasy (*ridda*) is forbidden, and it is punishable by death.

Conservatives call into question the idea of natural reason as an independent source of ethical knowledge. According to conservatives, following past traditions (*taqlid*) and returning to established norms in times of crisis are two cardinal rules of Islamic orthodoxy.[18] This group included Qayam-ud-Din Muhammad Abulbari (1878–1926), Ahmad Raza Khan Barelvi (1856–1921), Haji Imdadullah (1815–99), Mahmud al-Hasan (1850–1921), and Sayyid Kazem Shariatmadari (1905–86).[19]

Islamic Neoconservatives

Within Islamic thought and context, the traditions of Salafism (*al-Salafiyya*) and Wahhabism have urged believers to return to the pristine, pure, and unadulterated form of Islam practiced by Mohammad and his companions.[20] These traditions are known for their "intolerance toward any perceived deviation from the dogmatic interpretation of Islam that [they] preach."[21]

The proponents of these traditions, who may be characterized as radical as well as ultra-orthodox Islamic groups, are critical of modern, secular Western ideas, practices, and institutions that are contrary to Islam. They are also opposed to the doctrine of *taqlid*—whereby legal rulings of one or more schools of Islamic jurisprudence are unconditionally followed. These groups advocate *ijtihad*—that is, Islamic reasoning in matters relating to Islamic law.

Some neoconservatives, also known as neofundamentalists, place greater stress on mores and purity; they are less concerned with the immediate capture of political power than with grassroots activism aimed at the moral reconstruction of the individual and the gradual transformation of society into one that is more Islamic. These groups have consistently attempted to penetrate or to take over the institutions of civil society; they have shown more conservative approaches toward women's role in society.[22]

Other members, in contrast, tend to pursue an ultimate goal: "to establish an Islamic state based on the comprehensive and rigorous application of the *Shari'a*."[23] The members of this group are not drawn exclusively from the ranks of the *ulama* (Islamic scholars). They regard the conservative approach, as represented by the orthodox *ulama*, as unrealistic, and they oppose modernist Islamic groups that emulate Western ideas, practices, and institutions that neoconservatives regard as alien to Islam.[24] Neoconservatives see human rights as a hegemonic instrument of the Western world that, if adopted, would lead to moral decay of Islamic societies. With some reservations, the Taliban movement in Afghanistan may arguably be seen as an extreme manifestation of neofundamentalism of a sort.[25]

Islamic neoconservatives see the principal reasons for the Muslim world's decline as colonialism, neocolonialism, and disunity within the Muslim world. They emphasize a constitution that is Islamic. Most of them have come to accept Western parliamentary democracy and its corollary "popular sovereignty."[26] The neoconservative leadership generally consists of Islamic scholars and activists. Examples include Sayyid Abul A'la Maududi (1903–79), Hassan al-Banna (1906–49), and Sayyid Qutb (1906–66).

Still other Islamic neoconservatives or neofundamentalist groups act globally, and for them borders are no longer barriers. They are organized by transnational nonstate actors and organizations. Although they represent a tiny fraction of Islamists, they have been very effective in targeting Western countries. Since the September 11 attacks, such groups are associated with Al-Qaeda more generally. There are clear differences over tactics and strategies among global jihadists, mainstream Islamists (e.g., Muslim Brothers, independents, and clerics), conservative Islamists, and *ulama*. Mainstream Islamists, such as Hassan al-Turabi, leader of Islamic Front in Sudan, and Sayyed Mohammed Hussein Faddallah, spiritual founding father of Lebanon's Hezbollah, both questioned Al-Qaeda's claim that its attacks on the United States could be religiously legitimate and sanctioned.[27]

Global jihadists tend to interpret the U.S. invasion of Iraq as a direct, external assault on their community and religion—that is, on their Islamic identity. The war in Iraq since March 2003 has strengthened global jihadists' hands, as they have increasingly penetrated Iraqi borders. Drawing our attention to a nuanced and subtle distinction between mainstream Islamists, experts underscore the point that Western commentators and policy makers, who have turned their attention to Al-Qaeda and like-minded extremists, have often overlooked the fault lines among global jihadists and the vast societal opposition to them.[28] Among the four types of Muslims highlighted and analyzed in this chapter, the ability of global jihadists to transform their society and obtain fundamental freedoms is minimal and thus is the least relevant to the particular purposes of this volume.

Islamic Reformists

Islamic reformists, in contrast, are receptive to non-Islamic ideas, practices, and institutions. They stress the continuity of basic Islamic traditions along with the material progress that they deem necessary for human and economic transformation within an Islamic framework. Reformists believe that shari'a is historically conditioned and needs to be reinterpreted in light of the changing needs of modern society. Reformists refer to the 1990 Cairo Islamic Human Rights Declaration as a document that brings the Muslim world closer to certain articles of the UN Universal Declaration of Human Rights, making it possible to promote intercultural dialogue with the West over the general themes of human rights.[29]

Unlike the Salafists, who advise Muslims against integration into European societies, the associations emerging from the Muslim Brothers have chosen since 1989 "to root themselves in civil society."[30] Some reform-minded observers even see in the Islamic mystical belief system a type of ideology that is in sync with universal values. Within the context of the Islamic ecosystem, Ali Paya argues, there is a certain type of belief system, known as mysticism, which emphasizes such basic values as freedom, tolerance, equity, responsibility, love, and respect for all earthly manifestations of God.[31]

To advance the idea that Western and Muslim traditions share commonalities in their thinking related to freedom of conscience and religious liberty, Abdulaziz A. Sachedina demonstrates that "the Western notions of natural law and conscience are present in the spiritual and ethical utterances and presuppositions of the Qur'an . . . that in the notion of *fitra* (innate disposition) and *qalb* (the heart) we have the constitutive elements of the Western notion of synderesis and conscience."[32]

On the position of women within Islamic societies, reformists argue that the *hijab* empowers women, allows them increased physical mobility and therefore more access to power and space, and, more significantly, protects them within their own sociocultural milieus. Viewed from this perspective, the *hijab* is a profound symbol of Muslim identity and piety.[33] To the extent that Muslim women have actively chosen to veil as an expression of their own sexual, religious, and national identity, viewing *hijab* as a symbol of their subjugation is fundamentally flawed.[34] For many Muslim women, wearing the veil is indeed an act of empowerment that allows them to remain in the workplace with dignity and respect as well as to move freely in public space—a space dominated by males.[35] The forced imposition of the veil, however, is a form of cultural control by male elites that has much to do with the patriarchal attitudes and practices.

In recent years, Iranian women have negotiated concrete gains from the Islamic Republic in such matters as divorce, marriage, alimony, and child support. They have seen little reason to regard the system as inherently opposed to their interests.[36] Ziba Mir-Hosseini demonstrates how women's struggles in the course of these negotiations have produced a modicum of legitimacy and satisfaction. She argues that "one neglected and paradoxical outcome of the rise of political Islam in the 1970s has been to help create a space within which Muslim women can reconcile their faith with their feminism."[37] Within the context of Iranian politics, Mir-Hosseini insists, feminist readings of the shari'a have become both possible and inescapable given that Islamic sources have presented no oppositional discourse in national politics.[38]

The reformist concept of the Islamic state asserts that consultation (*shura*) by Muslim rulers with their citizenry is a requirement. Reformists invoke other democratic concepts and ethical constructs within the Islamic traditions, including *ijtihad* (independent reasoning), *ijma* (consensus of the religious scholars), and *baya* (holding the leaders to certain standards of accountability). These socioethical constructs demand democratic accountability and respect for social justice by the authorities.

Integral to Islamic civilization, reform, pluralism, and tolerance is the role of individual reasoning and reinterpretation (*ijtihad*). Muqtedar Khan expounds on the fear and skepticism of reason in Islamic jurisprudence, arguing that "it is important for the revitalization of Islamic civilization that the relationship between reason and revelation be properly understood."[39] While revelation is a source, Muqtedar Khan continues, reason is a tool. The sources of shari'a are akin to *data* that need to be processed into *information* that can be used in specific conditions. It is reason that processes data into information. Reason and revelation are inseparable. Reason is much broader in scope than analogical reasoning mentioned in traditional Islamic jurisprudence. "It is time," Muqtedar Khan points out, "we opened the doors of *ijtihad* not just to allow individual reasoning in legal issues, but to make reason one of the central arbiters in all issues."[40]

Some reformists have argued that divine law does not reflect the general consent of the people. Abdolkarim Soroush, an Iranian philosopher, argues that "divine legislation in Islam is said to have been discovered by a few and those discoverers think that they have privileged access to the interpretation of this law."[41] Having questioned the monopoly over interpretation by one group or class, Soroush argues the need for a dialogical pluralism between inside and outside religious intellectual fields.[42] Human rights, according to Soroush, lie outside religion and are not a solely legal (*fiq'hi*) intrareligious argument; rather, they belong to the domain of philosophical theology (*kalam*) and philosophy in general.[43] Some values, he argues, cannot be derived from religion. Human rights are the case in point. The language of religion and religious law (*fiq'h*) is essentially the language of duties, not rights. Rights enjoy a modern primacy over duties in our times.[44]

By contrast, Sheikh Rached al-Ghannouchi, leader of the Tunisian An-Nahda political party, represents a different view of reform. For Ghannouchi, the central question is how to free the Muslim community from backwardness and dependence on *the other*. Reconciling Islam and modernity, according to Ghannouchi, involves introduction of democracy and freedom, neither of which is opposed to Islamic principles. For Ghannouchi, the community, not the individual, remains the ultimate reality and objective.[45] Democracy and freedom of thought are tools that Muslims should use to achieve their community's goals and defend its interests.

The ranks of Islamic modernists include Rifa'ah al-Tahtawi (1801–73), Sayyid Jamal al-Din al-Afghani (1838–97), Muhammad Rashid Rida (1865–1935), Muhammad Iqbal (1873–1938), and Ali Shariati (1933–77).[46] Among the contemporaries, one can refer to Mohammad Khatami (president of Iran, 1997–2005), Chandra Muzafffar (Malaysia), and Nurcholish Madjid (Indonesia).

The Muslim Secularists

Secular Muslims are a significant part of the political, economic, and cultural elite that rules most of Muslim societies. Though a minority in all

Muslim societies, they possess a disproportionate degree of wealth and power while comprising the most assertive and vocal segment of their society.[47] Many secular elites have explored alternative forms of plural personal laws. Their engagement in mass politics, however, has left them exposed and vulnerable to the tumultuous vicissitudes of the mass-based Islamic movements.[48] Secular Muslims look to the experiences of the secular West as guiding models in an effort to promote their country's development. Secularists often support policies and programs that are grounded in pragmatic foundations. Muslim secularists are reluctant to replace secular laws with shari'a. To secularists, Islamic practices, such as *shura* and *baya,* have failed to uphold individual political participation and to elicit democratic accountability from governments.

In recent years, we have seen the convergence of some religious and secular women on matters relating to divorce law, child custody rights, and alimony. These reformist women, both religious and secular, have worked together to build a consensus on at least some issues, including the prevention of domestic violence and the promotion of gender equality. Since the late 1990s, these groups have participated in elections, have been active as legal staff in Islamic courts, and have significantly contributed to the literature on women's rights in Iran. The result has been vibrant intellectually, imbued with flourishing ideas about universal human rights and women's rights.[49]

Iranian feminists—Islamic and secular—have argued that the global movements for democracy and women's rights are inextricably intertwined and that women's quest for equality and emancipation is universal rather than Western.[50] In opposition to the early years of the Islamic Republic that emphasized a restrictive and homogeneous gender identity, Iranian women have, since the 1990s, successfully constructed more inclusive, multiple, and fluid identities based on the creative synthesis of Iran's local traditions, Islamic influences, modern aspects, and Western/global pressures.[51]

A new configuration of Islam, revolution, and feminism is emerging in Iran.[52] Women's press in Iran has become a primary vehicle to demonstrate how secular and Islamically oriented women have reconstructed and redefined the status and role of women. A coalition of secular and Islamic feminists, some of whom became members of the Majlis (parliament), has begun to work with "reformist parliamentarians to contest the codified and institutionalized privileges of men over women."[53]

After winning the 2003 Nobel Peace Prize, Shirin Ebadi, who is known as a secular Muslim feminist, noted that "the Qur'an does not contradict human rights. It is not Islam that is responsible for the failure to honor human rights, but the corrupt regimes in Muslim countries, which to my regret use religion as a justification for their illegitimate governments."[54] Supporting reformed Islam, Ebadi has argued that human rights abuses throughout the Muslim world are politically contingent acts perpetrated by state elites, facilitated by a patriarchal culture, and reinforced by Islamic extremists—all in the name of Islam.[55]

As ardent exponents of modernization, secularists have at times appeared as effective populist politicians (Mohammad Ali Jinnah and Zulfiqar Ali Bhutto of Pakistan, Anwar Sadat of Egypt, and Saddam Hussein of Iraq). Current secular leaders of the Middle East and North Africa, including King Abdullah (Jordan), King Hassan II (Morocco), Ben Ali (Tunisia), Qaddafi (Libya), Mubarak (Egypt), and Musharraf (Pakistan), are similar in some ways and different in others. With the exception of Iran (since the 1979 Islamic Revolution), Sudan (under the Bashir/Turabi alliance), and Afghanistan (under the Taliban), the Muslim world is ruled by secular regimes (see Table 1).

Muslims' Quest for Identity in the West

During the long process of modernization and secularization since the sixteenth and seventeenth centuries, Europe defined Islam as the other, with Islam having a reputation for embracing fanatic and militant ideologies. The image of Islam has been distorted in the Western world: "The view of Islam as a faith that made no separation between religion and politics deepened its image as fundamentalist, dangerous and backward."[56] Furthermore, as one observer reminds us, "most European countries do not officially recognize Islam as the second largest religion in Europe. It follows that Islamic communities cannot enjoy many of their civil and religious rights."[57]

Much has been made of the issue of women's dress in Europe. In both England and France, headscarves were seen as posing a threat to these countries' cultural pluralism and multiculturalism. In England, the negative responses to the female Islamic headscarves in the schools have been justified in the name of maintaining a homogeneous social image, while at the same time claiming that the *hijab* emphasized women's inferior status in Islam and was antithetical to the idea of gender equality.[58] In France, where the expression of Muslim or Arab identity was deemed a regressive ten-

TABLE 1. RESISTING AND ACCOMMODATING GLOBAL NORMS IN THE MUSLIM WORLD

	Forms	*Agents*	*Sites*	*Strategies*
Conservatives	Custom and traditions (*hijab*)	Clerics and *ulama*	Mosque	Seeking local alliances
Neofundamentalists	Moral reconstruction of the individual	Islamic activists and scholars	Local and transnational communities	Grass-roots activism
Reformists	Reconciling Islam with modernity, emphasizing individual choice (*ijtihad*)	Dissident clerics and moderate Islamists	National and state-level activities	Seeking ideas, allies, and intercultural dialogue with the West
Secularists	Equality and freedom	Politicians, human rights activists, lawyers, writers, and journalists	National, transnational, and global spaces (the Internet)	Synthesis with the West

dency and thus inhospitable to the continuing process of national integration, such resistance finally culminated in the passage of a law in February 2004 banning the veil in public schools.[59]

There is a fear among some that Muslim immigrants will become the majority in Europe, a concern that is exaggerated.[60] There are 15.2 million Muslims in the fifteen countries that joined the European Union prior to 2004—approximately 4 percent of the total population there.[61] Even the addition of Turkey's 68 million Muslims would increase the Europe's overall Muslim population to only 15 percent.[62] Birth rates, however, have fallen among native-born Europeans in a number of countries. The Continent's Muslim population, in contrast, represents a stark exception to this trend. Europe's Muslims are noticeably younger than its non-Muslims, and their average birth rate is roughly three times as high.[63]

There is also fear of radical Islam. Muslim immigrants tend to cluster around large cities (London and Paris), often in huge housing projects that are culturally and economically isolated and marginalized from the mainstream society. These Muslim ghettos naturally have high crime rates, poor education, and rampant unemployment—factors that render them all the more vulnerable to the lure of radical Islam.[64]

Terrorist attacks by radical Muslims (such as the bombings in Madrid in the spring of 2004) are taken as substantiating negative stereotypes about Islam and all Muslims. Family members who come to join their relatives in France are viewed as a drain on public resources and social services.[65] Human rights are not fully observed in some parts of Europe, given persistent racial violence against those identified as foreign and continuous discriminatory police action against them. Differences in the treatment of natives and migrants in gaining access to and enjoying a full range of civil rights is yet another hurdle to achieving equal rights.[66] Under such circumstances, the transnational flow of labor in the globalizing economy is bound to strengthen the proposition that "one's identity and position matter to one's proper claims to rights."[67]

Some observers provide a contrasting view of the West's expanding Muslim population. They argue that the increasing presence of Islam in the West may accelerate a process similar to the Christian Reformation. Western Islam is likely to become more secularized. Over time, Muslim communities in the West may develop a substantial influence on secularization and minority rights in the Middle East itself.[68] Muslims in the West may promote certain socially conservative Islamic values that are not necessarily inconsistent with mainstream, conservative values of Westerners, such as promoting family values, restricting abortion rights, castigating sex and violence in the movie industry, and maintaining drug-free communities.[69]

As Islam becomes domesticated in the West, especially in North America, it will inexorably take on many aspects of Western culture and society in the process. Islam's inherent capacity to invent and reinvent its traditions as well as to alter and be changed by various cultures and societies cannot be underestimated.[70] This is, in Frederick M. Denny's words, "a great advantage in parts of the world that are highly secularized and lukewarm if not indifferent or even hostile to religion. Muslims can freely call their fellow humans to Islam in a great variety of ways . . . , especially in the West."[71] This view is also shared by those who argue that the most important battle to win Muslims' hearts and minds in the coming decade "will be fought not in Palestine or Iraq but in these communities of believers on the outskirts of London, Paris, and other European cities, where Islam is already a growing part of the West."[72] If integrated into economic prosperity in the West, this new generation of Muslims is likely to offer a valuable vision of faith and democratic transition to their countries of origin.

Still another view holds that an Islamic presence in the Western world on a significant scale may begin to reverse the perceived cultural homogenization: "Values will begin to mix, tastes compete, and perspectives intermingle, as a new moral calculus evolves on the world scene."[73] In the fluid postmodern age, individuals can no longer escape multiple and overlapping identities. One can be both a devout Muslim and a loyal citizen of a non-Muslim country. Such eclecticism, which reinforces tolerance of others, lessens the likelihood of cultural confrontation. Islamic doctrine has always encouraged global participation.

Aside from the phenomenon of multiple identities, a new style of assimilation has, since the early 1990s, emerged among many Muslim minority communities: integration without full assimilation.[74] The alarm caused by extremism, such as the bombing of the World Trade Center in New York and the September 11, 2001, attacks in New York and Washington, has obscured the reality that most Muslim communities in the West are strongly adaptationist in style.[75] For these Western Muslims, the debate is no longer about Islamic governance; instead, it concerns issues of pluralism and tolerance.[76]

Furthermore, the networks of associations among Muslims in some European countries, such as France and Germany, have helped maintain and strengthen cross-border feelings. Such overarching solidarity does not point necessarily to the existence of a unified and homogenous Muslim network in Europe. "Islam in Europe," Valeri Amiraux notes, "is a complex series of entities, not a community. September 11, 2001, should prevent any temptation to confuse believers and activists."[77]

Undoubtedly Islam provides a unique locus of identity for Muslim immigrants by giving them a basic sense of meaning and selfhood.[78] The growth of pluralism in the West has facilitated the building of a distinctive Muslim religious and sociocultural space. Caught between Islamic and Western cultures, that space is not eroded by pluralist social environments.[79] In short, while assimilation is resisted, integration is conceded by Western Muslims who wish to preclude the risk of losing their sense of identity.

The difficulties that Muslims face in terms of integration without the loss of identity are not unique to the Muslim minorities in the West; they are typical among minorities throughout the world. Today, at least one third of Muslims live in minority situations and represent a broad range of understandings of Islam.[80] This situation demands intra-Muslim ecumenism and the necessity of promoting interreligious ties with other faith communities.

The key here is the principle of reciprocity in the freedom of religious expression and movement. It is just as important to note that Christians and Muslims collaborate on many global problems such as international trade, poverty, hunger, starvation, migration, refugees, ecological and environmental issues, and the dangers of spreading weapons of mass destruction and deadly diseases like AIDS. It is no longer plausible to perceive of Christian-Muslim relations in terms of relations between Islam and the West, because today the centers of Christianity and Islam have shifted to Africa, Asia, and the Americas, and the fluid nature of modern society has led to a retreat from geographic separation.[81]

In Cyberspace

The unprecedented communication between or among Muslims in cyberspace (the Internet) has contributed to a wide variety of debates and exchanges about civil society, the rule of law, and democratization. This has created a religious public sphere in which all Muslims can participate. Many Islamic groups and parties have set up Web sites, like the Ikwan al-Muslimeen (Muslim Brotherhood) in Egypt, the Jama'at-e Islami in Pakistan, the Islamic Movement in Palestine (Hamas), and the Hizbollah in Lebanon, illustrating how Muslims are using technology to create a virtual pluralistic community.

This so-called *umma* that Islamists are promoting is a transnational one, or even a virtual one, through the Internet. Islamists who once pushed for the creation of an Islamic state—so the argument runs—have given way to neofundamentalists who tend to concentrate on individuals and shun purely political issues.[82]

The claim that the increased information and knowledge about Islam on the Net has resulted in the formation of a virtual community of Muslims is well documented. This claim nevertheless fails to address how such a global electronic web of people, ideas, and interaction on the Internet, which is unrestricted by the borders of the geopolitical world, would lead to or undermine moral convergence with the rest of the world. Cyberspace could simultaneously intensify identity issues and those related to transnational ties and interests among varying individuals, groups, and communities.

Similarly, the central theoretical problem for populist Islam is the absence of a clear link between cyberspace and the consolidation and growth of Islam.[83] Although the Internet has accelerated pluralism in the Islamic community, largely in terms of the availability of information, its impact on believers' minds is as yet unclear.[84] What is clear is that these cyber communications are affecting processes of identity formation, demonstrating less coherence and correspondence with established institutionalized sources of information in the community.[85]

The Social Construction of Human Rights

In the late 1940s, when the Universal Declaration of Human Rights (UDHR) was drawn up, representatives of Muslim countries expressed qualms about some of its articles (e.g., Articles 16 and 18) but nevertheless participated in drafting its text. There seemed to be, at least initially, a consensus in the postwar period on the need to construct a harmonious cosmopolitan order. In this context, the idea of universal human rights appeared to have had a wide appeal. The subsequent international human rights movements became a terrain of struggle not only among different interpretations of those rights but also regarding the ensuing claims of ownership of the international standards.

It is important, however, to recognize that Muslim views were divided. Yet, as Susan Waltz points out, no Muslim country actually voted against Article 18 (freedom to choose and change one's religion).[86] Some objections were raised regarding Article 16 (marriage and the family) by delegates from Egypt, Saudi Arabia, Iraq, and Syria on the grounds that some of its components conflicted with Islamic laws and rules. But in the end, no Muslim countries voted against Article 16 or steered away from it in the name of Islamic law. When the Declaration was submitted to the General Assembly, no Muslim country actually cast a vote against it. Saudi Arabia was the lone Muslim country that opted for abstaining, along with South Africa and several Eastern European countries at the time.[87]

When the draft UDHR was submitted to the Third Committee in 1948, Waltz continues, there were opportunities for participation and discourse among Muslim countries. The UN official records indicate numerous interventions from Afghanistan, Egypt, Iraq, Lebanon, Pakistan, Saudi Arabia, and Syria during the detailed review of the UDHR. Egypt and Lebanon particularly offered some key amendments to the draft prepared by the commission.[88]

After the UDHR won the support of a majority of countries, representatives of several Muslim countries played an important role in the subsequent development of two additional UN covenants—the International Covenant on Civil and Political Rights (ICCPR) and the International Covenant on Economic, Social and Cultural Rights (ICESCR). Despite some objections to certain articles, all Muslim countries voted in favor of the covenants, including Saudi Arabia. During the 1950s and 1960s, when the foundations for the covenants were laid out, several key individuals from Muslim majority countries contributed to the drafting of the instruments. These include Jamil Baroody (Saudi Arabia), Bedia Afnan (Iraq), Abdul Rahman Pazhwak (Afghanistan), Abdul Kayaly and Jawaat Mufti (Syria), Begum Aziz Ahmed (Pakistan), Abdullah El-Erian (UAR), Mohammed Chackchouk (Tunisia), Abdul Latif Hendraningrat (Indonesia), Wan Mustapha bin Haji Ali (Malaya), and Halima Embarek Warzazi (Morocco).[89]

Interestingly enough, Muslim delegates repeatedly expressed concerns about the logical coherence of the draft texts in terms of civil laws and Islamic law. They were cognizant of crafting global standards of good governance that were all-encompassing and involved all governments. Representing Pakistan in 1948, for instance, Shaista Ikramullah asserted that "it was imperative that the peoples of the world should recognize the existence of a code of civilized behavior which would apply not only in international relations but also in domestic affairs."[90] The significance of Muslim states' participation in assembling those human rights standards notwithstanding, the fact remains that resistance to the new globalization-era human rights regime is not out of antagonism to human rights but from a recognition of the problems inherent in creating a solid global basis for human rights, given the disparities of power and wealth among nations and the intricacies of global politics.

Consider, for example, the way in which powerful states have reacted to international norms. These states have routinely disregarded international standards if doing so has been in their interest.[91] Given this reality, the challenge rests in persuading weak states to adhere to international norms. The human rights system today faces more challenging conditions than most of its proponents had previously imagined or anticipated. It is in this context that Muslim countries' challenges to the universality of human rights must be understood. When invoked against the universality of human rights, some experts argue, culture has become a proxy for many different concerns, including preserving national sovereignty, prioritizing economic and social rights, placing the right to development over civil-political rights, or even opposing Western double standards in applying rights.[92]

In the 1980s and early 1990s, Muslims attempted to define their own Codex Islamicus for human rights by drafting the Cairo Declaration on Human Rights in Islam, known as the Universal Islamic Declaration of Human Rights (UIDHR). Some experts have pointed out that the UIDHR uses formulations in the English and Arabic versions that convey contradictory impressions. These different impressions have little to do with mandates of Islamic law more generally. It seems fair to argue that the violations of human rights (e.g., religious freedoms) in the Muslim world are a result of official policies and repressive regimes.[93] Regardless, Muslims' efforts to codify their own human rights illustrate that Muslim states are in fact responding to intellectual pressures of social modernity. But it does not suggest that Islam is transforming from a trans-statist to a sub-statist doctrine. For many Muslims, however, Islamic personal ethics represent a code of conduct they willingly undertake as an act of private worship.

An inward-looking view has also emerged among some segments of Muslim societies, including the media pundits, intellectuals, and business elite.[94] Muslim societies' internal preoccupations are arguably far more significant in the long run than anti-Westernism.[95] Significantly, Muslims have come to realize that the nature of state-society relations would have to undergo a drastic change were they to enjoy democratic rights and basic freedoms. All Muslim states have ratified at least one international human rights treaty. Over 70 percent of the members of the Organization of the Islamic Conference (OIC)—that is, forty of its fifty-six member states—have ratified both the International Covenant on Civil and Political Rights and the International Covenant on Economic and Social Rights.[96] With the exception of Somalia, all OIC member states have ratified the UN Convention on the Rights of the Child. The United States remains the only Western country that has refused to ratify the Convention on the Rights of the Child.

The Muslim world has, in defense of the downtrodden and the underprivileged, taken on the challenge of addressing structural causes of injustice by acknowledging that human rights are not solely confined to civil-political rights. The achievement of economic, social, and cultural rights (especially the right to development) must be regarded as an important component of safeguarding human rights. The Muslim world has rightfully pointed to the fact those economic rights proclaimed in the Universal Declaration of Human Rights, especially Articles 25–1 ("everyone has the right to a standard of living adequate for the health and well-being of himself and his family, including food, clothing, housing, and medical care") and Article 28 ("everyone is entitled to a social and international order in which the rights and freedoms set forth in this Declaration can be fully realized") cannot be fulfilled for the vast majority of Third World inhabitants living in abject poverty in view of the current unjust international economic order.

To avoid abstract and false universalism under the rubric of the Universal Declaration of Human Rights, the Muslim world's participation in the rights-creation process is imperative. The articulation of a "right of civilizational participation" is integral to the normative reconstruction of a legitimate world order based on cultural identity, difference, and self-definition.[97] This reconstruction can and should be achieved without sacrificing fundamental freedoms, including civil-political rights as well as economic and social rights. Rather, what is needed is a rethinking of the Western human rights framework that recognizes diversity of cultures while conferring and protecting individual and collective identity. The right to one's identity must be safeguarded within the framework of the right to cultural self-determination.

With regard to Western participation in a cross-cultural discussion of human rights, Jürgen Habermas argues that the contest over the sufficient interpretation of human rights has to do not with the desirability of the "modern condition" but with an interpretation of human rights that does justice to the modern world from the standpoints of other cultures as well as our own.[98] "The controversy turns above all," Habermas writes, "on the individualism and secular character of human rights that are centered in the concept of autonomy."[99] The concept of autonomy, when uncoupled from religious and cosmological worldviews, could promote inclusion and the principle of tolerance. The latter enables others' equally entitled coexistence within the same political community.

While shoving into the background the relevance that different cultures give to religion, Habermas points out that the conception of human rights provided the solution to a problem that once confronted Europeans—when they had to surmount the political consequences of confessional fragmentation. Now similar situations pose serious cultural and political challenges to non-Western societies. To avoid cultural conflicts of our times, Habermas concludes, "collective actors must, regardless of their different cultural traditions, agree for better or worse on norms of coexistence. The autarkic isolation against external influences is no longer an option in today's world."[100]

Critics of universal human rights as enunciated in the UDHR argue that claims of universality of human rights need to be negotiated within the international discourse with a view toward building a consensus among different civilizations. The neglect of civilizational participation for Islam has produced a series of partially deformed institutions, practices, and perceptions. There is also a wide range of intracivilizational differences in Islam that need to be democratically and nonviolently negotiated as part of constructing a human rights paradigm.[101] The participation of different civilizations in the formation of human rights norms is both desirable and necessary. Cultural differences must be negotiated "as part of an effort to create a world in which all people should be free to deliberate, develop, and choose values to help them live more equitable and fulfilling lives."[102]

The present mentality, critics insist, that sets the universal against culture must be discarded. Andrew J. Nathan questions the universal forms of rationality and the manner in which such a notion of rationality tends to undermine culturally particular values. According to Nathan, it is a fallacy to argue that whatever is culturally valued cannot be conceived of as universal. It is important to realize, Nathan continues, that all social facts and all values are culturally situated. Such recognition would dissolve the dilemma between the universal and culture and "might open new prospects not only for the human rights debate but for the study of culture more generally."[103]

While Western scholars view human rights as liberating ideas and tools, some Muslim analysts regard the human rights movement as a postcolonial tool of cultural imperialism. Enlightenment philosophers began with the individual and his or her sense of experience as a core value, thus privileging the individual over the community. Muslim philosophers, in contrast, began with the nature of community as a core unit of analysis. The Islamic principles, which emphasize a communitarian view of human rights, accord priorities to the rights of state, society, and collective identities and interests over individual rights.[104] Given these cultural and contextual differences, and given the existing inequality of power, wealth, and levels of economic development in the world, the real question becomes this: how are we to foster a global consensus on international human rights? One viewpoint holds that a cross-cultural dialogue may indeed be essential for "mitigating differentials in power relations in the present context of economic and technological globalization."[105] This observation, however, admits that until such differentials in the global power structure and levels of economic development are properly redressed, it is hard to imagine how meaningful progress toward building such a consensus is practical and sustainable.

Conclusion

Globalization has reinforced different, and sometimes contradictory, processes and trends. It has given rise to worldwide flows of information, trade, and ideas on the one hand and it has revitalized religious and cultural identity (both individually and collectively) on the other. It is not clear how people living in a globalizing world would empathize with the culture of "the other." Moreover, it leaves unanswered the question of how the grand, abstract Universal Declaration of Human Rights can be linked in any effective way to the concrete and situation-specific lives of people in the Muslim world.

The permeation of rights discourse in the Muslim world, made possible largely by increasing international communications and mass education, has opened up an enormous rhetorical as well as institutional space for many Muslims who hope to reconcile their cultures and faith with universalism.[106] At the same time, the expansion of self-awareness and civilizational identity has reinforced a return to Islamist rights talk. That is, Islamic identity has been reasserted through activities aimed at protecting and promoting human rights within the Muslim world.

As globalization has intensified, concerns have been raised over whether Muslim countries will lose the ability to control their own economies, their status in the global distribution of power, and, most important, their cultural assets. The ways in which identity and rights intersect will become increasingly crucial to the discourse of universal human rights in coming years. Our fourfold typology of Muslim viewpoints might provide some answers, albeit tentative, to the question of whether the human rights paradigm has gained in legitimacy throughout the Muslim world.

It is desirable and necessary to have Muslims' participation in human rights discourse in an effort to retain what is still universally valid and to adjust to changing moral and political contexts. The best way to develop a set of nonethnocentric universal values, arguably, is through argumentation.[107] It is also the case that participants in the intercultural dialogue must be open to internal and external legitimate criticisms. The willingness to critically reflect on one's own local culture and practices is of great importance in maintaining any sustainable intercultural dialogue. Establishing a human rights framework that is not only visible in the actual practices of the states but also is reflective of cultural/moral diversity is a good place to start the intercultural dialogue. The diversity of Muslim countries and Islamism must also be appreciated in any discussion of Islam's role in world affairs. The common good of both humanity as a whole and the planet itself requires the renegotiation of principles and procedures between and among cultures and civilizations that constitute the global civil society. This renegotiation is premised on the idea that global inclusiveness recognizes universal norms while allowing for cultural distinctiveness.[108]

The task of expanding the dialogue between the Muslim and Western worlds must be a mutual one. The Muslim world's archaic and unfit traditions and laws (such as stoning to death in the case of adultery, amputating a hand for theft, and proscribing apostasy in situations of voluntary renunciations of one's religious faith) must be discarded. Similarly, the Western world's normative hegemony and cultural intrusions into Muslim countries' local circumstances must be discontinued. Western countries have failed to demonstrate consistent acceptance of collective and group rights as well as economic, social, and cultural rights (e.g., the right to education, employment, adequate standard of living). Their policy makers have thus far shied away from providing any concrete definition and implementation processes by which such human rights are taken seriously.[109] Western countries must become full parties to the UN Covenant on Economic, Social, and Cultural Rights if a general consensus on universal human rights is to emerge (the United States has yet to endorse the socioeconomic and cultural rights presented therein).

Both civilizations must engage in the cultural mediation of the local and global.[110] As John O. Voll has so aptly reminded us, as scholars "we cannot accept the differences between cultures as being so great as to be unbridgeable."[111] A global consensus has emerged on certain rights that are so fundamental and nonderogative that no form of cultural diversity can justify their absence. These include, among others, free elections, political participation, free press, peaceful protest, individual and organized dissent, and the rule of law. To this list, one must add freedom from torture, freedom from hunger, freedom from discrimination, and freedom from extrajudicial killing. To argue that these rights are context sensitive and culturally contingent is politically self-serving and morally suspect.

Chapter 3
Gender, Identity, and Negotiating Rights

Historically regarded as cultural transmitters and protectors of national values, Muslim women have become a new subject of debate. This impassioned debate on women's roles in Islam is also seen by many as a source of moral and social disorder. Defying both conventional and patriarchal ideologies, Muslim women today have become a powerful voice for change. Interestingly, certain elements of Islamic feminism and secular feminism are working together to push for legal and educational reforms.

The spread of mass education and mass communication has facilitated a new awareness among Muslims, dissolving barriers of space and distance and opening new grounds for interaction and mutual recognition, both inside these countries and beyond. Increasingly, local issues have taken on transnational dimensions.[1] This era of social transformation has profoundly impacted Muslim societies. No group has been more drastically and immediately influenced by such transformation than women, who have struggled to reform laws and construct new rules.

By addressing shared problems, such as preventing domestic violence and gender discrimination, Muslim women have come into contact with women's movements and organizations across the globe, developing transnational ties and identities. There clearly are some divisions among women's organizations and groups over issues such as *hijab* (Islamic dress code), which has become a symbol for the defense of the faith, family integrity, and Islamic identity as well as some religious beliefs. Nevertheless, the convergence between certain elements of Islamic feminists and secular feminists has pointed to the existence of pragmatic grounds for cooperation between the two.

Muslim women encounter three fronts simultaneously. First, they represent an Islamic identity that more often than not is in conflict with modern political regimes and state elites. Second, they must fight against Islamic fundamentalists, whose ideas, institutions, and goals they vehemently reject. And finally, and just as important, they face a mundane confrontation with a prevailing patriarchal culture within which they live. Questions of women's rights are exacerbated by difficulties Muslim women encounter in a patriarchal culture in which women are often characterized by stereotypes.

The "borderless solidarity" has led to the promotion of women's rights across and within cultures, but it stands in a problematic relationship to broader, more complex social issues. Although this global solidarity is resisted in many parts of the Muslim world, women's empowerment is seen as the most effective antidote to extremism in the Muslim world. This chapter attempts to contextualize gender analysis in the cultural, economic, and political domains while addressing three questions: (1) Why have Muslim women become the agents of change, reform, and democratization in a globalizing world? (2) What impact has globalization had on Muslim women and the rise of Islamic feminism? (3) How can Muslim women maintain the integrity of their culture while at the same time remaining receptive to universal values, ideas, and institutions?

Reconceptualization of Gender Identity

Globalization has prompted the simultaneous but possibly contradictory emergence of transnational advocacy networks, which defend collective identity transcending national borders, and cross-national alliances, which challenge certain modern norms as false universalism.[2] The gender-based divisions in the world conferences on women's issues attest to this reality.[3] At the same time, concerns with preventing domestic violence and improving the social-legal status of women have opened up a new discursive space for the dialogue between Islamic and secular feminists. This development has made resistance and empowerment central to any processes of change in women's status and rights in the Muslim world.

Many obstacles stand in the way of Muslim women's struggle for equality, some of which are linked to the political economy and others to sociocultural contexts, religion, and cultural traditions. John L. Esposito points to the multitude of barriers: "Muslim women's battle is about gender, class, and political and economic power as often as it is about religious faith and identity."[4] The relationship between Islam, the state, and gender politics can be better understood as the various modes of control that states have either averted or established over local, kin-based, religious, and ethnic communities. The persistence of communal politics during the processes of state consolidation tends to undermine women's rights. The "Islamization" package—as a means of establishing Islamic credentials—introduced by General Zia ul-Haq conferred legal sanction on crude forms of sexual discrimination, against which Pakistani women's organizations vehemently protested.[5]

With the sprawling identity politics—that is, the increasing politicization of religious and ethnic identities—women's issues were left to local communities and cultural traditions. Governments struggling to consolidate their legitimacy chose tactically to surrender control of women to their immediate communities and families, thus depriving female citizens of their full legal protection.[6] In those Muslim countries where the state itself supports religious groups, as in Iran, Pakistan, or Saudi Arabia, such patriarchal authority stretches beyond the state to the clergy, police, or other unrelated men, who consider it their duty to monitor the dress and conduct of women.[7] Tighter controls over women and restrictions of these kinds have forced many Muslim women to seek change from within such communities by reconstructing their identity and religiosity, especially as these communities' economic and political dependence on the rest of the world increases. Of particular relevance to this book are the ways in which women redefine religion and negotiate modernity.

Over the past two decades, the tension between political regimes and Islamic identity has intensified. Central to this tension is the debate over the role and status of women, who have come not only to demand but also to represent the vast social changes transpiring in the Muslim world. Increasingly, women's place in society and in the family has become a primary focus of potential change in Muslim societies. Much of the progress made by women has thus far been in the legal-political arenas. The family personal status law remains resistant to change, in large part because the "family" continues to occupy a central place in Muslim societies, both culturally and historically.

How to reconcile the family with the right of women to act against their husbands—particularly in cases of inheritance, marriage, divorce, child support, and women's reproductive choice—remains an unresolved issue. The 1956 Tunisian Code of Personal Status (CPS), which profoundly altered family law and the legal status of women, represented one of the initial reformist policies publicly known in the Arab world. This was, in one expert's view, a manifestation of the different vision of society held by Habib Bourguiba and demonstrated after his victory over other factions immediately following the proclamation of the nation's independence.[8] The

CPS changed, among other things, regulations on marriage, divorce, alimony, custody, and to a lesser extent inheritance. The code decreased the prerogatives of extended kin in family matters, giving women great rights by broadening the range of options available to them in their private lives. The code abolished polygamy, terminated the husband's right to repudiate his wife, allowed women to file for divorce, and increased women's custody rights. Absent any feminist movement or women's mass protest movement in Tunisia in the 1950s demanding such reforms, the move can rightly be labeled a reform from above.[9]

A similar attempt at reforming personal status law occurred in Morocco, albeit several decades later. With the support of King Mohammed VI, Morocco has recently adopted a new family law, in which women are granted property rights within marriage as well as the ability to initiate a divorce. The minimum age of marriage for women was raised to eighteen from fifteen. The law also tightened restrictions on polygamy, which is subject to the judge's authorization, and introduced stringent legal obligations on the husband to provide similar living conditions to all wives. Accordingly, women now have the right to choose monogamy.[10] Abdeilela bin Kiran, the leader of Morocco's Party of Justice and Development, an Islamist group that has made huge electoral gains in recent elections, has praised the family code, arguing that "it is in keeping with Islam."[11]

In post-Saddam Iraq, the guarantee of 25 percent female participation in the Iraqi interim government, known as the Transitional National Assembly, fares better than the 14 percent representation by women in the U.S. House of Representatives. Women's rights activists in Iraq are also pleased with the document that indicates Islamic law (shari'a) would be just one of several sources of future legislation.[12]

Muslim feminists blame male jurists rather than the sacred texts, including the Qur'an and the Hadith, for perpetuating inequality between men and women.[13] The existing male-centered practices and institutions have reinforced the notion that women are "seductresses and potential sources of moral and social disorder."[14] In such a context, nationalism is often invoked in gendered politics, and women are thus presented in their symbolic role as mothers, the physical reproducers of the nation, and transmitters of culture. Symbolism is manifested in the ways in which women protect their bodies and behavior.[15] The role and status of Muslim women, one observer points out, has become a highly politicized and charged symbol in cultural battles between the Muslim world and the West as well as within the Muslim world itself.[16] The cultural and political dominance of the West renders the use of Western rights-based language and the issue of the liberation of women vulnerable to the charges of lacking cultural authenticity.[17]

Despite conservative resistance, the views regarding women's role in Muslim societies have undergone a profound change. Due to educational reforms and increased female literacy rates, Muslim women have become a significant new force with more visibility in public life. Consider, for example, the case of Islamic feminists in Iran. Islamic feminists and secular feminists disagree over whether religious interpretations are the appropriate strategy for confronting legal and social oppression of women. Factions of the religious and secular camps, however, have found a common ground in their attempts to push for reforms of family law, including divorce law, inheritance, custody rights over children, and alimony.

The feminist monthly magazine *Zanan* has sought to bridge the dichotomy between secular and Islamic feminists in Iran by becoming an outlet for well-known secular and non-Muslim women as well as its traditional Muslim women's perspective. The journal has embarked on a radical interpretation of Islamic sources concerned with women's rights, opening up a new discursive space for dialogue between secular and Islamic feminists. The magazine's most impressive success has been to bring modernized religious women together with their secular, nonconformist counterparts.[18] This convergence has unleashed new dynamics for improving women's legal status and social positions.[19]

Furthermore, *Zanan* has tacitly insisted on temporality or secularity (*asri shodan*) of religion.[20] Such an inclusive strategy of convergence may prove to be the most effective way for transforming Iranians' cultural, attitudinal, and legal orientations. For now, at least, it has shifted the focus from the ongoing oppression of women in the Islamic Republic of Iran to an appreciation of resistance, empowerment, and change.[21] Its major drawback, however, is the lack of attention to real socioeconomic problems and political variables in the broader society. Political intransigence continues to block any real progress in women's socioeconomic situations.

Although the unilateral right to divorce remains the exclusive domain of men, the divorce laws have improved the position of women vis-à-vis men. In 1992, an amendment of divorce laws produced more reforms. All divorcing couples must go through a process of arbitration. Courts added a new right to compensation for the divorced wife, in the form of *ujrat al-mithal* (wages for the household and child care she undertook during the marriage). This compensation has given the wife greater financial security upon divorce. In 1997, the *mehr* (dower) was inflation-indexed by the parliament. In 2001, the ban on single women receiving government scholarships to study abroad was lifted.[22]

Between 1956 and 1966, the female literacy rate in Iran increased from 8 percent to 17.9 percent. In 1971, some 25.5 percent of women were literate. Before the revolution, 35 percent were literate, and by the late 1990s the rate had reached 74 percent. Under the shah's regime, about a third of university students were female. By 1999, women made up fully half of new admissions. In 1999, one in three Iranian physicians was a woman. In the postrevolutionary era, many women gained access to higher education, making it possible for them to enter public domains.[23]

Today, Iranian women are among the most educated and accomplished women in the Muslim world. Sixty-four percent of university graduates in Iran are female, with practically no restrictions on selecting fields of study previously banned to them. I am neither suggesting that Iranian women are far better off in terms of their rights under the Islamic Republic than during the Shah's era nor justifying the limits to external pressure. Rather, my position is simply that human rights ultimately result from concrete social struggles. They are earned—not given—and must be fought for and won on the national turf. The struggle is gradual but based on grassroots and social movements. There is tremendous potential for international norms to enter domestic law and policy through the efforts of social movements and "forces from below."[24]

Producing sustainable change in women's rights is inescapably slow and fraught with difficulties. More than one hundred reformist newspapers have been closed since President Muhammad Khatami won the 1997 Iranian election. Many journalists and student activists have been jailed. Torture and other human rights abuses have been rampant and systematic. And yet, Iranian human rights activists and lawyers have struggled consistently to promote their cause. But the possibility of a foreign military attack on their country represents a colossal disaster for their cause. In the case of Iran, military incursion is not a proper tool for protecting and promoting human rights, and it will risk undermining local efforts aimed at improving these rights.[25]

Curbing violence against women has been a dominant theme in Malaysia since the Domestic Violence Act (DVA) was enacted in 1995. The DVA, though a clear indication of progress on gender issues, criminalizes violence against married women.[26] Women's groups have been concerned with the incidence of rape, the problem of sex workers, and trafficking in women.[27] The Sisters in Islam (SIS), a local NGO established in 1992 in Kuala Lumpur, has become a prime example of the way Muslim women can encounter reactionary, politicized Islam in the context of a multiethnic and multireligious society. The core members turn directly to the Qur'an for support and justification of women's rights and equality. They emphasize reinterpretation and application of universal Qur'anic principles to modern Malaysian society.

In Malaysia, cultural traditions or customs, known as *adat*, define and determine women's role and their participation in society in positive, non-hierarchical ways. The rule of *hijab* (Islamic dress) entails no female seclusion and segregation of social space within Malay's cultural traditions, as it does throughout much of the Middle East.[28]

Economic globalization has created a unique situation in which the role of the state in promoting socioeconomic conditions has become more crucial than in the past. Some human rights scholars have argued that an alliance between human rights advocates and state elites, who are inhospitable to human rights, may prove to be the most effective way to maintain or reestablish social control over free markets essential to guarantee economic and social rights for all.[29] In parts of the Muslim world (Jordan, Tunisia, Sudan, and Saudi Arabia), this pragmatic pursuit, coupled with women's struggle against Islamic extremists' agenda, has led to the emergence of an alliance between the government and women known as state feminism.

Neither feminism nor women's rights movements are solely of Western origin. In several Asian and Middle Eastern colonies, "the women question" arose in the early twentieth century alongside or in connection with anticolonial nationalism. Some feminists even traveled to participate in international conferences.[30] Feminists in the Muslim world, as elsewhere, are diverse and represent varying viewpoints. Aware of their identity and rights, as well as their place in history, many Muslim women have become avid enthusiasts of globalization. In a globalizing context defined by common problems and shared standards as well as by transnational identities and ties, Muslim women's central role will be to shape the terms and establish the conditions under which discrimination is countered and social and legal reforms are advocated.

Some scholars call on human rights advocates in Muslim societies to seek, articulate, and engage Islamic justifications for the rights of women. They maintain that adopting such a method of discourse is indeed integral to—and not just a substitute for—the political struggle for the protection and promotion of women's human rights.[31] Others warn about using Islamic rationales as part of an appeal to the laws of Nature, laws that have discriminated against women by making them different from men.[32] Such a pattern of hypocrisy on women's rights issues, they note, is not unique to Islamic societies; it is an example of the worldwide rhetorical strategy to bypass the principle of women's equality as established in international law and such UN human rights instruments as the Convention on the Elimination of All Forms of Discrimination against Women (CEDAW).[33]

Still others note that Muslim women must transcend the colonial experience and traditional patriarchal politics if they are to achieve their task of self-authentication. "They should refuse to identify themselves as against the world outside," insists Mahnaz Afkhami, an Iranian secular feminist.[34] The new vehicles of international communication, such as the Internet, have spread further interest in *ijtihad* (independent reasoning), leading women to challenge male-centered values, institutions, and legal systems.

The spread of the Internet and the growing access to it in Muslim societies have resulted in at least two types of women's mobilization: feminist organizations within Muslim countries and the international solidarity network or transnational feminist networks (TFNs), such as Women Living under Muslim Law (WLUML). These networks bring together women from different countries around a common agenda, such as rights, economics, reproductive health and rights, and antimilitarism.[35]

Heba Raouf Ezzat, an Islamist writer and political scientist in Cairo, has led a fight against outmoded thinking on women by other Islamists. "God in the Qur'an never put restrictions on a woman in a ruling position," she wrote. "Contrary to what the traditional Muslim scholars teach, a woman in a leading political position is not against God's system or against the Qur'an. It might be against the chauvinistic views of some men."[36]

Women's access to resources of participation in the larger society has been increasingly aided by several factors, including the growing necessity for more women to earn a cash income, the market expansion in women-oriented and women-run social and political movements, the rise in demand for female literacy levels, and the concern with population planning and its effects on national economic goals.[37] In brief, many Muslim women have come to see globalization as a liberalizing and empowering process with far-reaching implications for gender relations.[38]

Dissenting Voices and Actions

The explosion of new possibilities and feminist thought points to dramatic changes in the Muslim world. Two forms of change can be discerned: structural and ideational. The material or structural change is associated with the socioeconomic transformation and growth that Muslim societies have undergone. The rising educational and employment opportunities for women in the Muslim world have helped to shape new ideas and attitudes with profound implications for such societies. The availability of educational resources in such countries as Qatar, Morocco, and Jordan has led to women's rising political participation.

Women studies' scholars have begun to pay attention to the messages and instruments of communication that the state, Islamic groups, and NGOs in civil society have used to enhance women's status vis-à-vis the family and reproductive rights.[39] Exposure to ideational forces, via extended schooling and education, has spurred the debate over customs, habits, and conformism, influencing the way in which women confront traditional and legal restraints on their rights. The upsurge of interest in the Arab-regional and UN conferences on women in Cairo (1994) and Beijing (1995) represents the growing impact of ideational factors.

Cultural Mediation

One important, if not dominant, aspect of life in the Muslim world is that *cultural politics*—a process of conflict over cultural norms and symbols—is inseparable from *sexual politics*, that is, women's struggle for power and authority at domestic, community, national, and international levels. One of the most drastically visible ideational challenges facing women's rights in the Muslim world is the issue of gender identity. During much of the twentieth century, the issue of Islamic identity of Muslim countries has shaped the debate regarding the role and status of Muslim women. As a symbol of national identity, Muslim women have faced a daunting challenge to promote "modernity" and the notion of "becoming modern" without losing the integrity of their culture. They have for a long time struggled to maintain their identity in a modern way. Foremost among the symbols of identity are the "dress code" and an alternative "Islamic moral/social order."

Six decades after the death of Ataturk, Turkey is pushed to redefine its Muslim identity on both social and political levels.[40] The top-down modernization by secular elites over a period of almost seventy years has brought Turkish women positive consequences. The imposition of eight years of compulsory schooling and the enactment of the law that tries to prevent intrafamily violence are two examples of such achievements. In 1981, Turkey became the only Muslim country where abortion was legal on request.[41] In reaction to a secularization process in the country, the "New Muslim" women's movement emerged, which attacked not just the Western world and Turkey, brought into being by the Kemalist reforms, but also attempted to dissociate itself from orthodox Islam.[42] Ironically, the secular feminist movement, whether Kemalist or radical, by siding with the state and the army to counterbalance the influences of this "New Muslim" movement, has "lost the search for new solutions and new alliances."[43]

The Pahlavi dynasty (1925–79) in Iran and its modernizing programs led to Islamic resistance, expressed by using the chador (*hijab*) as a symbol of resistance against the shah's regime. In the post-Islamic revolution era, the Family Protection Law of 1967, which promoted secular laws and placed some limitations on men's ability to divorce their wives willfully, was canceled and the legal age for marriage, which had been raised to eighteen by this law, was lowered to fourteen.[44] The reformist women in the second decade after the revolution pushed successfully for the restoration of the Family Protection Law of 1967. Yet many cultural and traditional constraints affecting gender relations, such as individual rights, *hijab*, or sexual freedom and preferences, continued to characterize social relations. The reformist women's movement proved to be a crisis-oriented one that failed to fundamentally challenge patriarchy.[45]

In recent years, however, a noticeable split has appeared between traditional religious women and nonconformist Islamic feminists in favor of reform, on the one hand, and a convergence of religious and secular women on some matters relating to divorce law, child custody rights, and alimony, on the other (see Table 2). While for some young Muslim women, *hijab* may be a sign of piety or a political statement, for others, it is increasingly becoming a declaration of identity and fashion sense.[46] Of particular relevance to this chapter is the continuing struggle of reformist women, both religious and secular, to build consensus on at least some issues, including the prevention of domestic violence and the promotion of gender equality.

Since the late 1990s, as Mehrangis Kar reminds us, these groups have participated in elections, have been active as legal staff in the Islamic courts, and have significantly contributed to the literature on women's rights in Iran. The result has been a vibrant intellectual setting imbued with flourishing ideas about universal human rights and women's rights.[47] Increasingly, new configurations of Islam, revolution, and feminism are emerging in Iran.[48] In fact, the women's press in Iran has become a primary vehicle for demonstrating how secular and Islamically oriented women have redefined the status and role of women. A coalition of secular and Islamic feminists, some of whom became members of the Iranian parliament in 2000, has begun to work with "reformist parliamentarians to contest the codified and institutionalized privileges of men over women."[49]

Their divergent views on some issues notwithstanding, an unprecedented degree of gender solidarity has emerged between secular and modernist-Islamist women, thus strengthening their alliance. Mahboobeh Abbassgholizadeh, the editor of *Farzaneh: Journal of Women's Studies and Research* in Tehran, has noted that Islamist women are no longer the sole heirs of the revolution: "We have realized that our sectarian views of the first post-revolutionary years led to the isolation of many competent seculars, which was to the detriment of all women."[50]

Iranian women, however, continue to lack the organizational infrastructure to build a sustainable civil society in postrevolutionary Iran.[51] Women have lost any enthusiasm for political power, revolution, and ideology. Rather, they seem to be more concerned with the "control of their own lives within political, social, and economic institutions, whatever the ideological configurations of those institutions."[52]

Just as revealing is the phenomenon of Islamic feminism in Egypt. Heba Raouf Ezzat, herself a supporter of the Muslim Brotherhood and a practicing Muslim, defends the Beijing "Platform for Action" but resents attempts by the state to impose a Western secular view of the world on Egyptian society and women. Islamist women have a public presence that has enabled them to win elections and thus become a force in the parliament.[53] Islamic religious modernity, as opposed to secular Western modernity, is linked not just to legitimacy but also to considerable power in social and political space.

Many Muslim women join Islamists to find a legitimate place for their identity, social presence, and political activism. The so-called fundamentalist threat, however, has put many secularist and feminist groups on the side of the government, with the price of being silent about the violations of human rights perpetrated by the state in the process.[54] Another fundamental problem is that the majority of women in Egypt remain excluded from the globalization process because of their lack of presence and representation in Egyptian politics.[55]

In Pakistan, the key identity problem since the inception of the country in 1947 has been deciding whether it is an Islamic state that is committed to implementing the shari'a (Islamic law) or simply a state for the Muslims of the subcontinent.[56] Some state elites saw in modernization an instrumental value that could be used to push for the emancipation of women. Improving the position of women came to be seen as the central element of modernization by the secular nationalists.[57] The alliance between the women's movement and the modernizing state in Pakistan under Ayub Khan (1947–70) and Zulifkhar Ali Bhutto (1970–77) must be seen in this context. A manifestation of this push is women's organizations such as the All Pakistan Women Association (APWA) started in 1949 by the wife of then prime minister Liaqate Ali Khan.

Passage of the Muslim Family laws Ordinance of 1961 under Ayub Khan marked an era of confrontation between Ayub Khan and the *ulama* and Jamaat-e-Islami, a religiopolitical organization that has particularly influenced the intelligentsia and youth of the South Asian subcontinent. During Zulifkhar Ali Bhutto's tenure, there was continued support for women's rights as part of the government's modernizing agenda.[58] Under General Zia Ul Haq (1977–88) changes occurred in three areas of law—the Hudud Ordinance of 1979, the 1984 Law of Evidence, and *qisas* (retribution) and *diyah* (blood money)—that dramatically affected women's status and lives. The Hudud Ordinance referred to fixed punishment and laws against theft, fornication, consumption of alcohol, robbery, illegal sexual intercourse, rebellion, and apostasy. The Law of Evidence required that in the case of rape, four Muslim adult truthful male eye-witnesses testify that the act of rape has occurred. *Qisas* referred to the laws of retaliation and *diyah* laws had to do with compensation paid to the heirs of a victim. In the case of *diyah* laws, the blood money for a woman was half that of a man's. These laws were—and continue to be—emblematic of discriminatory attitudes and practices against women. The challenge to the Islamization programs of Zia Ul Haq came from the urban professional women who organized the Women's Action Forum (WAF). Some members of WAF relied on Muslim feminist theologians, such as Riffat Hassan, and worked at a feminist interpretation of Muslim laws and history. This approach offered a possibility for expanding the base of the WAF beyond middle- and upper-class professional women to include women from the lower middle class and the working poor.[59]

The cultural centrality of family and its importance in preserving the desired moral order have become intricately linked to women's struggle for rights. The imposition of Western cultural practices on Muslim families is disruptive. In recent years, the women's movement in Pakistan has evolved from the politically oriented WAF to the project-oriented NGOs, and this has shifted the movement's focus from abstract ideological struggles toward women's practical needs. Asma Jahangir, for example, successfully defended a case involving an adult woman's right to marry of her own free will. In early 1997, a Lahore High Court decided by a 2-to-1 margin to validate the marriage of twenty-three-year-old Saima Waheed against the wishes of her parents.[60] One senior advocate of the Supreme Court of Pakistan strongly rejected Asma Jahangir's rationale, arguing that the most troubling aspect of this case was the portrayal of the institution of the family as "oppressive," claiming that such a characterization undermines the love, the protection, the intimacy, and the connection that the family provides. This was said to explain the peril of externally imposed cultural practices on Muslim families.[61]

Contrary to Huntington's "clash of civilizations" paradigm, the heterogeneity of cultural and religious beliefs has not precluded the emergence of cross-national alliances that challenge the course of modernity. The gender-based divisions in the world conferences on women's issues attest to this reality. Jane Bayes and Nayereh Tohidi argue that the 1995 United Nations Fourth World Conference on Women in Beijing was the site of competing trends between a new transnational, cross-cultural conservative and religious alliance against equal rights for women, on the one hand, and the growing globalization of women and gender politics, on the other. Bayes and Tohidi argue that the societal and structural conditions, such as cross-time, cross-class, and cross-cultural variability or diversity in the status of Catholic and Muslim women, demonstrate that religion is not the only or even the primary variable in determining women's rights in shaping gender relations.[62]

Sudan has mainly an agricultural economy with a sparsely developed urban population, with the exception of the capital, Greater Khartoum; in this country, Sondra Hale points out, "the cultural positioning of women by men is relevant to the Sudan situation, i.e., women are seen as the embodiment of the culture and expected to serve the culture/society through particular forms of labor."[63] Sudanese women have distanced themselves from Arab identity or an "authentically Arab" identity by displaying more willingness to be liberated from certain patriarchal Arab cultural traditions and customs, while returning to *pure* Islam. Under shari'a, they have insisted, women would have a higher status and more respect.[64]

TABLE 2. MUSLIM WOMEN AND CULTURAL POLITICS

	Ontology	
Epistemology	Cultural Relativism	Universalism
Anti-foundationalism	Islamic feminists and state feminists (communitarian pragmatism)	NGO feminists and post-Islamist feminists (cosmopolitan pragmatism)
Foundationalism	Conservative religious women (communitarian traditionalism)	Secular feminists (liberal and natural rights advocates)

State Feminism

Economic globalization has created a unique situation in which the role of the state in promoting socioeconomic conditions has become more critical than in the past. Some human rights scholars have argued that an alliance between human rights advocates and state elites, who are generally known to be unsympathetic to human rights, may prove to be the best way to maintain or (re)establish social control over free markets necessary to guarantee economic and social rights for all.[65] In parts of the Muslim world, women tend to think that the appropriate focus for them to deal with the processes of globalization and threat of Islamic radicalism is the political community—namely, the state. This pragmatic orientation has led to the emergence of state feminism, in the process creating varied opportunities and posing many difficulties for women (see Table 2 and Table 3).

The Jordanian Women's Union (JWU) has aimed at changing a variety of laws to advance greater equality between the sexes while improving family relations and curbing domestic violence. Yet this and other women's organizations, such as the General Federation of Jordanian Women (GFJW), are unlikely to play a vanguard role in the country's political development. In 1992, Prince Hassan established the Jordanian National Committee for Women (JNCW). Likewise, the Jordanian National Women's Forum (JNWF) was created with Princess Basma as its head and with logistical and financial support coming from the governorates and ministries. As its mission was the implementation of the government's National Strategy for Women, this proved to be a quasi-governmental organization.[66] This em-

TABLE 3. GENDER, IDENTITY, AND NEGOTIATING RIGHTS

Identity-Related Questions	*Forms*	*Agents*	*Sites*	*Strategies*
Who am I and what are my obligations and rights?	Shari'a-based reform	Islamic feminists	Localists (communitarian)	Cultural mediation
Who will I be without the state support?	Civil law reform	State feminists	Nationalists (pragmatic)	Seeking allies
How could I legitimate and empower my claims?	Governance and democratic structures	Nonstate feminists	Domestic and transnational advocacy networks (pragmatic)	Grassroots and social movements, as well as food and aid programs
What are my rights and how do they shape my interests?	International law and conventions	Secular feminists	Globalists (cosmopolitan)	Universalist (international norms, media, instruments, regimes; NGOs; rights groups)

bryonic Hashemite state feminism has not been without its limitations. It has marginalized authentic civil-society activity and closed a political opening initiated during the 1989–94 period. The weakness of civil-society institutions is in turn the key domestic reason for the continuation of such top-down NGOs, which undermine women's meaningful participation in the political system.[67] It should be noted, however, that JNWF has succeeded in putting "honor killing" on the national agenda.

In Tunisia, this type of state feminism within the broader construct of a corporatist political system has faced similar difficulties. Caught between the regime, which offers tolerance and a modicum of secular empowerment, and Islamists, who offer the reassurance of cultural authenticity and traditionally defined gender roles, Tunisian women face hard choices. Emma C. Murphy portrays the colossal challenge facing the government:

"However much largesse it is inclined to hand down to women from its bureaucratic heights, it has made few inroads into countering the social conservatism upon which political Islam feeds."[68] The Islamic paradigm, Murphy argues, entails a message that "offers women a solution to the contradictions of a society that demands they not only be the guardians of family honor and purity, but also participate in a modern, technologically advanced, and socially liberal environment."[69]

While considerable progress was made in women's status in the 1990s, "women do not achieve high ranks in more traditionally male-dominated ministries, such as the Ministries of the State and Interior, Justice, National Economy, Finance, or Foreign Affairs."[70] With regard to economic liberalization programs, Murphy writes that structural adjustment programs (SAPs) and economic liberalization programs are not gender neutral: women are the first to be laid off when wage cuts are implemented or when poverty rises. The female unemployment rate has increased in the early years of economic reform. But more important, women are caught in a cultural dilemma. Economic liberalization becomes synonymous with the enforced importation of alien cultural values. In trying to "gain cultural emancipation, women lose their economic freedom."[71] To prevent women from being drawn to Islamic groups, Tunisian governments have tried to incorporate women into the regime and accommodate their interests within government policy and legislation.[72]

The restructuring of the economy in Sudan, Sondra Hale notes, has thrown women into new or reinvented roles that directly involve them in rebuilding the Islamic nation while seeking out "authentic" Islam for their rights and emancipation.[73] The shift in identity construction of the woman citizen—mother, Muslim, militia woman, and national service volunteer—has sharpened since the regime has come under attack militarily and in international critiques.[74] In reality, Hale argues, state feminism, as manifested in the "new Muslim woman," indicates that women are active in the workforce but only under conditions that fulfill the requirements of the party/state and of the *umma*—that is, the Muslim community.[75]

Saudi Arabia's state feminism has led to the emergence of elite women with *wasta*, connections in high political places.[76] Not surprisingly, women who break through the established gender paradigm are carefully dressed in full *hijab* (Islamic dress code), invoking models of liberated women from an Islamic past while adhering closely to Islamic values. The traditional gender paradigm has been incorporated into the mandatory religious studies curricula to satisfy the country's powerful and culturally defensive *ulama* (scholars of religion).

Contesting Patriarchy

In the contemporary Middle East, the family is a powerful signifier, and there is a strong conservative move to reinforce women's maternal roles, even as the nuclear family setting becomes prevalent.[77] It is important to remember, as Valentine Moghadam argues, that patriarchy should not be conflated with Islam but rather should be placed in a social-structural and development context. Patriarchal structures of Muslim societies, however, are not timeless but undergo change as a result of economic and political developments.[78] Modernized patriarchy or "neopatriarchy" features the dominance of the father within the household and at the level of the state. Women inherit less property than men do; they are required to obtain permission of father, husband, or other male guardian to marry, seek employment, start a business, or travel. Men still enjoy the right of unilateral divorce.[79] Outside the household, the source of patriarchal control is political-juridical—that is, the state and legislation.

The Arab region of the Muslim world, according to the *Arab Human Development Report 2002*, is hampered by three key deficits: the freedom deficit, the women's empowerment deficit, and the human capabilities/knowledge deficit relative to income. Out of seven world regions, the Arab region had the lowest freedom score in the late 1990s and also had the lowest value for voice and accountability.[80] Similarly, the Arab countries suffer a noticeable deficit in women's empowerment. Arab women occupy 3.5 percent of parliamentary seats, the lowest in the world with the exception of sub-Saharan Africa.[81] Although they have made great strides in girls' education, female enrollment rates are lower than those for males at all levels. These countries also lag far behind other regions of the world in female enrollment in higher education.[82] Likewise, the Arab region has the lowest level of access to information and communication technology (ICT), as measured by the number of Internet hosts per thousand people, of all regions of the world, even lower than sub-Saharan Africa.[83] Further, with the exception of Kuwait and the United Arab Emirates, all Arab countries seem to be equal in their ICT deprivation, regardless of their Human Development Index.[84]

Arab women's campaign to push their governments to allow women to enter parliament has met with resistance by Muslim groups such as the Egyptian Muslim Brotherhood throughout the Arab world. But progress has been made. Qatari women voted in 1999 elections for municipal councils and they ran for office, albeit unsuccessfully. The Sultan of Oman appointed two women to the country's advisory council (Majlis al-Shura). Bahrain has named its first female ambassador; and in Saudi Arabia, a royal princess was named assistant undersecretary for education.[85] In Jordan, a new law now prescribes a heavy sentence against the practice of "honor killings" of wives or female relatives by a man.[86]

The Arab women from eighteen nations met in the Arab Women's Summit in Jordan (November 2002) and demanded equal representation in the form of quotas. They also acknowledged that the problem was not simply the lack of legal reforms or low female literacy rates but a patriarchal culture in which "women do not vote for each other. [In the last election] they didn't elect a single woman in Jordan. Women want men to rule."[87] The militarization of states and numerous bloody conflicts in the region have helped keep power in the hands of male leaders.[88]

Under Taliban rule, the women of Afghanistan were not allowed to study at schools, universities, or any other educational institutions. A year after Taliban rule was removed from the country's political scene, millions of girls and women have returned to school and work. International agencies and NGOs, unable to operate under the anti-Western Taliban, have returned to major cities. Although the lot of Afghan women appears to be improving, much needs to be done to secure these new improvements and reduce the hardships of their lives. The women of Afghanistan today challenge the nature of foreign aid, historically premised on military and other strategically oriented objectives, lest they be excluded from such assistance.

Several networks and NGOs have worked to assist the women of Afghanistan. The Afghan Women's Network (AWN), the Afghan Women's Council (AWC), and the Revolutionary Association of the Women of Afghanistan (RAWA) have all used advocacy networks, fund-raising, and education to aid Afghan women.[89] Moreover, the UN Commission on the Status of Women (CSW), established in 1946 as a functional body of the UN Economic and Social Council (ECOSOC), has urged the transitional government of Afghanistan to fully respect the equal rights and fundamental freedoms of women, give high priority to the issue of ratification of the CEDAW, and consider signing the CEDAW Optional Protocol. The CSW draft resolution (March 25, 2002) urges the government of Afghanistan to repeal all legislative and other measures that discriminate against women and girls; to ensure the full, equal, and effective participation of women and girls in the country's civil, cultural, socioeconomic, and political life; and to enable the equal rights of women and girls to education.[90]

Women's rights advocates in Iran have attempted a feminist rereading and interpretation of the Qur'an, in which they demonstrate its emancipative content and dispute existing patriarchal interpretations and codifications. Many Islamic and secular feminists argue that the Qur'an has not prohibited women from becoming judges, making a distinction between Islam and patriarchal traditions. Echoing a similar viewpoint, one progressive Iranian cleric regards gender inequality in shari'a as a mistaken construction by male jurists: "Gender is a social and human concept and does not enter the divine realm, thus it could never have been a consideration for the divine Law-Giver."[91]

Advocates of women's rights have questioned male privilege in areas such as divorce, child custody, and inheritance, while calling for the adoption of international conventions and standards. They have participated in the Beijing Plus Five deliberations in June 2000, formed links with global feminists outside the country, and have received support from Iranian expatriate feminists and other feminist organizations and networks across the globe.[92]

Education, central to demographic transition in the Muslim world as elsewhere, is the single most important determinant in the age of marriage. Many surveys have found links among education, declining fertility rates, and rising age of marriage in Middle Eastern countries.[93] Access to education and the expansion of schooling for girls continues to be an important factor in the decline of patriarchy. Social change as such has caused a conservative backlash within Muslim societies: "The relative rise in the position of women is seen by conservative forces as having the greatest potential of any factor to destroy the patriarchal family and its political, economic, and demographic structure."[94] The profound family changes under way in some Middle Eastern regions indicate the impact of such socioeconomic transformation. "Whereas a few decades ago the majority of women married before the age of twenty," Moghadam writes, "today only 10 percent of that age group in Algeria and 18 percent in Iran are married."[95]

Fighting Poverty

In poverty-stricken settings, such as Bangladesh, development-oriented and sustainable solutions to socioeconomic problems have become integral to the campaign against gender-biased traditions and practices. This is not to underestimate the importance of other barriers. The majority of people in Bangladesh, as Najma Chowdhury notes, "tend to define the role and status of women through a prism that is layered with religious conservatism."[96] These religious beliefs, when combined with cultural orientations, Chowdhury continues, lead to subservient status for women: "A man can marry four times; girls inherit half the share of boys; a man can divorce at will and may only make the utterance thrice to annul the marriage; custody rests with the father after a certain age; women's sexuality is to be restrained; girls are encumbrances whose marriage will require the payment of dowry."[97]

In recent decades, the modernization program in Bangladesh has led to educational opportunities for women and created expanded roles for women, especially in employment. A cultural trend is emerging that promotes liberalization, defends a new role for women, and fosters a reappraisal of traditional gender roles.[98] A growing number of feminists in Bangladesh regard international women's conferences such as the Beijing Platform for Action (PFA), adopted at the end of the Fourth World Conference on Women (1995), as an important vehicle in globalizing women's issues, networks, and alliances (see Tables 2 and 3).

Local NGOs there have proven instrumental in safeguarding women's rights to health, education, and social well-being. They have also played an unusually significant role in empowering Bangladeshi women by focusing on meeting women's strategic needs, including increasing women's bargaining capacity, reducing violence against women, and enhancing their influence over political and socioeconomic decision making. Known as a country of NGOs, Bangladesh is home to many community development NGOs that aim at eradicating poverty and achieving gender equality. These organizations focus on credit-based income-generating activities as part of a larger struggle while going beyond women's economic empowerment by encouraging poor women to unite in support groups.[99] The Grameen Bank in Bangladesh, which has given micro-credits and loans to the poor who could not afford to offer banks property as collateral, has treated "credit" as a human right.[100] The largest rural finance institution in the country, the Grameen Bank has more than 2.3 million borrowers, 94 percent of whom are women.[101] The women are mostly welfare mothers who borrow as little as $300 a month. In nearly all cases, they have repaid their loans.[102]

Views of Women's Rights

To understand gender issues and the roots of violations of women's rights, we also need to address two basic questions: How do Muslim men view women's rights? How are Muslim men's attitudes and identities constructed in relation to women's rights? There are enormous variations in men's views of women's freedom within the Muslim world. The relationship between Muslim men and women will no doubt continue to change but exactly how this will occur remains uncertain. In recent decades, awareness and disapproval of human rights violations on a global scale have risen dramatically; consequently, those countries in which abuses of women's rights occur have been the recipients of political and diplomatic pressures regardless of their regime type: secular or Islamic.

That said, the most steadfast supporters of women's human rights come from among male secularists in the Muslim world. Secular modernists have argued that human rights can exist only within a secular context—not within a religious framework. Secular reformists point out that women's rights will be fully protected only in a completely secular state with a secular constitution and laws, with only a few Islamic provisions in family law. Regardless of whether secular or religious leaders rule, the truth remains that politics trump human rights throughout the Muslim world. In Pakistan, for example, reforms in family status law have been averted largely because of the influence of Islamic groups within the parliament and courts.

The reform-minded Islamic scholars in the Muslim world have also demanded gender equality and a more flexible Islamic legal system. Having played a critical role in the ongoing discourse of Islamic reform, modernist scholars tend to develop a new critique of the conventional and orthodox interpretations of Islamic laws by calling for a new *ijtihad* (independent reasoning). For these reformists, enlightened interpretations of the Qur'an and creative ways to apply *ijtihad* are indeed the cornerstones of a "dynamic theology."[103] In Iran, modernist thinkers such as Abdolkarim Soroush and Hojjat ol-Eslam Seyyed Mohsen Sa'idzadeh address the issue of gender equality from within the framework of Islamic jurisprudence. Sa'idzadeh views gender inequality in the shari'a not as a manifestation of divine justice but as a mistaken construction by male jurists that runs counter to the very essence of divine will as revealed in the Qur'an.[104]

Today, women's lives and their social status are determined more by historical, socioeconomic, and political conditions than by religious texts or theological debates. This reality is reflected in the writings of many male Muslim scholars such as Mohammed Arkoun, Abdulaziz Sachedina, Tariq Ramadan, M. A. Muqtedar Khan, Chandra Muzaffar, Hasan Hanafi, and Mohsen Kadivar.[105]

Turning their attention to legislatures, Muslim men and women have utilized a strategy of legal activism. As a result of a long battle by Egyptian women and sympathetic men to reform personal status law, in January 2000, the Egyptian parliament passed the Law on Reorganization of Certain Terms and Procedures of Litigation in Personal Status Matters.[106] This law was the culmination of a fifteen-year campaign to facilitate divorce for women, organized by a divergent coalition of activists, lawyers, government officials, civic leaders, legislators, and scholars of history, law, sociology, religion, and philosophy.[107] The women and their male supporters in the Personal Status Law (PSL) coalition became a new transnational movement of Muslim intellectuals and activists that contested dominant frames legitimated by religious authorities with close connections with the more conservative Islamist groups.[108] The PSL coalition turned religion into an asset by conducting its campaign in an Islamic frame while engaging in civil and legal collective action that was acceptable within the confines of an illiberal rule in Egypt.[109]

In addition to reformist scholars and enlightened Islamic jurists who interpret Islamic texts, many novelists and filmmakers throughout the Muslim world have publicized women's suffering and offered ways to restore their dignity. The image of women in cinema, however, has been projected in contradictory ways. Arab cinema has played a dual role in concert with its commercial interests. Whereas some movies have generalized values of sexual discrimination, others have reflected the wishes of new generations of women seeking freedom and full selfhood as autonomous human beings.[110]

Likewise, Iranian journalists, novelists, and filmmakers have created an important site of cultural and political negotiation, where notions of self, other, place, and displacement are articulated in complicated and sometimes contradictory ways. Clearly, the boundaries of such imaginary cultural spaces transcend the nation. In many ways, cinema has become a crucial space for national as well as transnational exchanges and encounters.[111] In postrevolutionary Iran, women filmmakers have chosen to question the unrealistic image of women portrayed in Iranian cinema by making films themselves. Male directors have increasingly followed women's lead in the realistic portrayal of women and their presence.[112] Cinema has become a major arena for the debates surrounding the nature of Iranian culture and identity. Despite the restricted political contexts in which the films are produced, the international success of Iranian cinema has served as a channel for reconciliation between Iranians of divergent views at home and abroad. In short, as experts remind us, cinema has become "an important medium—through viewing and debate—for negotiating Iranian cultural identity."[113]

In looking specifically at globalization and its impacts on women in the Arab Middle East, some studies have shown how technological and communications advances have helped the formation of a new global political culture that fosters a common moral responsibility and human solidarity. Men and women around the world have increasingly united in common causes such as social justice, environmentalism, and labor rights. The women's movement has benefited from some aspects of globalization, which have resulted in the formation of international conventions on women's rights, such as the Convention on the Elimination of All Forms of Discrimination against Women (CEDAW).[114]

Economic liberalization programs in many Arab countries, however, have failed to address numerous areas of gender disparity, such as levels of employment, income, and access to education. Structural adjustment programs have led to increased hardship for women, in large part because they have often included cuts in government spending, especially in the areas of public-sector employment, education, and social services, such as antipoverty programs.[115] The rise of Islamism in such countries as Tunisia is in part a backlash against SAPs and globalization. The Islamic paradigm, experts note, offers women an alternative to a modernizing society that expects them not only to be the guardians of family honor and purity but also to participate in a technologically advanced and socially liberal environment.[116]

Modernization presents Muslim women with conflicting interests and competing identities while at the same time challenging their ability to fulfill traditional roles and modern expectations. Given that Islam and cultural traditions continue to influence women's roles in Islamic societies, modernizing experiences raise a central question: How should Muslim women view themselves? In some situations, living with contradiction and duality in a modernizing society may create ambivalence: to participate in or retreat from society. Some Muslim women try to determine who they are and what they seek to become through their own efforts—that is, accommodation or resistance. These women are eager to create a new and independent identity for themselves.[117]

When young Muslim women embrace the modern norms surrounding social and sexual expressions, some may find it difficult, unsettling, and conflictive. In the face of change and uncertainty, they are likely to return to traditional values, which are predictable and easily managed, even as they risk losing economic and political advancement in the long run.[118] For men, the spread of the Islamic movement reinforces their cultural identity/ ideal of the male as the breadwinner, poses no threat of losing jobs to women by making female employment less socially acceptable, and restores their dignity that has been lost by the bewildering process of social transformation. Although men feel secure in their perception of their place in society insofar as they find cultural harmony with what appears to be an inevitable changing economic order, women are becoming increasingly cognizant that such adjustments come at a cost to them and with a dissonance in their "place."[119]

In addition to male domination in patriarchal societies and neopatriarchal states, another formidable challenge to institutionalized recognition of women's rights comes from Islamic radicals and traditionalists. The rise of religious militancy has unleashed two opposing trends: (1) the intensification of women's subordination and (2) the emergence of a backlash in the form of women's legal rights in particular and women's rights to religious freedom more generally (see Table 3).

Islamic fundamentalists (traditionalists) and neofundamentalists (radicals) see major threats emanating from the pace and quality of social change. Education for women, they insist, "has dissolved traditional arrangements of space segregation, family ethics, and gender roles."[120] Both of these groups promote the segregation of the sexes and enjoin women to adopt *purdah*—that is, veiling and seclusion. They also stress extreme modesty in dress in educational institutions.[121] Traditionalist Islamists reject the right of any Muslim to tamper with the practice of polygamy. Both the traditionalist and the revolutionary Islamists believe that the court testimony given by one man is equal to that of two women.[122]

In Saudi Arabia, the official education policy of the kingdom, written in 1970, places Islam at the center of the curriculum. The school texts for women review the *mahram* rules (a *mahram* is a woman's closest male relative and her guardian, usually her father or husband, or someone to whom the woman could not be legally married) and apply them to women's work, while listing permissible places for women to work. Girls are taught comprehensively about "the duty of obedience that a wife owes her husband, such as pleasing a husband sexually upon request, not leaving the home without his permission, and taking care of the house and children."[123] These texts create a closed system that precludes creativity, experimentation, and logical reasoning.[124]

Especially problematic is fundamentalists' attempt at controlling women's bodies, sexuality, and reproduction. To fundamentalists, as Asma M. Abdel Halim notes, women's sexuality is destructive of society, family, and social norms. Their interpretations of the shari'a have focused on sex and sexuality as the determining factor for women's rights and duties. They reject the concept of "gender" in an attempt to delink the status of women from their sexuality.[125] "Muslim women's claim to their human rights," Halim writes, "is destined to be treated by fundamentalists as a move by lustful women seeking to Westernize life in Muslim societies."[126]

Conclusion

Strategies for promoting women's rights in the Muslim world must be specifically tailored to the realities of these societies. The imposition of external standards, such as CEDAW, as a precondition for exogenous support must be carefully examined. The strict application of external standards can do more harm than good. Equally problematic is counting on state initiatives to create processes and institutions of fair governance. State-guided reforms are politically calculated, slow, and inconsistent. The patriarchal structure of Muslim societies, private and public, account for some of the fundamental barriers to women rights. Given these realities, the real question is how best to protect women's rights in the Muslim world. In many Muslim countries revolution is highly unlikely and outside intervention is widely regarded as illegitimate.

The task of textual reinterpretation, though critical to challenging religious fundamentalism, is insufficient in and of itself. The reform in political economy and legal empowerment of women are imperative. Socioeconomic development and women's collective action are the most effective tools to reform archaic laws and traditions. Grassroots movements have a decent chance to initiate reforms via the activities and ideas of nonconformist dissidents. They represent a force from within that legitimately challenges the status quo.

Claims that human rights are universal need to be negotiated and challenged within the internal discourse of contemporary Muslim societies. To create common values and norms through dialogue and debate appears to be the most sustainable form of enhancing human rights. The convergence between Islamic and secular feminists on matters relating to negotiating culture and human rights has gained more public appeal than focusing on distinct or profound differences among such groups.

Chapter 4

Searching for a Modern Islamic Identity in Egypt

Egypt is home to one of the world's oldest civilizations. The vast majority of its people are Muslim, and Islam is the state religion. Although Egyptians' identity has been shaped by their own distinct geography, history, and cultural traditions, the content of their identity is surely Arab-Islamic. Egypt also has the largest Christian population in the Middle Eastern and North African region. The Coptic Christians are the largest non-Muslim religious group there. The country has undergone a profound social transformation in the twentieth century. The rise of commercialized agriculture unleashed a transformation of rural society that resulted in the land reform measures of the 1950s and 1960s.[1] By the early 1980s, however, surging population growth and rising production costs had eradicated many of the land reform's earlier gains.

The 1952 revolution greatly expanded educational opportunities. University enrollment grew rapidly through the 1970s, swelled by the ranks of middle- and lower-class youngsters in search of more sustainable employment.[2] Although Islam remains a critical element of social life, within it have emerged multiple identities, with variations and sometimes conflicting subdivisions. Egypt's demographic features make it an extremely interesting Middle Eastern country. Half of the Egyptian people are under twenty years of age and two thirds are under thirty.[3] This means that many children depend on adults for their livelihood, a situation that severely strains the economy. The Egyptian government and economy have proven ill-equipped to meet the demands for food, shelter, education, and jobs for this young population.[4]

This chapter contextualizes the struggles between secularist and Islamist movements in Egypt, which vie over constructing identity and gaining power in the country. Although cultural Islam has become a symbol of resistance to Western-style modernity and secular globalization, political

Islam is searching for a middle ground in national politics. At the same time, mainstream Islamic forces have increasingly transformed themselves into a more accommodating force at the national level.

Social and National Integration

Unlike many countries in the Middle East, Egypt has a high degree of social and national integration. While this has helped create a strong sense of national identity, it has also made ruling the country and stifling dissent much easier for the ruling elites. Egypt's military defeat in the 1948 Arab-Israeli war coincided with social and political instability that had started in the early 1940s as a result of increasing class disparities, unbridled and sprawling urbanization, and labor unrest. During the 1923–52 period, no popularly elected Egyptian parliament ever completed its term, and the average life of a cabinet was less than eighteen months.[5] The corrupt royal family, the lack of reform, and Britain's stubborn refusal to withdraw from the Suez Canal Zone led to the 1952 revolution of young army officers.

On July 23, 1952, the army engineered a coup, seizing state control. King Farouk abdicated in favor of his infant son. In June 1953, the monarchy was terminated and a republic was declared. All political parties, including the Wafd and the Muslim Brotherhood, were abolished. In the ensuing years, the state dominated society and the economy—a period also known as Arab Socialism. Egypt, spearheaded by Gamal Abdel Nasser, was a veritable police state from 1953 to 1970, when Nasser died.

The post-Nasser era witnessed gradual economic liberalization and a partial opening of the political climate by President Anwar al-Sadat. President Sadat launched a program of economic liberalization, known as the *infitah* (opening up), which was based on free-market economics, while leaving the Egyptian state in firm control of the political process.[6] By 1977, however, political unrest had broken out throughout Egypt, largely after the government attempted to withdraw subsidies from the basic commodities under pressure from the International Monetary Fund. Following these riots, President Sadat shifted his ruling style from one of patrimonial and paternalistic piety to that of a pseudo-monarch. He came to govern Egypt according to his own personal whims and interpretation.[7] In 1977, Sadat began rapprochement with the United States and Israel. He was assassinated by Islamist militants in 1981.

His successor, Husni Mubarak, has pursued a zig-zag pattern of democratization, cautiously allowing multiparty parliamentary elections at regular intervals. Egypt under Mubarak has failed to successfully integrate Islamist groups into the political process. By 1992, Islamist groups controlled most university student unions and professors' associations as well as a number of organizations in civil society, including societies of engineers, physicians, pharmacists, and lawyers.[8]

Egyptians have vacillated among several identities: Egyptian, Arab, and Muslim. Egypt's Arab identity was marginalized after the country's 1967 defeat by the Israelis, but its Islamist identity gained more prominence. The 1979 Iranian Revolution provided an impetus for Islamist groups to influence the country's politics. After a severe earthquake in October of 1992, Egypt's Islamic organizations provided faster and more effective health services and assisted more in reconstruction aid than any government agency. Their protests against U.S. military attacks against Iraq in 1991 and 2003 have further solidified Islamist positions and fueled resentment against American intervention in the region.[9]

Identity Construction in the Post-Colonial Period

In contrast with many countries in the Middle East and North Africa, Egypt lacks a precise date when it became "independent." Instead there was a process beginning with the anti-British movement of 1919 and the ratification of the constitution of 1923, and continuing through international recognition in 1937 and the departure of the last British soldier in 1956.[10] During World War II, Egypt was turned into a British base of operations. The war helped strengthen the rising Egyptian capitalist class, as the production value in industrial projects significantly increased.[11]

After the war, competing forces associated with the Palace, political parties, and Imperial Britain, coupled with deteriorating socioeconomic conditions, bridged the gap between various forces, including labor, intellectuals, the petite bourgeoisie, lawyers, teachers, students, and the democratic wings of the political parties. These developments culminated in Egyptian demands for a revision of the Anglo-Egyptian Treaty of 1936, which had legalized the British military presence in the Suez Canal.[12] British support for the creation of Israel in 1948 increased anti-British sentiments in Egypt. In 1948, Egypt entered the war with Israel in an effort to defend the Palestinian cause. On July 22, 1952, a group of young Egyptian army officers led a coup that ousted King Fu'ad, who had succeeded his father,

King Farouq. The Egyptian monarchy ended on June 18, 1953, when a republic was proclaimed.[13]

The emergence of nationalism in the postwar period, according to experts, embraced three distinct features. First, it became equated with "modernity." Second, it rested on military might and discipline. Third, it stressed the unity of the Arabs. These strands, personified by Gamal Abdel Nasser, came to characterize Arab nationalism during the 1950s and 1960s.[14] Some experts argue that Nasser's triumphant return to Cairo from Alexandria on July 28, 1956, after announcing the nationalization of the Suez Canal, marked a new era in which the oppressive past had been cast aside by a competent and decisive leader, and Egypt had gained a measure of independence and pride.[15] At his death, however, some analysts observe that the hopes he had raised and the Arab public he had lifted with his promises entered a period of disenchantment and despair.[16]

In the first half of the twentieth century, there was clear ideological conflict between pan-Islamism and Egyptian nationalism. Egypt's intellectuals rejected pan-Arabism during that time, but their attitude altered as the Israeli-Palestinian conflict intensified and the Arab League was formed.[17] Nasser's family background, childhood, and experience in the 1948 war with Israel inclined him toward Arab nationalism.[18]

The rise of Arab nationalism reached its peak during the Nasser era. But this nationalistic phase, which culminated in the fulfillment of a manifest destiny, turned out to be a transitory political identity.[19] Several challenges to nationalism have arisen. The first "post-nationalist" reality is that of subnational political cleavages, many of which are assuming increasingly distinct political identities. *Saidi*, or Upper Egyptian identity, is intermixed with religion and tribalism/familialism that has amounted to a rural revolt.[20] *Saidi* identity is unlikely to be eroded by force; it could be tempered were the region to be more thoroughly integrated into the political economy.[21]

Christians and non-*Saidi* Islamists pose another challenge to the ruling elite, in part because they are not exclusively of the rural hinterland and in part because they do enjoy international cooperation and support. Coptic communities in the West, including those in Australia, Canada, and the United States, have placed enormous pressure on the Egyptian government to stop discriminating against Copts and to defend them more effectively from the depredations of radical Islamist activists.

The Islamist challenge is even more profound than the Coptic one, given its wider appeal to a larger proportion of the population. The roots of Islamic identity in twentieth-century Egypt can be traced back to 1928, when Hasan Al-Banna (1906–49), an Egyptian schoolteacher, founded Jamiyat al-Ikhwan al-Muslimin (the Society of Muslim Brothers), also known as the Muslim Brotherhood. The Brotherhood was intent on creating an Islamic society and state based on the shari'a that would empower Egyptians to shake off the vestiges of European rule.[22] To this end, the Brotherhood founded hospitals, schools, and other social service institutions with a view toward reaching out to schoolteachers, lawyers, physicians, police officers, students, and civil servants. Its political goals were to rid Egypt of the British as well as to transform the Egyptian government into an Islamic one.[23]

Since its inception, the Ikhwan has promoted Islamism with the goal of reforming the society. The most famous theoretician of the Ikhwan was Sayyid Qutb, who was influenced by the Pakistani theologian, Sayyid Abu al-Ala Mawdudi. Qutb in turn influenced the thoughts of Ayatollah Ruhollah Khomeini of Iran, as well as such Egyptian radical Islamic groups as al-Tak fir wa al-Hijrah and al-Jihad. The latter carried out the assassination of Anwar al-Sadat in 1981.[24]

President Anwar al-Sadat, who succeeded Nasser in 1970 and who sought the support of the Ikhwan against leftists in his government, helped in rebuilding the Ikhwan. He refused to grant the Brotherhood unconditional legal status as a political party, however. In 1979, following Sadat's peace initiative with Israel, his support of the Brotherhood dwindled, as the latter heavily criticized this initiative. By 1981, when Sadat was assassinated, many of the group's members were arrested. While not being implicated in the assassination, the Ikhwan established itself as a nonviolent opposition movement. The organization has ever since moved into the mainstream of political life in Egypt. Under the leadership of Umar al-Tilimsani, the Ikhwan accepted political pluralism and parliamentary democracy, forging an alliance with the Wafd Party in the 1984 parliamentary elections. By 1987, the coalition collapsed and the Brotherhood formed a new Islamic Alliance with the Socialist Labor Party and the Liberal Party to contest the 1987 parliamentary elections.[25]

In the parliamentary elections of November 2000, many members of the Brotherhood were independently elected to parliament, thus rendering the Ikhwan the largest holder of opposition seats in that body. By avoiding theological and divisive debate over the nature of law and the Islamic state, taking a progressive stand on women's rights, advocating the elimination of Western secular influences and ideologies, and providing much-needed

civic institutions, the Ikhwan has become the most broadly based representative of the Egyptian people.[26]

Sayyid Qutb (1906–66), al-Banna's ideological successor, worked as a
teacher in the public schools and joined the Muslim Brotherhood in 1951.
In the ensuing years, Qutb was arrested, jailed, tortured, and finally in 1966
he was executed along with other Brotherhood members implicated in a
conspiracy against the Egyptian President Gamal Abdel Nasser. The Brotherhood was disbanded and its activities banned by President Nasser. During
his time in prison, Qutb wrote one of his most famous works called *Ma'a-
limi fi al-tariq* (Signposts along the Road), in which he claimed that the
cause of Muslim weakness was not the careless imitation of previous generations of Muslims but the uncritical adoption of alien moral and practical
philosophies as well as the granting of sovereignty to dictatorial regimes.
His key solution to these problems was to attempt to overthrow the government rather than to work from within the established political system.[27]

The Ikhwan has increasingly become a major advocate of dialogue and
slow reform rather than revolt. No longer do Islamic movements in Egypt
seek the violent overthrow of the government or a return to a medieval age.
The Islamic revival is broad based, reaching Egyptians of every social class
and all walks of life. Egypt's "Popular Islam" has become a grassroots
movement emerging from the streets, bent on creating an Islamic order by
transforming the social structure of Egyptian society from below.[28]

The existence of a group of "haves," the major beneficiary of globalization and privatization, also poses a challenge to the official political identity of Egyptian nationalism. For many of these "haves," the residue of
radical Egyptian Arab nationalism is unattractive and counterproductive.
Today's Egyptian capitalists are less nationalist and more globalist in that
they are driven by the economic realities of globalization far more than by
the Egyptian political game. National identities have taken on different
forms as dominant modernizing sociocultural features and globalizing economic and political aspects have become pervasive. "Heterogeneity of political identity," as Robert Sprinborg notes, "both historically and today, is
thus a perception increasingly shared."[29] Egyptian government must come
to terms with the growing gap between Egyptian and Arab identity imbued
with Islam, on the one hand, and increasingly discontented Christian and
regional minorities, on the other. Also disillusioned are the so-called globalized economic elites and impoverished masses, whose leaders tend to gravi-
tate toward Islamist projects.[30]

The tradition of emphasizing Egyptian unity presents a major obstacle to a process whereby identity is continually altered through its articulation and conversion into public policy choices within pluralistic institutions. Political identity in Egypt is gradually becoming more heterogeneous and fragmented in a globalizing world. Egyptian political arenas lack the political structures that would make negotiation, bargaining, and compromise possible while mitigating conflicting identities. Nor do they have the mechanisms through which a newly forged "multicultural" identity could emerge. The Egyptian government, which is likely to frustrate even debate on issues related to these conflicting identities, is struggling to manipulate symbols of Arabism and Islam, on the one hand, and globalization, on the other. The juxtaposition of sprawling slums, such as Bulaq al Daqrur, with fast-food-outlet-infested upper-middle-class suburbs, such as Muhandisin, demonstrates both class divisions and contentious political identities. This growing gap may in the future become too broad for the government to bridge.[31]

Contesting Identities in the Post-Arab Nationalism

This failure of a secular-liberal discourse has led to the resurgence of radical Islam. Islam appeals because it is an alternative to the secular nation-state, to a Western, nonindigenous, non-Islamic form of social organization and political process. For many young Egyptians, modernity has brought uncertainty, confusion, and a real crisis of identity.[32] Modern Islamic movements have galvanized the imagination of the middle-class devout and technically educated youth in Egypt. Deeply humiliated by the defeat in the 1967 war with Israel, these young men turned to Islam for answers to their frustration. Seeking Islam in this sense was part of the drive to restore the identity and dignity of Muslims. The key question is this: What accounts for the success of modern Islamists compared to the leftist secularists or Marxists?

The success of modern Islamic radicalism can be attributed to several factors. To begin, it is based on an indigenous ideology that is antiforeign and anticommunist. The deep and pervasive roots of Islam make it easier for modern Islamic radicals to promote their ideology. Defeat in the Arab-Israeli war was equated with the failure of socialism under Nasser. Although Nasser was not discredited, the ideology and policies—premised on socialism—were. But, more important, the strong sense of communion that Muslim groups provide for their members is of great importance. "The typical recruit," A. Saad Eddin Ibrahim, an Egyptian sociologist, writes, "is

usually of recent rural background, a newcomer to a huge, impersonal city.
. . . The militant Islamic groups, with their emphasis on 'brotherhood,' and
mutual material and spiritual support, become the equivalent of an extended family. This function in particular is not matched by other, rival
political movements."[33]

Many Islamic organizations started as community-based self-help
projects. The Muslim Brotherhood is typical. The Brotherhood runs medical clinics and job training programs, subsidizes cheap food, and collects
garbage. It provides social services that the Egyptian government has failed
to do. The Brotherhood is highly organized, has established an effective social base, and is seen as quite legitimate by a majority of Muslims. Islamism
as such is viewed by some Muslims as an alternative to socialism, Arab-
nationalism, military dictatorships, and monarchies.

The Rise of Islamic Activism and Identity

The surge in Islamic activism and identity among urban, educated youth in
Egypt in the 1980s and 1990s underscored the importance of Islamist
da'wa—or the project of ideological networks and outreach—in integrating
recruits for collective action associated with the movement's goal of gaining
political power through nonviolent means. The contemporary Islamic drive
has focused on family values, traditional sexual mores, and cultural authenticity.[34] Egypt's new generation of Islamists has advocated peaceful transformation by concentrating their efforts largely on changing the individual
through preaching and worship, in a gradual process of enlightenment
known as *tarbiyya*.[35]

Anwar al-Sadat's modernization plan, manifested largely by the Open
Door Economic Policy in 1974, aimed at accommodating tourists and upper
class Egyptians. The 1978–81 forced relocation of five thousand families
from Bulaq, in central Cairo, to a new public-sector housing complex in al-
Zawiya al-Hamra—a low-income neighborhood—resulted in many tensions caused by social dislocation, urbanization, and alienation in Cairo.
These families joined older waves of migrants who had fled to Cairo and
others whose urban housing had been erased in the early 1960s. As these
conditions were turning the Bulaqis into dangerous and backward members of the society, the mosque celebrated their culture and provided
community, relief, and social services to them. Many of these residents,
particularly women, turned toward the mosque and found social networks,

solace, and a moral compass there. Their renewed religious identity helped them to embrace positive aspects of modernity and reject its negative influences.[36]

Many institutions have begun undermining the state's secular policies. Universities, the courts, the *ulama*, doctors, lawyers, and engineers have created their own channels to apply religious values in Egyptian society. Students have organized underground Islamic-oriented groups and unions on university campuses. Middle-class professionals have created a syndicate movement, offering many doctors, lawyers, and engineers social services and an Islamic way of life independent from the state.[37] Similarly, the *ulama* have extended their authority beyond the religious domain to ban books and films that they consider offensive to the Muslim community. The courts have also banned from cinemas films that were deemed blasphemous to Islam.[38]

Islamist politics has tended to deploy the discursive strategies of religious orthodoxy as well as the mechanisms and practices of societal regulation with the goal of controlling the public space. Informal groups, such as Islamist lawyers, challenge moral code violations through the courts. Likewise, the state sponsors religious television programs and publications and has granted censorship power to al-Azhar authorities, elucidating the extent to which the Egyptian government engages in cultural politics. The state's participation in the battle over questions of morality and the cultural domain demonstrates the Islamization of state institutions.[39]

Most university graduates initially joined Islamic networks because of various rational or instrumental benefits—social as well as emotional.[40] As participants became increasingly integrated into movement networks, Islamists framed activism as a moral "obligation" that demands unwavering commitment to the cause of religious transformation. As the framing deepens, so does the groundwork for riskier political actions. Because they emphasize incremental change at the local level rather than confronting the regime, Islamic communal networks were perceived by new members as less risky venues for social activity.[41] Many university graduates argued that the single greatest problem facing Egyptian society was moral anarchy or crisis (*azmat al-akhlaq*), or what Egyptian youths called "normlessness."[42]

While selective incentives, social networks, and outreach facilitated initial recruitment, ideas and religious duties seem to have gained more importance in laying the groundwork for high-risk activism and commitment.[43] Broadly speaking, it is on the platform of ideas that the Islamists achieved their categorical success. By helping people to question dominant

beliefs and norms, the Muslim Brotherhood has given Egyptians a new Islamist critical consciousness, one that is "counter-society" in its ideals and
is clearly detached from the society's mainstream cultural forces and the
country's state institutions and elites. This new subculture has provided the
ideational framework for new kinds of political activism, embracing different forms of opposition to authoritarian rule.[44]

Conservative Islamist Discourse

Islamists tend to pursue different strategies to Islamicize social arenas and
to appropriate the public sphere. The conservative Islamist forces follow the
strategy of working within existing institutions while jockeying for political
power. The Muslim Brotherhood has found in the professional syndicates
an arena for expanding its ranks and developing a broad base among a key
segment of society.[45] Other organizations have developed to achieve Islamic
groups' political objectives. Private voluntary organizations, which are connected to mosques, have been established by the Brotherhood, the Jihad,
and the al-Jama'at al-Islamiyya.[46] Some experts define some of these groups
as neofundamentalist or extremist groups (see Table 4).

The state has promoted its own brand of Islam, sponsoring religious
newspapers and television programs, and extending the powers of al-Azhar
in censoring un-Islamic intellectual and artistic productions.[47] The state's
position in cultural politics is in keeping with the conservative Islamist discourse while maneuvering to cope with the challenge of radical Islamism.
The definition of *takfir* (accusation of apostasy) and the charges related to
it are now espoused by both the state and official Islam.[48]

Conservative Islamist discourse attempts to reconstitute the domain
of struggle with secular forces in moral, cultural, and religious terms. This
discourse is articulated by Islamist political forces working within legal
channels such as the right-wing al-Ahrar (Liberal) Party and its ideologues.
The conservative Islamist discourse is largely represented in the al-Ahrar
Party's two publications, *al-Ahrar* and *al-Nur*, but it is also found in the
al-Amal (Labor) Party's press organ, *al-Shab*, as well as in various Muslim
Brotherhood publications, including *al-Mukhtar* and *al-Itisam*.[49]

The conservative Islamist discourse finds expression in the official
media as well. State-affiliated conservative clerics, such as Shaykh Sharawi
and Abd Al-Sabur Shahin, have their own forum for expressing their ideas
in state-run newspapers such as *al-Liwa al-Islami* and *Aqidati*. These forces
are known as "conservative" largely because of their willingness to work

TABLE 4. COMPETITION FOR POWER AND IDENTITY POLITICS IN EGYPT

	Goals	*Agents*	*Sites*	*Strategies*
Conservatives	Protecting custom and traditions (*hijab*)	Religious authorities and scholars (*ulama*)	Al-azhar Mosque and community organizations	Seeking local alliances with reformists and politicians through democratic processes
Neofundamentalists	Creating an Islamic state based on shari'a	Islamic Jihad, and al-Jama'at al-Islamiyya	Mosques, local and transnational movements	Grassroots activism via identity politics
Reformists	Pluralistic power sharing with secularists	New Islamists (Wassatteyya, Muslim Brotherhood, and Islamic feminists)	Local and transnational NGOs, civil society, media, and student movements	Seeking ideas, allies, and intercultural dialogue with the West
Secularists	Secular nationalism and national unity; controlling all formal power	Political figures; intellectuals; nationalists; human rights activists and lawyers; feminists; and the military	Feminist movements, national and international movements	Simultaneous accommodation and repression of its Islamist challenge

within the established political order, which promotes hierarchical and patriarchal values reinforcing the status quo. The writings associated with the conservative Islamist discourse are premised on two central narratives: (1) the confrontation with the Other (the West) and (2) the assertion of the superiority of Islam.[50]

The Other is perceived as morally corrupt and its cultural assault could negatively influence various institutions and sociocultural realms, such as schools, the media, the arts, and popular tastes. Contact with the West and the nation's permeable borders are considered dangers to Islamic identity. Revivalist Islamic discourses as such have emphasized "cultural authenticity" in contrast to Western cultural influences. Likewise, they have stressed the "moral and ethical" structure of society against the structural and economic insecurities caused by modernization.[51] The same is the case with internal forces that are conceived as enemies of Islam: Arab Marxists, nationalists, and secularists. All of them are identified with the West.[52] The conservative Islamist discourse views globalization, or opening to the outside world, as a cause of corruption more in cultural and ethical terms than in economic matters.

For the Egyptian radical Islamic thinker Sayyid Qutb, Islam's superiority is tied to its values of equality and justice.[53] Secularism is regarded as alien to Islam, which is both religious and secular (*din was dunya*). Secularization is seen as the object of Westernization.[54] The secular state and its institutions, including the banking system based on usury, are rejected. The alternative, the Islamic Banks and the Islamic Societies for the Placement of Funds (ISPF), were legitimized as Islamic.

The state uses dialogue with the conservative Islamist groups and repression to contain the activities of radical Islamists such as the Jihad. Meanwhile, a condition of balanced tension between the state and conservative Islamists goes on. The "oppositional" forces of moderate and conservative Islamists act as mediators between them and the state. While condemning violence, the Islamists fault the government for allowing transgression against Islam.[55] Islamic revivalism in Egypt hardly fits neatly into categories of premodernism or postmodernism. The new Islamists pick and choose from what the modern world has to offer.[56]

New Islamists

The New Islamists represent a moderate centrist (Wassatteyya—the Middle Way) and reformist Islamic mainstream vision, as embodied by the new

Wassat Party that emerged in the mid-1990s. Rooted in Egypt, this group's manifesto was published in 1991 by its founder, Kamal Abu Magd, a professor of law at Cairo University and an international legal authority. The New Islamist ideology emerged out of the Muslim Brotherhood, shaped as much by reaction to its failures as by its successes.[57] This group includes renowned Islamic scholars, jurists, historians, lawyers, and journalists: Yusuf al Qaradawy and the late Muhammad al-Ghazzaly, Islamic scholars; Fahmy Huwaidy, Egypt's most prominent Islamist journalist; Kamal Abul Magd and Selim al-wa, highly regarded lawyers and public figures in Egypt and the Arab world; and Tareq al Bishry, a distinguished member of the judiciary and renowned historian. Together they represent a major intellectual force in Egypt and beyond (see Table 4).

The New Islamists insist that moderate approaches to social change do not necessarily require the overthrow of existing institutions. Many laws in Egypt, they argue, do not contradict the shari'a. The *Wassateyya* tradition of centrist Islamic reform with deep roots in Egyptian history has been fostered by the intellectual legacy of Muhammad Abduh and Gamal Eddine al Afghany, the nineteenth-century reformers, as well as by some elements of the social activism of Hassan al-Banna, the founder of the Muslim Brotherhood.[58]

With regard to educational reform, the New Islamists argue that "real reform must rest on secure intellectual foundations that foster a broadly based sense of national identity and purpose."[59] They view rationality and realistic *ijtihad* (independent judgment and interpretation), as well as their roles in human affairs, as the cornerstone of their new understanding of education. On foreign policy issues, this group supports a defensive jihad against U.S. interventions in Afghanistan and Iraq while defending the rights of Palestinians. The New Islamist identity has emerged from embracing those elements that have drawn these individuals together and recognizing and respecting the distances that need to be bridged.[60]

Secularist Discourse

Secularists in Egypt are part of a wide-ranging ideological spectrum, including intellectuals, journalists, writers, legal advisers, feminists, and human rights activists. The country's policy makers and the military also are typical members (see Table 4). The shari'a has been the primary target of attacks by the secularists. Some of them deny its relevance to today's mundane affairs; others reject its divine origin; and still others argue that it can be interpreted in many different ways. A popular theory among secularists in Egypt, Azzam Tamimi writes, is that *"Shari'a*—as understood by Islamic scholars and Islamic movements—is alien to Egyptian society and is the product of Saudi influence on migrant Egyptian society."[61] Some experts have even referred to it as "petro-Islam" imported from Saudi Arabia and other Gulf countries.[62] The problem with secularist governments is their reluctance to accept the outcome of free elections. Results of elections held so far clearly demonstrate that secularists are unpopular with the masses.[63] In fact, secularists have been associated with dictatorship, the abuse of human rights, and the contraction of civil society in Egypt (see Table 4).

The Egyptian government under President Mubarak has narrowed considerably the public sphere for participation of diverse groups as part of a strategy of simultaneous accommodation and repression of its Islamist challenge.[64] The Mubarak regime has used systemic police violence against the opposition and Islamic groups. Frequent reports of torture and police abuse in early autumn of 2007 fueled protests across the country.[65] The Egyptian government has regularly suppressed the secular-leaning Kifaya movement, which has been dedicated to replacing President Mubarak, by beating and jailing several of its leaders. It has also dealt harshly with its strongest opposition political group as well as the country's most popular political opposition, the Muslim Brotherhood, by putting a thousand of its activists in jail. Labor organizers and an antitorture NGO have also been targeted. Antigovernment journalists and media are among the latest victims of the government's crackdown on the press.[66] Political analysts attribute this crackdown to two reasons. One is that American criticism of Mubarak has become a thing of the past. The other relates to the succession issue, with many journalists criticizing Mubarak's son, Gamal, as the leading candidate of the ruling National Democratic Party (NDP).[67]

Egyptian society today is embroiled in a vigorous internal debate about how to define national unity and construct a national identity. Nowhere is this debate over identity construction more evident than in the rivalry between Islamists and secularists. Some former secular thinkers and writers—such as Hassan Hanafi, Safinaz Qazim, Adel Hussain, Mohamed Amara, Anwar Abdel Malek, Magdi Hussain, and Khaled Mohamed Khaled—have now become Islamist proponents who view secularism as antithetical to Islam. Their backgrounds and views are too diverse to point to the emergence of new thinking or a new school of thought, yet their dramatic shift toward Islamism and the way in which they appropriate a new interpretation of Islam as the core of an "eastern heritage," which they must necessarily defend against Western cultural imperialism, is a common denominator.[68]

Other secular intellectuals—such as Hussein Ahmad Amin, the late Farag Foda, Fuad Zakariya, Muhammad Said al-Ashmawi, and Muhammad Nur Farhat—have refuted the Islamists' claim that secularism is peculiar to the European experience and that medieval Christianity was radically different from the conditions prevailing in Islam. Some of these secular thinkers, such as Farag Foda, who was assassinated by the members of al-Jama'at al-Islamiyya on June 8, 1992, have argued that an Islamic state would lead to sectarian strife and discrimination against Copts, who would be treated as second-class citizens. The debate over issues of national unity/identity has intensified in recent years, especially as Islamist attacks on Copts have been accompanied by ferocious intellectual debates as to whether Copts constitute a minority in Egypt.[69]

The increased interest in Islamic movements and constituencies during the 1970s and 1980s has challenged secular discourse in Egypt, forcing secular thinkers to redefine the notion of secularism (*almaniyah*). Secularism as such does not necessarily denote antireligious or anti-Islamic positions. While not sharing a conception of the term "secularism," secularists support the separation of religion and politics and generally take the concept "secular" to mean a nondogmatic view of religion. This view does not imply that secularists are without belief.

Islamists, in contrast, have frequently used *almani* (secular) interchangeably with *mulhid* (atheist) or even *kafir* (infidel). This interpretation has gained wide discursive power and acceptance in contemporary Egypt and has unleashed a fierce intellectual debate between Islamists and secularists as to what it means to be an Egyptian Muslim.[70] No secular group has been more intensely involved in the discourse over national identity than the secular-oriented Egyptian women's movement. We will explore this issue thoroughly in the next section of this chapter.

Suffice it here to say that secular-oriented women's movements, for example, refuse to accept the shari'a as the main or sole source of legislation. Instead, they view civil law and UN human rights instruments/conventions as frames of reference for their struggle.[71] Breaking with modernist conceptions of society and development (that religion is equated with "backwardness" and science is equated with "progress"), some Egyptian women activists view the modernist premises of rationality and progress and their connection with secularism as another male ploy to discriminate against women. Nadje Al-Ali makes this point poignantly: "They oppose the nationalist and liberal-modernist discourses that simply address women's rights in the public sphere as part of the process of creating new societies. Likewise, they reject authoritarian and undemocratic tendencies among both Islamist and secular constituencies."[72]

Egyptian secular women activists have engaged in the daunting task of subverting hegemonic discourses related to the state, Islamists, and conservative male intellectuals. There are, however, commonalities between Islamists and secular women activists: they both are opposed to foreign funding (because of its corrupting influence) and appear wary of Western cultural encroachment.[73] Both groups, for instance, emphasize cultural specificity, even though there are major differences between them. Further, the varying positions of different constituencies concerning women's issues make it impossible to draw sharp lines between those supporting universal rights and those advocating cultural specificity. Regardless, Egyptian women's movements actively engage in struggles over shaping authenticity, identity, power, and social change.[74]

An important organization for social change is the Arabic Network for Human Rights Information (ANHRI), a central repository for human rights information and Web sites in Arabic throughout the Middle East and North Africa. Today there are many millions of Internet users in the Middle East, but it remains difficult for users to find information about human rights. The ANHRI provides a central site where Arabic readers can easily find links to and information about all human rights groups and their work in the region. The network also focuses on and seeks the expansion of freedom of expression on the Internet in the Middle East. There are critical areas on which no groups in the region are working, such as the abolition of the death penalty and protecting the rights of Christian minorities. The ANHRI has created a space where these issues and other relevant information about human rights can be discussed freely, and where people who share an interest in these areas can communicate and have an intellectual exchange. The ANHRI, for example, has launched the so-called the Initiative for an Open Arab Internet advocating free use of the Internet without censorship, blocking, or spying. The initiative seeks to provide international and Arab information and Internet-related documents while defending Internet users, Web designers, and writers by organizing legal and media campaigns and highlighting practices restricting Internet freedom. With Arab governments expressing great animosity against freedom, the Initiative focuses on the Arab World. For this purpose, most information is provided in Arabic.[75]

The Gender Issue: Secularists versus Islamists

During the Nasser era, the regime incorporated the demands of middle-class women as part of its socially progressive agenda. This reform package was described by some experts as state feminism.[76] In 1956, the right to vote and to run for public office, which had been given to men in 1920, was extended to women. The regime celebrated the success of a few token professional women who were promoted into leadership positions, like Hikmat Abu Zeid, the first woman nominated to a cabinet position in 1962 as minister of Social Affairs, and Karima al-Said, who reached the position of the undersecretary of the Ministry of Education in 1965.[77]

These few success stories were not emblematic of the internalization of equality and empowerment. Furthermore, state commitment to women's universal access to work, education, and political participation was never extended to the rural working class, who represented the majority of Egyptian women. Land reform excluded women as an economic group from its gains. It treated women as marginal economic actors and introduced new definitions that reinforced their economic dependence on men. In the 1950s and the 1960s, the country's personal status laws denied women equal rights to divorce and tolerated polygamy.[78]

In the 1970s, Anwar al-Sadat pursued a project of economic liberalization (*infitah*), which also strengthened the Egyptian state's Muslim identity. The emergence of a political alliance between the Sadat regime and the Muslim Brotherhood in the 1970s marked a new era. As noted before, this alliance did not last long, as most economic and political policies ignored Islamic concepts and perspectives. Religion was marginal to legislation, except for the cases involving personal status laws.

Under the Sadat regime, the postcolonial state underscored the differences between religious affairs and the state's modus operandi. The political space given to the Muslim Brotherhood gave Islamist thinkers a competing platform from which to address the new middle-class audience whose consciousness had already been shaped by a modern educational system and professional training. Islamists succeeded in persuading a majority of middle-class college women and working women to adopt the Islamic mode of dress as a symbol of the synthesis of Islam and modernity.[79] Islamist thinking was articulated by Shaykh al-Sha'rawi and Zeinab al-Ghazali, who attempted through broadcast and printed media to link modernist and Islamic values and consciousness. Science and professional knowledge, they insisted, must be placed in the service of an Islamic upbringing. The goal of the educational system, however modern, was to represent gender and cultural difference. They insisted on reconsidering the basis of education and training in Egyptian schools, especially in girls' schools. They particularly emphasized child rearing, expecting women to absorb the personal and social costs of this process.[80]

An intense debate arose in Egypt over female genital mutilation after the 1994 International Conference on Population and Development (ICPD). While the mufti of Egypt publicly declared that female genital cutting had no place in the Qur'an, Sheikh Gad al-Haq Ali of al-Azhar issued a *fatwa* that "female circumcision is a part of the legal body of Islam and is a laudable practice that does honor to the women."[81] In 1997, pressure from international nongovernmental agencies as well as the reported deaths of girls who were circumcised in hospitals led to a renewed ban on the practice in public hospitals in Cairo.

These contestations illustrate the way in which conservative and revivalist Islamist discourses engaged the Egyptian state in "symbolic gender politics" as a means to fortify a national Muslim identity in opposition to transnational influences.[82] The conservative Muslims asserted that "authentic" national Muslim identity presented barriers to the attempts of liberal Muslims to alter popular support for female genital mutilation, but what actually curtailed national levels of support for this practice in Egypt was the passage in 1997 of national laws prohibiting it.[83]

In my visit to Egypt during spring 2007, I noticed that a great majority of Egyptian women wore the *hijab* (Islamic headscarf) on the street or on the subway in Cairo and Alexandria and especially on the campus of Cairo University. For some students, the *hijab* is clearly a declaration of identity and fashion. A growing number of young Muslim women in Egypt have actually transformed the *hijab* from tradition to fashion statement.[84] This statement is intended as a step toward making their personal choice and having control over their public appearance, a step that resituates Islamic feminism within the discourse of women's rights in Egypt's high context culture.

For others, the *hijab* empowers them to become socially active and protect their socioeconomic rights. For still others, it was a potent symbol of piety, one that definitely manifested their personal as well as ideological values and convictions. When I asked Mona El Baradei, professor of economics and dean of the Faculty of Economics and Political Science at Cairo University, why Egyptian women were not politically active, she offered a standard explanation: "[The] occupational role and domestic responsibilities of women [have] made it very difficult if not impossible for Egyptian women to intensely engage in the nation's politics."[85]

Having acknowledged the country's dramatic social and cultural changes of the recent past, El Baradei downplayed the extent to which the younger generations face an identity crisis. Egyptians, she asserted, had survived many years of British occupation (1882–1936) without losing their identity. The nation's territorial integrity and cultural continuity, as well as its unique history, have made the Egyptians adroit at balancing continuity with change. She said there was a good balance between globalization and identity construction in Egypt and that it was not uncommon in Islamic countries for their governments to pay heed to the people's general religious beliefs.[86]

Islamists and Mubarak's Regime

Since Sadat's death (1981), his successor, Husni Mubarak, has strengthened the country's ties with the United States. At the same time, Egypt's Arab identity has revived, fueled in part by resentment against Israel for the continued occupation of Palestine and its manipulation of U.S. foreign policy toward the region.[87] Islamic sentiment has also intensified among the Egyptian population as a result of deteriorating socioeconomic conditions and the U.S. invasion of Iraq, as well as by the U.S. backing of Israel against the Palestinians.[88]

A growing number of Egyptians do not even vote. A large number now endorse political Islam and insist that the nation's laws should be based on the shari'a.[89] Experts note that the Muslim Brotherhood survives in large part because of the lack of credible alternatives on the country's political scene.[90] Egyptian Islamists have been jailed, tortured, and silenced by several modernizing regimes, but no credible political philosophy has replaced the Islamists' influence, despite their lack of an effective political party apparatus.[91]

A cursory look at the evolution of the political party system in Egypt helps explain the rise of Islamic groups. The end of World War II led to the decline of the principal Egyptian nationalist party, the Wafd, which was loyal to the British against Germany during the war. By 1945, the Muslim Brotherhood posed the most formidable challenge to the Wafd, having positioned itself as an effective party capable of opposing communism.[92]

The war in Palestine, along with a burgeoning violent struggle between the Muslim Brotherhood and the Wafd, unleashed turmoil in Egypt that eventually ended in 1952 when the nationalist elements of the army seized power. On December 8, 1948, the Muslim Brotherhood was dissolved by government decree on the grounds that it led an armed insurrection against the government. On February 12, 1949, Hassan al-Banna was assassinated by government agents on a Cairo street.[93] During the 1950s and 1960s, Islamic activism was espoused in response to repressive conditions prevalent in Egyptian society. Islamists advocated the shari'a as the sole source of law.

Mark Huban explains the rise of the Muslim Brotherhood in such a repressive climate: "The society of which it is an integral part now lies in a state of intellectual repression; Egyptian political life is moribund and its leaders are more concerned about halting political evolution than risking a looser power structure in the search for a valid national identity. Within this void, the Muslim Brotherhood has proved durable, extending its role as a provider of welfare and as a social movement with broader roots than any other Egyptian political organization."[94]

The regime of President Husni Mubarak (1981–) has followed contradictory policies toward Islamists. Initially, Mubarak set out to create a broad national front against Islamist extremists by tolerating the moderate Muslim Brotherhood and cooperating with leftists and the Wafd Party. Because of this policy, social spaces, including syndicates, university campuses, and charitable and voluntary associations, were given an extensive measure of autonomy. The Muslim Brotherhood took control of such spaces by providing their constituencies with services that were either lacking or insufficiently provided by the state. These practices gradually conferred informal legitimacy and social recognition on the Muslim Brotherhood, both of which were derived from society but denied by the state.[95]

Sensing the rising competition and contestation from such activities, the state eventually reversed its policies and launched an assault against the Islamists.[96] State repression, some experts have noted, was "brutal, swift, and indiscriminate."[97] The Mubarak regime resorted to making mass arrests, taking "hostages," and detaining families and relatives (including the wives) of suspected militants until the militants turned themselves over to the authorities. Torture was indiscriminate and pervasive in prisons. Islamists, whether they belong to Islamic Jihad, the Muslim Brotherhood, or Gama'a Islamiyya, were all referred to military courts with no appeal process. The far-reaching repression, experts remind us, gave added incentives to other nonviolent activists to join the ranks of militants. Violence in the

Egyptian Islamic movement was not necessarily the domain of a fringe ter- rorist group. Islamists were reacting to the coercive and heavy-handed state policies that had jeopardized the organizational and societal gains of their movements.[98]

Radical Islamic groups launched a broad armed offensive exemplified by the assassination of the secularist journalist Farag Fuda in June 1992. These groups particularly targeted the tourist industry. On November 17, 1997, they massacred fifty-eight foreigners and four Egyptians in Luxor. The combination of repression and loss of credibility following this incident sig- nificantly undermined the viability of the jihad option in Egypt.[99]

In the case of the Muslim Brotherhood, it was not so much the build- up of legitimacy that threatened the Mubarak regime as the effort of this social movement to enhance its political impact. By the late 1980s, the Mus- lim Brotherhood associations continued to dominate student unions on university campuses. The services that these Islamic organizations provided included health care, cheap textbooks, funds, and accommodation.[100] The Brotherhood made populist appeals to workers and university graduates, bankers, financiers, and teachers' clubs, syndicates, and other organized networks on the university campuses.[101]

The Muslim Brotherhood became formally included in the political arena following its unprecedented electoral gains in the 1980s. The increas- ingly repressive nature of state policies toward Islamists throughout the 1980s and 1990s, however, served to escalate the Brotherhood's militancy and activism. Such acts included the assassination of state officials and pub- lic figures, the bombings of the Egyptian embassy in Pakistan, attacks on tourists and Egyptian civilians, and several assassination attempts against President Mubarak.[102]

The violence that ensued between Islamists and the state during this period not only led to the 1997 Luxor massacre but also resulted in thirteen hundred fatal casualties between 1990 and 1997.[103] By 1997, the leadership of Al-Jama' rethought its strategy on violence in part because the group's vio- lent tactics were progressively seen as repugnant by the Egyptian public. Equally important, their leaders saw themselves being alienated from politi- cal activity and being pushed into the category of terrorists. Consequently, the Al-Jama' leadership, both inside and outside the country, formally de- clared a cease-fire in March 1999.[104] The state's coercive strategies continued to preserve the authoritarian nature of Mubarak's regime.

Following the tragic earthquake in Egypt in 1992, the Muslim Brother- hood networks utilized their wide resources and connections to rescue hundreds of victims, further strengthening the legitimacy of their operations. These developments were likely to lead to the emergence of an independent and organized network capable of challenging the state's own networks, an eventuality that the Mubarak regime feared the most.

As noted above, in the 1990s, the Ikhwan began to expand its successes in social realms into political spheres, attempting to form political parties. During the first Persian Gulf War, the Ikhwan condemned equally Iraq's invasion of Kuwait in 1990 and the 1991 Western presence in the region. The latter widened the rift between the Mubarak regime and the Ikhwan. The earthquake in 1992 presented yet another opportunity for the Ikhwan to promote its political concerns by displaying banners that carried the slogan "Islam is the Solution."[105]

The Mubarak administration reversed its policies and launched a campaign against Islamists. In universities such as Asyut, Alexandria, and Zaqaziq, elected councils were disbanded and others appointed.[106] The regime's fear of the Muslim Brotherhood was accentuated by the victory of the Islamic Salvation Front in the 1992 Algerian elections. Likewise, the Ikhwan's expansion into the lawyers' syndicate in 1992 raised more concerns in the regime that the Ikhwan was capable of winning elections in that body.

In June 1995, militant Islamists attempted to assassinate Mubarak in Addis Ababa, raising the specter of Islamist violence. Since then, the regime has made no distinction between "radical" and "moderate" Islamists.[107] The internal discourse with the Muslim Brotherhood organizations indicates that some members speak against projecting the Ikhwan as a political opponent to the state. They argue that attempts at reform must come from inside the state and that opposition to the state from outside is bound to fail. But at the same time, the state cannot deprive the Ikhwan from formal recognition. With the welfare role of the state declining, in part as a result of globalizing forces and privatization programs, constituencies feel thwarted by a regime that is either unable or unwilling to provide them with similar services. This has created tensions in state-society relations and further complicated national governance.[108]

Recently, the Muslim Brotherhood has been prevented from participating in Shura Council (the Upper House of Parliament) elections. According to Gamal Eid, executive director of the Arabic Network for Human Rights Information (ANHRI), the clampdown on the Muslim Brotherhood continues. "The government is still continuing its strategy of suspending members of the Muslim Brotherhood," Eid notes, "due to the government's disagreements with the group."[109] Eid points out that the Muslim Brotherhood is the government's strongest opposition and is well accepted by the public. A joint committee in parliament is looking into the rights of political parties and is intent on questioning it on the floor of the People's Assembly.[110] Opposition deputies would call for implementing change in the Constitution's Article 5, which prohibits political activity based on religion and indeed bans the creation of religious parties.[111]

Increasingly, some Egyptian journalists argue for the need to allow vigorous secular opposition. They say that the ruling National Democratic Party (NDP) has monopolized power for the past three decades. Egypt has more than twenty legal political parties, but most of them carry no street clout. Hence, it is important to give other civil groups the right to form political parties to widen the nation's political and ideological spectrum.[112] The liberal-oriented Wafd and the Arab Nasserists have asserted that they would not field any candidates for the Shura Council. Diasdeddin Dawould, leader of the Nasserist Party, has said that "the constitutional amendments, especially the Article 88 that eliminates full judicial supervision, make staging free and fair elections impossible."[113]

2005 Parliamentary Elections

The strong showing of the Muslim Brotherhood in the 2005 parliamentary elections was attributed to many factors. Under international and domestic pressures, parliamentary elections were conducted in a relatively more open and credible system of elections. The regime's National Democratic Party (NDP) obtained a total of 311 seats. The Brotherhood obtained eighty-eight parliamentary seats, by far the strongest showing by an Egyptian opposition party in the past half century. This meant that 61 percent of the 144 candidates that the Brotherhood nominated won—a sixfold increase over their 2000 showing of seventeen seats.[114]

The Brotherhood movement represented a legitimate political opposition with its success based on widespread grassroots service provision in health care, education, and poverty alleviation programs.[115] Other opposition groups performed poorly. The National Front for Change and Reform won only twelve seats. The secular opposition parties, such as Tagammu, Nasserists, Ghad (Tomorrow), Karama (Dignity), and Wafd, failed to build a popular base. Several members of the Brotherhood led by Abul Ila Madi left the Brotherhood to attempt to form the Center (Wasat) Party. Other young leaders, such as Essam Al Eryan, remained in the Brotherhood but expressed support for transparent and democratic structure within the movement.[116]

The ruling party (NDP) has initiated and passed laws that seemed reasonably democratic on paper but that actually favored the party's standing and position. Preoccupied with regime stability, the Mubarak government has devoted extensive efforts to containing political space and preventing the formation of competing power centers.[117] To close political space to the Islamists, the Mubarak administration has allowed the Al Azhar religious establishment to exercise enormous influence over Egyptian society, provided that it avoids interfering in politics.

This Islamic establishment has dominated the public sphere; it has extended its monopoly over truth and morality and has exercised exclusive control over the mosques; it has shown a strong presence in all academic institutions, as well as in government agencies and many civil society organizations. In the absence of political competition and negotiations, Islamic identities and values, espoused by the conservative religious establishment, have become less subject to mediation and negotiation.

For the religious establishment, notes one observer, cultural authenticity has become a main symbol of sovereignty, in the same way that development of heavy industry was equated with the progress and independence of Nasser's Egypt. As is becoming increasingly obvious in other Muslim countries, the cultural field is where the ferocious battles are being waged. Religious censorship from Al Azhar extends to cultural products, the media, women's dress code, and sexuality. In such circumstances, defying the religious establishment leads to punishment and censorship, whereas joining the mainstream Islamic networks brings a multitude of rewards, including a new identity and way of life that is shaped by a network of social organizations. Members of these Islamic networks find a real opportunity to procure self-esteem and emotional belongingness.[118]

One of the central questions for the future of secularism in Egypt is whether the Muslim Brotherhood is going to be a part of a democratic order or whether they will pursue a more radical agenda. A pessimistic analysis explicates the risks entailed in trusting Islamic groups. The March 2004 political platform of the Muslim Brotherhood demonstrated the Brotherhood's mission: to build an Islamic state, a Muslim unity, and a multinational Islamist Caliphate, with little or no national vision or patriotic loyalty to Egypt. The foundation of this mission, which is based on a religious rather than a national identity, runs counter to the notion of a national state. This Islamic state, it is argued, will be upheld by a number of initiatives, including an economic system that is derived from Islam, an educational system focused on learning the Qur'an by heart, alms institutions in charge of distributing wealth and income, gender employment consistent with the preservation of traditional expectations, and cultural programs that are derived from Islamic sources.[119]

Globalization and Identity

Embedded in Egyptian society are multilayered national-cultural experiences that combine aspects of deep historical legacies and civilizational richness: Pharaonic, Coptic, Arab-Islamic, nationalistic, and Western cultures. This long history of blending a multitude of civilizations, argued Professor Mostafa Elwi Saif, chair of the Department of Political Science at Cairo University, makes it possible to better adjust to today's cultural shocks of globalization. To other scholars, such as Dan Tschirgi, professor of political science at the American University in Cairo, Egyptians represent an amalgam of a dozen identities. This reality is reflected in the country's having had four constitutions in the last fifty years, three or four different flags, and several national anthems. Yet just as important as these multidimensional cultural influences, Tschirgi points out, is the presence of a broader confusion or uncertainty over whether Egypt is Islamic or secular and whether Egyptians are Western or secular Arab nationalist in their identities. It may be that Islamic identity is merely a reaction to the corrupt, inept, and repressive government.[120]

One widely heard question in the public arena is whether Egyptians should look to and emulate Turkey's model. Some Egyptian journalists argue that the Arab world has much to learn from Turkey's experience of balancing religion and secularism. Galal Nassar writes that the secular parties that ruled Turkey in the past were marred with corruption and mismanagement. The Islamists under the Justice and Development Party (JDP) have achieved political and economic stability. The Turkish economy has grown enormously, inflation is down, and many reforms have been effectively initiated under the JDP. What matters most to foreign investors in Turkey is not Islamic headdresses or university regulations but political stability, a balanced budget, and a strong government.[121]

It should be noted, however, that cultural forces can hardly be understood by examining them within specific contexts. Culture must be seen as *intersecting* with social, political, and economic forces to generate specific outcomes in specific places and time periods.[122] The widening income gaps and the lack of expansion of the middle classes have further reinforced Islamic identity among many Egyptians. This economic reality, notes Tarek Selim, professor of economics at the American University in Cairo, should not obscure the fact that the Egyptians generally tend to be a risk-averse and culturally conservative people. On balance, however, Selim argues, the prevalence of Islamic identity in Egyptian society can be attributed to the certainty of moral guidelines provided by religion in an age of uncertainty caused by the forces of globalization.[123]

Many secular-minded Egyptians appear to be either sanguine or blasé about the effects of globalization. Khaled Ahmed, a student at the Sadat Academy for Management Sciences in Cairo, argued that "globalization has truly become localized in Egypt and that technological advancements should not be seen as symbols of Westernization or globally inspired tools of alien cultures." Rather, Ahmed insisted, the Egyptians feel that "they are part of the modernized and inter-connected world without necessarily having to become Westernized."[124]

Perhaps the impact of globalization in Egypt can be traced back to the mass migration of several million Egyptians to the Persian Gulf region in the early 1970s due to oil price hikes and better job opportunities in oil-rich countries there. Such migrations led to the prevalence of Islamic headdress among Egyptian migrants who eventually returned home. Understandably, Professor Saif noted, these migrations brought back to Egypt aspects of the conservative cultural traditions of the rich Persian Gulf Arab states.[125]

Conclusion

Despite the decline of Islamic radicalism and its revolutionary appeal, Islam has been an ascendant force in the lives of most Egyptians. The emergence of a broad Islamization of public culture in Egypt since the demise of the nationalist-secular ideologies of the 1970s attests to this reality.[126] Egyptians' increasing embrace of Islam as the primary source of their identity can be traced back to their humiliating defeat at the hands of the Israelis in the 1967 war. Increasingly, during the 1980s and 1990s, many young Egyptians, alienated and frustrated, joined Islamist movements in a search of supporting networks and value systems more compatible with Egypt's socioeconomic situation than the consumerism of the West.[127]

This Islamic awakening led to the emergence of the Islamic moderate mainstream (Wassatteyya), who argue that the reformist movement of the Free Officers project, from Nasser through Sadat to Mubarak, was devoid of cultural and spiritual stamina.[128] Increasingly, it has become clear that reform is not viable without the incorporation of the Islamist mainstream into public life. Politically, however, President Mubarak's continued concern has been more with advocating the peace process—something that counts for maintaining U.S. support—rather than with democratization, economic reform, or political reconciliation.[129]

With the continued strength of the Muslim Brotherhood on the Egyptian political scene, a new battle is under way between Islamists and secularists over Islam's role in the public arena. It is in cultural arenas that Islam, which has become a defense of identity, continues to be a bulwark against an omnipresent Western modernity and globalization. The Muslim Brotherhood has gained a higher moral ground in reshaping Egypt's secular sociocultural order. The success of the Muslim Brotherhood on Egypt's political scene hinges on the ability of its leaders to promote a religious nationalism of a sort that narrows down the rift between Islamic identity and national identity. Ultimately, however, Egyptian ruling elites and Islamists must search for answers in civil society and democratic arenas, where the divide between them can be bridged through negotiations and political representation.

Chapter 5
Occupation, Sectarianism, and Identity Politics in Iraq

Thirty-five years of political coercion by the Baath Party did little to diminish a wide split between the Sunni, Shiite, and Kurdish populations. The Baath Party acted as an Arab nationalist movement whose pan-Arabism quashed cultural and political pluralism. Given the historical power disparities between these groups, the Shiites and Kurds continue to see themselves as different from the Sunnis.[1] While the Kurds are Sunni, they are less driven by religious identity than the Shiites are. A significant number of Shiites today are likely to push for some expression of their religious identity through the state. Their insistence on Islamic law and enshrining of Islamic family law is emblematic of such desire.[2]

The conflict in Iraq has brought to power a Shiite religious coalition and has in many respects resurrected an identity politics that further feeds into sectarian and tribal scrambles for power. The surging Shiite and Sunni identities have heightened insecurity caused by insurgency, extremism, assassinations, and in some cases even ethnic cleansing. In places like Ramadi, the local Sunni population failed to stop insurgents from forcing the city's Shiite inhabitants to leave. In Basra, a predominantly Shiite city, Shiite extremists have murdered Sunni clerics, leaders, and people, sparking a Sunni exodus from the country's second largest city.[3] After the British exit in September 2007, Basra has become a city where Shiite parties, militia, and criminal gangs vie to fill the power vacuum. Al-Qaeda is not a factor; the violence is caused not only by sectarian tensions but also by deep-seated political and tribal rivalries for power.[4]

History and theology, Vali Nasr rightly argues, might have constructed the identities of rival groups, but today's competing interests are far less likely to be linked to religious ideas than matters of concrete power and wealth doled out along communal lines.[5] Until the political issues of power and wealth distribution are properly addressed, stability in a multiethnic society like Iraq will hardly be sustainable. What makes the process of nation building in Iraq paradoxical, however, is the fact that the U.S. occupation and war simultaneously heighten Arab solidarity and the Shiite-Sunni divide. The former generates anger and resentment that cut across ethnic and sectarian divides, conceivably constructing a common Iraqi identity that will grow in opposition to the United States.[6] The latter takes apart Iraqi nationalism, while pushing the parties toward their own particularistic identity.

At present, as Graham E. Fuller reminds us, Islamist politics overwhelms national politics: "Islamism, as a basic feature of Muslim and especially Arab politics, is destined to play a major role in the future of Iraqi politics. A huge moral and ideological vacuum has now emerged in Iraq, and Islam is tailor-made to provide a new moral compass to the people."[7] Both Shiite and Sunni Islamists are determined to retain the "Muslim character" of Iraq, especially in the face of continued U.S. occupation.[8]

This chapter seeks to analyze the extent to which the U.S. invasion of Iraq has placed the issue of Arab identity at the center of Arab public debates and the Arab media. Just as the Palestinian issue has become a part of personal and social identity for many Arabs, so has the Iraqi situation.[9] The U.S. intervention has complicated the prospects for the formation of a new national identity in Iraq by liberating and empowering the country's Shiite majority. The question thus posed is this: How has U.S. intervention altered Iraqis' political views and identities? This chapter is an attempt to explain how the occupation of Iraq has undermined a sense of "nation-based identity" by unleashing identifiable sectarian politics and motivations.

The Occupation and Resurgent Identities

The war in Iraq has led not to the establishment of a liberal democracy, as presumed or claimed to be the case by the Bush administration, but instead to an opportunity for the majority of Iraqis to redress age-old grievances and injustices having to do with the unfair distribution of power and wealth among the country's major communities. As a result, the Iraqi Shiite majority has risen to power and the Kurdish minority has moved closer to their aspiration for sovereignty. These developments have vividly disturbed the country's sectarian balance, foreboding serious consequences not only for Iraq but also for the whole region for many years to come.

Since the invasion of Iraq in 2003, a sense of cynicism and anger over

U.S. aims and actions in Iraq has prevailed in much of the Middle East and the larger Muslim world. Powerful visual images of the American occupation have become a part of the collective memory and political consciousness of the Muslim world.[10] With the U.S. occupation of Iraq and the Bush administration's inability to push Israeli-Palestinian talks forward, public opinion polls throughout the Middle Eastern and North African region show "devastating evidence of the broad popular antipathy toward the United States."[11]

The occupation of Iraq has portrayed mixed and conflicted images: abominable pictures of rampant looting of the cultural wealth and heritage of the country shortly after the capture of Baghdad, gruesome images of the abused Abu Ghraib prisoners, and spectacular images of public participation in Iraq's first legitimate parliamentary elections. All these developments have constituted new identities for a people who have lived under several repressive regimes ever since Iraq won its independence from British mandate in 1932. Pictures of American soldiers forcing naked prisoners into compromising positions have certainly caused not only a huge embarrassment for the U.S. military operations in Iraq but, more important, humiliation and pain in the Muslim world. The prisoners' scandal has intensified trans-state identities—Arabism and Islam—across the Muslim world. This is hardly surprising given the widespread feeling among Arab Muslims of belonging to a distinct Arab world (*al-am al-arabi*).[12]

The impact of the U.S. invasion on Iraq's economic conditions and social life has been profound. Despite the symbolism of the handover of sovereignty to the provisional government, the U.S. military has remained in control. The dissolution of the Iraqi army and national police force threw out of work more than half a million people and alienated many who were dependent on those lost incomes.[13] More important, in a country vulnerable to sectarian and ethnic divisions and retaining few unifying national institutions, this act severely undermined the country's stability. The decision of the Coalition Provisional Authority (CPA) to cleanse the political system of Hussein sympathizers—that is, the de-Baathification effort—crippled the Iraqi police services. The ensuing purge of all Baathists from the state bureaucracy, professions, and academic ranks also proved to be costly.[14] Consequently, a prolonged foreign occupation that was built on de-Baathification, dissolution of the army, and the closing of factories left many Iraqis outside the economic and political life of the country.[15] This policy built steady opposition to the U.S. presence in Iraq. The obsession with punitive measures sidestepped a more conciliatory approach toward national integration for some time, at which point an organized, hostile insurgency erupted.[16]

But even more striking was the failure of the U.S. government to set up provisional institutions after the fall of Saddam Hussein, a major blunder that created a huge vacuum only to be subsequently filled by communally identified factions and organizations. Indeed, it could be argued that the U.S. managers of Iraq's occupation lacked a postwar reconstruction plan. The subsequent attempts at privatizing oil companies by the U.S. government on Washington's terms—not on Iraqis'—failed, as many Iraqis opposed such measures.[17] Increasingly, Iraq looked like a collapsing state headed for resurgent sectarian and ethnic tensions.

The violent resistance by the Sunni Arab minority, who saw the new order imposed on Iraq as threatening to their interests, defied the country's postwar stability. The Shiite leadership, in contrast, saw an opportunity to assert their rights in Iraq after living for a long time under Sunni-dominated regimes that privileged the Sunni minority. This strategy paid off when the United Arab Alliance (UAA), backed by Shiite religious leaders, gained a majority of the seats in the January 2005 elections.[18] Nevertheless, the lingering U.S. occupation fueled nationalistic and social grievances of militant Islamic movements both inside and outside the country. These sentiments were further reinforced by the pervasive view among most Arabs who believed that the United States attacked Iraq to enhance its imperialist objectives—that is, gaining control of Iraqi oil and protecting Israel.

The subsequent rise in the Sunni and the Shiite Islamic militancy was expectedly directed at resisting the U.S.-led occupation. The resistance was motivated by nationalist and religious forces alike. For many observers, such a reaction was typical. The fact that much of the Iraqi resistance to occupation has had an Islamist dimension should not come as a surprise, given the extent to which religion still permeates national identity throughout the Muslim world, and given the failure of the secular nationalism and socialism once firmly embraced by Saddam Hussein.[19]

The communal and ethnic divisions also influenced the way in which reactions to the war and occupation were evoked. While both the Kurds and Shiite Muslims viewed the overthrow of Saddam Hussein as a form of liberation, the Sunnis saw it as an attack on their power, resources, and identity. The disjuncture between national and religious identities was obvious in the case of the Kurds, who were more motivated by secular and ethnically driven goals of independence than by Islamist orientations. Whereas the Shiite concerns were essentially internal and related to the issue of who should or would control the state, the Kurdish issue was more of an external nature and had much to do with the issue of how the Kurds could escape the authority of Baghdad en route to achieving their autonomy.[20]

Historically, the Baathist regime in Baghdad has ruled over a country with a confluence of interlinked identities, with the sectarian, tribal, and ethnic bonds covered by other layers of identities such as pan-Arabism and nationalism, as well as a range of different interests. With the removal of Saddam, the traumatized sectarian and ethnic identities have surfaced, posing a formidable challenge to the occupying forces' task of maintaining order.[21] Arab Iraqis, Sunnis and Shiites, Islamist or otherwise, became divided first and foremost along their political aspirations but later largely along religious lines. The invasion has actually strengthened Shiite Islamists, while at the same time turning the Sunni insurgency and Islamists into both an anti-American and anti-Shiite movement, further sharpening the divide between the two.[22]

Meanwhile, the torture of detainees in the Abu Ghraib prison shocked the world as an Army report noted that prewar planning had not included planning for detainee operations.[23] Further revelations about the U.S. government's practice of outsourcing torture—that is, the policy of seizing individuals without any due process and sending them off to be interrogated by repressive regimes known to have regularly practiced torture—pointed to another abominable strategy of jettisoning the rule of law to permit such inhuman treatment.[24] The images of the Abu Ghraib abuses projected by the Arab media throughout the Muslim world caused a great deal of resentment toward American troops. The occupation rapidly turned a contained dictatorship and the secular country of Iraq into an epicenter of fundamentalist-inspired insurgency. In the eyes of Iraqis and the rest of the Muslim people, the occupation of another Arab land by another imperial power further resurrected anticolonial sentiments reminiscent of the fierce resistance to the British and French mandates of the interwar period. Occupation also stimulated a new generation of young Islamic radicals with a safe harbor.

The Problem of Nation Building

The political reconstruction of Iraq proved to be a difficult task largely because Saddam's rule had created political fragmentation—not unity. By giving power to tribal chiefs, Saddam governed through tribal structures and went as far as claiming that "the tribes were a source of sectarian unity rather than division in Iraq."[25] The intercommunal divisions were widened by Saddam's firm grip on power, on the one hand, and his tactical alliances across tribal lines, on the other. In fact, Saddam's efforts to construct a new vision of Iraqi identity, one expert notes, based on a glorification of the Iraqi nation generated deep divisions within Iraqi society along subnational lines. The ethnic and religious fragmentation of Iraqi society was the culmination not of primordial proclivities but of Saddam's policies over two decades that, by denying the legitimacy of ethnic, regional, and sectarian identities, only accentuated their centrality as frameworks of political dissent.[26] The Iraqi invasion of Kuwait in 1990 and the subsequent defeat there eclipsed a sense of pan-Arabism among the vast majority of Iraqis and put an end to Saddam's reliance on rent extraction from the Gulf Arab states in the name of reaffirming its identity as the defender of the Arab nation vis-à-vis Iranian-style Islamic revolution.[27]

It is important to recognize that tribes constitute the only existing coherent social structures and power brokers in their respective regions. They have their own militias, rendering them potentially susceptible to violent intertribal power struggles. In the absence of a strong central authority to hold the country together, tribal structures are unlikely to provide a firm foundation for the country's political stability.[28] Iraqi regimes have often deliberately supported communitarian identities (religious, ethnic, and tribal) while undermining attempts to build a national identity on horizontal, cross-community lines. Iraqi politics, one expert argues, from the creation of the state since the end of World War I until the removal of Saddam Hussein, has been dominated by four interlinked structural problems. First, the state has dominated society through the use of high levels of organized violence. Second, the state has used its resources—jobs, development aid, and patronage—to win the loyalty of certain sections of society. Third, the state has used oil revenue to enhance its autonomy from society. And finally, the state has attempted to exacerbate and re-create communal and ethnic divisions as a strategy of rule.[29]

The postinvasion confusion and instability demonstrated that the occupiers lacked a sufficient understanding of the regional, communal, religious, and ethnic structures of Iraqi society—not to mention the Bush administration's failure to establish a compelling link between Saddam Hussein's regime and the operations of al-Qaeda. Furthermore, it was unclear how removing Saddam's secular regime would make it easier to effectively promote a democratic process aimed at addressing historical grievances among different communities. The occupation of Iraq, as Gilles Kepel noted, heightened belief in Europe that the United States used the rhetorical appeal of advancing Arab democracy merely to "mask its own strategic and energy interest in the Gulf."[30] The insurgency in Iraq raised a fundamental question for the sustainability of nation building and democratization there: Why did Iraqis confront an army who came to liberate them from tyranny?[31]

The January 30, 2005, elections of the provisional national assembly generated new hopes among Shiites and Sunni Kurds. The Sunni Arabs, who have ruled Iraq since its inception as a nation-state, chose with remarkable consistency to skip these elections. As a result, they had almost no representation in the new government, and they were, as a subculture, set adrift, in danger of becoming unconnected to the events now shaping Iraq.[32] The elections were undoubtedly a great moral victory for Iraqis, but the problem was that they voted along ethnic lines, and this created an impasse. The outnumbered Sunnis felt they were left out of power-sharing in a new Iraq dominated by Shiites. The victorious Shia appeared to be divided themselves. Nouri al-Maliki, the country's new prime minister, depended for a majority on members loyal to Muqtada al-Sadr, a radical anti-occupation Shia cleric with a powerful militia at his disposal.[33] Another reason for Maliki's inability to govern was the prevalence of violence and the absence of law. Many Sunnis took up arms against the new Shiite-dominated government of Maliki. By blowing up the Askariyah shrine in February 2006, Al-Qaeda-related groups succeeded in provoking further sectarian terror and revenge.[34]

Under such circumstances, elections provided no magic bullet for true sovereignty or the transfer of ethical responsibility.[35] It may just be that invasion is not the best way to establish democratic institutions, proper political culture, and an effective rule of law.[36] Furthermore, the privatization of war compounded the task of nation building in Iraq. Emerging details regarding the prevalence and privileges of private security companies in Iraq demonstrated the growing but unregulated role of private contractors in U.S. military activities. The September 16, 2007, gunfire in Baghdad, in which seventeen Iraqi civilians were killed by Blackwater employees, sparked rage and debate over the role of these privately employed agents in Iraq. Some contractors remained outside the jurisdiction of U.S. courts, civil or military, for improper conduct in Iraq.[37] Many analysts argued that there were inadequate controls over who can work for these private military firms and for whom these firms can work.[38]

Many questions exist about the clientele of these private contractors. Although military contractors have worked for democratic governments and the UN, and have even promoted causes associated with humanitarian and environmental organizations, they have nevertheless been hired by "dictatorships, rebel groups, drug cartels, and, prior to September 11, 2001, at least two al-Qaeda-linked jihadi groups."[39] The issues of who had jurisdiction over them and who could prosecute them, both internally and externally, remained unanswered. In cases where contractors committed misdeeds, it was often unclear how, when, where, and which authorities were responsible for investigating, prosecuting, and punishing such crimes.[40]

The Shiites' Political Resurgence

Unlike Sunni Arab and Kurd, names that denote a particular ethnic or cultural identity, Shiite in Iraq is neither a sociological, political, or cultural classification.[41] The Iraqi Shia are identified as holders of particular Islamic beliefs that distinguish them from other Muslim believers, especially the Sunnis. The sheer size of their population today renders them a potentially potent constituency. Shiites comprise about 90 percent of Iranians, nearly 70 percent of the people living in the Persian Gulf region, and some 50 percent of those in the arc from Lebanon to Pakistan—approximately 140 million people in all.[42]

The word "Shiite" refers to "partisans" or a party that supported Ali, the Prophet Muhammad's son-in-law, who later became Islam's fourth caliph. The party emerged during a civil war from 656 to 661, in which several battles were fought between the Shiites and the Sunni over the issue of succession to the Prophet's reign. Shiism suffered defeats at the hands of the Sunni, and today's Shiites tend to commemorate those occasions. Several Shiite Imams, including Ali and Hussein, are buried in the holy cities of Najaf, Karbala, Kazmiya, and Samarra. All these resting places are located in Iraq, making it a place of special spiritual significance to the world's Shiites.

One of the key origins of the Sunni/Shiite divide, or perhaps a major doctrinal difference between the two, stems from a Shia contention that the Sunnis reject: that the Prophet Muhammad selected Ali to be the first *imam* of the Islamic state and thus rejected the Shiite institution of the *imamate*, which recognized the divine right of Ali and his descendants to lead the *umma* (the community of believers).[43] Shiism later encountered its own dissidents, those who declared themselves Isma'ilis, Alawites, Zaydis, and Druzes. Although the Shiites constitute the majority in Iran, Iraq, Bahrain, and Azerbaijan, they are significant minorities in some Arab countries such as Lebanon, Pakistan, and Saudi Arabia. Shiites are often wrongly assumed to be Iranian, when in fact many of them are Arab and loyal to their Arab homeland rather than to Iran.[44] Shiite masses throughout the Middle East, however, are appraising the new situation, seeking new bargains with their leaders. "It is the sectarian balance within states," Juan Cole writes, "rather than primarily the relationship among states—though the two are obviously related—that is driving these political developments."[45]

The Shiite majority has traditionally been utterly underrepresented within decision-making echelons of the Iraqi state, even though they have had no difficulty accepting and even supporting the legitimacy of Iraqi nationalism or the validity of the Iraqi state. As a clear manifestation of their Iraqi nationalism, Shiite tribes participated in the 1920 revolt against the British and constituted the majority in the Iraqi army in the Iran-Iraq war of 1980–88.[46] Yet the war's legacy has not divided Iranian and Iraqi Shiites, in large part because they have suffered from the systematic repressive policies of the central government. In fact, the Iran-Iraq war, as Vali Nasr argues, "pales before the memory of the anti-Shiite pogrom in Iraq that followed the failed uprising in 1991. Today, Iraqi Shiites worry far more about the Sunnis' domination than about Tehran's influence in Baghdad."[47] Iraqi nationalism, however, has practically declined in the face of increasing connections between the Shiite communities in Iran and Iraq, buttressing Shiite identity and networks.

Fearful of the potential power of Shiite masses and fueled by the concerns of neighboring Persian Gulf States, especially Saudi Arabia, regarding the purported spread of Iranian political influence, Saddam turned to mass and summary executions and the destruction of vast areas of marshland in southern Iraq throughout his rule and particularly after 1988.[48] This mistreatment of Shiites was not a particularly Iraqi phenomenon. Historically, Sunni regimes throughout the Muslim world have maintained their political dominance by keeping the Shiites "weak and divided."[49]

Despite their nationalistic credentials, the Shiites had good reason to be concerned with the sectarian divide. First, the Iraqi state has been dominated by the Sunni minority since the inception of the state itself. Staunchly pan-Arabist and secular in their political orientation, the Sunni minority played a disproportionate role in shaping the identity of the Iraqi state. Shiites have traditionally raised questions about the proper role of religious leaders as well as the extent to which Iraq should be governed as an Islamic state—questions that lie at the root of the identity of the Iraqi state. Second and even more crucially, Shiite leadership has raised serious concerns about the insufficient representation of Shiites in the Iraqi political system.[50]

The development of political Shiism in Iraq began with the efforts of Ayatollah Muhammad Baqir al-Sadr (1935–80), who created Hizb al-Da'wa al-Islamiyya (The Party of the Islamic Call—al-Da'wa) in the late 1950s in Najaf.[51] Outside the country, the Supreme Council for Islamic Revolution in Iraq (SCIRI—al-Majlis al-A'la li'l-Thawra al-Islamiyya fi'l-Iraq) was formed in 1982 in Tehran. The political opening of Iraq also produced not only divisions between Shias but, more important, a new leadership: Grand Ayatollah Sistani, who represented SCIRI in Iraq. Some Shiite groups, led by Muqtada al-Sadr, downplayed the importance of Shiite identity and sectarian differences with Sunnis by focusing on fighting the United States and Israel. Muqtada al-Sadr blended Shiism, nationalism, and anti-Americanism in his approach to Iraq's emerging politics.[52]

Sistani, in contrast, pursued a policy of consolidating Shiites' gains in Iraq by fortifying their identity and culture. He was soon recognized by Shiites from Lebanon to Iran to Pakistan. Although born and raised in Iran, he never got involved in Iranian clerical politics.[53] He confined the role of Islam to providing values and moral guidelines for social order. His pragmatic style was based on promoting Shiite interests inside Iraq and Shia revival at the regional level based on an identity common to millions of Shiites in Iraq, Iran, Lebanon, Pakistan, and Afghanistan. Thus, the greater Shiite political resurgence and cultural identity would translate into more rights and power across the crescent from Lebanon to Pakistan. The main thrust of Sistani's message was that because greater democracy serves Shiite interests across the region, Shiite revival is—and ought to be—favorably disposed toward democratic change. Beyond pragmatic interest in democracy, many Shiites embraced democracy as an idea.[54]

The intra-Shiite scramble for power and multiple loyalties cannot be divorced from the struggle over distribution of Iraq's wealth and resources. Given that the bulk of Iraq's estimated two hundred billion barrels in potential oil deposits are in Basra, the militias' jockeying for Basra's riches is understandable. According to most estimates, potential Iraqi reserves account for approximately 16 percent to 20 percent of Middle East reserves. Producing at full capacity, Iraq can generate nearly $90 million a day through exports to support its own reconstruction.[55]

Many personal and social freedoms have eroded with the rising tide of hard-line Shiite Islamists in Basra. Likewise, the Sunni areas are seeing the growth of religious conservatism. Many commentators attribute this rise of conservatism to the U.S. intervention, arguing that "Iraq and other places [in the Arab world] are under attack . . . by the West and there is a lot of return to religion in order to empower themselves to fight the infidels."[56] Although the desire for a clerical state is not widely shared among the Shiites, Iran has successfully forged ties with Shiite forces across the Iraqi spectrum by bolstering aspirations and sentiments of different Shiite groups. Iran's powerful allies, such as the Supreme Islamic Iraqi Council and elements of the Mahdi Army, have fortified Shiite control over Iraq by forcing the Western intruders and the so-called enemies of faith out of the country.[57]

The Shia revival, Vali Nasr argues, depends on three pillars: "the newly empowered Shiite majority in Iraq, the current rise of Iran as regional leader, and the empowerment of Shiites across Lebanon, Saudi Arabia, Kuwait, the UAE, and Pakistan."[58] These three pillars are interconnected, and each reinforces the other. Together they assure a greater Shiite voice in Middle Eastern politics and are certain to push for a new power distribution in the region.[59] The Shiites have become increasingly cognizant that only the U.S. occupation stands between them and the ultimate attainment of political power so long denied.[60] They have much to gain if the democratic process succeeds in Iraq.

Some commentators have viewed with skepticism the idea that a "broad Shiite revival" is spreading throughout the Middle East, arguing that Shiite populations are influenced by local, social, political, and economic conditions. Nationalism has thus far managed to outweigh Shiism. Moreover, international relations and the pursuit of national interests have severely restrained the formation of transnational movements, such as Shiite revival, based on shared meanings and belief systems. Shiism as such is a flexible identity constructed by the particular circumstances and contexts in which Shiites live.[61] It is important to bear in mind, they note, that the key motivations behind the "Shia Crescent" concern the nagging geopolitical considerations in the region, stretching over nearly three decades. The sectarian argument has served and continues to serve as a way to confer legitimacy on Sunni rulers' policies.[62]

The Erosion of Sunni Hegemony

The most constant factor in modern Iraqi politics and its power structure has been its domination by the Sunnis, as evidenced by the fact that virtually every regime in Iraq since its inception—irrespective of its underlying social basis—has perpetuated Sunni dominance.[63] Experts point out that "Sunnis have either administered or ruled the territory that is now called Iraq for the last 1,500 years."[64] To keep the Sunnis in line and prevent the divisions within them from threatening existing power structures, most rulers have adopted a policy of patronage and coercion.

The fact that Sunnis are a majority in the Arab and the entire Muslim world has resulted in strong Arab nationalist links between Baghdad and other regional Arab capitals. That explains not only why the Sunnis associated themselves with the Iraqi state identity—be that monarchy or republican—but also why the Arab Sunni heartland of Iraq was central to Saddam's survival and legitimacy.[65] Since the demise of Saddam, however, the Sunnis have heard the death knell of their unmitigated hegemony in Iraq, as they have lost the power to define and construct the identity of the Iraqi state.[66] This has facilitated the decline of Sunni-led Arab nationalism and the emergence of a new political identity for the Shiites.

Sectarian politics and conflict in Iraq have increased simultaneously with the growth of Sunni extremism, anti-Americanism, religious conservatism, and jihadi activism in the region. The Sunni militancy—al-Qaeda, Wahhabi, and Salafi activists—along with the network of Muslim Brotherhood organizations throughout the Middle East, North Africa, and Europe, are bound to pose a major threat to U.S. interests.[67] The war in Iraq presented a rare opportunity to the extremist activists in both Jordan and Syria, who have often been chased away by Jordanian and Syrian security forces, to come to Iraq. These elements over the decades prior to the Iraq war introduced fundamentalist thinking in al-Anbar province and have created networks that would facilitate the insurgency after the war. The emergence of Abu Musab al-Zarqawi as the leader of insurgency immediately after the Iraq war, for instance, reveals the extent to which Jordanian Salafis were involved in Iraq.[68]

Led by the Sunni militants, the insurgency could very well turn into a bloody civil war, with the consequences of involving Jordan, Syria, and Iran. The surging militancy of Iraq's Sunni Arabs, and their alliance with radical Jordanian Salafis, will most likely pose longer term menaces to the Jordanian political regime as well.[69] The rise of Shiite power in Iraq, growing Iranian influence, and the ethnic separatism that jeopardizes regional stability are concerns shared by many of Iraq's Arab neighbors, especially Saudi Arabia. Riyadh fears that its own Shiites will grow restive, undermining Saudi control of its vast oil reserves in the Eastern Province.[70]

In the aftermath of the 2005 national elections, in which 77 percent of the electorate, including Sunni Arabs, voted, neither of the Sunni coalitions (the Iraqi Accord Front or the Iraqi National Dialogue Front) joined in forming an alliance with the United Iraqi Alliance (UIA), the principal Shiite coalition. This illustrated the fear of the Sunni minority who were in danger of losing power through free elections to the Shia majority in the first country ever in the Arab world in which such democratic transition had transpired. In fact, some of the Sunni political fronts have become more willing to negotiate with U.S. officials in the hope of slowing the obviously inevitable empowerment of the Shiites.[71]

Recognizing that the tide is changing, the U.S. government also made a portentous shift in foreign policy by moving away from supporting the government of Prime Minister Nouri al-Maliki as a way to force a bottom-up approach on certain issues. Fundamentally important in this shift was funding and arming of Sunni tribes and communities in Anbar Province, whose members have in the past relentlessly attacked U.S. forces.[72] Arguably, the Sunni mainstream's participation in constitutional negotiations may owe much to their strategic calculation of the cooperation with the United States. Quite understandably, many in Nouri al-Maliki's Shiite constituency regard the insurgent groups as terrorists with whom they will not negotiate. Most Shiites view the U.S. rapprochement with mainstream Sunni insurgent groups as a way to weaken Shiite power.[73] Defeating extremist Sunnis and their outside collaborators in Iraq presents a paradox for U.S. policy toward Iraq. The moderate Arab regimes, such as Jordan, Saudi Arabia, and Egypt, who are opposed to extremist elements in Iraq, tend to support insurgency insofar as it undermines the overall Shia influence in Iraq. It is not clear who the U.S. forces are fighting: the insurgents, or an externally infiltrated extremist group, or the rising Shiite factions.

Some commentators argue that rather than focusing on defeating and killing insurgents, U.S. forces should concentrate on providing human security and opportunity to the Iraqi people, thereby undercutting the popular support that insurgents need.[74] Aside from the patience required for defeating the insurgency, it is important to keep in mind that firm resolve to overcome any resistance to U.S. policies is not enough. Stephen M. Walt poignantly argues that U.S. power is now much more feared than welcomed around the world: "If anti-Americanism continues to grow, Washington will face greater resistance and find it harder to attract support. Americans will feel increasingly threatened in such a world, but trying to counter these threats alone will merely exacerbate the fear of U.S. power and isolate the United States even more."[75]

The Kurds: Revival of Ethnonationalism

The growing uncertainty over the Kurds' demand for autonomy has further complicated the outlook of democratic rule in Iraq. Since April 1991, after the first Gulf War, the Kurds' region in northern Iraq has enjoyed an autonomous status. This situation, however, preserved the territorial integrity of the country. The issue of independence became a part of a referendum, as hundreds of Kurds erected tents at official polling places in Iraq's Kurdish areas and asked voters to take part in an informal referendum on whether Kurdistan should be independent or part of Iraq. According to the referendum's organizers, the tally turned out to be overwhelmingly (98.76 percent) in favor of independence.[76]

Although Kurdish leaders have officially spoken of a democratic, federal, pluralistic, and united Iraq, they have long espoused the notion of an independent Kurdistan. Massoud Barzani, the leader of the Kurdish Democratic Party, has openly expressed his aspiration for an independent Kurdistan. Peter Galbraith, a former American diplomat who watched the collapse of Yugoslavia and was monitoring the voting in Kurdistan, noted that the breakup of Iraq was inevitable largely "because the Kurds had finally got close to independence and were in no mood to stop now."[77]

During constitutional negotiations, the Kurdish leaders settled for a constitutional draft that preserved their region's de facto independence and financial autonomy while granting them full control over the disputed province of Kirkuk. More important, the Kurds insisted on a fixed amount of Iraq's national budget and full sovereignty over their region's petroleum, including the right to export it.[78] The oil fields in Kirkuk represent almost two fifths of the country's proven petroleum reserves. This fact, among other things, has convinced the Kurds to keep all their options open, especially their attempt to expand into oil-rich territories. The Kurds' uncertain history and future has alerted them to this reality.[79]

The implications of who claims Kirkuk are varied and many, as this ethnic-sectarian conflict could potentially spread beyond the Iraqi borders. Aside from oil fields, Kirkuk is a setting for all the ethnic-sectarian conflicts characteristic of Iraq. Kirkuk is home to the Turkmens, who have always looked to Turkey as their protector. While Kirkuk is the center of the Turkmen population in Iraq, the city is seen by the Kurds as "a touchstone of their identity."[80] The competition for staking a claim on Kirkuk will likely pit the Turkmen against the Kurds, threatening to convert Iraqi internal politics into a regional conflict.[81] Turkey's long-term interest in preventing the formation of an independent, oil-rich Kurdistan is a familiar subject of internal debate within Turkey given its own large and rebellious Kurdish minority. The neighboring countries of Iran and Syria have pursued similar interests.

The question persists: To what extent will a future Iraqi polity have to take account of vertical communal identities? The Kurdish minority is likely to push for some form of autonomy in a federal structure.[82] The fact that Iraqi Kurds have been autonomous since 1991 and have operated separately from Baghdad has created structural problems that would make it painful for the Kurds to return to their pre-1991 situation. The dominant language in northern Iraq is now Kurdish, with no pressure on children to learn Arabic. Kurdish national universities advance their own educational system and the Kurdish administrations have established their own standing military forces. "The Kurds have tasted freedom," experts argue, "and will want to keep it."[83] This accounts for why the Kurds are reluctant to transfer their loyalty and commitment from tribes, villages, and ethnic and sectarian groups to the larger central political system. The real danger is that Iraq's assembly and its interim constitution may serve as a purely strategic instrument of the occupiers. Some Islamist leaders in the Middle East view the U.S. democracy initiative as an attempt to consolidate U.S.-Israeli hegemony in the region, both by promoting pro-U.S. regimes and by spreading Western secular, liberal values to the detriment of Arab-Islamic identity and culture.[84]

The Prospects for Democratic Transition

In the years following the removal of Saddam Hussein's regime, the U.S. foreign policy of promoting democracy in Iraq met with a series of disappointments, as hopes for the expansion of civil society, the rule of law, and political transition from authoritarianism did not materialize. Internally, different ethnic and sectarian drives motivated the Shiites, the Sunnis, and the Kurds. The expectation that democracy would rapidly alter Iraqi society was not fulfilled, and the strategy that the electoral process and elections would prove crucial in bridging sectarian gaps was fraught with tensions.

The subsequent Shiite revivalism became a cause of concern for major Arab Sunni countries, such as Saudi Arabia, which was worried that Iran could stir up their local kingdom's own Shiite minority.[85] But more to the point, these difficulties raised a central question regarding the effectiveness of the military intervention in promoting democracy.

A quick look at the history of U.S. involvement in nation building demonstrates why military conquest could not necessarily pave the way for social and political reform without the authorization of an international body, such as the United Nations. To be sure, U.S. nation-building operations have yielded some lucid successes (Japan, Germany, and Taiwan), some dismal failures (Haiti, Vietnam, and Somalia), and some inconclusive results (the Philippines and Kosovo).[86] The pitfalls encountered in previous rebuilding efforts in other places such as Bosnia, East Timor, and Afghanistan loom large. Lawlessness, poor oversight, and ethnic strife have rendered past rebuilding efforts precarious.[87] Some studies suggest that in only four countries—West Germany, Japan, Grenada, and Panama—did the types of democratic governance systems that the United States sought to establish continue after ten years. In the cases of Haiti, Nicaragua, Cambodia, and Vietnam, tyrannical regimes quickly emerged after U.S. forces left the country. In Lebanon (in the early 1980s) and Somalia (in the early 1990s), U.S. nation-building efforts utterly failed.[88]

Historically, intervention, proxy wars, and occupation in the Middle East by great powers have been motivated by purely instrumental interests and political, not democratic, considerations. One observer notes that America created violent and radical political Islam inadvertently as part of its Cold War strategy. In the Afghan war (1980–89), America supported *mujahideen* (freedom fighters) to dislodge Soviet forces from Afghanistan. The jihadi *madrasas* (religious schools) in Pakistan trained both the Afghan refugee children who later helped form the Taliban regime and the Arab-Afghans who were later networked by al-Qaeda. The U.S. policy makers turned this ideological tendency (Islamism) into a political organization. The Afghan war gave it organization, numbers, skills, resources, and a coherent strategy. In short, "America created an infrastructure of terror but heralded it as an infrastructure of liberation."[89]

Can occupation deliver on democratic objectives? There is a widespread skepticism that military occupation of Iraq will be justified on such grounds. Historically, the idea that Iraq would gradually become an independent, self-governing nation-state under British tutelage met with resistance and contempt. In the 1920s, Sunni and Shiite clerics and nationalists united in their opposition to British occupation, issuing a fatwa authorizing rebellion.[90]

The application of the lessons of U.S. occupation of Germany and Japan to Iraq is also problematic. One observer argues that these lessons will apply rather lightly to Iraq. The Germans and the Japanese were not part of any wider fellowship or nation, whereas Iraqis belong to a much larger Muslim global community in addition to their Arab identity. It is not difficult to understand why the invasion of Iraq is bound to inflame a new cycle of hatred among Muslims that can only benefit Islamic militants.[91]

Another study suggests that the historical experience of Germany and Japan in the postwar period showed that military occupation may increase the likelihood of democratization and that wise policy choices could surely improve its chances. That experience, however, was unique and not easily replicable today. The outcome of such interventions, Eva Bellin finds, "is largely shaped by factors, both domestic and international, that cannot be controlled by military engineers operating within the confines of current cultural norms and conventional limits of time and treasure."[92]

Several factors and endowments rendered it possible for both Germany and Japan to become democracies. Prior to the outbreak of World War II, both Germany and Japan were highly industrialized countries with advanced levels of economic development that generated impressive GNP per capita. They were both relatively homogenous ethnically, with a significant consensus about their sense of social solidarity and national identity. Both Germany and Japan emerged from World War II with state institutions intact. Both retained an effective police force, judicial system, and civil service with which to govern.[93] Both had extensive experience with democratic rule prior to World War II and had committed leaders, whose embrace of the democratic project helped anchor democratic projects at home. Additionally, context-specific factors such as the experience of total devastation and defeat, the fear of communist threat and takeover, and the imposed freedom of occupation bestowed by contemporary cultural norms made it possible for democracy to endure in these countries.[94]

These endowments crucial to democratic outcomes—levels of economic development, ethnic homogeneity, strength of state institutions, historical experience, and elite leadership—are factors conspicuously lacking in Iraq. The cases that are better matched to Iraq in initial conditions are Haiti and Bosnia, both of which have yet to become stable democracies with sustainable economic and political units.[95] The continuing violence and growing intercommunal strife over land, resources, and political power can slide the country into further chaos. A legitimate government, effective security forces, satisfaction of Sunnis that they would not be discriminated against in a Shiite-dominated Iraq, and thus a reduction in the Sunni support for the insurgency, could prove to be keys to a functioning political regime in Iraq.[96]

A larger and deeper question remains—whether democratizing and transforming Iraq and the rest of the Middle Eastern countries would be sustainable. In the case of Iraq, experts remind us, *taifiyya* (sectarianism), not democracy, is the central element of political solidarity.[97] It follows that the Shiite community's commitment to democracy is based on its control of the political system, which is likely to further intensify sectarian identities among the Sunnis and Kurds.[98]

Furthermore, the devastating UN-imposed economic sanctions on Iraq during 1990–2003 strangled the Iraqi civilian population, placing the lives of many Iraqis in great peril. The oil-for-food program failed to offset the impact of sanctions and thus to prevent the collapse of the health system and the deterioration of water supplies. The death of more than 600,000 Iraqi children as a result of the economic sanctions led the UN to reexamine its sanction program by exploring the possibility of imposing the so-called smart sanctions, which would target ruling elites, not innocent citizens.[99] The inhumane impacts of economic sanctions triggered a strong sense of sympathy for the Iraqi people across the globe. Also, the vibrant Iraqi middle class that had emerged by the mid-twentieth century and that provided the basis for a civil society was muted by a decade-long economic sanction and Saddam Hussein's repressive rule.

Today, organized crime and banditry are deeply entrenched. The military, security services, bureaucracy, and legal system need to be drastically reformed. The economy needs radical transformation to render it competitive in global markets.[100] The humanitarian burden on Iraq has been enormous. Nearly sixteen million Iraqis, according to the World Food Program, continue to rely solely on food rations distributed through the oil-for-food program to meet household needs.[101] Moreover, surging violence has created what is becoming one the world's largest refugee crisis. Some 40 percent of Iraq's professionals (doctors, teachers, and businesspeople) have fled the country. Some fifty thousand people a month are leaving Iraq, according to UN sources. Most have been escaping to the neighboring countries of Jordan and Syria. These refugees face tough restrictions in host countries, preventing them from finding jobs or gaining access to basic health care and other public services.[102]

Reversal of the U.S. policy of promoting democracy in the region—due in large part to the failure of U.S. policy in Iraq—has lightened the pressure on autocratic but pro-U.S. regimes in the Middle East to democratize, as long as they support Washington in its impending or future confrontation with Iran, Syria, and Shiite Islamists. But more to the point, with the rising Shiite Iran, the Bush administration has muted its call for reform in the region by redirecting policy to reembrace Sunni Arab allies who typically run authoritarian regimes. To contain Iran, the United States is now reaching out to Saudi Arabia, other Persian Gulf states, Egypt, and Jordan through large arms deals and new talks on such issues as the Israeli-Palestinian conflict, which is widely perceived in the Arab world as the greatest source of tension.[103]

Saudi Arabia and Egypt are back in Washington's good graces and are thought of as "moderates" as long as they have an interest in resisting Iran's regional domination.[104] Ultimately, however, U.S. interests would be served by a political settlement that would contain the scope of sectarian violence. The absence of a credible political process and road map to peacefully resolve sectarian grievances would render state building in Iraq impossible. The key here is to work toward a new power distribution not only in Iraq but also in the region. The newly empowered Shiite majority in Iraq, the rise of Iran as the regional leader, and the strengthening of Shiite groups across Lebanon, Saudi Arabia, Kuwait, the United Arab Emirates, and Pakistan all attest to the Shia revival throughout the region. Although U.S. confrontation with al-Qaeda in Afghanistan has never provoked responses on the Arab streets, sectarianism risks spawning such a backlash.[105]

What Lies Ahead

Historical and theological influences have shaped Iraq's sectarian and tribal undercurrents for a good part of the twentieth century. Such a simple statement, however, belies the complexity of dynamic debates about a wide variety of political and socioeconomic factors that have contributed to deepening the divide between various ethnic and religious groups. Nation building was never a finished business under Saddam's regime. The sectarian conflict that the Iraqi war has rekindled will make the nation-building process an even tougher task. One lesson learned from the British experience of occupying Iraq (1920–32) stems from the consequences of imposing order on an increasingly resentful population. The U.S. invasion of Iraq led to a similar occupation, bringing under its control a population who had lived under Saddam Hussein's all-pervasive state with its structures of patronage and violence.[106]

The power hierarchy in Iraq was persistently dominated by the Sunnis, who, while a minority numerically, always assumed the state identity and viewed their ruling elites as the guarantors of that identity. The Shiites, in contrast, while the numerical majority, were grossly underrepresented in the Iraqi decision-making structure and were widely discriminated against, despite the fact that they identified themselves as Arabs—both nationally and from a cultural standpoint. After the removal of Saddam, the Shiites have sought a greater voice and a new power distribution. The Kurds, while Sunni, were marginalized both geographically and politically within Iraq; they were driven by strong ethnic undercurrents and presented a major challenge to the Iraqi state identity and Iraqi nationalism more generally.

Today, both the Shiites and the Kurds have much to gain from the democratic process. The Sunnis, in contrast, have lost power and the ability to define state identity. The resurgence of Islamic culture and identity is bound to shape the future of Iraqi Shiite politics, while Sunni resistance will most likely be directed toward both the surge of Shiite power and U.S. occupying forces. What is more, Sunni extremists view anti-Shiism as being synonymous with anti-American jihad in Iraq. In northern Iraq, Kurdish clans and their leaders appear unlikely to merge with other Sunni Arab Islamist movements in the foreseeable future as long as Kurdish aspirations have not been met and a distinct "nationalist cause" remains among the Kurds.[107]

To conclude, anger and resentment toward the Anglo-American military occupation, along with the humiliation and shame caused by the mistreatment of Iraqi prisoners in Abu Ghraib, have incited a new cycle of hatred among Muslims that has only emboldened radical Sunni Islamic groups. Using Islam as a grassroots counter-hegemony, Iraqi militant Sunni groups have beefed up an insurgency capable of disrupting the country's postwar democratic process and reconstruction. Similarly, the continuing occupation of Iraq also fuels a sense of disillusionment, impotency, and social disempowerment among the Shiites. Together, the occupation of Iraq and the subsequent Shia-Sunni tensions that have gripped the country invite recruitment of more terrorists.

If the Iraqi situation reaches the level of a "civil war," the partition option may become a realistic option. Regardless, any postwar reconstruction of Iraq should commit itself to tackling the underlying structural problems of power sharing and distribution of state resources that have for so long marred Iraqi politics. The U.S. invasion of Iraq is having a profound impact on Iraqis' national identity in that it has seriously diminished any realistic chance of nation building there. After all, nation building was never intended as a moral or strategic basis for invading Iraq. The widespread sectarian violence and ethnic divide serve as an ominous reminder that occupation and war will lead to paradoxical consequences in potentially explosive and divisive societies by dismantling the national identities of some while reinforcing local identities and aspirations of others.

Chapter 6

The Melding of the Old and New in the United Arab Emirates

Known as the trading hub of the Persian Gulf and Middle Eastern region, the United Arab Emirates (UAE) is managing to preserve the balance between forces of tradition and modernity. Externally, the country manifests the growing impact of rapid modernization and globalization. But at the same time, the tribal sheikhs continue to play an extremely important role in the country's political system. Patriarchal ideology and culture run deep and are firmly in place in the UAE. Ruling elites typically operate within very specific tribal confines. Islam continues to be a unifying force within the country, conferring on its nationals a sense of belonging in addition to shaping their thinking and views about the challenges facing the country.

In many respects, the country has transformed into a modern state, but its conservative cultural traditions and political structures are well entrenched and resistant to radical change. Democratization does not have the same urgency as in some neighboring Persian Gulf countries, and there is little need for formal social support groups given that extended families and the tribal society remain intact.[1] The changing attitudes and values of the younger generation, however, merit particular attention. The country's politically conformist yet savvy media also deserve special attention, especially with the rise of anti-American sentiment among local Islamic groups throughout the Persian Gulf monarchies. This chapter investigates the unique character of state and society in the UAE in an attempt to reveal the formation of new but contradictory identities among its youth and women.

A Sociocultural Background

An introduction to the United Arab Emirates would not be complete without a brief mention of the nation's emirates and tribal makeup. Abu Dhabi occupies 88.3 percent of the country's total area; it accounts for 90 percent of the federation's oil and gas production and 60 percent of its gross domestic product (GDP).[2] Dubai, with less than 5 percent of the UAE's total area, has become a regional commercial and transportation center, generating 70 percent of the nation's non-oil trade.[3] Sharjah, with slightly more than 3 percent of the land, has focused on light manufacturing and port facilities, despite the fact it has oil and gas deposits.[4] The emirates of Ra's al-Khayma, Fujairah, Umm al-Qaywayn, and Ajman constitute the remainder of the country. Nearly all UAE nationals and expatriates are Muslim. Tribal affiliations are of particular saliency among the emirates, whose rulers are drawn from the prominent families of the dominant tribes.[5]

Cultivation and the permanent inland settlements in Fujairah contribute greatly to international trade through its ports of Julfar and Jumeira. The pearling industry, almost six thousand years old, was for decades the backbone of the region's economy.[6] In 1588, the Italian explorer Gasparo Balbi described Dubai as the center of pearling,[7] and as late as the end of the nineteenth century, the economy and social life of old Dubai was based almost entirely on the pearling industry. In the nineteenth and early twentieth centuries, fishing, pearling, trade, and agriculture were the key sources of income for the inhabitants of the emirates.

The period immediately prior to the advent of Islam saw an abundance of fairs and busy markets occurring throughout many of today's emirates. A magnet for early trade and commerce, Dubai was the scene of regular economic transactions. Indian, Russian, Persian, Southeast Asian, and Chinese merchants sailed to different parts of the UAE to explore and invest in the vast market opportunities and activities there. The advent of Islam reinforced rather than disrupted the tribal system, promoting social cohesion and fortifying the common will in the face of adversity. In fact, Islam brought to the tribal society a law that had its point of reference outside the tribal structure.[8]

With the expulsion of the Portuguese in 1633, European merchants, especially the British, began arriving in search of new sources of pearls for the flourishing European markets. The British came in the early 1800s, and the first treaties between the ruling sheikhs and the British were concluded in January 1820.[9] In an effort to curtail tribal disputes and preserve trade, the British signed the General Treaty of Peace with the nine rulers of the coastal sheikhdoms in 1820. This treaty outlawed plunder, piracy, and undeclared wars. The treaty also bestowed legitimacy on the independence of Sharjah, Ajman, and Umm al-Qiwayn from Ras al-Khaimah, which had been the capital of the Qawasim (the ruling dynasty and leaders of the Persian Gulf pirates from the early eighteenth century) and their allies. As a result, new sheikhdoms gained distinct geographical names instead of the old tribal designations that characterized the landscape.[10]

The lower Persian Gulf region was entirely isolated during the second half of the nineteenth century due to piracy, arms dealing, and the slave trade—all of which served as pretexts for British intervention. By the end of the nineteenth century, Britain had solidified its control over the coastal sheikhdoms by forcing them to sign protectorate treaties (1892) that made London responsible for the external affairs of the emirates. This policy further increased the region's isolation from the outside world.[11] Several subsequent agreements generated a collective name for the independent Sheikdoms—the Trucial Coast—laying down the foundation for the United Arab Emirates in the twentieth century.[12]

With the discovery of oil, Britain altered its regional strategy and paid considerable attention to internal affairs, largely to facilitate the signing of oil concessions and to maintain its monopoly over them. After World War I, Britain ruled over the region singlehandedly. The absence of clearly defined or well-delineated borders between individual emirates became a significant issue in light of the growing importance of oil. Consequently, the sheikhdoms entered a long and complicated period of negotiations and conflicts.[13]

The British presence in the Persian Gulf lasted for nearly 150 years. On December 1, 1971, the British forces withdrew from the Trucial States, paving the way for the formation of what today is the United Arab Emirates.[14] The UAE adopted a permanent constitution in 1996. Ras al Khaimah sought independence, but it lacked the necessary resources and the international support to survive. It thus joined the federation in 1972.[15]

Some experts have suggested that the idea of a union finally came to fruition not because of the imperative of pooling military forces for the purpose of a formidable defense or as a successor to the British protective shield. Rather, the UAE came into existence mainly as a result of the perception by political elites of "the inability of the emirates taken individually to assume the responsibilities of statehood in a highly complicated world and in light of the meager material and human resources each commanded after over a century of dependence on a foreign power."[16]

All of the nationals of the emirates were Sunni Muslims, following the Malaki and Hanbali denominations. A tiny minority in the eastern part of the country followed the Shafi school of thought.[17] The Shia were mostly from Iran; their numbers grew significantly after World War II, mainly among the merchant community.[18] This group successfully adjusted to Emirati society and, after unification, became part of the society, although it was not fully absorbed in it.[19]

The discovery of oil and the effects of petroleum income had enormous implications for the country. These effects brought about tremendous growth and change, along with shifting demographic trends caused not by the improvements in living conditions and health standards but by a massive influx of expatriates seeking work in a country whose oil wealth was disproportionately larger than its local population. During the first two decades after unification, health services, power and water supplies, and transportation systems developed rapidly.

These developments were accompanied and followed by huge economic growth, rising public awareness, an economic opening to the outside world, and the emergence of an educational movement that produced a generation of well-educated Emiratis.[20] But at the same time, demographic trends have posed a number of problems for the UAE's "national" inhabitants. Constantly reminded of being a minority in their own country, some experts note, the citizens of all seven emirates have unified around their undisputed privilege.[21]

The Power Structures of the Sheikhdoms

The political system is a mix of presidential and parliamentary elements, with the largest power concentrated in the executive Federal Supreme Council, whose members are the rulers of the seven emirates. The federation consists of three other main bodies: the Federal Council of Ministers (FCM), the Federal National Council (FNC), and the Federal Judiciary. The FCM or cabinet serves as the executive authority for the federation and is responsible for implementing general policy inside and outside the country, preparing the public budget, and formulating laws and decisions. The main weakness of the FCM is that it is an institution that belongs to the Supreme Council and therefore is committed to the implementation of its decisions.[22] The FNC is a consultative body that is empowered to deliberate and propose amendments to legislation and to draft union laws. Members of the FNC are typically selected by the rulers of the emirates and tend to be drawn from among the young educated men or from their most loyal supporters within each emirate.[23] The Federal Judiciary includes the Federal

Supreme Court and Courts of First Instance. The Federal Supreme Court's five judges are appointed by the Supreme Council of Rulers. These judges determine the constitutionality of federal laws and arbitrate on inter-emirate disputes as well as disputes between the federal government and the emirates.[24]

The UAE is a federation in which decentralization and political accommodation are embedded in the structure and modus operandi of the state.[25] The constitution defines the federation as a two-tier system of government, in which the political echelon is represented in two separate powers: the federal authority and the local authority.

The emirates have a patriarchal-monarchical executive system. The rulers are regarded as the heads of the states and the heads of their tribes as well as all other tribes residing in their territory. The rulers enjoy unmitigated tribal power and more crucially mediate between their people and the central government.[26] While the federation has noticeably matured over the years, one expert argues, it is nonetheless little more than a loose confederation holding together several uncoordinated and ultimately autonomous regional power bases.[27]

The political authorities have managed to win the traditional and indigenous Bedouins' allegiance through financial aid, the provision of various services, and opportunities to work in government jobs. The authority in the Bedouin community, however, is exercised on a dual basis. This means that there is a formal authority linked with central government, and at the same time there is a Bedouin popular authority that enjoys some degree of autonomous decision making.[28] Although a large number of Bedouins have left the desert and joined oil companies and their offices in urban centers, they still maintain their domestic family structure and conventions. They have arguably responded to changing lifestyles without losing their identity. Traditional and personal ties and networks still play a crucial role in UAE society.[29] The camel and camel racing are at the center of the cultural life of the Emiratis. The speed contests, an important part of social gatherings in the desert, have grown into a full-fledged sport with the Emirati political and commercial elite.[30]

The Federal National Council, while having only consultative powers, was given a greater role in the 1990s. Its forty members are appointed by the rulers: eight each from Abu Dhabi and Dubai, six each from Sharjah and Ra's al-Khayma, and four each from the remaining emirates. Actual legislative authority resides in the Council of Ministers, which initiates most laws, oversees implementation of federal laws, and determines the federal budget.[31] In many areas, including foreign affairs, defense, and finance, each emirate acts and pursues its goals autonomously. Each individual emirate pursues its own oil policy. Dubai and Sharjah, for instance, maintained business as usual with Iran despite the fact that the federal government tilted toward Iraq during the Iran-Iraq War (1980–88).[32]

Apart from the Supreme Council of Ministers, the UAE lacks a political culture and strong federal institutions.[33] Tribal history and loyalties to individual rulers continue to be a key part of UAE politics. Individual rulers still hold sway in UAE society and will most likely do so for some time to come. A large and fully independent middle class is nonexistent in the UAE, although new technocrats have just begun to build the basis for such a class, a transformation that may take many decades to complete.[34]

There are very few legally defined boundaries, and each emirate has border disputes with other emirates or the neighboring country of Oman. Sometimes these rivalries become violent. This was the case in 1987 when Abu Dhabi and Dubai supported different candidates for the ruler of Sharjah, and Abd al-Aziz Mohammed al Qasimi attempted a coup against his brother's government there.[35]

With the UAE's decision-making structure at the federal level chiefly dominated by hereditary rulers and their appointees, the country appears to have a mixed neopatrimonial government of apparently modern institutions placed under powerful traditional authorities.[36] Additionally, the unicameral and nonelected parliament continues to remain in a paralyzed state, lacking powers to exercise its constitutional rights and typically incapable of questioning or restraining the executive.[37]

For a long time after the UAE became independent, the ruler of Abu Dhabi, Sheikh Zayid al Nahyan, served as the federation's president and helped mediate its various disputes. Sheikh Zayid used Abu Dhabi's wealth and his political prowess to bridge the gap between the country's "tribal" and "modern" influences. While Abu Dhabi annually provides about 75 percent to 90 percent of the country's federal budget, Dubai covers the remainder.[38]

Political parties, however, have been regarded by the country's ruling elites as less desirable and unnecessary institutions with the potential to pose a threat to national solidarity and political unity. Although civil society is weak, it is not entirely absent. It is linked to a great extent to the newly developing middle class. Its development has been contingent largely on the emergence of the legal and executive institutions of the society itself.[39]

Economic and Demographic Trends

The UAE has large reserves of natural resources and the most developed non-oil private sector in the Persian Gulf.[40] Although the UAE economy is largely based on vast oil and gas supplies, this wealth is not divided evenly among the populace or within the federation. Nearly 94 percent of the country's proven oil is located in Abu Dhabi.[41] The indigenous people in Abu Dhabi call themselves "Dhibiani" (that is, people from Abu Dhabi) and tend to consider themselves superior to indigenous people from other parts of the UAE.[42] While Abu Dhabi and Dubai are rich modern cities, many remote and secluded villages lack running water, reliable electricity, and basic health care. There is little transparency in UAE budgets.[43] The shortage of water supplies remains an acute problem.

The UAE's population has soared by more than 5 percent annually and has the highest growth rate in the Arab world. Between 1985 and 1995, the nation's population grew by 5.75 percent annually and maintained high growth of 5.38 percent during 1995–2002, nearly double the combined Arab population growth of 2.6 in 1985–95 and 2.4 percent in 1995–2002.[44] Only 20 percent of the population is native-born.[45] To redress the demographic imbalance, government has adopted several policies. In 1996, for example, a permanent constitution was drafted in which specific steps were enunciated to "Emiratize" and develop other resources besides oil. The government adopted a policy to encourage citizens to have more children. Furthermore, a three-month grace period was issued to all illegal immigrants to leave the country and nearly one million rushed to be gone before the expiration date. This development illustrated the country's demographic dilemma, revealing the extreme vulnerability that the nation and its citizens felt.[46]

Experts have attributed the population growth rate to the absence of birth control, high fertility rates among nationals and government incentives for them to produce more children, the large foreign community, and constant expansion in non-oil sectors. Because of the country's shortage of human resources, both skilled and unskilled, the steady growth of the UAE economy has attracted hundreds of expatriates. The economy depends on these noncitizens—nearly 90 percent of the workforce in the UAE is expatriate. The large expatriate population has in fact transformed the country. To reduce this dependency and to achieve the stated national goal of "Emiratization," government has imposed minimum quotas for the employment of nationals and banned the import of unskilled labor from certain countries.[47]

Given these factors, the UAE has one of the world's highest population growth rates.[48] Estimates by the country's Ministry of Planning indicate that the UAE's total population, including nationals and expatriates, surged from around one million in the early 1980s to 2.4 million in 1995 and continued its fast pace to hit nearly 3.75 million at the end of 2002.[49] There are more than two men for every woman in Dubai due to the short-term labor migration patterns. While the country's young population is growing at a mercurial pace, its elderly population is growing at 10.3 percent annually.[50]

The long-term dependency on foreign labor creates structural difficulties for the country and could pose a potential threat to the nation's security. There may be no workable solution for the country's labor imbalance in the years to come. The expulsion of 300,000 expatriates in 1996, which led to high inflation and labor shortages, undermined the country's steady economic growth. Furthermore, most of the expatriates expelled returned to the UAE by mid-1997.[51]

Political and Economic Reforms

With vast oil reserves and comprehensive welfare packages for their citizens, the countries at the southern tip of the Persian Gulf have had "at best a limited recognition of the need for political and economic reform."[52] The rulers of these regimes tend to see their countries as "personal fiefdoms rather than a land for all their citizens."[53] As the population grows and oil wealth remains constant, the likelihood of buying off dissent will decrease. Drastic reforms are unlikely, as ruling families of these countries depend heavily on tradition to legitimize their rule. Moreover, most political and economic reforms would negatively affect each ruling family's own power and wealth, rendering it difficult to gather consensus among key decision makers even as they recognize the need for change.[54]

Furthermore, the Persian Gulf monarchies will find it increasingly difficult to control the intellectual environment. Given the political violence and instability in other parts of the region (Palestine, Afghanistan, and Iraq), violence will be perceived by some as an acceptable form of political action. Despite the stability of the emirates and the rulers' success in staving off local unrest, there is always a vulnerability to radical Arab thinkers and their ideological and political messages. Thus far, UAE leaders have skillfully managed to adopt policies that maintain the traditional political structure and resist fundamental political reform. Hence, the state has combined policies of political repression with accommodation in order to limit internal conflicts.[55]

The UAE's monarchies, according to one scholar, have managed to construct multidimensional "ruling bargains between themselves and their local constituencies, thereby securing both political stability and much needed sources of nondemocratic legitimacy."[56] Alongside vast economic networks of trade with the rest of the globe, "there [have] also existed remarkably flexible and relatively decentralized political structures that [have] allowed for direct channels of access to the rulers and highly effective systems of mobile and consultative democracy."[57]

Regarding political reform, the indigenous population—not foreign workers and international businesspeople and residents—are fully entitled to socioeconomic and political rights. The local people's interests and rights are paramount. There is a strong sense of identity among Emiratis, and the Emiratization of life is very visible in Abu Dhabi, where people display the strongest sense of indigenous cultural and national identity.

What democratic traditions exist are largely restricted to the original and local Arab population—with strict limitations on expatriates. For example, migrants from India constitute the largest group of expatriates living in Dubai and are allowed to have their own communities and observe their own traditions. They are entirely free to engage in their own cultural activities and enjoy their festivals at all times. They must, however, obey the laws of the land: they cannot, for example, open their shops before 4:00 P.M. on Fridays. Minorities or foreigners—as they are often called—can buy properties only in some designated areas. They are not eligible for citizenship, regardless of how long they have resided there or whether they have invested in or own a business or factory there.

A child born to a local Emirati father is considered a citizen. In the case of foreigners or expatriates, no citizenship by birth will apply. Minorities cannot set up their own company or any enterprise unless they have a local sponsor. All the companies' assets must be placed under the sponsor's name. This rule applies across the country with the exception of the free zone areas. Minorities cannot buy land for industrial activities or residential purposes except in a few projects under the direct supervision of the government. On balance, it is safe to say that minority rights are nonexistent in the UAE. There is no written civil law, as everything is based on Islamic law (shari'a). Personalized law, for example, allows the ruler of Dubai and vice president of the UAE, Sheikh Mohammed bin Rashid al-Maktoum, to have unlimited powers over residents of Dubai—citizens as well as noncitizens.

Beyond such restrictions, minorities are free to exercise their faith and religious beliefs. These policies, however, have not precluded the creation of a multinational, multicultural, and multiracial society in Dubai. Yet contradictions abound and the middle-class Arab population faces an identity crisis. One young Arab expert defended his Arab identity in connection with his faith and religion: "Our civilization is not in our façade or modern buildings; rather, it is in our minds, brains, ideas, values, and beliefs."[58]

Local Arabs (nationals) tend to intermingle with each other, excluding foreigners as much as possible. Local Arabs are typically reluctant to invite foreign guests inside their homes for celebration or dinner, but they may take them to the most expensive and luxurious restaurants to show their generosity and sense of hospitality. Locals have their own schools, and few send their children to non-Arab schools. Interestingly enough, during the holy month of Ramadan, local sheikhs open their homes to all—irrespective of nationality, class, race, or creed—to break their fast. Ramadan has such an equalizing impact that power and ethnic differentials are overlooked in the name of generosity.

Youth in the UAE

Recent figures show that 40 percent of the population of the UAE is under the age of ten. There are concerns that a large young population could enhance the likelihood of political instability. A rapidly growing population, as experts assert, is an asset that brings with it liabilities.[59] Most Emirati men wear the traditional long loose white robe (*kandoora*, also known as a *dishdash*) and a turban. While teenage boys often wear *kandoora*, many replace the traditional headgear with baseball caps, worn backward. Underneath their traditional dress (the *abayah*), Emirati girls wear the latest Western fashions. Teens seem to blend what they like from Western and Arab cultures.[60] Many Emirati families can afford to have servants at home because the salaries for foreign housemaids are so low ($300 to $400 a month) that even families who are dependent on government subsidies can afford at least one maid. Hence, foreign servants can play an important role in raising children.[61]

The lifestyles of nationals and non-nationals differ greatly. Emirati teens almost certainly know their relatives extremely well; they live with them in an extended family and socialize with them as much as they do with their classmates. For many nationals, "distant relative is a contradiction in terms."[62] Non-nationals, in contrast, are more likely to live in nuclear families. Both Emirati and non-national parents have more control over their children's lives than do parents in the West.[63]

In the last thirty years, literacy has soared dramatically in the emirates. Girls outnumber boys in school. The literacy rate in the UAE is 83 percent for males and 89 percent for females.[64] Almost all schools in the emirates are single-sex. After the fourth grade, boys and girls attend separate schools. Likewise, universities are single-sex, with separate campuses for male and female students.[65]

Social restrictions apply much more rigidly to girls than to boys. This is especially true of premarital sex, which is forbidden by both religion and custom.[66] In fact, religion is a key part of teen life in the UAE, but the way people act according to their beliefs varies. Most Muslim girls believe that their religion requires them to cover their hair in public, and all Muslims consider drinking alcohol contrary to Islam; but some teens feel that covering one's hair is a personal choice and that drinking is a minor infraction.[67] Other young people follow the letter and spirit of their religion far more rigorously, and some teens regard the conservative aspects of their religion a way of reasserting their cultural and religious identity. Many young Muslim men and boys routinely attend Friday prayers in the mosque, and many boys and girls customarily say their prayers every day. This merely means that "Islam is an important part of who they are and that they respect their religion and culture."[68]

The Conformist Mass Media

The first daily paper appeared in the UAE in 1970. A number of newspapers such as *al-Ittihad* started as weeklies because there were no local printing presses and the papers were produced in Beirut and transported to the Persian Gulf. Since 1970, several major daily newspapers have been published that have loyalist content: *Al-Kahlij* (the Gulf), *Al-Ittihad* (Unity), *Akhbar al-Arab* (Arab News), *Al-Bayan* (the Dispatch), *Al-Fajr* (the Dawn), *Al-Wahda* (Unity), *Khalij Times*, *Gulf News*, and *Gulf Today*.[69] As of 2003, of the nine daily newspapers, three were government sponsored: *al-Ittihad* and *al-Wahda* in Abu Dhabi, and *al-Bayan* in Dubai. The Dubai government has sponsored *al-Bayan* since 1980; it is the sole government paper founded after independence.[70]

Since 1999, the UAE government has fostered independent and private media institutions. In April 2001, Information Minister Sheikh Abdullah bin Zayid said that in an era of satellite dish, "governments can no longer control the dissemination of information to their citizens. The public will no longer accept media that are seen as being government-controlled and that seek to provide them with a limited and partial view of events."[71] Increasingly, however, newspapers are becoming privately owned and the trend is toward increased privatization.

Even so, the press tends to be loyalist and politically conformist, and generally does not assault the basic tenets of national policy; it refrains from criticizing the ruling elites, and it shows little real diversity of treatment or views on essential issues. Giving adequate publicity to government activities, the loyalist press rarely provides thorough and independent investigative reporting. UAE newspapers have often independently criticized the work of various ministries, such as health, labor, and education,[72] but such criticism is filtered through government censors.

After the 1991 Gulf War, the UAE government showed more flexibility toward addressing issues such as the open expression of opinion and the promotion of democracy. Since Sheik Abdullah bin Zayid became information minister in the 1990s, he has supported more freedom of expression in the country's media.[73] Government influence is derived from its legal authority and its financial capacity. Although the press is essentially privately owned, it is subsidized by government funding. Generally, there is an unwritten but widely recognized ban on criticism of the government, and the Press Law of 1980 made it illegal to criticize the ruling family. All published material is also subject to censorship under Federal Law 15 of 1988.[74]

As to why the mass media continue to be politically conformist, relatively passive, and nondiverse, it is important to recognize that Saudi Arabia, Qatar, Oman, and the UAE have no independent parliament and no institutionalized political opposition. Dissent is not expressed publicly. The climate of public consensus puts immense pressure on newspaper editors and writers to support the political status quo and the regime. The press has consistently shown its sensitivity to the political context and has regulated itself to conform with the broader consensus and public opinion.[75] With the encouragement of the Information Ministry in late 1999, *al-Ittihad* did criticize in several issues the alleged inefficiencies in the delivery of services by the Ministries of Health and Education.[76]

Women's Issues

Women in the UAE enjoy one of the highest female literacy rates in the Arab world.[77] Even with such well-educated women, the sheikhdoms of the UAE have hardly accepted, let alone implemented, a policy of women's participation in politics.[78] As of March 1, 2004, no seats in the UAE parliament were held by women.[79] Of the major international human rights instruments, the UAE has accepted only the International Convention on the Elimination of All Forms of Racial Discrimination (1965) and the Convention on the Rights of the Child (1989).[80]

Some experts point out the paradoxical life and limited choices of women living in the UAE: "The UAE is a contradictory society. It loves its daughters and, like an overprotective father, restricts them. The diversity of female college students is a prime example of what the UAE says that it wants for its young women. However, emirate women are limited by the decisions of men, who are by tradition and belief the leaders of their world. By today's Western standards, emirate women are submissive and without full authority."[81]

Locally, indigenous women stand out from others by their distinctive dress. "Women take care to retain a distinctively local way of using their *abayah*, the black outer garment. The use of very darkened car windows, which is allowed only for the conveyance of local female family members who shun the public gaze, reenforces the image of a separate identity."[82]

Female students are in the majority at all educational levels in the country. During 2000–2001, more than 95 percent of female students entered higher education in the UAE.[83] In spite of this positive attitude toward their educational achievements, women continue to confront obstacles. They cannot go abroad for study alone but must be accompanied by their husbands, brothers, or fathers. Women must negotiate with their fathers what major they will choose, and despite their advanced degrees, they find few opportunities for employment.[84]

Among other restrictions, under UAE civil law, women are entitled to only forty-five days of paid maternity leave, although this may be extended to ninety days. A woman's share of inheritance is half of a man's share. On the other hand, there is no law mandating *hijab*, and some women do not wear it. In many cases, the *abaya* (a long, black, wrinkle-free overgarment) is a status symbol among adolescents—a symbol that the wearer is a citizen.[85]

Regarding political participation, the UAE is not a democracy, and thus its citizens do not vote in periodic elections. Until recently, women could not be appointed to government offices. In 2001 for the first time, five women were appointed to the Sharjah Consultative Council, a first movement toward allowing women to participate in the nation's governmental system.[86] Sheikha Fatima bint Mubarak, chairperson of the General Women's Union in the UAE, created the Women's Federation in 1973 to develop opportunities for women. These opportunities include fostering education and eliminating illiteracy, developing women's self-image and self-esteem, encouraging women to play an active role in social development, and influencing social policy. UAE women see in Islam a guarantee of rights that can serve as a model for the rest of the world. The UAE was elected to a four-year membership on the Women's Committee of the fifty-four-member UN Economic and Social Council beginning in 2002. This committee established a national database on UAE women, a rare source in the Arab world.[87]

Contradictions and Identity Crisis

The confederate nature of the UAE allows traditions to remain localized in different parts of the country. There are federal rules, laws, and regulations that apply to the core of governance, and issues such as national currency and foreign policy remain the exclusive domain of the federal government. Beyond that, each emirate applies its own rules, laws, and codes of conduct, making it impossible to apply the same yardstick to all the seven emirates that make up the UAE. Given this diversity, it is hard to precisely define the state and society in the UAE.[88]

Take, for example, Dubai. The local Arab population of Dubai is nearly 14 percent. Dubai is the second largest of the seven emirates comprising the UAE. Dubai's economic dependence on oil revenue is only about 7 percent while its major revenue—about 93 percent—derives from the non-oil, service economy. Dubai is the trading hub of the Middle Eastern region. Its Jabal Ali free zone has expanded the UAE's non-oil sector to 60 percent of total GDP.[89] The rest of the country is attempting to diversify its economy through expanding its infrastructure in order to accommodate more investment and offer free trade agreement to Western and Asian countries. Sheikh Mohammad bin Rashid Al Maktoum, Dubai crown prince and UAE defense minister, has pushed for a truly globalized economy, and his vision to build Dubai into a prosperous trading hub has actually been realized.

Mindful of tradition, the government of Dubai adheres to the essence of Islamic culture and its Arab Bedu heritage. People have unrestricted access to those in power. This interaction allows fewer tensions or grievances to be accumulated over time.[90] Islamic culture, however, is not strictly implemented in Dubai. Some resident experts argue that the economic strategy of globalization renders impossible the full or strict application of the shari'a. Creating an environment conducive to the global economy, they note, is the highest priority of the government officials there. Where values conflict, religious practices take a back seat to economic strategies. In short, religion is not an issue in Dubai.[91] This is not the case in Sharjah, where alcoholic beverages are not sold and Islamic laws are closely observed. There are no nightclubs in Sharjah. There are, in contrast, many nightclubs in Dubai, and one can enter these without showing any form of identification—Arabic or otherwise.

Throughout the UAE, the Internet is controlled. Pornographic and politically sensitive sites are blocked. No radical Islamic groups or ideologies can reach people via the Internet. The federal government has invested heavily in blocking such sites. It is not clear, however, whether this is an effective way to protect the state and society from the onslaught of globalization. Although pornographic sites on the Internet are censored, sex on the street level in Dubai is blatantly available as the sexual trade and trafficking flourish—arguably with the implicit approval of this emirate's ruling elites.

Two key questions arise in this context: How will Dubai meet the challenge of the future in such fast-changing times? How is the character of the state and society protected? Some people deeply resent the extent to which their country has become modernized and Westernized. Even in relatively calm areas of the Persian Gulf, such as Kuwait, young Islamists have pressed the government to ban satellite dishes and VCRs to fight these new assaults on traditions.[92] The security agents in Kuwait, Qatar, Oman, and the UAE are nevertheless less active given the low level of internal opposition that these regimes face. Yet they carefully monitor the large expatriate labor populations there and guard against foreign-backed political violence. Security forces also closely monitor intellectual and spiritual leaders to prevent them from making any antigovernment statements.[93]

Arguably, the sheer variety in the UAE allows globalization and Islamic tradition to coexist. The native population can rely on the expatriate workforce to support its nontraditional economy; Dubai can have alcohol, nightclubs, and the Internet, while passing on the benefits to more traditional emirates. There are paradoxical dynamics here nevertheless. The persistence of traditional political structures and forces in the face of different bargains that ruling elites practice vis-à-vis modern and global forces of change will at some point in the future present problems for the country. The lack of transparency and democratic reforms are bound to emerge as troubling issues for the ruling sheikhs. The impact of globalizing forces on the UAE's cultural traditions and national language—Arabic—has generated considerable criticism and fueled strong backlashes, often from the highest levels of government.

The Arabic language seems in danger of becoming increasingly marginalized, as English has fast become the lingua franca for almost all private sector activities.[94] Many young UAE nationals are now well acquainted with Hindi, having been brought up by Asian caregivers.[95] In a 1999 survey, nearly half of respondents favored English instruction; about 30 percent wished to have mixed English and Arabic instruction; and only 23 percent preferred to be taught only in Arabic.[96]

To revive and preserve their cultural heritage, especially when faced with the global threats to indigenous cultures, many Emiratis have chosen to firmly maintain their cultural traditions such as camel racing. The camel and camel racing continue to serve as the basis for "building the state's ideological and political identity and machinery for re-enforcing social cohesion and sense of belonging among otherwise segmented, but not isolated, tribal and economic groups in the Emirati society."[97]

While there are many emirate-level identities and loyalties, as well as pan-Arabic sentiments in the UAE, the greater awareness of communal solidarity arising from the union of the seven emirates appears to prevail over others. Increasingly, a sense of a UAE/Emirati identity is emerging, with a great number of UAE citizens now seeing themselves primarily as Emirati rather than "Arab" or some other localized identity.[98]

Post-9/11: Some Implications

Since the September 11, 2001, terror attacks on the United States, most of the Persian Gulf monarchies have come under increased U.S. pressure to introduce democracy, improve their human rights records, and crack down on the activities of Islamist extremists.[99] To avoid a major policy difference with the United States, all of the Persian Gulf monarchies introduced some political and educational reforms. The Persian Gulf political elites, however, viewed the U.S. pressure as a major external threat to their political stability. They asserted that such pressures would create public opposition, which, in turn, might jeopardize ongoing gradual reforms that could lead to more political instability and intolerance.[100]

Reform in the UAE faces a major hurdle. While social and economic institutions have supported modernization policies, the political system has resisted change. The political structure continues to be pyramidal and hierarchical. Sheikhs and merchants are the main beneficiaries of their family role and they support a private-enterprise system. Young Emiratis become successful business partners, and many of them have received advanced education in the West. The West, in turn, has shaped this young generation's outlook. When they return home, many became potent forces for change.[101]

Another, but different, influence was the 1991 Gulf War. Many Islamists, for instance, felt "humiliated" at being defended by Christian forces. During the war, many *ulama* (religious scholars) were forced to support their government's decision to accept the deployment of U.S. troops on their soil. After the war, many citizens took part in the debate over public issues regarding their daily lives, their identity, and what it meant to be an Emirati. Major concerns emerged over such issues as Islamic identity, modernization, demographic trends, and increasing Westernization. The Islamist groups participated in this national debate, trying to regain their true cultural identity and raising Islamic awareness. The emphasis on Islam demonstrated how people's perceptions and values continued to be shaped by their faith. Interestingly, many young Emiratis who studied in the West and returned home shied away from echoing pro-West sentiments.[102]

The Ministry of Education initiated a series of education reforms, including the formation of local committees to oversee these changes. Their aim was to review school textbooks published by the government and to eliminate any materials that might contain discriminatory language toward the West. Despite public criticism, the ministry remained committed to such reforms.[103] Additionally, Dubai's prince, Sheikh Mohammad bin Rashid Al-Maktoum, has ordered the formation of the Dubai Executive Council (DEC) as part of the government's effort to empower the public to participate in the decision-making process. Although these councils fall far short of actual participatory government, public interest in matters relating to policy making has increased.[104]

Conclusion

In the UAE, natives are in the minority, and labor migrants, including Arab and non-Arab expatriates, make up more than three quarters of the country's population. Under these circumstances, national identity simply reflects the dynasty that rules the state rather than the wider population of these countries. The ruling family has become both the symbol and the representative of the UAE.[105] The ruling elites have nevertheless managed to maintain a balance between a basically traditional political structure and the impact of modern and global forces. Without undermining the neopatrimonial and rentier networks on which the UAE's federal system rests, the ruling families have introduced liberalized economic structures. They have rapidly transformed a tribal and feudal society into a modern country, in which Islamic traditions of tolerance and respect for the followers of other religious practices are fully protected.[106] Despite their small numbers, Emiratis maintain a strong sense of national identity and coherence. They are not threatened by the many and varied shades of culture imported by the expatriate majority.[107] The ruling elites' efforts at developing and expanding a stronger civil society, however, have fallen far short of what they have pledged.

Massive oil and gas revenues have made it possible to fund major local development projects and reforms. Yet, the political will to initiate equally ambitious democratic reforms has been conspicuously lacking. The UAE media, especially broadcast media, remain more cautious than their Qatari and Bahrani counterparts. A confluence of factors accounts for the country's weak civil society and associational life. These include, among others, cultural heterogeneity resulting from the massive expatriate labor force, increasing levels of government cooptation, royal patronage, and in some cases greater control and repression.[108]

Some within the nation's ruling families have raised serious concerns over the increasing "cultural contamination" that has resulted from the exposure to globalizing forces, claiming that such influences will potentially erode much of the traditional cultural and political structures. On balance, however, the new leadership seems to be eager to absorb the shocks of globalization while maintaining the country's cultural and national integrity and identities. The process of social change in UAE society contains a paradox. Just as the country's wealth and socioeconomic dynamics have initially undermined the position of traditional life of the indigenous people, so have they also strengthened the position of the advocates of local cultural traditions.

Chapter 7

Secularism, Turkish Islam, and Identity

Led by Mustafa Kemal Atatürk in 1923, Turkey was the first secular state in the Muslim world that placed all educational institutions under government jurisdiction. By 1929, Turkish secular ruling elites, known as Kemalists, had succeeded in eliminating Islam from political and public life. A Swiss-based civil code supplanted Islamic legal codes.[1] In recent times, however, this secularism from above, backed by the military, has increasingly come into conflict with the aspirations of practicing Turkish Muslims. Today, Turkey exhibits the complexity of political life in a Muslim country caught between competing forces of change and continuity, trying to strike a balance between maintaining its cultural identity and participating in global politics. Atatürk failed to create a Turkish nationalism that would also embrace Kurdish nationalism. Kemalism has clearly failed to create either a mass secular culture or a monolithic Turkish identity in a diversified and complex society such as Turkey. Instead, the political developments of the past half century point to the growth of multiple identities.[2]

The grassroots appeal of the Islamist movement across existing social and class divisions continues to call into question the conventional view that regards Turkey as a quintessential model of secular modernization in the Muslim world. From 1923 onward, Ayse Kadioglu writes, the new Turks were in a mental state best described as "voluntary amnesia," which reflected a desire to break with the past.[3] The state under the republic was bent on elevating people to a new level of civilization. Any opposition against this modern order was construed as an effort to revive the old religious order. This ideological stance was shallowly held and not espoused by all the classes; what is more, it was founded primarily on tenets constructed and imposed from above. This so-called Kemalist ideology could not substitute for Islam in the daily lives of the people, in large part because it was internalized only by the intelligentsia.[4]

The new republic under Atatürk focused on a broad-based Westernization of the country. The ensuing political, cultural, and socioeconomic reforms even after Atatürk's death in 1938 intensified the ongoing debate about secularism, nationalism, and modernization. Turkey entered World War II on the Allied side in 1945 and became a charter member of the United Nations in the following year. Uncertainties faced by Greece in the postwar period in stifling a communist rebellion and demands by the Soviet Union for military bases in the Turkish straits led to the declaration of the Truman Doctrine by U.S. president Harry Truman in 1947. The doctrine pledged to guarantee the security of Turkey and to shore up Greece's crumbling economic and political conditions, culminating in large-scale U.S. military and economic aid. Subsequently, in 1952, Turkey joined the North Atlantic Treaty Organization (NATO). From 1960 to 1980, the country was particularly marked by cycles of political instability, as several military coups (1960, 1971, and 1980) characterized these uncertain times.

The 1980s and 1990s unleashed new internal political dynamics that underscored the importance of Islamic identity for the Turks. The new discourse of the state elites was laden with references to the significance of religious values. Islam had finally been pushed to the forefront of Turkish politics as the antidote of communism.[5] Elements of civil society increased in number, Kadioglu notes, along with the new mission of the technocratic elites of the 1980s, who saw their goal mainly as "synthesizing Islamic values and pragmatic rationality"; this created a political atmosphere that allowed the search for a more historically rooted Turkish identity.[6] For the first time since the republic's inception, a pro-Islamic party came to power in 2003 without coalition.

To better understand secularism, Islam, and identity politics in Turkey, from both a chronological and thematic standpoint, I begin by presenting a historical background and structural setting for the reconstruction of modern Islamic identity in Turkey, followed by a discussion of the triumph of pragmatic politics in recent years. I next focus on the headscarf issue, which continues to be divisive, attesting to the lingering tensions between Islamists and secularists. In the following sections, I argue that Turkey's ties with the West and its attempts to join the European Union (EU) render it a unique case. The challenges facing the country's prospects for entry into the EU, including human rights conditions and the treatment of ethnic and religious minorities (Kurds and Aleviler), will be discussed. After an examination of these thematic issues, this chapter turns to an analysis of the shift in identity formation, with a view toward exploring Turkish Islam and how it has affected the fluidity of identities and the permeability of the boundaries of discourse.

Historical Overview

For more than six hundred years, the Ottoman society owed much of its longevity to a legacy of multiculturalism and self-rule that was a testament to the balance it struck among different ethnic and religious groups. The Ottoman caliphate tolerated Christian Armenians and Jews and was built on, in Robert D. Kaplan's terms, "territorial indifference."[7] This multicultural formula meant that minorities could live anywhere from the Balkans to Mesopotamia and as far south as Yemen without threatening the empire's sovereignty. Violent discussions over who controlled which territory emerged only when the empire collapsed in the aftermath of World War I.[8]

The Ottoman Empire's initial solution to this diversity was the *millet* system that gave some degree of autonomy to religious communities, with each *millet* essentially in control of organizing and funding its own religious and educational institutions.[9] The reforms introduced during the nineteenth and early twentieth centuries transformed the multinational state into a relatively modern one with a centralized bureaucracy. During the constitutional period (1909–18), the Ottoman Empire experienced the most democratic era of its history, with a multitude of political parties electing deputies to the Ottoman parliament, which initiated vast secular reforms.[10]

The pursuant ethnic and nationalistic violence in the Balkan wars (1912–13), instigated largely by Russia to push the Ottomans out of the European territories of the Ottoman Empire, threatened the survival of the empire. The Young Turk leaders ended this short-lived Ottoman democracy and establish an authoritarian regime that successfully managed to defend the empire. The Young Turks, however, led the country to its defeat and devastation in World War I (1914–18) when Turkey aligned with the losing Central powers on the side of Germany and Austria. The Ottoman Empire was partitioned. The Turkish War for Independence that followed partition (1918–23), under the leadership of Mustafa Kemal Atatürk and Ismet Inönü, deprived the efforts of the victorious allies to take over the territories occupied primarily by Turks. The stage was set for the establishment of the Turkish Republic in Anatolia and Eastern Thrace.[11]

The new republic under Kemal Atatürk (1923) was a drastic departure from its Islamic-Ottoman past. The most visible feature of Atatürk's reforms was the institutionalization of secular systems and practices in Turkey. The shari'a (Islamic law) was replaced by a secular code; polygamy was stamped out; all Sufi brotherhoods of "folk" Islam were banned. Religious schools and education were prohibited. The sultanate and the caliphate were abolished.[12] Despite the abrogation of certain religious practices and institutions, religion remained a strong force at the grassroots level. The competing forces of Islam and secularism as the basis of identity formation have since characterized the Turkish society.

In the post-Atatürk era, the Democracy Party (DP) benefited politically from widespread antiestablishment sentiment in rural areas. Beginning in 1948, leaders of the DP revoked some of the Kemalist secular reforms and displayed greater sensitivity to the all-encompassing Islamic identity of the vast majority of Turkish Muslims. In the May 1950 election, the DP won 408 seats and its leader Celal Bâyar became the president of the new assembly. One-party rule was replaced by multiparty competition for power, paving the way for the reassertion of Islamic groups and their entrance into the political arena.[13] The DP's majority in the assembly, however, diminished substantially in the 1957 general elections. The rivalry among different parties between 1957 and 1960 led to unrest and a series of crises in Turkish democracy, culminating in military interventions in 1960, 1971, and 1980. During the 1970s, when the electoral process in Turkey further exposed the defects inherent in the multiparty system, major parties—the Justice Party (JP) and the Republican People's Party (RPP)—sought the support of the Islamic parties, such as the National Salvation Party (NSP, 1972–81) and its successor, the Refah Partisi (Welfare Party, 1981–97), as coalition partners, in an effort to remain in power.[14]

Throughout the 1980s and 1990s, the society grew bifurcated and polarized, evolving further away from a state-centric milieu toward a dynamic, associational one. In the meantime, in the early 1980s, the waves of Islamic revivalism that swept across the Muslim world reinvigorated the Turkish cultural heritage. Religious education was made compulsory for all primary and secondary schoolchildren in 1982.[15] The issue of women's dress proved to be a highly contested issue in the years to come.

Around the same time, a new brand of Islamist intellectuals (*Islamci aydin*) tried to advocate a modern Islamic perspective that was both critical and appreciative of social and ethical dimensions of religion. These included such popular writers as Ali Bulac, Rasim Ozdenoren, and Ismet Ozel, who were highly critical of Turkey's secular intellectuals and their attempt to substitute worldly materialism for religious values.[16] Post-1980, Turgut Özal's Motherland Party (MP) acted on the premise of advancing state control of religion within a more flexible and democratic political context. In many respects, the economic and political liberalization during the 1980s transformed Turkish society, strengthening Islamic identity and Turkish nationalism. The 1991 election results fortified the religious and extreme right at the expense of the center-moderate right and strengthened the left at the expense of the social democratic left.

The dualistic tensions inherent in contemporary Turkish identity manifested themselves in 1996, when Necmettin Erbakan, representing the Refah Partisi, and Tansu Ciler, representing the Dogru Yol Partisi (True Path Party), formed a coalition government. Erbakan was forced to resign and the governing coalition collapsed under pressure from the Turkish military in February 1997. This so-called soft coup plunged the Turkish state into a renewed legitimacy crisis.[17] It demonstrated that protecting secularism the Turkish way comes at the price of selectively sacrificing democracy.[18]

The battle between secularists and Islamists resurfaced in 2008 when the country's top constitutional court reimposed a ban on women's wearing headscarves at universities. This battle reflected the increasingly politicized nature of the country's legal system. The judicial quarrel renewed the old debate on the constitution's strict separation of religion and politics. The underlying tension demonstrated that the struggle for finding a right balance for the role of religion in the Turkish public sphere remained unsettled. The governing party (Justice and Development Party, AKP) is locked in a power struggle with secular groups that exercise large sway over the military and other state institutions. AKP officials have indicated that the court's verdict is binding and should be obeyed in an attempt to reassure the Turkish people that supporting the secular foundation of the constitution is indeed a bipartisan hallmark of the country's democracy.

Both the 1997 soft coup and the 2008 judicial clash over the headscarf issue have shown that the country's constitutional secular underpinnings continue to shape the role of religion and its proper limits in the public arena. The army, a major part of the establishment and state, reserves the right to interfere in religion any time it deems it necessary to do so. Secularism as such is an official ideology to which all parties, nongovernmental organizations (NGOs), groups, and individuals must adhere. Many NGOs, such as Insan Haklari ve Mazlumlar Için Dayanişma Derneği (Organization of Human Rights and Solidarity for Oppressed People), see secularism as a vehicle for safeguarding as well as promoting the coexistence of different religious identities. Secularism is not an end in itself; rather, it is a means to enhance interfaith tolerance and communal coexistence. Preserving freedom of religion, however, is the end. In Turkey, secularism is not a style of management; it is a political vehicle for regulating religious affairs.[19]

Reconstruction of Modern Islamic Identity

In the postwar period, the political liberalization experienced in Turkey opened up a political and intellectual space for Islamic groups and elements. The Democratic Party argued that the secular culture of state-ruling elites "had no relevance to the daily life experience of the people, while the social norms and practices of Islam represented something very real in their lives."[20] The emphasis on religious tolerance provided the DP with a cultural basis for opposing the Republican People's Party. Some conservative factions within the RPP also underscored the importance of blending Turkish nationalism and Islam.[21]

Following the RPP Seventh Party Congress in 1947, RPP governments initiated several new policies, including the allocation of foreign currency for pilgrimages to Mecca, the restoration of religious instruction for primary school students, the introduction of *imam-hatip* (religious leader who delivers Friday sermon) training courses for a period of three years by the Ministry of Education, and the opening of the Faculty of Theology at Ankara University in January 1949.[22] The DP electoral success put it at the helm between 1950 and 1960, when the DP aimed to integrate local popular cultures into the secular political state. Between 1951 and 1954, a total of 616 mosques and historical shrines were repaired. More than 5.5 million Turkish lira were allocated to that end.[23] The state, however, maintained widespread control over all religious institutions, and students who became prayer leaders and preachers were in fact employed by the state.[24]

The Islamic social movements grew in the early 1980s within a political context in which the military council and the ensuing governments reintroduced Islam as part of Turkey's official ideology to dismiss or contain Marxist and other violent movements of the 1970s.[25] Increasingly, the Turco-Islamic synthesis replaced the secular Kemalist ideology on utilitarian grounds. As a result, the number of *imam hatip liseleri* (schools training personnel for religious services), mosque-building activities, religious foundations and *tariqas* (religious brotherhoods) increased in both numbers and influence. Religious courses were made mandatory in primary and secondary schools. Major school curricula and books were rewritten in more conservative terms, if not strictly in religious terms. Moreover, Turgut Özal's Motherland Party (Anavatan Partisi, ANAP) placed more conservative people in state cadres. Religious press and publications, as well as radio and TV channels, operated freely.[26]

The roots of the formation of modern Islamic identity in Turkey can be traced back to the Nur movement. Founded by Naksibendi spiritual leader Said Nursi (1877–1960), this movement was bent on creating a modern and pragmatic Islam in Turkish society. Later, Fethullah Gülen's ideas and activities (known as Turkish Islam) led an Islamist political movement that had a major impact on the political debate in Turkey over the role of Islam in state and society.[27] Gülen's movement avoided stressing Islam directly in its colleges. Rather, it adopted a kind of quiet and gradual moral ideology that—while not confronting the official Kemalist ideology—promoted conservatism and demanded religious and cultural recognition.

Linked to Gülen's movement was the Science Research Foundation (Bilim Arastirma Vakfi, BAV), which has undertaken a new mission of spreading an Islamic version of scientific creationism in Turkey. Radical Islamic sects (*tariqas*) have supported the BAV's mission to combat evolution. Established in 1991 by Sheikh Adnan Oktar, BAV has become a radical fundamentalist foundation bent on promoting the Qur'an as the ultimate truth[28] (see Table 5). The movement led by Gülen, however, advanced a moral ideology that was restricting but docile. It was so invisible that some experts described it as "a sort of Anatolian Confucianism."[29] This movement represented a moderate Islamic and democratic alternative to radical Islamist movements in Turkey. Gülen called on people to "rediscover the self" that had been "embodied within Islam and the Ottoman past."[30] Gülen attempted to construct a new social contract in which the multiculturalist Turko-Ottoman tradition plays a dominant role. The movement has brought many diverse groups together to discuss social, cultural, and political challenges facing the country. Utilizing the new opportunity spaces and global discourses on multiculturalism and human rights, the Gülen movement has opened new spaces for a different imagination of Islam in the public sphere[31] (see Table 5).

In the 1980s, Islamic groups provided alternative solutions to the failures of secularizing programs to transform traditional society into a modern one capable of addressing the issues of justice, development, participation, and identity. The neoliberalization programs advocated by Turgut Özal (since 1983) provided "opportunity spaces" for Islamic groups and, in fact, pushed their intellectuals and social movement to the forefront of politics. The growth in literacy and print media and the formation of reading groups have fostered interpretive communities. As the country's political opening and market economy gave Muslims a chance to carve their own social and political spaces, a new Islamic political identity was

TABLE 5. COMPETITION FOR POWER AND IDENTITY POLITICS IN TURKEY

	Goals	Agents	Sites	Strategies
Conservatives	Protecting Turkish Islam	Fethullah Gülen and other mainstream Islamic groups	Mosque and community organizations, and religious NGOs	Seeking local alliances with reformists and politicians through democratic processes
Neofundamentalists	Creating an Islamic shari'a-based state	Tariqas, the BAV, Kurdish Hezbollah, UICS, and IBDA-C	Mosque, local, and transnational communities (Europe and Turkey)	Grassroots activism and political violence (suspected of assassinating secular journalists and intellectuals)
Reformists	Turkish-Islamic synthesis: promoting security, economic growth, social justice, and EU accession	AKP Prime Minister Erdoğan and President Abdullah Gul	Local and transnational NGOs, civil society, and media	Pragmatic Islam: seeking ideas, allies, and intercultural dialogue with the West
Secularists	Defending the secular regime and Kemalist ideology	Secular elites, intellectuals and journalists, human rights activists, lawyers, and the military	National, transnational, and global spaces (the Internet)	Economic globalization, trade with the West, integration into the EU

formed in Turkey. The growth of mass education and mass communication, instead of undermining the influence of Islam, has "led to its redefinition as a dynamic form of political and social consciousness."[32]

The Turkish case indicates that such openings have rendered Islam responsive to the practical needs of both the state and the market economy. That is why Gülen has "appropriated Islam as a new bourgeois political identity rather than a counterforce against new openings in society."[33] Islamic social movements in Turkey, M. Hakan Yavuz writes, offer principal forces and agents of democratic change and pluralism. These movements "are not fueled by a deep-seated rage and frustration with the authoritarian policies of the secular elites, as is the case in Algeria and Egypt."[34] Politically active Muslims in Turkey have utilized Islam to construct their own version of modernity. Yavuz also describes this process as "vernacularization of modernity," which is aimed at redefining the discourses of modernity, nationalism, secularism, democracy, human rights, the liberal market, and personal autonomy.[35] Significantly, Islamic groups seek to explain religious symbols and values in terms of rationality and the overriding exigencies of reason and evidence (epistemology), a process Yavuz labels as "internal secularization of Islam."[36] The interaction between ideas and lived sociopolitical experience has transformed Islam and Islamic identity in Turkey.

Other experts have used the concept of "vernacular politics" to illustrate how everyday concerns and interpersonal relations—not Islamic dogma—have helped Islamic parties gain access to community networks. The Islamists have often appealed to voters' specific identities and sensibilities by fostering local cultural values and community-based support systems. Localized and informal networks have been largely responsible for the increasing success of Islamist political actors throughout Turkey. Such politics have successfully mobilized Islamic groups in Turkey's recent elections despite their conflicting agendas.

Jenny B. White explains "vernacular politics" as a value-oriented political process that is deeply rooted in local culture, interpersonal ties, and community networks. This process is also linked through civic organizations to national party politics.[37] Religion, which is used as a local cultural idiom—not as a coherent ideology or political agenda—provides a degree of protectionism, trust, and mutual support among different community groups.[38] In this sense, religion tends to unify diverse Muslim groups living in urban areas such as Istanbul, even as they pursue a different political agenda.

Islamic identity is also generally seen as a site of contestation—not as a constant ideological or behavioral understanding—across time and space.[39] When Prime Minister Erbakan was forced to resign and his party (the Welfare Party) was banned, the Islamists formed a new party called the Fazilet Partisi (Virtue Party, VP) with Recai Kutan as its leader. It became obvious that each time the Islamist party was dissolved its successor has pursued moderate policies and programs. Kutan, for instance, abandoned the rigid Islamist positions; he no longer supported leaving NATO or introducing Islamic banking.[40] The Virtue Party was dissolved by the constitutional court in June 2001. While Erbakan's supporters formed the Saadet Parisi (the Felicity Party), the reformist wing of the Virtue Party formed the Adalet ve Kalkinma Partisi (AKP, Justice and Development Party).[41]

The victory of the AKP in the 2002 elections—primarily attributed to political pluralism, autonomous civil society, and upward social mobility—demonstrated the growing strength of the Islamist movement. Islamic groups have exhibited far more moderation in their policy platforms than in the past. Since coming to power in 2002, the Erdoğan government has enthusiastically supported democratic rights and reforms as well as Turkey's entry into the European Union. Some scholars view the AKP as "a success story of Turkish democracy."[42] Others attribute the AKP's success to its increasing ability to occupy the political center, where a great majority of Turkish voters stand politically. This reality is most frightening to Turkey's traditional elites and the military.[43]

Yet tectonic problems over Turkey's identity continue, as evidenced by the tensions in spring 2007 over the disputed presidential candidacy of Abdullah Gul, currently the foreign minister with Islamist credentials. The Turkish Army warned against Mr. Gul's candidacy. Secular-minded protesters supported the army's position in several demonstrations in Istanbul. After failing the second time to gain approval in parliament, Gul withdrew his candidacy on May 6, 2007.[44] In a subsequent interview, when asked if he thought Turkey should adopt shari'a (Islamic law), he replied, "No. There is no possibility of introducing *Sharia* in Turkey. We are harmonizing Turkey's laws with the EU's standards in every area. Is this *Sharia*?"[45] On the issue of Islamic headdress, Gul explained, "I have no intention of forcing or even asking anyone to wear a headscarf. It is a matter of personal choice. Not all the women in my family wear them. If I do not ask my family to do it, why would I ask others?"[46]

Radical Islamic groups in Turkey have not attracted as much attention as moderate Islamic groups because of their small size and apparently limited threat. The "Hezbollah Muslims" appeared for the first time on the

Turkish political scene in 1984, proclaiming support for the Iranian revolution. In southeast Turkey, Islamic radical movements emerged in poor towns and villages with a large Kurdish population. Influenced by Khomenini's teachings, they were identified by the local population as Kurdish Hezbollah.[47] The members of Hezbollah are predominantly Sunni and seek to unite the Kurds in Europe and Turkey. Two other radical Islamic groups are the Union of Islamic Communities and Societies (UICS) and the Great Eastern Islamic Fighters Front (IBDA-C); the IBDA-C, although an Islamic movement struggling for the creation of an Islamic constitution and state, uses leftist slogans in its publications and is anti-Semitic and anti-Christian in its propaganda and terrorist activities. It shares Al-Qaeda's Sunni-Salafi ideology and openly challenges Turkey's government as the main barrier to reaching its goal. The IBDA-C is widely believed to have been involved in the assassination of a number of secular journalists and intellectuals in Turkey.[48]

The Union of Islamic Communities and Societies (UICS), also known as the Anatolia Federal Islamic State, attempts to organize Muslims in Europe, especially in Germany, to achieve their ultimate goal of establishing an Islamic state in Anatolia. This group's members met with Bin Laden in Afghanistan in 1997 and have sent operatives there for training. Its leader, Metin Kaplan, was arrested in Germany and extradited to Turkey, where he received a sentence of life imprisonment in June 2005; since then, UICS's members have remained silent and dormant.[49] On balance, radical Islamic groups were and continue to be marginal in their political influence and violence. Turkish society sees Al-Qaeda and its ideology as overwhelmingly negative, viewing them as a serious menace to the country's security as well as to international security.[50] The marginal influence of radical Islamic groups can be attributed to many factors unique to Turkey, including the secularist Kemalist ideology and legacy, the dominant form of Turkish nationalism, and the Turkish pluralist system that allows Islamic parties to participate in the political process[51] (see Table 5).

Triumph of Pragmatic Politics

No longer can black and white perspectives, devoid of domestic nuance and national subtleties, explain the effects of the victory of the Islamist-influenced AKP in parliamentary elections on July 22, 2007. The AKP's "silent revolution" is now evident everywhere in Turkey. Under the AKP, average annual growth has exceeded 7 percent (nearly four times the EU figure), a record $20 billion in foreign direct investment has been achieved, and $40 billion in tourism earnings are expected by 2013.[52] There is a consensus among many European and American diplomats that Prime Minister Recep Tayyip Erdoğan is "the man most fit to lead Turkey."[53]

As the AKP received nearly 47 percent of the vote, this victory has marked yet another milestone in the construction of Turkey's new identity cast in an evolving brand of political Islam—that is, pragmatic Islam (see Table 5). There are obvious but compelling incentives to find pragmatic compromises in Turkish politics in order to avoid political confrontation between Islamists and secularists. Turkey's powerful military, the guardian of the secular system since 1923, has made it abundantly clear that it would intervene if it believes the ruling party's actions run counter to the secular principles enshrined in the country's constitution.

The election results conveyed two important messages: (1) that economy trumps religion in Turkey, and (2) that moderate Islamic identity can be reconciled with secular principles. These elections, which demonstrated the triumph of economic prosperity over religious beliefs, could influence Turkey's drive to become the first Muslim-dominated country to join the EU. This victory meant that Turks were more worried about economic instability than the threat of more Islam in government.[54] It also illustrated the way Turkey's moderate Islamic leadership kept personal piety and religious identity out of the public sphere. Islam in Turkey, some Turkish experts such as Ihsan Dagi write, has a unique historical, cultural, and social context that precludes it from becoming overtly "political."[55] The AKP is not an example of "Islamic democracy." Its victory has nothing to do with Islam and its voters are not essentially motivated by Islamic concerns. Instead, AKP voters' demands are influenced by such secular issues as employment, health care, education, social security, and basic rights and liberties. In Turkey, Dagi notes, people avoid mixing religion with political choices.[56]

Historically, there have been four regime changes in Turkey when the military crushed elected Islamist politicians. A 1960 army coup led to the execution of Prime Minister Adnan Menderes and two of his senior ministers and the imprisonment of many of Menderes's followers. Military pressure removed governments regarded as anti-Kemalist in 1971 and 1980. And in 1997, the army ousted Prime Minister Necmettin Erbakan, an Islamist-minded technocrat.[57] Facing a similar situation, Prime Minister Erdoğan and his AKP associates advocate amending the Turkish Constitution so that presidents would be elected by direct popular vote instead of by successive parliamentary polls, as is presently the case. Mr. Abdullah Gul was nevertheless elected as the eleventh president by the Turkish Grand National Assembly, winning 339 votes in the 550-member parliament. Gul, who assumed his duties on August 28, 2008, emphasized in his inaugural address before the parliament that he would remain decisively neutral, while supporting secularism, human rights, and Turkey's efforts to join the European Union. His central message was loud and clear: "secularism—one of the main principles of our republic—is a precondition for social peace as much as it is a liberating model for different lifestyles."[58] Many experts had stressed that the biggest challenge for Gul would be to reassure the army and the nationalists that his religion would not undermine the nature of the Turkish secular constitution and nation.[59]

The Headscarf Issue

The headscarf is widely perceived as one form of public expression of a religious conviction. Not only does it relate to the principles of the neutrality of the secular state, but it also concerns the individual's religious freedom. There are various opinions concerning female dress code in Turkey in particular and in the West more generally. For some Turkish women, according to Baskent Kadin Platformu (Capital City Women's Platform), a Muslim women's NGO in Ankara, wearing the headscarf is a common cultural tradition. Far from carrying a symbolic meaning, as is wrongly claimed by officials, wearing the headscarf is merely a natural part of daily life.

Veiled women, according to a Turkish scholar, have come to be seen by the country's secularists as obstacles to civilization. The modernization that colonialism claimed to export made the veil an open target of attack.[60] The issue of women has occupied a central place in the colonial narrative of Islam—a narrative that views Islam as inherently oppressive to women. Turkey's Westernized and native Orientalists have consistently pointed to the inferiority of Muslim traditions in this context. Atatürk himself particularly referred to the incivility of veiling and expressed an uneasy feeling of embarrassment at being derided by the so-called civilized world.[61]

The AKP's attempt in February 2008 to lift the ban on headscarves—supported by the opposition Nationalist Action Party (MHP)—was regarded as an attempt at providing greater religious freedom. This legal move was rejected by Turkey's constitutional court on June 5, 2008, when the court ruled that the Turkish Parliament had violated the constitutionally enshrined principle of secularism. This development highlighted the AKP's failure to redraft the constitution that was drawn up in 1982 under the then military regime brought to power by the September 12, 1980, military coup.[62] This has led to further tensions between Islamists, who head the government, and secularists, who run the military, courts, and bureaucracy. On March 14, 2008, the chief prosecutor of the Court of Appeals asked the Constitutional Court to ban the ruling AKP on the grounds that it had violated the country's secular principles; he also demanded a five-year political ban for members of the AKP, including Prime Minister Erdoğan and President Gul. Following the proceedings of the closure case, the court issued a compromise verdict on July 30, 2008, which ruled against closure of the AKP but decided to impose a financial penalty on the grounds that the party had become a focal point for antisecular activities.[63]

Even though this case proved that the country's Constitutional Court was unable to eliminate the AKP as a political force, its verdict appears to have caused the party to return to reforms it had advocated in earlier years. The implications of the Court's decision were profound. Immediately thereafter, Prime Minister Erdoğan became more supportive of EU accession as a means to forge wider social and political coalitions. Likewise, the verdict might lead to a process of rethinking secularism, even by the radical secularist bloc, which may come to embrace a "moderate secularism" in an attempt to respect the religious identity and concerns of masses of people. No less significant was the fact that after this non-closure decision the EU demanded more reforms, which basically meant adopting less religious and more secular positions.[64]

Today, Islamic feminists argue that women in Turkey have to choose between headscarves and their jobs in certain positions. Girls wearing headscarves cannot attend any university or school. Teachers wearing the Islamic *hijab* are not allowed to work in such places. Even civil institutions are reluctant to employ headscarved personnel because of the official press.[65] Lawyers, dentists, and pharmacists, among others, are prevented from wearing the headscarf by their professional organizations. Journalists in Islamic dress are not granted a yellow press card. There are no employment opportunities for Muslim women with *hijab*, except in areas such as breeding hens, milking cows, and other agricultural jobs. It is said that male relatives of headscarved women also suffer from discrimination, even when they are soldiers, governors, or government bureaucrats.[66]

Following the 1980 coup, a law was passed that made it illegal to wear the headscarf in certain places, including public offices and university classes. The state argued that the headscarf was a political symbol that brought the shari'a (Islamic law) not only to the university classrooms but also to the country as a whole. During the 1980s and 1990s, secular elites felt insecure, as many female Muslims wearing *hijab* entered the job market and successfully managed to get prestigious jobs. In 1999, Merve Kavakç, a female deputy, became the first female parliament deputy who was denied her position in parliament because she insisted on wearing the headscarf.

Despite these limitations, Islamic feminists in Turkey tend to see the positive side of secularism when they compare themselves with women in other Muslim countries. They argue that if secularism is defined broadly, it would suit their rights better. Broadly defined, secularism promotes tolerance and respect for difference. A secular vision of modernity that allows for the full expression of cultural difference is far more desirable than a theocratic and conformist system that imposes a strict control over society. But if secularism is defined narrowly and unilaterally by the state, such rights will be severely limited.[67]

In the West, while some view the headscarf as an agent of women's oppression, others see it as a sign of the unwillingness to integrate into the Western world's democratic institutions. Muslim women born in France, for instance, may wear the headscarf as a way to affirm their identity publicly against the dominance of French culture.[68] Importantly, headscarves can be seen as, among other things, an expression of a conscientious Muslim identity.[69]

The Aleviler

The Alevis are practitioners of a heterodox form of Islam in Turkey. They are also referred to as Qizilbash, or Red Heads, for the distinctive red turbans they have traditionally worn. Alevi beliefs are a combination of pre-Islamic, Zoroastrian, Turkoman shaman, and Shia ideas. The Alevis share beliefs with the Ahl-I Haqq religion, such as the veneration of the Prophet Muhammad's son-in-law, Ali. Alevis have long been the subject of discrimination. Aleviler (plural for the Alevi) resent their designation as a minority in large part because the new Turkish Republic was based on a secular Turkish nationalism in which no other minorities were recognized except those referred to in the Lausanne Treaty—that is, the Greeks, the Jews, and the Armenians. The term "Qizilbash" is an epithet of abuse in modern Turkey. Until recently, Aleviler used to hide their identity.[70]

The religious practice of Aleviler is the *jam* (or *cam*), which is a kind of religious ritual that involves chanting and dancing in the presence of an old man, who is the equivalent of an *imam* or prominent religious leader. When asked to compare Aleviler with Sunni Turks, a young and committed Alevi asserted that "Aleviler put emphasis on human beings rather than on God, whereas Sunnis fear God." Under EU pressure, the Turkish government has forgone its repressive policies toward Aleviler.[71]

Doğan Bermek, a prominent Alevi head and one of the founders of Cem Vakfi (Cem Foundation), argues that the basics of the republic have been seriously undermined since 1950 when the transition toward a multiparty system culminated in the incorporation of nonsecular parties into Turkey's political processes. Furthermore, Bermek continues, until 1980, Aleviler had the option of avoiding religious lessons in schools if they so desired. Since 1982, however, religious lessons have become mandatory. This development has strengthened Sunni identity to the detriment of the human rights of such religious groups as the Aleviler. The Aleviler, Bermek asserts, have contributed greatly to the sustainability of secularism in Turkey, both historically and in recent times. Yet, they have been subject to formal and informal social violence, such as the deadly riots that killed several hundreds in Kahramanmaras in southeastern Turkey on Christmas Day in 1978, including many Qizilbash.[72]

Until the sixteenth century, tolerance of the Aleviler was the key to the Ottoman Empire's tradition of cultural diversity and multireligious acceptance. After 1517, Sunni Islam was imported to the Ottoman Empire. Ideas of equality, tolerance, and respect for difference, as well as basic human rights, were intimately associated with the Aleviler's way of life and culture. Today, Bermek insists, such values are undermined by a government led by the AKP.[73] Will the protection of the rights of minorities present a problem for Turkey's entry into the European Union?

Today's Islamists in Turkey share a common cause with the West: "the need for political reform in Turkey."[74] This simply means by seeking globalization and integration into the EU to counter the Kemalist state and elites, the new generations of Turkish Islamists have effectively surrendered their utopian dream of an Islamic state.[75] Ironically, however, Turkey's experience further reaffirms the possibility of Islamic democracy. It may be, as Noah Feldman poignantly observes, that "the more truly democratic Turkey becomes, the more Islamic it is likely to be."[76] Progress toward democracy in Turkey is indeed a prelude to its full integration into the European Union. The Turkish people must be treated fairly and equally; their Muslim identity need not be seen as a handicap to EU-Turkey relations.

The Kurdish Problem

One of the central obstacles to joining the EU remains the country's human rights situation. Of particular relevance to Turkey's human rights condition is the treatment of the minority Kurds. The Kurdish issues relate, among other things, to identity matters. The Kurds have historically viewed Atatürk's drive toward Turkish nationalism and secularism as a threat to their own distinct cultural identity. Many Kurdish national movements in Turkey aspire to a free climate in which to claim their Kurdish identity. The ethnic Kurdish population in Turkey is growing faster than is the ethnic Turkish population. Further, younger people make up a considerably higher percentage of the Kurdish population than of the Turkish population. Istanbul is home to the largest Kurdish population in the world.[77]

The Kurdish community is using MED-TV, a satellite television channel with studios in Belgium and London, to foster its ethnic political movement in Turkey. This movement, which is deeply rooted in the dream of an independent Kurdistan, promotes Kurdish identity via global communication and technologies. Although the Kurds have embraced the idea of forming a political movement based on regional, ethnic, and linguistic identity, which appears to be resistant to globalization, they have relied heavily on global technologies and languages of globalization to accomplish this goal.[78]

The modern Kurdish national movement in Turkey emerged out of the intellectual drive caused by the Marxist movement that formed during the 1960s.[79] In November 1978, Abdullah (Apo) Öcalan created the Kurdistan Workers Party (Partiya Karderen Kurdistan, PKK), which actually began its revolt in August 1984. The PKK uprising represented the longest Kurdish rebellion in modern Turkish history and the PKK became the single most important political force to ever engage in a violent guerrilla war against the Turkish state and the army. The PKK became a militant organization, leading the insurgency for years. Its ideological basis blended revolutionary Marxism-Leninism and Kurdish nationalism.

Gradually, the Turkish army defeated the PKK by increasing political and military pressure on Syria, which had supported the PKK. In 1998, Turkey finally secured the expulsion of Öcalan from Syria. He was captured in Nairobi, Kenya in February 1999 by Western intelligence services and turned over to Turkish commandos; they flew him to Turkey, where he was put on trial for high treason.[80] Öcalan was convicted and condemned to death in 1999, but this sentence was commuted to life imprisonment in 2002. The PKK was formally dissolved shortly thereafter and transformed into a new organization, KADEK (Congress for Freedom and Democracy in Kurdistan), which pledged to be nonviolent and democratic.[81] Thus, the PKK rebellion ended, with the party evolving into a political organization intent on transforming the Turkish state into a Kurdish-Turkish federation.

Since its inception, however, the PKK had justified its armed struggle against the Turkish government on the grounds that the Turks had suppressed the distinct Kurdish identity. A key facet of the Kurdish movement over the past several decades, as analysts observe, was to foster among Turkish Kurds a sense of national consciousness. The emergence of such a Kurdish awareness was strongly discouraged within Turkey.[82] Turks expressed serious concerns about the resurgence of ethnonationalism among Kurds as well as enhanced awareness of varying ethnic identities within the country, fearing that such a level of consciousness could result in a separatist movement.[83] Many pro-Kurdish organizations and analysts argued that insofar as the Kurds are concerned, their use of force to defend their right to self-determination should not have been subject to laws governing treason or other national laws. The charge of treason for actions undertaken in the defense of the Kurdish people, they insisted, thus had no legal basis. The right to self-determination, they argued, made Öcalan's trial and conviction on the grounds of treason illegal.[84]

The Kurdish people, who supported Erdoğan in the 2002 national elections, prefer to be part of Turkey if Turkey is a member of the EU rather than to have an independent state. Similarly, the presence of a Kurdish diaspora has increased EU involvement in the satisfactory resolution of the Kurdish issue. The EU continues to view Turkey's treatment of its Kurds as a significant factor affecting the country's application for EU membership. In one survey, 13 percent of Kurds advocated independence; 43 percent advocated federation; 19 percent advocated local self-government; and 13 percent desired autonomy.[85]

In the May 2007 crisis over the Kurdish issue in Iraq, the Turkish military was contemplating an all-out invasion of northern Iraq. Some observers argued that this was a well-calculated decision before the July 22, 2007, elections to bolster the position of the military vis-à-vis Erdoğan's AKP. The military's stated policy of fighting against the PKK and the forces of Massoud Barzani was not a new policy and in fact it has been going on without success for the last twenty years. The Barzani tribe has been a major political force in northern Iraq for the last fifty years. Likewise, the formation of an autonomous Kurdish entity in northern Iraq under U.S. protection has been going on for the last fifteen years.[86]

Turkey's cross-border raids to strike at the PKK in northern Iraq continued during the fall of 2007. By mid-December 2007, Turkish troops had crossed into Iraq on several occasions and Turkish bombardments of PKK rebel targets were among the largest airstrikes in years against the Kurdish separatists.[87] Pressure grew on Prime Minister Erdoğan to act, as the PKK attacks had surged against Turkish troops and civilians. Iraqi President Barzani, whom the Turkish military accuses of harboring the PKK, has repeatedly said the United States should fulfill its "moral and legal commitment to protect the country's sovereignty and defend the Iraqi people."[88] Meanwhile, the military has been attempting to redesign Turkish politics in such a way that it could reassert its hegemony over the political system, which has been lost as a result of Turkey's move toward the EU in recent years. The military and their allies have tried to reverse the EU entry talks. They prefer a coalition of political parties, such as the ultra-nationalist parties: the Nationalist Action Party (MHP) and the Republican People's Party (Cumhuriyet Halk Partisi or CHP), with their anti-EU and anti-globalization positions.

EU-Turkey Relations

Historically, Turkey has benefited immensely from its ties with the West. Turkey was a founding member of the Council of Europe and the Organization for Security and Cooperation in Europe (OSCE). Today, Turkey is a member of the North Atlantic Treaty Organization (NATO) and the Organization for Economic Cooperation and Development (OECD). Its importance in the post–Cold War era has risen since the Central Asian Republics and the Caucasus gained their independence. This area, as Recep Tayyip Erdoğan, the prime minister of Turkey, reminds us, not only represents a newly emerging energy landscape but it is also in desperate need of consolidating political stability and achieving sustainable development.[89]

The rejection of Turkey's full membership in December 1989 by the European Community (EC) was widely regarded in Turkey as being based on cultural and religious grounds. This feeling of being excluded from the West had a profound impact on the self-perception of the Turks, irrespective of secular and Islamist persuasion.[90] Recognizing Turkey's geopolitical and economic significance for the EU in the post–Cold War era, the EU pushed for a compromise solution that neither shut the door for future membership nor granted Turkey immediate accession.

The Custom Union (CU) agreement of 1995 provided that solution. This agreement opened the Turkish market of seventy million consumers to EU companies, but it also provided Turkey with economic ties to the EU. For the Turks, the CU was the harbinger of membership to come. For the Europeans, however, the CU was a way of maintaining economic ties with Turkey while keeping Turkey outside Union membership—at least for the foreseeable future.[91] The decision of the EU at the Helsinki summit of December 10–11, 1999, to include Turkey among the list of candidate countries for possible membership and to lift the Greek veto of Turkey's membership did create a new opportunity—provided that Turkey completes a series of economic and political reforms—for accession talks.

The EU, in turn, demanded that Turkey fully comply with the Copenhagen criteria for membership, resolve the Cyprus problem and bilateral issues between Greece and Turkey, and assist reforms in security areas such as NATO-ESDI (European Security Defense Identity) relations.[92] The EU also insisted that Turkey abolish the death penalty and grant Kurds the right to education and broadcasting in Kurdish. Turkey has complied in both cases. On December 17, 2004, the EU responded positively to Turkey's internal reforms by finally deciding to begin accession talks with Turkey. Full membership, however, may take ten to fifteen years to realize, during which time the EU will monitor the reform processes in Turkey.[93]

The Copenhagen membership criteria were these: (1) the applicant country has to be a member of the European family of states, (2) it must be a democracy in which respect for human rights and protection of minorities is upheld, (3) it must maintain a strong market economy with freedom of movement of goods, capital, services, and people, and (4) it must work toward fulfilling the aims of political, economic, and monetary union and adopt the EU legislation—*acquis communautaire*.[94] On the criterion of Europeanness, the debate often revolves on the issue of cultural constraint on what constitutes Europeanness. There is in fact nothing in the EU founding Treaty of Rome (1957) or in any other unwritten rule that requires the EU states to be Christian.

Several EU states have significant Muslim minorities. In response to the question of whether Europe wants that many Muslims within its community, Robert D. Kaplan notes, "Europe has no choice. It is becoming Muslim anyway."[95] While economic ties with Turkey will foster Islamic moderation in Europe, Turkey's membership is certain to reinforce secularism in Turkey.[96] The EU should capitalize on this unique opportunity. "Though American troops are fighting and dying in Iraq," Kaplan writes, "ultimately the Europeans, because of geography and their own demographic patterns, have more at stake in the stabilization of the region. And the surest way to advance that stabilization is to make Turkey part of Europe."[97]

Since the Helsinki agreement on Turkey's candidacy, the EU has closely observed that country's progress toward democratization and human rights. There are serious concerns regarding the judiciary and the State Security Courts (SSCs) and the human rights of minorities. Classroom instruction in Kurdish is allowed throughout the country but only with restrictions.[98] The question facing the EU is whether Turkey is ready for European-style democracy. Turkish people insist on EU membership in the hope of containing or controlling the power of corrupt bureaucrats, the state, and the army. Turkey's membership in the EU, they argue, is likely to lead to democratic norms (e.g., equality) in the political system.[99]

As for demographic trends, Abdullah Gul, Turkey's then–foreign minister, argued that the Turkish population was expected to stabilize around eighty-five million by 2025, much less than the one hundred million in some European projections.[100] Given the demographic trends in Europe over the next few decades (falling birth rates and population decreases in some cases), the young population of Turkey can prove to be an asset rather than a liability for the EU.[101] Prime Minister Erdoğan has underscored the importance of a Turco-Greek strategic equation within the context of the EU. "If Turco-Greek rapprochement is possible today," Erdoğan notes, "it is because we have a common ground through which mutual perceptions are formed most accurately. That common ground is the EU."[102] Furthermore, Erdoğan sees a wider gamut of regional and extra-regional issues that constitute a common ground for cooperation between Turkey and the EU. Developments in Iraq, the Balkans, the Caucasus, and Afghanistan as well as policies to confront Al-Qaeda have great potential for cooperation between the two.[103]

Erdoğan has also asserted that the view of Islam held by the Turkish Muslim masses and the AK Party's posture can be described as conservative-democratic with strong Islamic roots. This perspective runs counter to what the Al-Qaeda terror network stands for. "The confrontation between Islamic terror and Muslim-Democratic states," Erdoğan insists, "represents the coming internal clashes within Islamic civilization."[104] Some experts have even suggested that despite the nature of Turkey's secular state and serious limits to its ability and willingness to foster political change, a secular and democratizing Turkey could offer significant lessons for the initiation and promotion of democracy and a reform process among the Arab countries of the Persian Gulf region.[105]

Many of Europe's voters view cultural differences as the main reason Turkey should not join the EU. Few European politicians have attempted to tackle this issue, since they have no compelling answers. Turkish accession is unpopular, some observers argue, because it forces Europeans to confront questions about European identity. That is to say, it forces Europeans to confront fundamental uncertainties about who they are, which values they share, and how open their societies can and should be."[106] Criticizing the view that is skeptical of Turkey's potential to enter the EU on political or cultural issues, Erdoğan writes, "Those who support the exclusion of Turkey on religious, cultural or some superficial definitions of borders do not realize that they are in fact hindering the integration of the Muslims who already live in the EU."[107] Turkey has an enormous stake in becoming a member of the EU.

Since the CU entered into force, a growing number of European companies have invested in Turkey. Further benefits will come as soon as negotiations start. By 2010, approximately forty-two thousand Turkish students could begin to study abroad under the EU's Erasmus program for student exchange.[108] By 2007, Turkey expected to receive close to two billion euros in aid from the EU.[109] Turkey has attempted to harmonize its laws and regulations with those of the EU in such areas as asylum policy, drug trafficking, migration policy, policy cooperation, and other related issues.[110]

The Shift in Identity Formation

For the AKP, the enormity of the challenges ahead will require a willingness to strike a delicate balance between Islamic and secular forces. The question that has bedeviled the observers of Turkish politics persists: How would Islamic leaders translate this enormous grassroots support at the local level into political strength at the national party level, while keeping their end of bargain, which is to respect the country's secular laws and rules? Secular politicians at all levels may be surprised by a public more aware of such global values and standards as human rights and the rule of law than conventional wisdom holds. A shift in the position of Turkey's Muslim intellectuals became obvious when the AKP garnered 34 percent of the votes in the 2002 general elections and 42 percent of the votes in the 2004 local elections, while the Saadet Partisi (the Felicity Party), which adhered to the pro-Islamist line of Necmettin Erbakan, received only 2.5 percent of the total vote cast.[111] The AKP, under the leadership of Recep Tayyib Erdoğan, the former mayor of Istanbul, has moved to the political center by breaking away from the Milli Görüs Hareketi (National View Movement). Erdoğan has introduced drastic reforms (on the Kurdish issue, human rights, and civil-military relations) and passed several harmonization packages; and made risky compromises to resolve the Cyprus dispute.

Furthermore, by pledging to work with an International Monetary Fund (IMF) program, the AKP has reasserted its pro-globalization position.[112] More significantly, after taking office, Erdoğan asserted that secularism is the basis of Turkey's unity. His acceptance of secularism is summarized in this bold statement: "Islam is religion. Secularism is just a style of management."[113] These newly adopted policy approaches demonstrated that intellectual leaders of post-Islamism have been searching for a rapprochement with the West as an effort to rethink modern political notions such as democracy and human rights, integration into the globalization process, and Turkey's entry into the European Union.[114]

Emerging out of the soft coup of February 28, 1997, in which the military forced Erbakan's resignation, the post-Islamists searched for ways to overcome the policy of exclusion and elimination. They have actually demanded the formation of a genuinely liberal democratic regime in Turkey. Their opposition to the Kemalist regime is no longer expressed in the name of Islam but, rather, in modern jargon such as democracy, human rights, and the rule of law.[115] These notions provide a "discursive legitimacy" and supremacy over their opponents who cannot deny such modern notions.[116] In some odd ways, resorting to the universal language of political modernity rather than Islam's particularities, as Ihsan D. Dagi writes, has "served to justify the presence of an Islamic political identity."[117]

Many of the new Islamist intellectuals have adopted a post-Islamist position, replacing in their writings notions of Islamic worldviews and civilization with those of universal values such as fundamental rights, civil society, plural democracy, and the rule of law. Ali Bulac, for instance, has supported Turkey's entry into the EU by adopting the Copenhagen political criteria that the EU has set as a precondition for Turkey's membership. Recai Kutan, the chairperson of the Milli Görüş Hareketi (National View Movement) emphasized the importance of meeting the EU standards on democracy, calling for a civic constitution that would fulfill the Copenhagen criteria for basic rights and liberties.[118]

Significantly, in the post–Cold War era, the Turkish people have begun to rethink religiosity and work for the realization of individual freedoms. The issue of identity has become invariably intertwined with their freedom and equality. In a carefully calculated but sustainable way, the AKP has used human rights as an effective venue for its very survival, in part because the Erdoğan administration feels insecure, but also because of the rising prominence of human rights on the global scene. The AKP has sought to secure a "legitimate" place for itself in Turkish politics by its insistence on protecting and promoting human rights in addition to the popular legitimacy that it has enjoyed at the ballot box.

The recognition of democratic values and constraints—such as democratic governance, transparency, accountability, and respect for the secular foundation of the country's constitution—has had a transformative impact on Turkish political culture and conservative masses more generally.[119] Turkish democrats have come to symbolize a new way of thinking—a paradigm shift of sorts. Legitimacy lies at the heart of this rethinking. These developments are likely to speed up reforms that would undermine the Kemalist/secular state.[120] The globalization of ideas, norms, and technologies has actually worked against the Kemalist balance, revealing a curious irony: new forces of change now originate equally—and perhaps even more—from inside the society.[121]

Conclusion

By imposing an overarching secular and official ideology on society, the Turkish state has arguably created an identity crisis of sorts. Under such circumstances, the Turkish people have no option but to choose subnational identities. They are at times forced to opt for a Kemalist ideology and identity if for no other reason than without it the country's stability may be jeopardized. In the past, those who adopted the establishment's official ideology were granted perks and privileges. The political climate of the 1980s and 1990s, however, opened the Kemalist Pandora's box from which emerged multiple and fluid identities that refer to different sects of Islam and the Kurds.[122] The globalizing and polarizing political dynamics of the early twenty-first century have brought Turkey back to square one: how to strike a synthesis between Islamic and secular tendencies, values, and identities.

Whether Turkey's leaders can bridge secular and modern Islamic identities is a matter of deep interest, as the dispute between Islamists and secularists continues unabated. Some observers aptly capture the existing tensions between state and society relations: "If the secular establishment takes away the Islamic identity, how can it expect Turkish people to die for their country if need be?"[123] Although there is some disagreement over what factors would play a role in shaping Turkish identity, Islamic identity is undeniably a major facet and marker of it. In this fundamental sense, Turkey is no different from other Islamic societies, where religion—more than language and ethnicity—has typically defined political, social, and personal identity.[124] Atatürk tried to confront this reality by changing the Muslim culture. He utterly failed to do so, as evidenced by the rising Islamic identity in recent decades in Turkey.

In today's Turkey, however, views concerning Erdoğan's policies differ. One Alevi journalist with a Kemalist orientation argues that Erdoğan is using the EU as a major vehicle to reduce the power of the army. He is using the legal system to eliminate barriers toward establishing an Islamic state.[125] Others point out that Erdoğan defines himself as a "conservative democrat." In many respects, Erdoğan is much closer to Turgut Özal than Necmettin Erbakan. That is to say, Özal successfully brought four currents of thought together: Islamic, liberal, nationalist, and socialist. Erdoğan seems intent on achieving the same goal.[126] His party (AKP), however, has tried to redefine and reconstruct itself constantly and in the process has become part of the identity problem in Turkey.

Still others see Erdoğan as a nonideological and pragmatic leader who could successfully lead Turkey. He favors intercivilizational dialogue and regional détente and displays a strategic sense of global politics.[127] Yet the discomfort of secular women in Turkey continues, as was demonstrated by Turkish women's participation in anti-Islamist demonstrations in May 2007 in Istanbul. The secularists' fear of Islamists lingers on, even as the AKP has presided over strong economic growth and the continuation of the European Union accession talks, and has in fact adopted no Islamist-oriented laws.[128] Turkey's membership in the EU could potentially redefine the meaning and values associated with Islamic and Western identities. Unless the EU respects Turkey's national and cultural identity, the Turks will have no chance of becoming part of greater Europe. The interplay between identity, power, and human rights in Turkey should not go unnoticed. By persistent human rights improvement, Turkey's leaders can gain moral and political ground to make a compelling case for entry into the EU.

Chapter 8

The Reemergence of Populism in Iranian Politics: Constructing New Identities

The 1979 Islamic Revolution led, among other things, to a cultural transformation in which the Iranian masses demonstrated their wish to defend their religious and cultural identity. In the course of the revolution, many Iranians took the view that the shah's Westernizing and modernizing programs posed a threat to Iran's national and Islamic identity and widened class disparities. The resistance to the shah's repressive regime indeed became a reaction to what threatened not only Iranians' religious and cultural heritage but also their economic and personal security.

Following the revolution, the religiopolitical establishment attempted a re-Islamization of the society. In the post-Khomeini era, the Islamic Republic went through several phases to win popular support and to safeguard its political longevity: from radicalism to pragmatism in the 1980s; to political reform, the rule of law, and the dialogue of civilizations throughout the 1990s; to populism and economic reform rhetoric in the 2005 presidential election.

To explain how the rise of populism in Iran has transformed the notion of identity, it is essential to examine the impact of global forces on the internal political and social dynamics of the Iranian society. Globalization works like a double-edged sword, posing a threat to the people's indigenous identities by expanding transnational ties and interests between and among groups while at the same time intensifying local identities—be they ethnic, racial, religious, cultural, gender, or class. In much of the Muslim world, globalization also brings the threat of Westernization, posing an even greater threat to local identity. To protect against this perceived or actual threat, Islamists argue that modernization and Islamic identity must be blended in such a way that the religious and cultural identity of Muslims is maintained. Differently put, they wish to Islamize modernization.

Increasingly, Iran's ruling elites, cultural elites, and public at large have been drawn into a debate over the global dynamics of change, with some edging toward a convergence with the rest of the global community and others maintaining the more traditional Islamic stance against the intrusion of "alien values" and "alien ideals" into their local cultural traditions. Powerful ideas and norms such as democracy and human rights have reached different segments of the Iranian population, resulting in the social construction—in both cultural and political senses—of new identities and interests as well as shared meanings that Iranians assign to themselves and others.

The socioeconomic, cultural, and political dynamics of change have created a bifurcated society, in which some people emphasize their national identity and others underline the importance of their religious identity. Globalizing influences have widened this split while paradoxically strengthening both sides of Iran's religious and cultural divide. Following a brief overview of the internal developments of Iran since the 1979 Islamic Revolution, this chapter addresses the way the issue of identity has been constructed and has evolved within the context of Iranian society and polity.

The revival of populism in Iranian politics has generated new forms of identities and agencies. Obviously, the sociocultural liberalization of earlier years has broadened the cultural and religious divide among Iranians, precipitating the formation of many and varied identities. While youth have benefited from social freedoms and social transformation, the improvement of economic conditions has been largely overlooked at the expense of promoting political reforms and civil society. To put the formation of new identities in context, particular consideration is given to economic conditions and the question of why such circumstances led to the reemergence of populism in Iranian politics.

The Islamic Republic of Iran

The shah's fast-paced modernization and Westernization led to widespread corruption and mismanagement and a huge gulf in living standards between rich and poor; it also severely undermined the traditional social structures and values of a society in which religious mores still held a central place. Opposition to the shah's regime was mobilized and organized under the banner of Islam, demonstrating that Islam played a key role as both a rallying cry for change and a symbol of protest. Some experts have pointed to the persistence of Islamic identity among Iranians as evidence that Iranian patriotism and Islamism are closely intertwined. Despite strong interest in Persia's ancient past, they have argued, Islam has upheld its primacy in Iranian self-identification.[1] John L. Esposito captures the spirit of the revolution: "Islamic symbols, rhetoric, and institutions provided the infrastructure for organization, protest, and mobilization of a coalition of forces calling for reform and in the end for revolution."[2]

Similarly, the secularization of governmental institutions and the educational system caused negative reactions in the religious community as did the exodus of the brightest students to U.S. and British universities.[3] Some modern, Western-educated intellectuals, such as Jalal al-e-Ahmad and Ali Shariati, wrote of the dangers of "Westoxification," an excessive dependence on the West that threatened to strip Iranians of their independence and cultural identity.

Moreover, Shiite Islam provided the discontent and disoriented masses a common set of symbols, historical identity, and values, which were internally authentic and predicated on a non-Western alternative.[4] Some experts have pointed out that Shia religious identity has provided a unifying force and has indeed become inextricably intertwined with Iranian national identity to the present.[5] Others have argued that Shiism has been integral to Iranian identity and has in fact been a source of political legitimacy since the sixteenth century, when it was first declared the state religion of Iran.[6] Because of its involvement in politics from its origins, Shia Islam has provided a history and system of belief that has kept it in the thick of political crises. "In Iranian history," John L. Esposito and John O. Voll wrote, "Twelver Shiism (*Ithna Ashari*) has often been apolitical, finding a tolerable accommodation with the state. However, at critical points throughout history, Shia belief, leadership, and institutions have played an important role in Iranian politics and society. Shiism has been interpreted and utilized to safeguard national identity and independence and to mobilize popular support."[7]

The disruption caused by the growing political, technological, and cultural influences of the West led to an upheaval in Iran that principally challenged Western notions of modernization. The shah's modernization campaign, as one observer noted, proved to be a fundamentally misguided program of adopting Western technologies and agricultural methods that were often inappropriate to Iranian environmental and economic conditions; the shah's virtual mania for overdeveloping his military merely compounded the mismatch between government and society.[8]

The people's sense of threatened identity, repression, and relative deprivation combined in a revolt against a decadent and corrupt regime.[9] The resultant social breakdown, caused by a widespread sense of alienation and dislocated identity, was converted into a social movement spearheaded by Ayatollah Ruhollah Khomeini (1902–89). Khomeini reasserted his role as protector of Islam and the Shia community vis-à-vis the tyranny of the shah's regime. It is, however, important not to forget that the collapse of the regime of Mohammad Reza Shah Pahlavi (1919–80) was in many ways precipitated by his unrelenting drive toward Westernizing and modernizing programs that blatantly undermined a sense of national and cultural identity.

Khomeini's ascendance to power was followed by the prolonged crisis over holding U.S. hostages (1979–81); the Iran-Iraq war (1980–88); the dismantling of opposition groups, both at home and abroad; the issuance of a *fatwa* (death decree) for Salman Rushdie, author of the novel *The Satanic Verses* (1989); and the Islamization of all facets of life. Khomeini's death in 1989 left behind disruptive interfactional disputes and the lack of a credible successor to maintain his agenda with the same commitment and tenacity. Ever since, many of Iran's seventy million people have become vastly disillusioned with the clerics' reign of power. The government has incarcerated tens of thousands of its opponents without due process and has "systematically tortured prisoners to extract false confessions and public recantations."[10]

The post-Khomeini era gave way to an Islamic pragmatism in both Iran's foreign policy and domestic reforms. Factional disputes and the primacy of the economy over ideological issues emerged as the key developments in Iranian politics in the post-Khomeini era. A national referendum abolished the post of prime minister and replaced it with a popularly elected president as head of the government—an officer who did not need to be approved by the Majles (parliament). As such, many powers were transferred from the clergy to the state. These changes also enabled President Ali Akbar Hashemi Rafsanjani, the Islamic Republic's first president, to implement his reforms while relying on a platform of moderation and pragmatism.

Although the Majles was important in promoting popular sovereignty in the post-Khomeini era, it failed to provide genuinely broad political participation. Parliamentary elections were manipulated, among other things, by interfactional disputes. Rafsanjani's liberalization program (1989–97) faced many obstacles: low levels of private investment, low growth rates, budget bottlenecks, and mounting foreign debt. Furthermore, corruption and mismanagement hugely complicated the state's liberalization programs.[11]

Rafsanjani's first term (1989–93) brought only slight relaxation of the strict enforcement of Islamic social codes by the so-called morals squads and security police. During his second term (1993–97), his political engagement brought about further relaxation of the strict Islamic codes of behavior. Meanwhile, an emerging debate surrounding civil society brought the discussion of the common standards of moral decency and human rights to the country's domestic forefront. The protection and promotion of women's rights entered a new phase when Zahra Mostafavi founded the Association of Muslim Women to fight for greater access to higher education for women. In 1992, President Rafsanjani created the Bureau of Women's Affairs and appointed Shahla Habibi as his adviser on issues pertaining to women.[12] But it was not until the election of Rafsanjani's successor, Mohammad Khatami, who removed cultural restrictions on the printing of books and magazines previously banned, that the real discourse about reform transpired.

Khatami: Cultural and Political Reforms

In a decisive electoral victory on May 23, 1997, Mohammad Khatami became Iran's new president. Khatami's landslide victory—he received almost 70 percent of the popular vote—was a firm rejection of the hard-line clerics who had dominated Iranian politics since the 1979 revolution. Khatami's supporters—mainly youth, women, intellectuals, left-of-the-center political activists, and ethnic minorities—demanded greater social and political freedom and more political pluralism.

On the domestic front, Khatami brought greater freedom and tolerance not just to the political regime but also to the social sphere. As a direct result of his policies, freedom of the press was reasonably maintained, at least until the beginning of 2000. Since early 2000, however, the conservative judiciary has shut down more than one hundred reformist newspapers and magazines and jailed many reformist journalists, intellectuals, and political activists. Almost all of the sixteen reformist writers and activists who attended the Berlin Conference—organized and sponsored by the Heinrich Böll Foundation, an arm of the German Green Party—April 7–8, 2000, were put on trial.

On June 8, 2001, Khatami swept his way into the presidency for a second term by winning 78.3 percent of the vote. This victory implied a mandate for reform, as it was accompanied with the reformers' electoral triumph in the sixth Majles elections held on February 18, 2000, and subsequently on May 5, 2000, in which reformists won 189 of the parliament's total 290 seats.[13] Although these victories emboldened ordinary people to speak more openly about public policies and their shortcomings, the reformers' initiatives in parliament were repeatedly stopped. On August 6, 2000, legislation prepared by reformers to ease the press law was blocked by the country's Supreme Leader Ayatollah Ali Khamenei.[14] Subsequently, several reformist newspapers were closed and many reformist leaders were arrested. One observer characterized this situation as a de facto coup.[15]

The assertion of Iran's Islamic identity, one expert notes, seems more preoccupied with debates over women's dress and conduct in society than with the execution of effective political and economic policies.[16] As pressure and popular discontent steadily mounted, people began to talk increasingly about the collapse of the system from within. Meanwhile Khatami remained in office and the parliament remained in reformist hands, but the conservatives used extensive control over other branches of the state apparatus to prevent the president and parliament from implementing their reform agenda. During his first term, Khatami's policies arguably led to improved gender relations in society at large. He bolstered women's freedom in many areas and appointed several female deputy vice presidents for technical affairs and sports. As a result, female students now compete equally with male students for university seats in all engineering fields previously reserved solely for male students.

Khatami greatly contributed to the strength of civil society in Iran by opening up the political arena, by espousing the formation of new political parties by civil groups, and by supporting the rule of law. He laid the groundwork for introducing transparency into the political texture of society via the institutionalization of law and a multiparty system. He abolished the president's slush fund, spoke favorably of all aspects of a civil society, and publicly acknowledged both the negative and positive achievements of Western civilization. Khatami frequently referred to the "dialogue among civilizations and cultures" as the most effective way to achieve global détente. Under his administration, Iran has accepted the Chemical Weapons Convention, and many restrictions were placed on the religious vigilantes and militia who spied on people's private lives to enforce Islamic social codes—that is, codes of dress and behavior.[17]

Despite Khatami's significant progress toward liberalization, the decisive question remained unanswered: How would his mandate translate into political capital and power? One measure of Khatami's success, therefore, was how far his government was prepared to go to limit the authority of the supreme leader. The fact remains that Khatami was unable to implement concrete policy reforms during either of his terms.

In the meantime, the conservative forces took majority control of Iran's seventh parliament (2004–7) in the February 2004 elections. This victory was made possible by the help of the Guardian Council, a body that blocked the candidacy of over one thousand reformist candidates. Several other factors explained the conservatives' reversal of fortune in the seventh parliament. Those included, among others, lack of unity among the reformists, Khatami's inability to confront the conservatives, and the idiosyncratic constitution that confers wide-ranging powers on the judiciary and the office of the Supreme Leader, as well as on other conservative bodies. Arguably, the conservatives did not achieve their victory through brute force and repressive measures. A new generation in their ranks employed a more pragmatic rather than puritan approach to enhancing their public appeal.[18]

Khatami was unable to convert his popularity into real reforms, and popular frustration and dismal economic conditions have proven incapable of dethroning the conservatives, so can the democratic gains for which the Iranian people fought so tenaciously in recent years be rolled back? A cursory look at the globalizing trend shows that the gains achieved and identities constructed under such dynamics are irreversible.

Globalization and Identity Formation

Broadly speaking, three reactions to globalization can be discerned in Iran. One group considers globalization a tool of the great powers in their attempts to continue controlling global politics and economics, and it sees two choices for action: to either resist globalization or to be integrated into the global forces of ideas, transformed cultures, and evolving economic systems. The new era of transformation, so runs the argument, is old wine in a new bottle. Social movements, Islamic or otherwise, represent a collective form of resistance to globalization and they are invariably intertwined with the rise of counter-hegemonic consciousness.

A second group views globalization as inevitable, irreversible, and evolutionary (not controlled by the West) but sees only one choice for action: accommodation. This, not resistance, is the key to protecting one's security and balance vis-à-vis the onslaught of globalization. The members of this group have sought to adjust their religious beliefs and understanding to accommodate scientific and instrumental knowledge—that is, modern rationality.

A third group sees globalization as a paradigm shift that the Muslim world cannot avoid. This shift requires changes in lifestyle, value system, and cultural and mental attitudes toward local, national, and universal realities. This group also seems to argue for accommodation, or adjustment, or change in response: almost a need to "surf" the wave of globalization by "adjusting the sail" of Islam. The proponents of this view argue that Islam is growing as a religious identity, but it is also in need of a paradigm shift. There are two points to be made here. First, as the French scholar Olivier Roy argues, globalization has deterritorialized culture and politics for the Muslim diaspora in the West, but at the same time—the second point—it has intensified cultural politics in the homeland.[19]

While some religious-minded Iranians are skeptical about the globalization of culture, others assert that globalization, by enlarging the space of interactions between different countries and communities, could empower and extend the scope of religious identity. The skeptical view holds that globalization results in the fragmentation of religious identity at local, regional, and global levels, culminating in hybrid and mixed cultural identities. The optimistic view emphasizes the notion that religious identity has never been stable and homogenized and that the increase in global access of communication could reorient a sense of religious identity, extending it to other parts of the globe.

A sense of legitimacy is arguably essential to upholding self and collective identities. The discourse about the intersection of cultural dynamics and identity construction can no longer overlook human rights issues. Today, both Islamic reformists and militants in Iran turn to international law and human rights to advance their ideological and strategic goals. This approach has become integral to any systematic way of thinking about evolving Iranian politics and communities. For many Iranians, the issue of identity is a matter of self-assertion and recognition of Iranians by the rest of the world. The latter is even more important given that the dialectic of local and global experiences is bound to produce paradoxical effects.

Likewise, many Iranian women have underlined the need for "internal legitimacy" to successfully negotiate their rights with the state. Since the second decade of the Islamic Revolution, Iranian women have gone on the offensive, putting enormous pressure on the state for changes in social and legal policies affecting them. It is generally argued that greater individualism has emerged in the current women's activism than had existed previously—an attitude grounded in and encouraged by the global forces of modernity.

The state's efforts to impose a collectivist identity on Iranian women has backfired, leading them to seek a balance between the extremes of Western individualism and Islamic collectivism. Increasingly, women have tried to separate their identity from group affiliations—be they religious, family, or ethnic—while turning to individual definitions based on their own accomplishments.[20] As a reflection of this attitude, most Iranian female activists today are less interested in totalistic ideologies, political power, and revolutionary tasks than in penetrating various professions in fields of the public arena such as the film industry, literary works, and mass media.[21]

Coping with competing and conflicting ways of life is among the greatest challenges facing Iranians residing outside their homeland, who too often find themselves caught between the pull and push of local and global forces. It is clear that asserting homeland traditions and customs while trying to win recognition from the countries in which they reside is no mean task. Ultimately, it is up to the Iranian diaspora in the West to decide which aspects of their indigenous culture to retain and which parts to give up.

The growth of mass education and mass communication, instead of undermining the influence of Islam, has led to its redefinition as a dynamic form of political and social consciousness. Global forces have created in Iran a world of multiple and shifting identities. The cultural conflicts in which many Iranians find themselves are clashes over who controls modernity and who can stake out a claim to authenticity and legitimacy. The language of legitimacy today is human rights and democratization. It is no coincidence that the key to Iranians' successes in both political and social processes, as in Turkey, Yemen, and Jordan, is their attempt to incorporate modern norms and standards into their policies without losing the integrity of their culture. The corrective to militant Islamism, which represents a tiny minority of the world's 1.2 billion Muslims, is to integrate mainstream, moderate Islamists into the political process. Without inclusionary politics, the Islamic radicals are likely to prevail in the political struggle over who gets to define globalization and who gets to control modernity.

Identity Formation and the Women's Movement

The youth vote and women provided the bedrock of support for the election of Khatami. Iran is a young nation—some estimates show that 70 percent of the population is under the age of thirty. Young people who are part of the wired world, with access to satellite television and the Internet, led protests against the state in 1999, 2002, and 2003.[22] These young people became disillusioned with the government of the moderate cleric President Mohammad Khatami, whom they strongly supported in two elections: 1997 and 2001. In fairness, it is important to know that President Khatami's reform efforts in parliament were often blocked by the conservative clerics and the country's Supreme Leader Ayatollah Ali Khamenei.

Nowhere, however, is the impact of globalization so drastically felt and visible than in the issues of gender and class. Although the status of women during the revolutionary era deteriorated considerably, their basic opportunities in heath care, educational attainment, and access to economic resources noticeably increased during the postrevolutionary period. "The greatest irony of all," Eric Rouleau wrote, "is that making the chador [*hijab*] compulsory has given a powerful boost to the emancipation of women."[23] The chador has made possible the mass enrollment in schools and universities of girls whose traditional families were reluctant to send them to schools during the shah's era. Women with modest Islamic dress have also entered the labor market and have demanded full equality under the law, especially in such areas as inheritance and divorce.[24]

Furthermore, the globalizing dynamics of the 1990s, prompted by the international conventions held in Rio de Janeiro (1992), Vienna (1993), Cairo (1994), Copenhagen (1995), Beijing (1995), and the Hague (1999), have had important implications for women's rights all over the world, intensifying the pressure on the Islamic Republic of Iran to take necessary measures to improve women's situation in the legal, socioeconomic, political, and educational domains.

These global forces helped forge shared meanings and identities as well as local structures such as women's rights groups in addition to becoming an effective vehicle for voicing transnational demands for the promotion of gender equality. Globalization as such also induced the social construction of identity. This perspective, however, reinforced the skeptical view that cultural imperialism manifested itself through female attitudes and behavior and that excessively Westernized codes adopted by women posed a cultural danger. The women's liberation movement was thus viewed as an explicit attempt to pursue hedonism and individualism—two Western influences seen as propelled by the forces of globalization and disdained by conservatives. To shield women from such influences, the conservatives argued that it was necessary to closely monitor their public appearance, sexuality, and social activities.

Tension also persisted over the government's inability to generate a balance between women's expectations and the state's capabilities. If not properly managed, it was argued, this imbalance was likely to lead to a major social crisis in a society in which females constitute 64 percent of university graduates and the nationwide literacy rate of women between the ages of fifteen and twenty-four has risen to 97 percent.[25] It has become more difficult for educated women to find a suitable match (marriage partner) given the custom for women to marry at their status or higher.

Today, women's testimony in court counts for half that of men and they cannot travel on their own without the permission of their husbands. Under Iran's blood money law (*diyah*), a woman's life is worth half that of a man. Men continue to have a unilateral right of divorce. With no social institutions to translate women's frustration into organized resistance, the likelihood of a social upheaval is weak in the short run.[26] Looking into the future, however, the prospects for change are more encouraging.

Internationally acclaimed filmmaker Tahmineh Milani has produced movies reflective of women's struggles in Iran's male-centered cultural contexts. Movies such as *Two Women*, *Red*, and *The Hidden Half* have portrayed women's social problems, including the negation of their identity as human beings and the requirement that they live with judgments imposed on them by archaic legal and cultural traditions and social forces.[27] Some of these movies clearly demonstrate injustices associated with the man's unilateral right of divorce.

Feminists, such as Mahboobeh Abassgholizadeh, who directs an NGO training center in Tehran, argue that the main objective of the women's movement in Iran is not to acquire a share of political power but to create social changes that would benefit women. Unless there is coordination between the movement's internal rules and those of its shareholders, the women's movement risks being manipulated for purely instrumental reasons as well as becoming a pawn in the politicians' political game.[28]

Still others note that Iranian society is far more developed than the Iranian state. Some parliament deputies, such as Elahe Koolaee, predict that the gap between the society and the state makes a gender crisis inescapable.[29] Mostapha Tajzadeh, a journalist and former adviser to President Mohammad Khatami, echoes the same view, arguing that Iranian leaders have adopted a wrong approach toward women's social demands in the past, intensifying and radicalizing the feminist problem. A more progressive attitude, Tajzadeh noted, could have had a moderating influence on feminism in Iran.[30]

During the first decade of the 1979 Islamic Revolution, as pointed out by an Iranian feminist, the women's struggle was spearheaded by "revolutionary women." These feminists were primarily concerned with the communitarian viewpoint and a traditionalist question of identity: "Who am I?" The second generation of feminists in the late 1980s, who were communitarian in one sense but pragmatic in others, came to be known as "religious reformists." They were deeply concerned with addressing the question of "what is my duty?" By the 1990s, the third generation of feminists, who combined aspects of cosmopolitanism with pragmatism, came to be known as "Islamic feminists." They were largely concerned with the question of "what are my rights?" as they emphasized rationality over sacred texts and dynamic jurisprudence.[31]

Shirin Ebadi, the 2003 Nobel Peace Prize winner, epitomizes a secular feminist who shares certain views of the third generation of Muslim feminists.[32] Islamic feminists generally support international human rights covenants and conventions, especially the Convention on the Elimination of All Forms of Discrimination against Women (CEDAW). Winning the Nobel Peace Prize has empowered Ebadi to further expose the inherent contradictions of Iran's conservative ideology. This development has predictably renewed the debate on the intersection of globalization and Islamic feminism in many circles.[33]

The term "Islamic feminism" has invited controversy, both within the country and abroad. Politically, the antifeminist Islamic patriarchy sees it as a sign of Western cultural imperialism, noting that Islamic feminism glosses over the complexities of the socioeconomic and political transformations of Muslim countries.[34] On the contrary, some Iranian feminists abroad view Islamic feminism as one element of a more holistic social change in Iran. This phenomenon, they maintain, should be seen as a faith-based response of a certain stratum of Muslim women in their attempt to negotiate with state elites while recognizing the egalitarian ethics of Islam. The true testament of Islamic feminism and its limits for women's empowerment, Nayereh Tohidi continues, must be accounted for in its deeds more than in its theological or theoretical inconsistencies.[35]

Other secular Iranian feminists abroad have argued that Islamic feminists are playing an important role in broadening the discursive universe while expanding legal literacy and gender consciousness. Islamic feminism as such is "a legitimate—and historically necessary—strategy to improve the status of women and to modernize religious thought."[36] The detractors of Islamic feminism, they claim, deny women's agency and dismiss the reform movement as irrelevant. They define "feminism" essentially as Anglo-American radical and liberal feminism. The broader notion of a global feminism has no place in their critique.[37]

Women's Struggles against the Legal System

In Iran, marriage before puberty (age thirteen for girls and fifteen for boys) is legal, This simply suggests that males and females will be legally eligible for marriage with a noticeable age difference. This runs counter to the universal standards of human rights, which specify equality in all matters relating to marriage and family relations.[38] According to Iranian civil law, a father or the father's side of the family has the right to enter into a marriage contract for their baby girl or baby boy. Only the father and his side of the family will be in a legal position to cancel such a marriage if they decide that it compromises the boy's or the girl's welfare. The girl or boy will have no say in confirming or denying the choice of her husband or his wife in the future. This legal practice is also inconsistent with Article 11, section (a) of the Cairo Declaration on Human Rights in Islam: "Human beings are born free, and no one has the right to enslave, humiliate, oppress or exploit them, and there can be no subjugation but to God the Most-High."[39]

"Blood money," or *diyah,* is the payment by a murderer to the victim's family in return for the family's waiving its right to insist on the death penalty; *diyah* for women is set at only half of that for men. Also, according to current Iranian civil law, the witness of two females is equal to that of one male. These criminal and judicial rules clearly contradict modern standards of gender equality and human rights.[40]

Freedom of movement is another example of gender discrimination in Iran. Women cannot leave the country without their husband's written consent. Unless mentioned as a marriage condition, women's freedom to choose the place of their residence is limited. These laws run counter to the law relating to the free movement of persons and the freedom to choose their residence and domicile.

Women have also resisted the segregation of knowledge—that is, restrictions placed on studying certain subjects—and educational opportunities in the form of restricted areas of specialization in universities.[41] Under pressure from the Muslim female reformists, the High Planning Council of the Ministry of Culture and Higher Education removed the ban on integration. The influence of modern and reformist thinkers, particularly Ali Shariati, was drastically visible in the ideological and practical activities of the reformist Muslim female elites. Following Shariati, these women have relentlessly maneuvered within the cultural, religious, and political limits of Islamic tradition, seeking a different interpretation to that which has been provided by the clergy. This activism has resulted in an increased autonomy for women vis-à-vis the state's policies and practices. The clerics have arguably failed to organize the conservative Islamic state to reassert cultural identity in a modernizing society that has grown alienated from its cultural traditions . Relying on force and coercive measures to resolve internal sociocultural contradictions has proven counterproductive.[42]

The Rise of Populism: New Forms of Identity and Agency

Iran's 2005 presidential elections demonstrated that for some Iranians concerns about political reform, human rights, and social freedoms were a thing of the past.[43] The elections showed that sociocultural liberalization may backfire in the form of resistance and that there were ethical problems with pushing for pro-market policies without any regard for the lower and middle classes. Questions persist: Whom does privatization or an unbridled free market serve? And who should shape its development? Iran's runoff elections, in which both the poor and middle-class people rejected Ali Akbar Hashemi Rafsanjani as the embodiment of a privileged political class and as the ultimate insider, illustrated that there were enormous cultural and economic gaps in Iranian society.

Moreover, the youth and the poor proved to be the key to Mahmoud Ahmadinejad's victory in the 2005 presidential elections. To the young generation, the fact that any of the candidates had fought the shah and overthrown him in 1979 meant nothing. Born after 1979, these young Iranians had not experienced the shah's repressive regime and were not impressed with the revolutionary credentials and rhetoric of the 1980s. They wanted a candidate who would redress their numerous economic grievances and who could actually provide job opportunities for them.[44] Not surprisingly, campaign slogans that pledged to meet the socioeconomic demands of this generation succeeded more than those promising to safeguard the ideals of the Islamic Revolution. In sum, pragmatism was more significant than ideology.[45]

The flaws of the election process notwithstanding, the 2005 elections demonstrated that reformists have essentially failed to come to grips with reality on the ground. One political analyst put it: "The reformists had forgotten about the poor people."[46] Ahmadinejad, who took more than 61 percent of the vote in the second round, scored a victory that some observers equated with another revolution in the Islamic Republic in which a new generation of hard-liners returned Iran to the fundamentals of the 1979 Islamic Revolution, when the dispossessed and underprivileged were indeed given hopes of a better life.

In a final television appearance before the runoff campaign, Ahmadinejad described the plight of the average Iranian: "making the equivalent of about $150 a month and crushed by bills and inflation hovering around 15 percent, how can such a person have dignity in front of his children and wife?" And "how can a family respect him if he cannot even take care of them?"[47] Ahmadinejad revived the notion of full Islamic identity during his presidential campaign by emphasizing a return to the true Islamic principles of social justice and equality. Contrary to the belief that there was already a movement toward reform and secular nationalism and away from Islamism,[48] a new brand of Islamism (grassroots and populist) was embraced by the lower and middle classes, as evidenced by Ahamdinejad's strong showing in the election.

Not surprisingly, the populists have capitalized on the confusion and contradiction resulting from globalization in a country where religion and high-context culture continue to play a central role in people's lives. The rise of populism will pose equally serious challenges to the women's movement toward gender equality while at the same time redefining the meanings of identities and interests. Clearly, poor economic conditions will prevail over Iran's drive toward social transformation. The reemergence of populism could potentially undermine progress toward cultural politics, social freedoms, and women's rights. The new administration may be reluctant to sign certain international human rights instruments, including the Convention on the Elimination of All Forms of Discrimination against Women (CEDAW, 1979) and the Convention against Torture and Other Cruel, Inhuman or Degrading Treatment or Punishment (1984).[49]

For years, the conventional wisdom held that freedoms and the open social climate espoused during Khatami's era cannot be rolled back. But since Ahmadinejad became president, women, labor activists, and students who have spoken against government policies have been arrested. Academics have received directives to cease contacts with foreigners lest the country go through a velvet revolution. Such a tightened security atmosphere is likely to suffocate any possible change from within Iran. Amnesty International noted that the number of executions had risen from 177 in 2006 to more than 210 in late 2007.[50] Widespread student demonstrations in Iran in November and December 2007 drew particular attention to and protests against the death penalty.[51]

The struggle to gain power and shape identity politics continues unabated, as the conservatives and neofundamentalists appear to have forged a formidable alliance excluding reformists, who have received tacit support from the secularists. While the conservatives hold all formal power, the reformists rely on social and soft power (see Table 6). Islamic conservatives tend to represent Islamic scholars and *ulama*. Their allies, known as neofundamentalists, emphasize themes such as social justice and welfare rights and tend to view Islam as a highly egalitarian religion. Social justice, they note, is the backbone of Islam. It was this message that proved to be an empowering call for the majority of the people who participated in the 2005 national elections. Although many Iranians embrace the notions of social justice and welfare rights, they also tend to adopt a much broader perspective of rights that is notably inclusive of civil and political rights.

Reformists, both inside and outside government, typically define Islamic modernity in terms of the ability to adjust to the imperatives of time and space. Islamic modernists have tried to build a bridge between secular and Islamic domains. In their quest for legitimacy, they have found it essential to adapt to emerging secular, modernizing pressures as well as to transnational standards of morality. Reformists' struggle can best be summarized in one major task: how to balance cultural "authenticity" with cultural "modernity." Islamic reformists also provide a competing alternative to the conceptions of Islam, identity, human rights, and Iran as a static society devoid of internal self-criticism. They argue that internal diversity of perspectives and rights must be mutually recognized and negotiated.

Despite the fact that secularists are not part of the power structure, they provide a dynamic illustration of contemporary Muslim responses to the role of religion in politics and identity formation. The secular intellectuals and writers in Iran are still viewed by many as the "real arbiters of society's creative cultural works."[52] Iranian cinema produced numerous internationally recognized films in the 1990s, some of them by secular producers and filmmakers. Addressing such concerns as the environment, globalization, and the rule of law, secularists point out, is not entirely religious in character. Secularists' participation in shaping culture enraged the

TABLE 6. COMPETITION FOR POWER AND IDENTITY POLITICS IN IRAN

	Goals	Agents	Sites	Strategies
Conservatives	Protecting Custom and traditions (hijab)	Majlis, judiciary system, electronic media, and revolutionary guards/ Basiji	Mosque and community organizations	Seeking local alliances with Islamic populists
Neofundamentalists	Islamist state, Islamic populism, and social justice (committed to revolution)	Presidency and the armed forces	Three branches of the government	Seeking alliance with populist regimes across the globe
Reformists	Struggle for power; promoting democratization, reform, the rule of law, and civil society (committed to reform)	Media, student movements, civil society, women's organizations, and NGOs	Local and transnational NGOs, civil society, media, and student movements	Engaging with reformist ideas and movements across the globe
Secularists	Promoting Iranian nationalism and universal human rights	Intellectuals, writers, feminists, lawyers, and NGOs	National, transnational, and global spaces	Economic globalization and trade with the West

hard-liners, who saw their influence on society as a frontal assault not only on the Islamic Republic institutions and ideals but also on the divine convictions of the people.[53] There is no denying that the power struggle in Iran continues to revolve around the issues of *who* controls modernization, rationality, authenticity, and cultural assets. The domination of power by a particular group or faction, or an alliance of factions for that matter, will strip Iranians of channels of communication and dialogue, from both public and international standpoints.

It is important to recognize that the Bush administration's policy of sanctions and the threat of war toward Iran have lost all credibility in view of the U.S. National Intelligence Estimate released in early December 2007, which contradicted Washington's depiction of the Iranian threat. The Achilles' heel of Iran, however, continues to be its faltering economy. Capital markets are in shambles, investment is at rock bottom, and flight of capital is a lingering problem. Ahmadinejad's populist policies have raised inflation; labor unrest has become more visible across the country. Economic mismanagement and political repression are certain to add to public frustrations in the lead up to future elections for Majles or the 2009 presidential elections.[54]

Poverty in a Rentier State

Results from the elections of 2005 have demonstrated an anti-liberalization tendency by many Iranians who can buy sugar and rice for about one fifth of the retail price. This is a huge savings in a country where more than a quarter of the population lives below the poverty line—which is defined as a family of five with an income of less than $278 a month.[55] Those who participated in the elections sent a strong signal to the religiopolitical establishment that there were serious cultural and economic gaps in the society and that some civil and political rights must take a back seat to the people's overall economic security. According to economists, there is a massive class chasm in Iran, where some 76 percent of the national income goes to just 10 percent of the population.[56]

As in the rest of the world, the economy proved to be a deciding factor in the elections and many Iranians typically voted their pocketbooks. As Mark J. Gasiorowski points out, Ahmadinejad's campaign successfully emphasized the rising gap between Iran's rich and poor and the widespread corruption and rent-seeking that existed there, as well as his own moderate lifestyle.

These themes, Gasiorowski continues, seem to have brought large numbers of lower-class and lower-middle-class voters into Ahmadinejad's camp, including many who did not necessarily share his hard-line views on political, sociocultural, and foreign policy issues.[57] Ahmadinejad's emphasis on attacking inequality and corruption represented a refutation of the Rafsanjani and Khatami years. It should be noted, Gasiorowski cautions, that Iran's macroeconomic performance has been fairly positive and income inequality has been stable in recent years; thus, concern with a widening gap between rich and poor may indicate popular perceptions and mythology more than reality.[58]

Insofar as a cultural gap is concerned, this break stems from the fact that Islamic traditions have always placed social justice above civil-political rights. Religions are not about human rights; they are about ethical teachings, duties, and social justice. Both class and piety mattered in these elections, as the poor and pious largely voted for Ahmadinejad. This shows why Ahmadinejad's key slogan—"Islam without justice is not Islam"—struck a chord with many Iranians tired of corruption and economic decay.[59]

Ahmadinejad's populist message of economic equality won over the promises of neoliberal economic projects espoused by other candidates. Populism and revolt against the ruling elites have returned to the forefront of Iranian politics. This is a reversion to the Islamic revolution à la Ayatollah Khomenei. That the notions of liberal democracy and economic liberalization have yet to resonate deeply with the masses of Iranian people is a matter of simple economics. Iran's economy has been marked by a bloated, inefficient state sector, dominated by a rentier state with overreliance on the oil sector.[60] Direct foreign investment has faced many obstacles in Iran, including uncertainty and the inadequacy of domestic financial markets. The Tehran Stock Exchange has had a negligible impact on attracting foreign direct investment.[61] Ahmadinejad has said that he would spread Iran's wealth by slashing interest rates for corporate investment and also giving Iranians free shares in state-owned enterprises. Regarding the stock market and its transparency, Ahmadinejad has emphasized: "We need the bourse. It is a means of investment and very certainly it will develop with certain forms."[62]

Other experts have argued that unlike Western economies, Iran lacks the institutional infrastructure and the financial landscape necessary to operate an efficient capital market. As a result, Iran's experience with the stock market as the key privatization tool has been mixed. The stock market still lacks a proper signaling mechanism. This is in large part due to the low liquidity power of shares and inadequate disclosure of financial information by companies. These shortcomings must be resolved before the stock market can be used effectively as a privatization vehicle. A new strategy must be developed to stimulate the stock market and to foster broader participation by small investors. This strategy must alter the policy from a narrow focus on enterprise transfer to a larger embrace of revitalization of the stock market and mobilization of private savings to meet privatization objectives.[63] It is hard to conceive of any other solutions outside the realm of those connected to a more market-oriented economy and more efficient economic system and growth.

Although Iranian decision makers have underscored the importance of developing a viable stock market linked to the global economy, the problems of xenophobia and a preference for government ownership have presented major constraints to achieving this goal. More to the point, a concentration of economic power in large companies managing many state-owned enterprises has complicated matters.[64] The group Transparency International has recently ranked Iran about the middle of the pack in its 2004 "corruption perception" index.[65]

Relatively high oil prices in recent years have enabled Iran to collect some $30 billion in foreign exchange reserves, but this wealth has not eased economic hardships such as double-digit unemployment rates (11.2 percent—2004 estimate) and a rampant inflation around 15.5 percent (2004 estimate).[66] Currently, 800,000 Iranian youth enter the job market every year. The Ahmadinejad administration will have to double its job creation plan to meet the work requirements of this cadre, action that would require vast investments and a growth rate of more than 6 percent per year.[67]

Some 80 percent of the economy is state controlled.[68] In the late 1990s, the private sector accounted for only 14 percent of the country's gross domestic product. The remainder came from a combination of the public sector (the government) and the bonyads, institutions unique to postrevolutionary Iran that were set up to control assets held by the former shah's family and associates.[69] Bonyads, which were to operate as nonprofit organizations dedicated to assisting the poor, refuse to publish budgets or other financial statements and are independent from the state-owned enterprises whose budgets are part of the general budget of the treasury. These institutions control a large portion of the economy, have no shareholders, and are accountable only to the country's religious leaders.[70]

The state-owned industrial sector retains many dispensable workers, and there are many who are in fact underemployed.[71] According to one source, Iran's per capita income in 1977 was $2,450. By 2002, it was reduced to less than $1,500, near to that of the Gaza Strip.[72] Under President Muhammad Khatami, living standards continued to plunge. This decline came despite a tripling of world oil prices during the Khatami era.[73] Moreover, during this time, the unemployment rate among university graduates doubled to more than 22 percent. According to Zahra Shojai, Khatami's adviser on women's affairs, during 2000–2002, women's unemployment did increase from 30 percent to 60 percent.[74]

Furthermore, experts held that what really compounds the economic problems is the system of governance. The president, who is constitutionally in charge of dealing with economic affairs, is hindered by a lack of adequate authority to make basic changes.[75] During the 2005 presidential campaign, all presidential candidates (with the exception of Ahmadinejad) talked about privatization without even mentioning the corrupting influences that oil revenues have had on the management of oil resources. The Iranian government determined its long-term budget when the price of a barrel of oil was around $25. At the end of 2008, the price was hovering around $40. Many now demand that the country's national wealth be redistributed in the form of subsidies for the poor and tangible economic benefits in their lives.

Some Implications

The emerging populists on the Iranian scene tend to regard the "globalized vision of society" as detrimental to Islamic values. They question the market-oriented values of globalization and its cultural intrusions in societies where the state is held accountable as the main guarantor of economic and social rights. Experts have generally held that many of Iran's negative economic conditions could have been avoided or easily reversed had Iran's ideological straitjacket been removed from the policy-making process.[76] Many other issues have complicated Iran's economic situation, including the insecurity of individual citizens, the ease and frequency with which laws and regulations are revoked and modified, and the uncertainty about any future course of action.[77] Without a climate of stability, peace, and security, experts argue, people will engage in excessive and imprudent speculative deals that will have negative ramifications for the country's productive capacity and living standards.[78]

If the Ahmadinejad administration chooses to continue along a path of trade liberalization in the form of participation in a regional free-trade bloc, it could face many difficulties in the years ahead. Problems with these regional free-trade blocs, as experts remind us, are several. Trade blocs can increase common tariffs, are an inefficient way of conducting business, subsidize inefficient producers, deny competitive trade with better equipped nonmember countries, and result in the loss of government revenues.[79] Moreover, "members of free-trade blocs," one expert notes, "could potentially limit their access to more advanced and better technologies from the rest of the world. This could result from the promotion of intra-bloc trade that usually is common and pushed by member country governments."[80]

Another implication of Ahmadinejad's populism is that his protectionist agenda seems to be bound up with the notion of subsidies for the disenfranchised. For this reason, Ahamdinejad appears to be less interested in pursuing World Trade Organization (WTO) membership if it conflicts with his populist orientation.[81] The WTO, as such, occupies a less important place in his list of priorities , if for no other reason than that he is primarily concerned with internal ways to improve the economy and to upgrade the lot of the lower income classes. Likewise, even prior to Ahmadinejad's ascendance to power, Iranian officials have separated supporting Iran's membership of the WTO from any incentive to make concessions in nuclear talks.

As Iran has been marginal in exports and imports relative to total world trade, its absence from international and multilateral trade forums, such as the WTO, denies it a forum from which to defend and protect its interests. Being a member of the WTO and a partner in multilateral trade negotiations ultimately means participation in the decision-making process.[82] Similarly, international competition forces Iran to be much more judicious and far less cavalier in its choices of what and how much to produce.[83]

Turning to a different set of implications stemming from Iran's 2005 presidential elections, Michael Ignatieff reminds us of the Iranian paradox: "The Middle Eastern Muslim society with the most pro-American demands will strenuously resist any American attempt to promote democracy inside it."[84] This paradox clearly flies in the face of the so-called Bush doctrine of democracy promotion in the Middle East. Creating democracy with guns and bombs in Iraq, as it is portrayed in the Arab media, has made a secular country the hotbed of radical Islamic groups and has rendered this doctrine flawed in the face of rising insurgency there. To provoke a committed dissident movement via communication equipment of all kinds has proven counterproductive, as evidenced by Iran's presidential elections and the failure of satellite TV to beam rebellious messages into Iranian living rooms.

A congressional appropriation of $3 million to support democratic opposition groups inside and outside Iran, Ignatieff continues, is replete with uncertainties and unforeseen consequences.[85] Revolution via satellite TV from southern California has utterly failed to resonate strongly with the Iranian masses, who today question the sincerity and veracity of the American policy makers' attempt to advance the causes of democracy inside Iran. We are back to the basics: Is outside support the answer?

Applying pressure on the conservative clerical establishment to move toward reform and democratization may not be an effective way to achieve change. Provoking dissidents, however, without a clear plan to support them is equally flawed. While it is important to recognize that the Iranian people themselves must roll up their sleeves to fight for their liberation, it is wrong to assume that the Western world will automatically come to their rescue.

Considerable public discontent may or may not translate into revolutionary behavior, but it clearly enhances the chances of an internal explosion. The U.S. commitment to instigating a "velvet revolution" in Iran has led to a crackdown on human rights advocates, labor groups, and women's rights campaigners. The jailing of several Iranian-Americans—Haleh Esfandiari of the Woodrow Wilson International Center, one of Washington's most prominent foreign policy think tanks; Parnaz Azimal, a reporter of the Radio Farda and Persian Service of the Prague-based Radio Free Europe/Radio Liberty; and Hossuein Moussavian, an expert on nuclear programs—was apparently an Iranian reaction to the Bush administration's $75 million program to promote democracy in Iran, which was unveiled in 2006.[86] Shirin Ebadi, an Iranian lawyer and 2003 Nobel laureate, who dismissed the charges against Mrs. Esfandiari as baseless, argued that "the style of the Revolutionary Court regarding those charged with political crimes is such that it never allows lawyers to meet their clients or to be informed about the charge against them or the reasons for it. All of these actions I mentioned are against the law and we have always protested against such actions."[87]

Under such circumstances, the imposition of democracy from outside as well as throwing money at the problem may prove to be quixotic scenarios in Iran's case. As Ignatieff says, those who are deprived of democracy have much to teach to those who are not. The political task ahead for Iran's liberal thinkers is to find a way to link human rights and democracy to the economic grievances of the needy. We are faced with the old but perennial question: "Can democracy and human rights make any headway at all in a society deeply divided between rich and poor, included and excluded, educated and uneducated?"[88]

In Washington, State Department spokespersons keep comparing the emerging but limited democratic inroads made in Saudi Arabia, Egypt, Lebanon, Iraq, and Afghanistan, while missing the point that the Bush doctrine regarding the greater Middle East and democracy promotion faces formidable challenges and may in certain cases prove to be deeply problematic given the region's political history and culture, lack of institutionalized competition, and economic realities.

Some have speculated the U.S.-Iranian talks on May 27, 2007, in Iraq regarding the Iraqi crisis would lead to rapprochement between the two countries. It is too early to ascertain whether such talks reflect a major political shift on the part of the two governments. President Ahmadinejad continues to face many challenges, including the domestic economy, Iran's foreign policy toward the new Iraq, and Iran's nuclear program. One key question regarding the domestic economy persists: how to promote the privatization of state-owned industries, redistributing the wealth in shares of stock to each Iranian family, while at the same time pushing for subsidies and welfare packages such as health insurance and low-interest loans. Ahmadinejad's protectionist policies might prove to be costly if not disastrous for an economy hungry to join the globalizing world. Quite understandably, the same populist campaign platform that has brought him to power may spell trouble for him if his policies fail to narrow Iran's existing economic divide—a daunting task that no president has ever successfully undertaken in the short history of the Islamic Republic.

Regarding Iran's policy toward Iraq, sectarian and ethnic divisions (Sunni, Shiite, and Kurdish groups) within Iraq will present a new challenge to Iran's foreign and regional policies. From Iran's viewpoint, one expert writes, "a different Iraq requires the Sunnis' share of power to be redefined and balanced."[89] The impact of the engagement of a Shiite majority, characterized by factionalism and divisions, continues to be unpredictable. There is, however, considerable leverage for Iranian influence in Iraq; at the same time this influence could potentially drag Iran into unforeseen crises.[90] Although Iran has attempted to bring balance to the domestic scene in Iraq, different factions within the Islamic Republic try to keep close ties with Iraqi Shiites in order to counter the uncompromising U.S. approach toward Iran.[91] Essentially, however, at the highest levels, Iran has also sought to ease Shiite-Sunni friction in order to better project its leverage as the leader of all Muslims.[92] It is interesting to see what policy Ahmadinejad will choose vis-à-vis Iraq: active neutrality, engagement, or stabilization.

Iran's nuclear program presents another challenge. Unlike Khatami, Ahmadinejad is part of a system that has a complete monopoly over all levers of powers, including executive, judicial, and legislative branches that are now practically controlled by the hard-liners. This monopoly will surely give him more maneuverability vis-à-vis the West. But there are limits to it and he cannot overplay that card. While emphasizing Iran's fundamental right to the peaceful use of nuclear energy and technology, he must make a compelling case before the country's Supreme Security Council for resolving the nuclear standoff with the West.

The approval of UN Security Council sanctions, including a ban on Iranian arms exports and the freezing of the assets of twenty-eight individuals and organizations, has led to a broader consensus to apply pressure on Iran to relinquish its nuclear program. These sanctions would impose travel restrictions on individuals, ban arms sales to Iran, and block new financial assistance and loans to the Iranian government. It is estimated that one third of the people affected by the asset freeze had connections with Iran's Revolutionary Guard.[93] Iran has started enriching small amounts of uranium in more than thirteen hundred centrifuges. Playing on nationalist sentiments, Ahmadinejad has maneuvered the country into a position of strength vis-à-vis the West, although certain political divisions within the ruling elites have surfaced. While many Iranians are against the ruling hard-liners, they support Iran's nuclear program, in part because it is economically warranted and in part because it has become a source of national pride.[94] Some observers have argued that a transparent and democratic Iran could diminish the fears on the part of the West. Hence, linking Iran's nuclear program to its improvement on human rights can be more conducive to confidence-building measures in the long run.[95]

As noted above, however, the prospects for a military confrontation between the United States and Iran have receded with the release of the National Intelligence Estimate report in the United States in December 2007. The report, which was composed by sixteen U.S. intelligence agencies, emphatically concluded that Iran had stopped the military component of its nuclear program after 2003. This revelation exposed the extent to which the Iranian threat had been exaggerated. It has since become evident that the U.S. diplomatic attempts to isolate Iran have also failed. The EU, Russia, and China have resumed trade and commercial ties with Iran. Russia, for example, has continued its efforts to help construct the Bushehr nuclear facility. Likewise, many Persian Gulf countries, such as Saudi Arabia, have moved away from U.S. arguments for isolating Iran.

Conclusion

This chapter has shown that increasing disillusionment with the Rafsanjani and Khatami years has allowed the ascendance to power of a populist president whose message of fighting against growing class disparities and corruption has resonated strongly with the Iranian people. Additionally, sociocultural liberalization programs of the previous years have created a cultural and religious divide among Iranians, generating new demands, interests, and identities among the youth and the poor.

The youth in Iran feel no need, so manifest in the early revolutionary period, to assert another identity, an alternative "modernity" based on outright rejection of Western culture and the embrace of a politicized Islam as the "authentic" solution to all problems.[96] Rather, they feel that it is possible to pick and choose the elements that form an identity based on personal and individual needs and desires. The evolving demands of the new generation have serious implications for the regime of the Islamic Republic: either it must adapt to fulfill the demands of the young or become entirely illegitimate in the eyes of its citizens.[97]

As various discussions and illustrations in this chapter have suggested, understanding gender issues is also crucial to the future of Iran. Iranian women have emphasized their role in the public realm and imposed their own interpretations of Islamic laws and traditions to initiate legal reforms and adjust traditional cultural perceptions of women. They have in fact formed a new identity that is no longer based on tradition. As a result, they now perceive themselves as women and individuals rather than exclusively as mothers and wives.[98] While questioning traditional gender roles and identities, these women are also constructing their own religious models, thus acquiring autonomy vis-à-vis male religious authorities.[99]

Likewise, it is important to recognize that freedom and economic development are inseparable and that political and economic reforms are inextricably intertwined. The reformists' emphasis on political reform to the exclusion of economic reform came under question with the reemergence of populism. For now, however, political reforms have lost their raison d'être but not their vitality in the medium to long run. Economic recovery will most likely be followed by new demands for political reform and basic freedoms. Only time will tell whether the latest rise of populism will endure in a society that is not only rife with corruption and economic degradation but also simultaneously is pressed to come to grips with global economic forces. Ahmadinejad will be hard-pressed to carry out his pledges to the poor, even with unanticipated gains from high oil prices.

The growth of different but conflicting religious and national identities is likely to deepen contradictions inherent in Iranian policy and society. The ensuing tensions will further undermine clerical rulers' legitimacy and performance effectiveness. The formation of sustainable and new identities in Iran remains contingent upon reducing the climate of uncertainty and insecurity in the years to come. Much depends on how such ambiguity and instability is resolved.

Chapter 9

Negotiating Modernity and Tradition in Indonesia

Indonesia is the world's largest archipelago and the fourth largest country in the world. It is also the world's most populous Muslim country, a major producer of oil, and well endowed with natural resources. Its strategic location allows it to control a major waterway between the Pacific and the Indian Ocean. The security of these waterways is crucial to the passage of oil tankers and the international shipping trade. Indonesia is home to a blend of indigenous beliefs and a diverse array of cultures and civilizations as well as a variety of different ethnic and religious groups such as Hindus, Buddhists, Arabs, and Europeans. Indonesia's political and cultural history has been equally influenced by Hindu-Buddhist ideas from India and by Islam.[1]

Islam came peacefully to Indonesia through the trade routes. Despite some battles, Islam eventually settled into regions with Hindu and Buddhist temples and absorbed some of their mythologies.[2] There are more than 490 ethnic groups and 250 distinct languages in this scattered archipelago of some 3,000 islands. Different racial groups, such as Chinese, Arabs, and Europeans, constitute Indonesia's minorities. The major division lies between the Javanese and other ethnic groups as well as between orthodox (*santri*) and local (*abangan*) forms of Islam in Java. Most Indonesians are nevertheless linguistically and culturally part of a larger Indo-Malaysian world encompassing present-day Malaysia, Brunei, the Philippines, and other parts of insular and mainland Asia.[3] Many incidents of brutal communal violence in Indonesia predate the twentieth century, and in modern times, violence has persisted despite some strides made under democratization programs.[4]

Indonesia's ruling elites have constantly managed the country's decentralization and have attempted to resolve, with varying degrees of success or failure, numerous religious and ethnic conflicts, such as the separatist movement in resource-rich Aceh province.[5] President Sukarno (who ruled from 1945 to 1965) and President Suharto (who ruled from 1966 through 1998) institutionalized the tenet that domestic peace in Indonesia required a separation of church, state, and society. Much of Indonesian politics has been influenced by its leaders' attempts to institutionalize and manipulate traditionalist and modernist Muslims.[6]

The 1997 Asian economic crisis and collapse of Asian currencies caused the downfall of Indonesia's Suharto and led to the separation of East Timor as an independent nation-state. It is important to remember that opportunistic leaders of the postindependence era have played on repressed ethnic and religious tensions for political gains. Although clashes between different groups have been blamed on ethnic and religious hatred, economic troubles and political manipulations have been their root cause.[7]

Like the rest of the world, some experts remind us, Indonesia has witnessed a jump in religious vitality. As politics has liberalized in countries such as India, Mexico, Nigeria, Turkey, and Indonesia in the late 1990s, religion's impact on political life has increased vividly. The burgeoning influence of Nahdlatul Ulama (Renaissance of the Ulama or NU) and the Muhammadiya (followers of Mohammad) in shaping Indonesian ideas and society in recent years is typical.

In a 2002 Pew Global Attitudes Survey conducted in some Muslim countries, majorities or pluralities cited Islam as their primary identity, trumping nationality.[8] The upsurge of the new orthodoxies, such as the Nahdlatul Ulama, in Indonesia must be seen in this context.[9] The focus of this chapter is on Indonesia's ethnoreligious, linguistic, and cultural diversity as well as its class and racial divisions. The key to stability and economic growth in Indonesia is moderation of religious beliefs and practices.

As a multiethnic state, Indonesia has had serious concerns about the uneven impact of globalization on its populace, with its ethnic Chinese benefiting the most. Indonesian leaders have argued that globalization could weaken the government and undermine the notion of national identity, posing threats to the nation's social cohesion. Indonesians' concern over eroding values and social cohesion is widespread and legitimate.

A Historical Overview

Indonesia's postindependence era was marked by authoritarianism, state corruption, and economic mismanagement. The diversity of cultures in Indonesia and the historical experience of colonialism had done little to prepare Indonesians for democracy. Neither the Dutch nor the Japanese had helped to ready the colony for self-government. Given its key role in the National Revolution (1945–50), the military became deeply involved in politics.[10] Through thirty years of iron-clad rule, Suharto tried to integrate 214 million people from hundreds of different ethnic groups, spread across an archipelago of 3,000 islands, into a secular, multiethnic state. Indonesia's past did not make this easy. Hindu and Buddhist kingdoms had ruled the region until Islam arrived in the thirteenth century and became the dominant religion. The Dutch seized power in the seventeenth century, embarking on three hundred years of brutal colonial rule and Christian proselytizing that embedded in the culture a deep resentment of outsiders.[11]

Sukarno, the country's first president, crushed separatist movements on Sulawesi and other islands and created a national lingua franca—Bahasa Indonesia—to unify its people. After the political violence of the mid-1960s, Suharto seized power and launched the "New Order."[12] The transition from Sukarno's Guided Democracy to Suharto's New Order marked no shift in the country's authoritarian rule and the suppression of discussion of religion; ethnic differences persisted. The armed forces tried to head off the threat the revival of Islamic nationalism seemed to pose to its entrenched position in the political order. Under Suharto, the country sought to liberalize its economy without addressing the political change unleashed as a result.[13] Even so, during his thirty-two-year rule, as experts concur, Suharto's regime achieved one of the world's most impressive records of economic development.

By the end of 1993, one expert reminds us, Suharto was still struggling to maintain a balance between forces competing for power rather than building a more open society. He used popular demands for more openness as an excuse to contain military power, which Suharto viewed as the key threat to his position. His attempts to preserve his position amid these balancing acts left opportunities for longer-term political change.[14]

The April 1993 labor protests in Medan escalated into an anti-Chinese riot, in which one ethnic Chinese businessman was killed and more than 150 Chinese-owned shops, cars, and homes were destroyed or severely damaged. The eruption of this riot served as a reminder that anti-Chinese resentment was a potentially explosive force in Indonesia.[15] But the coup de grace came in 1998, when student unrest forced Suharto's resignation.

Although the 1997 East Asian financial crisis played a catalyzing role in the regime's demise, the deeper and more fundamental causes of the country's economic troubles and subsequent political turmoil had to do with accumulated institutional and political decay.[16] Suharto had the opportunity to initiate political reforms in the early 1980s after achieving a period of steady economic growth and political order. Instead, his regime failed to reform key political institutions, such as the legal system, and fell far short of opening up the political process. The status quo forces became more deeply entrenched inside the Indonesian state.[17]

The Suharto regime was eventually ousted by the Indonesian people on May 21, 1998. The ending of Suharto's rule was caused, among other things, by his failure to understand the fundamental changes brought about by the end of the Cold War. With the collapse of communism, Suharto's worth as a staunch anticommunist ally of the United States and the West as a whole had noticeably diminished in value. At the same time, Suharto himself underestimated the major changes that Indonesian society had undergone. The emergence of an increasingly large and assertive civil society demanded greater political liberalization and respect for human rights and the rule of the law.[18] Furthermore, as some analysts hold, the policy of the International Monetary Fund (IMF) toward Indonesia hastened Suharto's downfall. The IMF regarded Suharto's interests, associated with his extended family and cronies, as a major barrier to the implementation of necessary economic restructuring in the country. With the IMF withholding aid, Indonesia's economic crisis deepened, resulting in widespread demonstrations and riots and the subsequent downfall of Suharto's presidency.[19] Suharto's rule left a mixed legacy: thirty-two years of repressive rule, which was also accompanied by massive economic development, resulting in better health and educational services and improved living standards for most Indonesians. The 1997 currency crisis in Asia that intensified the country's already collapsing financial system, along with his repressive regime, ended his rule abruptly in 1998.

Despite initiating major political reform, his immediate successor, President Habibie, lacked the necessary legitimacy to survive. Abdurahman Wahid became Indonesia's first democratically elected president in October 1999, but his presidency proved weak and erratic. His government suppressed independence movements in East Timor and in the provinces of Aceh and Irian Jaya. A local political struggle also sparked religious clashes between Muslims and Christians who had lived in peace and harmony for approximately five hundred years in the Moluccas, a chain of islands three hundred miles east of Sulawesi, where more than three thousand Indonesians were slaughtered.[20] In mid-2001, Wahid was forced out of office and

Megawati Sukarnoputri—Sukarno's eldest daughter—ascended to the presidency.

The period since the downfall of Suharto has come to be known as Reformasi (democratic transition), as the role of the military in both business and politics had dramatically declined. In contrast to other Asian countries such as South Korea and Thailand, no successful military-operated business can today be found in the top ranks of Indonesian companies.[21] Increasingly, Indonesians have come to believe that their country's economic progress depends on their leaders' success in tackling an unreliable judicial system, a weak banking system, and corruption.[22]

Islam and the Anticolonial Campaign

Rich traditions of cultural cosmopolitanism and diversity provide a backdrop against which Islamic ideals are conceived throughout Indonesia. Although the vast majority of Indonesians are Muslims, there are considerable minority populations of other faiths, such as Protestant Christian and Roman Catholic communities in North Sulawesi, North Sumatra, and the eastern islands; Hindu communities in Bali; and Buddhist communities in other parts of the country. There are also numerous small-scale traditions that encounter the challenges of globalization and pressures to define themselves in terms of global categories such as "religion."[23] Although the archipelago was not invaded by outsiders and forcibly converted into Islam, states that had converted to Islam often waged war against those that observed the older, Hindu-Buddhist traditions.[24]

At the beginning of the twentieth century, Islam brought together nationalistic sentiments of unity as a common bond against Dutch colonialism.[25] Indonesian Islam is highly eclectic and syncretic, blending its rich Indic heritage in a loose and evolving union with Muslim elements.[26] Since the coming of Islam to Indonesia, religious life has combined with distinctive local Indonesian patterns, creating a vibrant Muslim culture. This culture continually shapes and is shaped by the changing conditions of life in contemporary Indonesia.[27] Historically, Indonesian Islam has been (and continues to be) vigorously cosmopolitan. This is so because Islam came to Indonesia during the thirteenth century through traders who brought with them religious scholars. Religion further permeated the country by elite conversions and political alliances.[28]

From 1300 to 1700, many communities in Indonesia integrated Islam into their local institutions and religious traditions, including educational, political, ethical, and legal systems.[29] With the institutionalization of Islam there, the focus on textual and educational traditions has sustained the dynamic participation of Southeast Asian Muslims within the broader context of transregional Islamic thought and culture.[30]

The writings of Hamzah Fansuri, who lived around the seventeenth century in Sumatra, indicated that Sufism (traditions of esoteric piety) was essential to Muslim cultural history in Southeast Asia. Sufi mysticism and its general tolerance of local traditions fostered the growth of Islam in the archipelago.[31] Throughout centuries, Sufism has been at the core of the integration of Islam and local tradition. Some of the Sufi orders (Tarekat, Qadiriya, and Naqshbandiyah) were among the country's powerful forces engaged in renewing and reforming the individual and society while providing an array of social networks resisting the colonial interests of their time. This legacy lingered on as Islamic networks continued to resist today's global system.[32] During the nineteenth century, resistance movements against Dutch colonialism inside and outside Java appealed to universally expressed—not locally or culturally inspired—ideals of Islam.[33]

The rise of modernist and reformist Islam in Indonesia began with building local educational institutions that paved the way for modernization and social change. Modernist Muslims laid the foundation for an organization called the Muhammadiyah. Founded in 1911 in Jogjakarta, East Java, by Ahmad Dahlan, this organization followed the teaching of Muhammad Abduh. Another association called the Sarekat Dagang Islamiyah (Islamic Commercial Union), which was founded in Jakarta in 1909, promoted Islamic teachings. Later in 1915, this organization became a nationwide political party know as Sarekat Islam (SI).[34]

In the following decades, Sarekat Islam suffered from internal struggles and fragmentation between Islamic, nationalist, and communist factions. The disintegration of Sarekat Islam began in the 1920s, when some Western-educated younger intellectuals, such as Sukarno, chose to form their own political organization in 1927—Partai Nasional Indonesia (PNI, Indonesian National Party). This party based its nationalist argument on the ideological notion of *kebangsaan* (nationalism).[35] Ahmad Hassan and Mohammad Natsir, the proponents of the Islamic ideological school, criticized Sukarno's emphasis on nationalism at the expense of religion. Natsir argued that the struggle for Indonesia's independence should be predicated on devotion to Allah (God) and that the country's nationalism must be Islamic in nature. As such, Natsir introduced the notion of *kebangsaan* Muslim (Muslim nationalism).[36]

Under the Japanese occupation (1942–45), the most influential Muslim organization, known as Masjumi, which was founded in 1943, persevered to shape ideals of Islam, law, and the state-society relations to this day.[37] During the 1950s and 1960s, the spread of Islamic views and ideals continued unabated. The turbulent toppling of Sukarno's government in 1965 was followed by the massacre of tens of thousands of Indonesians. Nearly eighty thousand of Bali's population died in the killing that followed the Jakarta coup of 1965.[38] In fact, more people died in Bali than anywhere else in Indonesia during the killings of 1965–66.[39]

During the 1970s and 1980s, the emergence of a new class of literate Indonesian Muslims led to the nation's mainstream religious revitalization. The new Islamic intellectual and modernist movements, spearheaded by Nurcholish Madjid and Abdurrahman Wahid, focused on modern interpretations of Islam. More popular forms of literature, such as novels and collections of short stories, came to convey ideas of Islamic reform in Indonesia. This approach appealed to several Malay-language authors who represented Islamic reform in the twentieth century, such as Sayyid Shaykh Abdul Hadi and Haji Abdul Malik Karim Amrullah, popularly known as Hamka (1908–89).

Hamka's formal schooling was brief, local, and in Malay and Arabic. To him, the basis of unity of Muslims under Dutch rule was Islam, not a Javanese Hindu past.[40] Hamka's argument, that Islam—not Java—is the basis for the country's unity, potently shook the Indonesian state at the beginning of the twenty-first century.[41] Under the influence of Hamka and other Islamic reformists, a public discourse on Islam has unfolded that extends beyond the circles of classically trained scholars and has become a prominent aspect of modern Indonesian society.[42]

There has also been an increase in the number of local periodicals stressing Islamic issues, including *Panji Massyarakat*, *Dahwah Kiblat*, and *Pesantren*. The works of foreign Muslim writers and intellectuals, such as Ali Shariati, Sayyid Qutb, Abu al-Ala Mawdudi, al-Ghazali, Hassan al-Banna, and Muhammad Iqbal, have been widely published in Indonesia. Following the 1979 Iranian Islamic Revolution, Shii ideas, thoughts, and books were translated into Indonesian.[43] Indonesian Islamic movements emphasize Qur'anic expression, aesthetics, and piety, aspects that allow Muslim diversity as a positive value.[44]

Islam and the State: Politics of Confrontation

Islam played a significant role in twentieth-century Indonesian politics. Given the country's ethnic and linguistic diversity, Islam provided the one common thread for the vast majority of the population. Islam, Fred R. von der Mehden wrote, "differentiated the Indonesians from their Christian masters and gave them a sense of identity with a universal cause."[45] When Japan occupied the Islands during World War II, it sought to foster public support by championing Islam against the Christian Dutch, on the one hand, and directing Indonesian loyalties away from the Middle East and toward an East Asian community, on the other.

The Japanese had sought to unify the Muslims to support its proposed Greater East Asian Co-Prosperity zone.[46] However, Japanese favoritism to the Indonesian Islamic movement provoked a hostile reaction among other nationalist leaders and their followers. Toward the end of the World War II, Indonesian nationalist figures who had not identified with the Muslim movement played an increasingly important role in occupation policies by seeking the abolition of the Masjumi (Consultative Council of Indonesian Muslims).[47]

Early in 1946, the Masjumi joined with other parties, including the Communists, the Partai Nasional Indonesia, the Socialists, and other military and social organizations in a united front against the Dutch. This marriage of convenience fell apart in 1952 when the Nahdatul Ulama (NU) seceded from the Masjumi. The younger generation of the Masjumi, who seemed to be both "Islam conscious" and "Indonesia conscious," drafted a modernist, Islamic, and socialist program that appealed to the short- and long-range socioeconomic needs of the Indonesian masses.[48] In 1960, the Masjumi Party was outlawed for supporting dissident elements fighting the central government.

In the aftermath of the 1965 coup, a large number of communists (400,000 or more) were killed by groups of young Muslims.[49] These tragic events caused the downfall of the Sukarno regime. In the ensuing government led by General Suharto, sharp cleavages developed between elements of the Muslim community and the Suharto regime. The most inflammatory issue arose over the marriage bill of 1973, when the Suharto regime attempted to place civil authority over marriage and divorce.

Under pressure from Islamic groups, the government withdrew the bill.[50] During the 1970s and 1980s, the Suharto government repressed radical Muslim activities. The movement to deemphasize Islam in politics reached its apex when the Suharto administration and its New Order institutions provided the normative and ideological base for the country: all organizations must affirm the state ideology Pancasila, which is based on five principles: belief in one God, national unity, civilized humanitarianism, representative government, and social justice.[51]

Islam and the State: Politics of Accommodation

Failure to create an Islamic state based on Islamic ideology led to shrinking access to power and the declining stature of Muslim political leaders and activists. Many developments contributed to the defeat of political Islam. These included the banning of the Masjumi (1960), the exclusion of its key figures in the leadership of the newly founded Parmusi (1968), and the curtailment of other political parties, which reduced the number of active parties from four—Nahdlatul Ulama, Muslimin Indonesia (MI), Partai Sarekat Islam Indonesia (PSII), and Persatuan Tarbiah Islam (Perti)—to one, the Partai Persatuan Pembangunan (PPP) in 1973. These developments, along with reduced representation in parliament and the cabinet and the denial of Islam as the basis of Islamic social and political organization (1985), further undermined the influence of Islam on the national scene.[52]

During the 1970s, a new generation of Muslim thinkers and activists aimed at transforming the legalistic-formalistic approach into a more substantive and integrative approach. With this strategy, the new Islamists sought to establish a "viable political synthesis between Islam and the state."[53] More and more Muslim political thinkers and activists have participated in both the executive and legislative branches. In the 1990s, there was an increase in the number of Islamic representatives in the parliament, although not necessarily through Islamic parties such as the PPP.[54]

The state's accommodation of Islam has permeated several areas. These include the passage of the education law that made religious instruction mandatory (1988); the passage of a religious court law that strengthened the position of Islamic courts in adjudicating marriage, divorce, reconciliation, and inheritance issues (1989); the establishment of the Indonesian Association of Muslim Intellectuals (Ikatan Cendekiawan Muslim Indonesia—ICMI) (1990); a compilation of Islamic law, a vehicle chosen to address the content of Islamic inheritance law (1991); a joint ministerial decision concerning the *zakat* (religious alms) collection and distribution agency; the reversal of a policy that forbade Muslim female high school students to wear the *jilbab* (headscarf) (1991); the introduction of an Islamic cultural festival, Festival Istiqlal (1991 and 1995); the development of mosques and religious educational institutions; instruction in Arabic on national television; and sending Muslim religious preachers to remote transmigration areas.[55]

Indonesia's moderate Islamists are not Western-educated secularists. Most of them emerged from rural *pesantrans* (religious schools). One such scholar, Ulil Abshar-Abdalla, a leader of the Nahdlatul Ulama, has declared, "We come from within the tradition. We can challenge the conservatives head-on."[56] After Suharto's fall, NU and the Muhammadiyah, with a large membership and networks of schools, provided an essential bulwark against extremists groups such as Lakar Jihad.[57] By mediating between the Muhammadiya and the nationalist parties, NU has helped sustain a multidimensional ideological field that has fostered inter-elite competition, negotiations, and compromises.[58]

An important indicator of the political moderation of Indonesian Muslims has been the decline in popular support for pro-shari'a parties since 1955. In the 1999 elections, according to one study, seven parties won considerable percentages of the vote. Only three of the seven were based on Islam: Hamza Haz's PPP, with 11 percent; the Crescent Moon and Star Party (PBB), with 2 percent; and the Justice Party (PK), with only 1 percent.[59] The remaining four, which together took a convincing 76 percent of the vote, were all committed to the secular state. These included Megwati's PDI-P, with 34 percent; the Joint Secretariat of Functional Groups (Golkar), with 22 percent; the National Awakening Party (PKB), with 13 percent; and the National Mandate Party (PAN), with 7 percent.[60] Golkar was the military-based state party. The PKB, headed by former president Abdurrahman Wahid, was the party of NU that opposed enforcing the shari'a. The PAN was founded by Amien Rais, national chair of Muhammadiyah for much of the 1990s; it received much of its 1999 vote from Muhammadiyah members. Its national board, which included several non-Muslims, vehemently opposed implementation of the shari'a.[61]

According to one survey conducted in 2002, Muslims who were strongly in favor of implementing Islamic law through the state were asked if they would agree to elect representatives who would seek to implement Islamic law. When given this choice, the respondents' support for Islamism dropped sharply from 71 percent to 46 percent. This result demonstrated that only a minority of respondents preferred politicians who advocated the implementation of Islamic law.[62] Moreover, in the 1999 national elections, only 14 percent of voters cast their votes for the three largest Islamist parties—the PPP, the PBBB, or the PK. A sizable majority (67 percent) took a neutral stance toward Islamism, with the remainder (19 percent) in favor of parties or candidates opposed to Islamism.[63]

Identity Politics in Cyberspace

The Laskar Jihad (Muslim Fighters for the Holy War) is one of the Islamist groups that have used the Internet to disseminate information and project an idealized Islamic image while constructing new identities. The Communication Forum of the Followers of the Sunnah and the Community of the Prophet (Forum Komunikasi Ahlus Sunnah wal jama'ah or FKAWJ) formed the Laskar Jihad, which fought Christian groups in the Moluccas in April 2000. Following the September 11, 2001, attacks on the World Trade Towers and other sites in the United States and the Bali nightclub bombing of October 12, 2002, Indonesia has become a center of attention concerning Islamic radicalism. Many recently formed Islamic groups, such as the Islamic Defenders Front (Front Pembela Islam or FPI), the Indonesian Mujahidin Council (Majelis Mujahidin Indonesia or MMI), and the Laskar Jihad, are radical in nature.[64]

These radical Islamist groups use their Web sites, chat rooms, and e-mails to further their ideological agendas. The Laskar Jihad's project is an example. The FKAWJ was founded in 1998 by Ustad Ja'far Umar Thalib of Madurese-Arab descent. Educated in the Middle East and influenced by Wahhabi Salafism, Thalib established the FKAWJ. The military wing of the FKAWJ was the Laskar Jihad, which was established in January 2000 in response to the tragic events that transpired in a Christian-Muslim conflict in the Northern Moluccas in December 1999, when several hundred Muslims were burned alive in a mosque where they had taken refuge.[65]

The Moluccan conflict, which broke out in January 1999, was fought largely along religious lines, between Christians and Muslims. An archipelago in Eastern Indonesia, the Moluccas was plunged into a civil war. As there was no governmental solution to the violence, the FKAWJ entered the picture. The FKAWJ started a jihad in cyberspace (http://www.laskarjihad .or.ed/) in 2000. The FKAWJ seemed to be coordinating online materials and was (and continues to be) surely the most notable speaker and actor for radical Islam in Indonesia on the Internet.[66] In the Moluccan case, the Internet is not only used to disseminate and exchange information about related events but also to broadcast requests for help and calls for common prayers and demonstrations. The Internet has generated a sense of belonging, identity, and companionship—a virtual community—among the Muslims there.[67]

The Laskar Jihad Web site has provided an ideal instrument for identity construction, using a variety of textual and audiovisual material and other site elements such as links, forms, and guest books. Its goal is the creation of an Islamic state and a unified Muslim community in Indonesia.[68] Nevertheless, many Laskar Jihad leaders have distanced themselves from Osama bin Laden as well as Al-Qaeda. In January 2002, the Laskar Jihad stressed emphatically that their organization had no connection to Jemaah Islamiya, which was accused of the Bali bombing in October 2002.[69]

The Asian Currency Crisis

The currency crisis, which started in Thailand in July 1997, spread in Southeast and East Asia and caused economic chaos in these countries as foreign investors withdrew their funds from the region. Shortly thereafter, the currencies of many of these countries depreciated by as much as 80 percent compared to the U.S. dollar, and share prices on stock markets in the region fell by as much as 90 percent.[70] The Jakarta composite Index, which had stood at 711 points in July 1997, plummeted to 406 by June 1998.[71] The financial sectors of many Southeast and East Asian countries became burdened with massive debts and bankruptcy.

The financial crisis created social turmoil resulting from skyrocketing prices, food shortages, and massive unemployment; it led to a political crisis of a magnitude that caused a change of government. A primary target of the unrest was the Chinese minority. Chinese-Indonesians have insisted in the past that their fundamental loyalties are to their current country of residence—not China—and that it is wrong to assume that they hold on to a "double identity" between their "country of residence and that of their ancestors."[72] Even so, there were major riots against the Chinese minority, along with a series of ethnic and religious conflicts in many parts of the country.[73] In all the severely affected countries in Asia, especially Indonesia, Thailand, and South Korea, reformers and political publics came to the somber realization that their political systems, characterized by rigidity, secrecy, and corruption, contributed to their economic liability.[74]

During the Asian currency crisis, Indonesia's private banks failed to recover the loans they had extended. Nonperforming loans, which accounted for 9 percent of all loans in 1996, increased to as much as 61 percent in 1998. Nearly 75 percent of these nonperforming loans were unlikely to be recovered. Some thirty-eight insolvent banks were closed down and seven other banks were taken over by the government.[75] By the end of 1997, 65 percent of all firms in the country had losses that exceeded their equity and were forced to declare bankruptcy.[76]

From 2,388 rupiah to the U.S. dollar in January 1997, the currency depreciated to 2,915 rupiah to the U.S. dollar on August 19, 1997.[77] By October 1998, the exchange rate had reached 4,000 rupiah to the U.S. dollar. Skepticism regarding President Suharto's willingness to implement economic reforms as part of the IMF rescue package resulted in furthering the slide in the value of the rupiah.[78] Following his reelection on March 14, 1998, President Suharto's new cabinet included a number of close confidants and family members, such as Dr. B. J. Habibie as vice president, Mohamad "Bob" Hassan as minister of industry and trade, and his daughter, Siti Hardijanti Rukmana (Tutut), as minister of social affairs. This signaled no major policy or personnel shift in Surharto's administration in the wake of the intensifying financial crisis.

Rising levels of corruption in Indonesia were attributed to two factors: (1) the numerous funds poured into business and real estate, with Indonesia receiving more than US$130 billion in foreign investment from 1988 through 1996 and (2) the impact of the president's family fortune on Indonesia.[79] Corruption, cronyism, and nepotism played a major role in the overthrow of President Sukarno's Guided Democracy in 1965 and in the collapse of President Suharto's New Order in May 1998. Moreover, the financial crisis defied claims by some Southeast Asian leaders that the region's success could be attributed to "Asian values." ASEAN, the Association of Southeast Asian Nations, as a regional organization was regarded as having failed to cope effectively with the economic challenges it faced.[80]

The monetary crisis (*krismon*), along with rising unemployment and prices, led to social unrest and political instability.[81] Public discontent rose as millions of Indonesians were plunged into poverty. In May 1998, student protests and street riots in Jakarta caused nationwide disruptions and erupted into violence. Six student demonstrators at Trisakti University lost their lives in confrontations with the police. On May 18, 1998, students occupied the grounds of Parliament House. The Speaker of the House announced on May 21, 1998, that a broad consensus in parliament held that

President Suharto had to resign. This engulfing crisis forced his resignation shortly thereafter.

Democratic Transition

The currency crisis intensified Indonesia's separatist and sectarian conflicts. Consequently, many Indonesians lost their trust in the ruling elites. Dr. B. J. Habibie, the vice president, was sworn in as the country's third president on May 21, 1998.[82] President Habibie announced more liberal terms for foreign investment, placing key decisions in this regard in the hands of the minister of investment. During President Habibie's seventeen-month tenure, he failed to put Suharto on trial for corruption and to resolve several other high-profile cases of corruption. These shortcomings, coupled with the crisis in East Timor, weakened Habibie's reelection bid by the supreme People's Consultative Assembly (MPR), Indonesia's highest deliberative body, in October 1999.

Nevertheless, Habibie's technological background and instincts for problem solving helped him to focus on legislative and constitutional reforms. Habibie also enjoyed enormous support from modernist Muslim groups. As a non-Javanese, he attracted support outside Java and Bali.[83] The MPR elected two leaders widely regarded as corruption-free: Abdurrahman Wahid as president and Megawati Sukarnoputri, daughter of independence leader and the country's first president, Sukarno, as vice president.[84]

The currency crisis, according to some experts, was the beginning of progress because people's trust in the government could only have been restored by free and fair elections resulting in cultural tolerance, fairness, and effective constitutional safeguards for the disadvantaged.[85] A broader consensus, however, held that Indonesia would experience a period of instability in the short run, largely because no government could meet the Indonesians' rising demands. After the 1997 currency crisis, twenty million people who were just above the poverty line fell precipitously below it.[86] The economic system created by Suharto (1978–97) largely benefited the Chinese-Indonesians. Hence the anti-Chinese sentiment became more readily apparent. This resentment is not new and has existed since the Dutch used the Chinese as intermediaries, thus setting them apart from indigenous Indonesians.[87]

The IMF and the United States, other experts noted, helped force Suharto out of power in an attempt to democratize the country. The post-

Suharto democratic transition has led to a proliferation of women's organizations that are intent on opposing violence and enhancing women's empowerment. Many basic freedoms, however, have been accompanied by extensive disorder and violence from which women have suffered disproportionately.[88] Women's rights continue to be marginalized by political conflict and politicians' larger agendas.

Indonesia has proved to be ill-prepared for democracy. Following the fall of Suharto, President Abdurrahman Wahid and some Nahdlatul Ulama members established the Islamic-oriented National Awakening Party (PKB), known as "the party of the NU Community."[89] Although a secular party, its supporters were exclusively NU loyalists, most of whom were peasant farmers or urban laborers. Wahid and other NU leaders at times used nondemocratic means to respond to any challenges to Wahid's authority.[90]

In April 2001, parliament passed a motion of censure against Wahid on the grounds that he had been involved in an improper state-funds transfer. Wahid's attempt to engineer a state of emergency that would allow him to dissolve parliament failed as the armed forces signaled no enthusiasm for this plan. With Wahid's health declining, his last desperate efforts to shake up the cabinet failed to rescue his rule. On July 23, 2001, the People's Consultative Assembly (MPR) dismissed him from office in a process tantamount to impeachment. Wahid was replaced by Megawati, who took the presidential oath of office the same day.[91] The daughter of Sukarno, Megawati inherited a precarious economic situation and became a symbol of opposition after Suharto had ousted Sukarno in 1967.

Indonesia's 2004 presidential elections dealt Megawati a decisive defeat. A retired General Susilo Bambang Yudhoyono was able to win in the second round of presidential elections in September 2004, defeating Megawati by 61 percent to 39 percent.[92] A widely held consensus after these elections led to the impression that Indonesia seemed to have met the challenge of establishing democratic legitimacy.[93] Yudhoyono restored Pancasila's integrity as a major base of tolerance.

On December 26, 2004, Indonesia was one of the Asian countries that were hit by a massive tsunami and was affected by it far worse than any other country. The disaster struck three months after a new president (Yudhoyono) was elected in Indonesia's first direct presidential election. The military's political fortunes at the time of the tsunami were at a low point. The national mood was against separatism after the loss of East Timor, which was the only part of the country colonized by the Portuguese and

dragged into union by invasion. The military had initiated a series of operations to crush the Aceh insurgency, but ironically, the tsunami presented
an opportunity to resolve the long-standing conflict. In coming to grips
with the reality of reconstruction after the tsunami disaster, one optimistic
view held that we might witness perhaps a foretaste of whether one of Asia's
longest-running civil wars would fade away, overshadowed by a much
greater calamity.[94]

It is worth noting that Indonesia's rich natural endowments have always allayed the fear of the country's rulers about recovering from such
natural calamities. Likewise, if properly utilized, such rich resources could
have enhanced the country's prospects for adopting democratic measures.
Of all the East Asian countries, experts note, Indonesia has the most natural
resources. Suharto had paid little attention to the task of institution building, and the country's low-level per capita income (approximately $2,650 in
1998) made the adoption of democracy immensely difficult at this time.[95]
The new political opening, Fareed Zakaria points out, also brought Islamic
groups to the forefront of Indonesian politics, as nearly one fifth of the
country's parliamentarians described themselves as Islamic politicians.[96] A
fast-paced shift to democracy proved disruptive, as it became increasingly
evident that a slow-paced political reform would have been preferable. It is
important to bear in mind that Suharto had achieved order, secularism, and
economic liberalization of a sort, despite his flawed regime.[97]

Women's Activism and Rising Feminist Power

The Indonesian women's movement historically has been framed, influenced, and constrained by two dominant forces: nationalism and developmentalism. The first women's congress in 1928 emerged at the same time as
the nationalist movement. Most participants framed their struggle in national terms, linking the pursuit of women's interests to those of national
unity and independence.[98] Women's support for independence during
1945–49 won the support of the male-led nationalist movement. The demo
cratic government of the new republic granted several legal rights to women
in areas such as constitutional equality, the right to vote, and equal pay in
the civil service. The nationalist movement under President Sukarno in the
late 1950s and early 1960s overwhelmed the women's movement. One of the
few mass-based women's organizations, Gerwani (Gerakan Wanita Indonesia—Indonesian Women's Movement), undermined the organization's

concerns, while giving up pushing for women's rights in order to support Sukarno's anti-imperialist orientation, in alliance with the Indonesian Communist Party (PKI).[99]

Suharto's presidency embarked upon wide-scale socioeconomic development, which had considerable advantages for the women's movement. The price, however, was the expansion of state feminism—that is, the mobilization of the women's movement by the state. The regime cleansed the women's movement by outlawing women's organizations such as Gerwani. It also controlled the Indonesian Women's Congress, Kowani (Kongres Wanita Indonesia), exploiting it for its own developmental goals. Women's political ambitions were in fact discredited and channeled into the impotent organizations that the state had created.[100] Middle-class women, however, began setting up new feminist organizations that at times claimed to defend the interests of poor women like overseas migrant workers. New Order discourse, however grudgingly, shifted toward the rhetoric of participation, empowerment, and opposition to domestic violence.[101]

As the economic crisis of 1998 intensified, dozens of women activists gathered in the office of the feminist magazine *Jurnal Perempuan* (Woman's Journal), determined to put pressure on the government to alleviate the negative consequences of the economic crisis for women and children. This development, which was followed by a rally on February 23, 1998, and the subsequent arrest of several women activists, along with a growing number of mass protests later, came to be known as the Reformasi movement.[102]

The 1998–99 crises made many women cognizant of their collective power and voice. Women's groups played a significant role in shaping social and political consciousness, in large part because of their strategic location in Jakarta. A pool of intellectuals and activists in Jakarta laid the foundation for organizing women's movements. These movements were spearheaded by Suaran Ibu Peduli (SIP, Voice of Concerned Mothers), Tim Relawan Divisi Kekerasan terhadap Perempuan (TRKP, Violence against Women Division of the Volunteers for Humanity), Koalisi Perempuan Indonesia untuk Keadilan dan Demokrasi (KPIKD, Indonesian Women's Coalition for Justice and Democracy), Komisi Nasional Anti Kekerasan terhadap Perempuan (Komnas Perempuan, the National Commission on Violence against Women), and the informal collectives that organized various peace rallies.[103]

The Reformasi movement demolished the ideological façade of the old regime. The Habibie and Wahid administrations acknowledged the flaws of the old ideas of tightly centralized nationalism and rapid economic growth.

They made conciliatory gestures toward the rising tide of regional dissatisfaction with Jakarta and tolerance of pluralism, realizing that they would be unable to buy off opponents with the gains of economic growth.[104] President Habibie issued a presidential decree setting up the National Commission on Violence against Women in response to the rapes, primarily of Chinese women, that occurred during the violent riots of May 13–15, 1998 and led to the fall of Surharto's regime. During these riots, with the Suharto regime on the brink, Chinese women in several districts of Jakarta were gang-raped by unidentified men. An essay surveying patterns of gendered violence in Indonesia in the 1998–99 issue of *Jurnal Perempuan*, suggested that the Indonesian Army had systematically used rape and sexual violence as a weapon of war against women political activists and the wives and female relatives of male activists.[105] The race-rapes in Jakarta became a central point of struggle for the Indonesian women's movement, which was in the process of forming its vision of itself and its future.[106]

Habibie's successor, President Abdurrahman Wahid, redefined the women's ministry, naming it the Ministry for the Empowerment of Women. Wahid appointed Khofifah Parawangsa to head the ministry.[107] Little progress, however, was made under Wahid on harmonizing Indonesian law with further UN human rights instruments besides those on antitorture and racial nondiscrimination that had been agreed to by the Habibie administration.[108]

Megawati Sukarnoputri's presidency (2001–4) failed to successfully address the main issues facing Indonesian women, such as female trafficking, the plight of women migrant workers, violence against women, and women's participation in politics. The biggest defeat for the Indonesian Women's Coalition for Justice and Democracy was the rejection by Megawati and parliament of the coalition's proposal that 30 percent of the parliament deputies (MPs) should be female. In recent years, women have occupied just 8 percent of the seats in parliament—a situation that indicates women's influence in shaping policies is woefully inadequate. Megawati's failure to promote women's rights and interests can be attributed, among other things, to the country's male-dominated political culture and the inferior position and role of women there.[109]

President Susilo Bambang Yudhoyono (2004–) is the first directly elected leader of Indonesia and is known as the personification of a tolerant Islam. In a speech in June 2006, he reasserted the notion of a state ideology (Pancasila), which is generally viewed as the country's commitment to secular government and of unity in diversity. Yudhoyono argues that Indonesia is a religiously neutral state in which shari'a (Islamic law) is largely confined to family law. When some strongly Islamic regions introduced more comprehensive shari'a-inspired regulations, such as dress codes and bans on alcohol and gambling, Yudhoyono did not support them. Yudhoyono included four women in his thirty-six-member cabinet. Many women's organizations argued that four women in the cabinet were not enough and that women's access to the political arena was routinely blocked.

The history of women's activism in Indonesia, according to Susan Blackburn, points to one reality: that the women's movement is weak in relation to the state in Indonesia. Only when the state has been weak have women had more freedom to organize, but even then they had to rely principally on their own resources. Women have achieved some goals in ways that do not directly involve the state.[110] But societal power dynamics, Blackburn continues, cannot be ignored: "Much can be done at the grass-roots level, through economic, social and cultural activism, to improve women's lives. Nevertheless, there will always be a need to influence state policies, at the very least to shelter women from some of their worst effects."[111]

Indonesian women feel ambivalent about globalization. The Asian financial crisis of 1997 had many negative repercussions for women's employment and welfare status. Likewise, the IMF's requirements that the government cut subsidies have adversely affected women. On the other hand, Indonesian manufacturing has benefited immensely from foreign investment, the increasing volume of world trade, and the opening up of export markets—and this sector is a key employer of women. Female migrant labor is likely to continue to grow and sex trafficking is on the rise.[112]

On balance, it is fair to say that the women's movement has often lacked a strong basis in society and has been fragmented.[113] Gender identities are complex, ranging from women's seclusion in local communities to their participation in the workforce in a globalizing economy. This complexity, coupled with women's limited possibilities for formal political participation in a country besieged by economic and political turmoil, makes it difficult to identify and articulate instances of female agency in Indonesia.[114] The women's movement in Indonesia is in transition. Ideologically, nationalism and developmentalism have lost their appeal. Regional diversity and ethnic separatism have asserted themselves. No universal ideology appears likely to gain prominence in Indonesia. Rather, there are competing paradigms, including human rights, Islamic models, and international feminism. Shifting and transient alliances have been and continue to be forged between organizations on particular issues like opposition to violence against women.[115]

The Political Arena: Competition for Power

There is no denying that Islam is and will remain one of the central elements of the Indonesian political landscape. Indonesian Islam continues to be a moderate, domesticated, and tolerant form of Islam. For half a century, Indonesia was governed by a complex power structure influenced by the military elites, businessmen, and feudal lords. The army and secular governments co-opted Islamic groups during this period. In the 1980s and 1990s, however, Islamic movements grew dramatically in Indonesia, as the political arena featured competition between and among Islamic groups (conservatives, reformists, neofundamentalists), secular nationalists, and the military.

Today, the country's ruling elite face the dilemma of how to achieve multicultural tolerance in the face of a surging Islamic revival. There are several basic Islamic orientations within the Indonesian Muslim community, with varying adherence to shari'a, pluralism, and religious tolerance. The indigenized Islamic orientation is a culturally integrated Islamic view that is prevalent among Indonesians living in east and central Java. Known as Javanists, these Indonesians rely on observant and learned Muslims to conduct major rituals. The members of this group constituted the core supporters of Megawati Sukarnoputri and her Democratic Party of Struggle.[116] The most conservative Muslim groups in Indonesia are represented by the Nahdlatul Ulama, which comprises Islamic scholars and their disciples. This group provided the political base for President Abdurrahman Wahid. Following the fall of Suharto, Wahid and other NU leaders established the National Resurrection Party. Although this is a secular party, its support came largely from NU loyalists, who were peasants and farmers or urban laborers.[117]

Wahid argues that Islam has served as a uniting force for many Indonesians across the archipelago and has become a key to the formation of the unitary state of the Republic of Indonesia. In a country that is both multiethnic and multireligious, Wahid continues, Islam has been culturally all-embracing and tolerant of differences. What distinguishes Indonesian Islam from other forms, Wahid insists, is that in Indonesia "religion serves more as moral support than a state ideology."[118] This moral rather than ideological template defines what it means to be a mainstream Indonesian Muslim. Islam in Indonesia has always fought against outside powers as well as local tyrants, mobilizing millions of Indonesians against oppressive authority.[119]

Islamic modernist groups and organizations are diverse and tend to push for a more explicitly Islamic political and social system through participation in the democratic process. One such group, known as Muhammadiyah, constitutes the largest modernist Muslim movement in Indonesia. The members of this group have refrained from direct involvement in politics. Other modernist organizations have had a more explicit political agenda. These include contemporary political parties, including the Partai Bulan Bintang (the Star and Moon Party) and the Partai Keadilan (the Justice Party), which have been active in politics.[120]

What is unique about identity politics in Indonesia is that the conservatives and the reformists work together and their Islamic agendas often overlap. For many Indonesian Muslims, to be Indonesian simply means to embrace an Islamic identity that clearly avoids being entangled in the complexity of power relations. Consider, for example, the two leading Muslim organizations, the Nahdatul Ulama and Muhammadiyah, which together have seventy million members, pursue different approaches to identity politics as noted above, but nevertheless concur on one thing: they both question the viability of an Islamic state not only in Indonesia but throughout the Muslim world. Concerned primarily with personal religiosity and community service, these two largest Muslim organizations have been big winners in the transition to democracy since Suharto's downfall. Their leading Muslim intellectuals, such as Norcholish Madjid and Amien Rais, a former speaker of parliament (People's Consultative Assembly—MPR during 1999–2004) and leader of the National Mandate Party (Partai Amanat Nasional—PAN), have consistently questioned the existence of an Islamic state according to the Sunnah—that is, based on the way and the manners of the Prophet Mohammad (see Table 7).

The Indonesian radical Islamists, largely represented by the Laksar Jihad Ablus Sunnah wal Jammah (Holy War Brigade of the People of the Muslim Community and Tradition) and the Jemmah Islamiyah (Islamic Community), provide a discourse centered on jihad and shari'a. Al-Ustaz Ja'far Umar Tholib, the leader of Laksar Jihad, is a veteran of the Afghan war who later received an Islamic education in Pakistan. Vehemently anti-

Table 7. Competition for Power and Identity Politics in Indonesia

	Goals	*Agents*	*Sites*	*Strategies*
Conservatives	Protecting custom and traditions *(hijab)*	Nahdlatul and Muhammdiyah *ulama*	Mosque and community organizations	Seeking local alliances with reformists and politicians through democratic processes
Neofundamentalists	Creating a theocratic state	Jemmah Islamiyah and Laskar Jihad	Mosque, local, and transnational communities	Grassroots activism via identity politics
Reformists	Pluralistic power sharing with secularists (neither theocratic nor Islamic state)	ICMI, Muslim intellectuals (Nurcholish Madjid and Amien Rais), and President Wahid	Local and transnational NGOs, civil society, media, and student movements	Seeking ideas, allies, and intercultural dialogue with the West
Secularists	Pancasila and national unity	Nationalists, human rights activists, lawyers, and the military	National, transnational, and global spaces (the Internet)	Economic globalization and trade with the West

Western, this group's members reject democracy and the secular state as un-Islamic.[121]

Neomodernist movements in Indonesia represent a new and different group of Muslims who are concerned more with Islamic values and ethics than with shari'a. Ironically, the proponents of this group come from both modernist and traditionalist backgrounds. A new generation of Muslim scholars has emerged, with strong theological and political commitments to democracy, Islam, and cultural pluralism.[122] Debate among Indonesian intellectuals about the role of Islam in society revolves around the secular ideology of Pancasila and its relevance to Islamic beliefs.

The strength of the Islamic resurgence in the 1980s captured the attention of Suharto and his advisers. As Suharto began to cultivate Muslim allies as a countervailing strategy against a growing opposition from the military, he found it even harder to forge a consensus among diverse Muslim groups. Under such circumstances, Suharto facilitated the creation of the Ikatan Cendekiawan Muslim Se-Indonesia (ICMI—the Indonesian Association of Muslim Intellectuals) in 1990—a move that fundamentally altered the New Order politics.[123] But ICMI was divided and never attained a unified position. Dissatisfied with ICMI's independent positions, Suharto shifted his patronage to ultraconservative Muslims, a strategy that had tragic consequences for his regime at the end. Suharto's actions also "reintroduced bitter sectarian divides into a military and a bureaucracy earlier purged of religious divisions."[124]

The failure of the Suharto regime in 1998, aggravated by the Asian economic crisis of 1997, was followed by a period of reform. The new politics reflected the split among nationalists, Islamists, and the military. Abdurrahman Wahid and his party attempted to move toward a more pluralist Islamic alliance in an attempt to win Muslim votes, thus emerging as a key power broker. Wahid's presidency (1999–2001) failed to create a consensus among different groups—secular-nationalists and Islamists. His resignation in July 2001 was attributed, among other things, to his erratic statecraft.[125] The subsequent government of Megawati Sukarnoputri attempted to pursue a pluralistic power-sharing arrangement with opposing groups. Her government, however, failed to address the nation's growing economic problems, snuff out government corruption, and reduce deep ethnic, social, and religious divisions as well as eradicate secessionist moves. Many Indonesians viewed Megawati's government as woefully weak.

In September 2004, Susilo Bambang Yudhoyono, an Indonesian retired military general and statesman, became the sixth president of Indonesia. Yudhoyono, who defeated incumbent President Megawati Sukarnoputri, has stridently refuted identity politics (having to do with ethnicity, religion, or class), arguing that such politics weakens the nation and its spirit of pluralism and tolerance. Although he espouses the state's accommodation of certain elements of Islamic law, such as on matters relating to marriage, divorce, endowment, and inheritance, he strongly opposes statist Islam—that is, a legalist and formalist political Islam.

Secular nationalists embraced the widely regarded notion that Indonesia is neither a theocratic nor a secular state, underscoring the importance of state policies to accommodate the interests of all Muslims.[126] At the same time, given the country's diverse socioreligious origins, Indonesian Muslims have found it imperative to articulate their interests in line with the Pancasila and national unity (see Table 7). Resorting to authoritarian and exclusionary politics, especially in relation to Islamic groups, will not bring stability nor is it a political agenda the military and secular nationalists covet. A national dialogue regarding the proper role of religion in the Indonesian state is both desirable and necessary.[127]

Conclusion

Most Indonesian Muslims are politically moderate and their various attitudes toward democracy reflect perennial struggles and debates over Islam's role in the country's politics, society, and human rights conditions. It is widely believed that Indonesia is neither a theocracy nor a secular state. Often, the Islamic agendas of the conservatives and the reformists intersect. For many Indonesian Muslims, an Indonesian identity is predominantly influenced or shaped by a state ideology based on national unity. Different Islamic ideologies exist but they are typically subsumed under a much broader national identity. Both the NU and Muhammadiyah activists have proven tolerant of religious differences and have displayed strong commitments to embracing democratic values and an Indonesian identity. The country's state ideology—Pancasila—has met resistance, as a minority of Muslims prefer to receive their schooling in residential learning centers, not public schools. In the Indonesian context, a different type of Islam is practiced, one that is less ideological and more practically and intellectually relevant to the needs of the country's Muslim majority.

The pervasive networks of progressive Muslim civil society organizations, led by the NU and Muhammadiyah, have had a moderating and democratizing influence on most Indonesian Muslims.[128] Islam is and will remain one of the most basic components of Indonesian identity. Indonesians' sense of patriotism and nationalism has also held the nation together, even as numerous political and economic crises have often edged the country toward disintegration.[129] Times of stability, as experts remind us, offer the best prospects for long-term policy formulation and planning, but whether women can effectively exploit these opportunities may depend heavily on state gender ideology and on the strength of the women's movement itself.[130]

The key to the country's political stability is an effective mediation by the ruling elites between Islamists and secularists. The intellectual transformation of Islamic political ideas and practices—from formative and legalistic to substantive and ethical—has led to an evolving stance of the state toward Islam. The emphasis on the state ideology—Pancasila—is grounded in the country's social, cultural, and religious heterogeneity.[131] But it is also a device by which to maintain a balance between accommodation and conflict. Although Indonesian leaders have generally encouraged bargaining and ideological pluralism, their political habits have proven deeply sectarian and often authoritarian.[132] The country's weak economic governance and flimsy financial governance have in the past intensified periods of financial crisis in Indonesia.

Finally, globalization has created a battle of ideas over defining the soul of Islam in Indonesia, as Islamist groups' push for a return to a purer form of Islam has gained wider appeal. In the post-Suharto era, however, most Indonesian Muslims do not appear to be in favor of implementing a formalist conception of the shari'a. Rather, they prefer to stress the ethical and social justice aspects of the shari'a.[133] Given the country's ethnic, religious, and cultural diversity, the vast majority of Indonesian Muslims are steadily moderate in their political views.[134] This moderation renders negotiating modern and traditional praxis not only feasible but sustainable.

Chapter 10

Construction of Muslims in Europe: The Politics of Immigration

Immigration has become one of the most significant political issues facing Europe, and Muslims have become the most important "other" in European public discourse. To better understand why, it is especially important to put in context the processes leading to the postwar reconstruction of Europe. The dynamics of reconstruction and its economic integration in the postwar period have led not to the growth of genuine "multiculturalism" and a "model of tolerance" but to emerging identity clashes between Europeans and their Muslim immigrants.

During the postwar period (1945–70), Europe relied heavily on migrant laborers to generate economic growth. The recession of the 1970s triggered rising unemployment and forced European governments to demand that this large pool of laborers go home. These migrant laborers, mainly Turks in Germany and Austria, proved unwilling to leave. By the 1990s, Germany, Austria, and Switzerland had begun to move toward providing citizenship to these minority laborers.

Since the 9/11 attacks on the United States, several contradictory trends have emerged in the Western world. On the one hand, we have seen the spread of Islamophobia and the increasing distrust and suspicion of the Muslim presence in the West. European societies have increasingly "converged in constructing Islam as a domestic threat to cohesive citizenship."[1] Their key political concern with the immigration issue arises from the perceived connection between international terrorism and Muslim immigrants. The designation "foreign enemy," previously applicable only to those outside Europe, has been increasingly applied to certain targeted domestic groups such as students or religious leaders. This so-called campaign against terrorism is likely to have significant consequences for Muslims living in Western countries.[2]

On the other hand, such a negative perception of Islam in European public opinion has created new opportunities for Muslims to express their own identities, claims, rights, and interests. For many Muslims, racism, discrimination, intolerance, and other kinds of injustice have generated a sense of shared vulnerability, of belonging to a community of suffering and exclusion. Religion has become a significant marker of identity and this sense of shared experience has led to the renewal of the idea of *umma* (community) in a non-Muslim context.[3]

Islam is now the second-largest faith in eight of the EU countries and an integral part of Europe. This situation has raised several questions, including whether Muslims can be incorporated as citizens and whether Islam is compatible with European political values.[4] Yet Europeans have failed to promote national identities in the immigrant communities. Ethnic and regional identities continue to persist. Additionally, one survey in the United Kingdom revealed that despite the fact that Muslims make up only a fraction of the total British population (less than 3 percent), "more people attend Friday prayers than go to Sunday church."[5]

Second- and third-generation Muslim immigrants continue to see themselves more as Muslim European and less as Algerian, Moroccan, or Turkish. As countries across Europe grapple with how to assimilate their second- and third-generation Muslims, a wide array of issues has added to worries that the increased presence of immigrants in Europe is destabilizing the continent's democratic process of integration-but-not-assimilation. These include the ban on headscarves in French schools, the possibility of Turkish membership in the EU, the difficulties of the Dutch model of "integration but not assimilation," France's failing integration model, and the cartoon episode in which the Danish newspaper *Jyllands-Posten* published twelve editorial cartoons depicting the Islamic Prophet Mohammad on September 30, 2005, leading to a widespread uproar in the Muslim world.

While some view the Muslim presence as a real threat to security (terrorism), others frame the threat in economic terms (jobs). Still others regard the key issue as an identity clash and the perceived cultural threat that Islam poses to the European way of life.[6] In this chapter, we will examine different types of identity formation (separate but equal, different but equal, respect and recognition, and resistance and protest) as well as different European models (assimilation and multiculturalism) to deal with the immigration issue.

Colonialism

The rise of political and cultural Islam in Europe can be traced to a form of anti-imperial opposition and identity. An influx of immigrants from European colonies provided cheap labor for European factories. The continued presence of Muslim guest workers in Europe rarely led to their gaining citizenship in the host country. Muslims in Europe, according to analysts, are a "voluntary minority," in contrast to those groups that became minorities in the wake of an occupation or invasion or other form of compulsion—such as slavery in the case of African Americans in the United States.[7]

Although for most of these immigrants, their original intention was a temporary stay, over time their presence developed into a de facto permanent immigration. Their relations with the host countries are conflicted. Many immigrants are unwilling to renounce their original citizenship, even though adopting the new citizenship would bring numerous practical advantages and would most likely be a more accurate reflection of the new center of their family's life and future.[8]

Most Muslims in Western Europe essentially came as migrant laborers or as refugees. They migrated because the economic opportunities were far better than in their countries of origin or because they fled political repression or war. Of the latter group, many stayed even when the military or political situation significantly improved at home. Europe offered safety, freedom, refuge, and an improvement in their overall life.[9]

Nonetheless, a combination of factors, such as unemployment, ghettoization, and social marginalization, has excluded Muslim immigrants from the mainstream European culture. Muslims are disproportionately at the margins of the school system. In Germany, for instance, large numbers are likely to end up in *Sonderschulen*, schools intended for mentally handicapped children. This is largely because language difficulties and behavioral problems attributable to unsuccessful assimilation render them unwelcome in the regular schools.[10]

Muslims are more severely affected by unemployment than the rest of the population. In 2004 in Germany, Turks had the highest unemployment rate: 20 percent.[11] Social marginalization has created a generation of young Muslims resentful of discrimination and ready to join Islamic groups, where they are kept away from drugs, alcohol abuse, and violent street gangs and crime, and where they are given a sense of importance and value.[12]

Diasporic Muslims: Demographics

A quick glance at the demographic dynamics of the Muslim diaspora in major Western countries is instructive. Birth rates have fallen below replacement rates among native-born Europeans in several countries, with no sign that this trend will reverse itself. The Continent's Muslims, however, stand in stark contrast to this trend. Europe's Muslims are considerably younger than its non-Muslims, and their overall birth rate is roughly three times as high. Given continued immigration and high Muslim fertility rates, Europe's National Intelligence Council estimates that by 2025, the Continent's Muslim population will double.[13]

According to a 2000 UN projection, the EU states would need 949,000 immigrants a year to maintain their 1995 population, 1,588,000 a year to maintain their 1995 working-age population, and a stunning 13,480,000 a year to maintain the 1995 ratio of working-age to retired residents.[14] Nevertheless, a volatile mix of European xenophobia and immigrant dissidence challenges these countries' national cohesion.[15]

More than twenty-three million Muslims reside in Europe, composing nearly 5 percent of the population, according to the U.S. Department of State's *Annual Report on International Religious Freedom 2003*. When Turkey is included, the figures jump to ninety million and 15 percent, respectively.[16] The waves of immigrants and asylum seekers from the Middle East and North Africa (MENA) have had more to do with the deteriorating economic conditions in the MENA countries than with labor shortages in Europe, a region with the world's lowest fertility rate.[17] Today, nearly 50 percent of Muslims in Western Europe were born there.[18]

Thirty-three percent of France's six million Muslims are under the age of twenty—compared to 21 percent of the French population as a whole; 33 percent of Germany's three million Muslims are under eighteen—compared to 18 percent of the German population as a whole; 33 percent of the United Kingdom's 1.5 million Muslims are under fifteen—compared to 20 percent of the British population as a whole; and 33 percent of Belgium's 364,000 Muslims are under fifteen—compared to 18 percent of the country's population as a whole.[19]

Some analysts have predicted that if current trends continue, Muslims could outnumber non-Muslims in France and perhaps in all of Western Europe by mid-century.[20] At the same time, we will be witnessing a dramatic decline of the general European population, which will fall by more than 100 million from 728 million in 2000 to approximately 600 million, and possibly as low as 565 million, by 2050.[21]

Europe's largest Muslim diaspora community is in France, which has an estimated six million Muslim immigrants.[22] These Muslims have migrated to France predominantly from Algeria, Morocco, and Tunisia. Because of a reduced workforce after World War II, France recruited immigrants from its North African colonies to work as laborers. The first migration wave took place between 1914 and 1918, during World War I, as these immigrants provided labor for industrialization and mining. In 1920, the demand for labor increased for postwar reconstruction.[23] Until 1960, a majority of Muslim immigrants were Algerian from the Tizi Ousou, Setif, and Constantine regions. Whereas in the 1970s, those who migrated to France in large numbers were male, in the 1980s, most immigrants were women and children.[24]

The second largest concentration of Muslim migrants in Europe is in Germany, where there are nearly three million Muslims, who are largely Turks and Bosnian Muslims, especially following the civil war in the former Yugoslavia.[25] Turks make up 67.9 percent of the immigrants, Bosnians 5.6 percent, Iranians 3.9 percent, and Moroccans 2.7 percent.[26] Because of labor shortages after World War II, Germany entered recruitment agreements with Turkey in 1962, Morocco in 1963, and Tunisia in 1965. The second wave of Muslim immigrants began in the mid-1970s.[27]

The 1962 agreement with Turkey was based on the understanding that Turks would not become Germans; they will remain *gastarbeiter* (guest workers). Permanent residence in Germany was never regarded in the 1962 agreement, and the tacit understanding was that Turks would only "temporarily" reside in Germany and that they would ultimately return to Turkey. It was not coincidental that the bilateral agreement for recruitment between the two countries was concluded in 1962, shortly after the construction of the Berlin wall, which effectively ended the influx of East German labor.[28]

The third-largest Muslim diaspora community is in England, which is home to an estimated 1.5 million Muslim immigrants, who are largely from Pakistan, Bangladesh, India, and the Black Caribbean.[29] The history of their immigration can be traced back to the colonial period.[30] There are approximately 1 million Muslim migrants in Italy. They are largely from Albania, Algeria, Bangladesh, Bosnia, Egypt, Iran, Morocco, other parts of Yugoslavia, Pakistan, Senegal, Somalia, Tunisia, and Turkey. The first wave of immigration to Italy began in the 1970s. During the 1980s and 1990s, immigrants arrived from the Maghreb, sub-Saharan African countries, Al-

TABLE 8. MUSLIM POPULATION IN SELECTED EUROPEAN UNION COUNTRIES

	1982 (millions)	2003 (millions)
France	2.500	5.000
Germany	1.800	3.000
United Kingdom	1.250	1.600
Spain	0.120	1.000
Italy	0.120	1.000
Holland	0.400	0.886
Belgium	0.350	0.364
Sweden	0.035	0.350
EU + Turkey	62.900	90.300

Sources: Ross Douthat, "A Muslim Europe?" *Atlantic Monthly*, January–February 2005, pp. 58–59; Timothy M. Savage, "Europe and Islam: Crescent Waxing, Cultures Clashing," *Washington Quarterly* 27, no. 3 (Summer 2005): 25–50, esp. 27.

bania, other Middle Eastern countries, and Latin America. Eastern Europeans began migrating to Italy in the 1990s, when the Cold War ended[31] (see Tables 8 and 9 below).

Diasporaic Muslims: Transnational Islam

The growth of the Muslim diaspora during the last quarter century has been marked by a rise in internal strife in their countries of origin and border disputes. This diasporic movement is distinct from the merchant trading and indentured servitude that have historically been the legacy of transnational Islam.[32] Some experts, such as Peter Mandaville, argue that diasporic Muslims in Europe have constructed a form of identity that can be called "interstitial identity" ("a third space"): one that participates neither in the politics of the majority non-Muslim society in which they reside nor in the politics of the country of origin. This creates, especially among the younger generation, forms of hybridized political identity that can be conceptualized as somehow in-between. Because of the context of translocality, in which these identities travel, a new mode of "relating internationally" is set in motion in which the boundaries of political community are invariably subject to re-articulation.[33]

Gone are the days when Muslims were obsessed with the somatics of prayer and correct bodily practice. At issue now are the wider questions concerning Muslim identity and relations between Muslims and non-

TABLE 9. EUROPEAN MUSLIM POPULATION

Country	Total Population in 2005 (millions)	Muslim Percentage	Muslim Population in 2005 (millions)
Northern Europe			
Denmark	5.40	3.02	0.16
Estonia	1.30	0.70	0.01
Finland	5.20	0.18	0.01
Iceland	0.30	0.04	0.00
Ireland	4.10	0.01	0.00
Latvia	2.30	0.38	0.01
Lithuania	3.40	0.14	0.00
Norway	4.60	1.04	0.05
Sweden	9.00	3.10	0.28
United Kingdom	60.10	2.50	1.48
Western Europe			
Austria	8.20	2.23	0.18
Belgium	10.50	3.60	0.37
France	60.70	10.00	5.98
Germany	82.50	3.70	3.06
Liechtenstein	0.04	3.43	0.00
Luxembourg	0.50	1.10	0.01
Monaco	0.03	0.50	0.00
Netherlands	16.30	5.40	0.87
Switzerland	7.40	3.10	0.23
Eastern Europe			
Belarus	9.80	0.10	0.01
Bulgaria	7.70	11.87	0.89
Czech Republic	10.20	0.20	0.02
Hungary	10.10	0.10	0.01
Moldova	4.20	0.20	0.01
Poland	38.20	0.10	0.04
Romania	21.60	1.00	0.22
Russia	143.00	19.00	27.65
Slovakia	5.40	0.02	0.00
Ukraine	47.10	4.07	1.95
Southern Europe			
Albania	3.20	70.00	2.17
Andorra	0.10	0.63	0.00
Bosnia Herzegovina	3.80	60.06	2.34
Croatia	4.40	3.00	0.13

TABLE 9. (Continued)

Country	Total Population in 2005 (millions)	Muslim Percentage	Muslim Population in 2005 (millions)
Greece	11.10	1.50	0.17
Italy	58.70	2.40	1.37
Macedonia	2.00	30.00	0.63
Malta	0.40	1.10	0.00
Portugal	10.60	0.50	0.05
San Marino	0.03		
Slovenia	2.00	1.55	0.03
Spain	43.50	1.20	0.50
Yugoslavia (Serbia and Montenegro)	10.70	19.00	2.03
Total	**729.70**	**14.33**	**50.90**

Source: "European Muslim Population," available at http://www.islamicpopulation.com/ europe_islam.html, last accessed on June 9, 2006.

Muslims. Reflection and comparison allow Muslims to develop their own reactions to the challenges of modern life in the West. To that end, they have developed something akin to a liberation theology that "allows them to be European without breaking with Islam."[34] "Western translocalities," Mandaville writes, "offer the aspiring Muslim intellectual the opportunity both to *express* and *encounter* alternative readings of Islam."[35]

As a result, diasporic Muslims in the West have come to know the Muslim other. The upshot has been dialogue, self-reflection, and a critical renewal of Islam. In short, as a collective exercise, we are seeing the deconstruction of Islam by Muslims themselves. It is not difficult to see why many Muslim opposition leaders from Bahrain, Syria, Pakistan, and Tunisia are all based in London.[36] The respect for and tolerance of autonomous and diverse religious communities in London provides a propitious environment to engage in activities aimed at individualizing the faith. Increasingly, as one observer puts it, we are witnessing the development—especially among young male and female Muslims—of a religiosity of believing that is evident by individualizing faith and identity based on personal choice. This religiosity of believing is supplanting a religiosity of communal belonging.[37] These young Muslims tend to individualize themselves *through* Islam rather than *from* Islam.[38]

A broader understanding of a reassertion of a global Muslim identity may arguably be a reaction to the existing social discrimination and stigma, racism, and rampant unemployment that Muslims have experienced in their adopted countries in the West. Many Muslims in England suffer high unemployment and endure poor standards of housing. According to a study commissioned to review the prospects of faith communities in England, 14 percent of Muslims over twenty-five were unemployed, compared with the national unemployment rate of 4 percent.[39] This study also revealed that Muslims face multiple deprivations, including poor levels of education and vulnerability to long-term illness.

To some observers, such as Olivier Roy, the shift from a diasporic to a universalist mode of Islamic identity has led to the emergence of a new group of radical Islamists who combine technical modernism, de-culturation—that is, the rejection of both traditional Muslim and modern Western cultures—and globalization, as exemplified by Web sites such as umma.net. This constructivist community is often based on a transnational religious identity and recommunalization of a supranational Muslim identity that produces a "virtual ghetto."[40] These Islamists are far more a product of a Westernized Islam than of traditional Middle Eastern politics. Radical Euro-Islamists as such are clearly more a postmodern than a premodern phenomenon.[41]

The Rise of "Islamophobic" Sentiments

In a growing number of European countries, the tensions between multiculturalism and assimilation are coming to a head. While Muslim immigrants seem willing to integrate, they tend generally not to assimilate by emphasizing diversity and tolerance for religious and cultural difference. The attempt to underscore the importance of difference and tolerance has wider appeal among the second- and third-generation Muslims living in the EU, even more so as times goes by.

On the individual level, change and continuity in religious identities and practices of young Muslims in Europe assume two types of tendencies: "privatization" and "Islamization." Privatization represents an individual choice and an increased emphasis on individual reflection, personal autonomy, and personal authenticity. Islamization, in contrast, refers to a religious identity that links the individual to a global Islamic *umma*.[42] To a majority of young Muslims, religious identity remains linked to a sense of ethnic belonging. National and ethnic identities and religious communities remain interchangeable. Religion is bound up with constructing identity and difference in many ways at both individual and collective levels.[43]

In Sweden, a new realization has begun to spread that the Swedish welfare state, which is premised on consensus, cannot be easily adapted to a society in which a seventh of the working-age population is foreign-born. Sweden now has a Muslim population of 200,000 to 400,000; the higher estimate would place it among the most heavily Muslim countries in Western Europe.[44] Although Sweden's immigrants are far from the poorest in Europe, they are among the most excluded. Moreover, the "structural discrimination" within the society demonstrates that the immigrants encounter inequalities "because of their lack of access to capital and social networks."[45] Sweden's biggest immigration problem may not be related as much to crime, unemployment, and Islamic radicalism as to the fact that "its newcomers understand perfectly well what this system erected in the name of equality is and have decided it doesn't particularly suit them."[46]

In Holland, the official euphemism for an immigrant and his or her child is *allochtoon*. There are three million *allochtonen* in the Netherlands—roughly 20 percent of the population. Muslims, two thirds of them Moroccans and Turks, account for approximately a million.[47] As of March 15, 2006, anyone applying to immigrate to Holland will have to pass an exam in Dutch and watch a video about gay couples and nude beaches.[48] In this way, the Dutch government is attempting to presensitize immigrants to possible cultural differences. This is intended to minimize conflicts rather than to dissuade immigrants from taking up residence in the Netherlands.

In the United Kingdom, France, Austria, and several other countries, under the new immigration laws, cultural integration into society is dependent upon the successful completion of a test that contains questions measuring the applicant's language ability and cultural knowledge. Those who fail the tests are forced to leave the country (Austria), pay fines or suffer cuts in their social assistance payments (the Netherlands), or find their residency rights removed or constrained (France).[49]

During the late 1980s and early 1990s, dramatic local and global dynamics, such as the Gulf War and the *fatwa* placed on the author Salman Rushdie, along with changing attitudes toward migrants, led many young Muslims to reconsider their position in Dutch society. Many Muslim organizations and actors adopted a strategy of "pillarization" for Islam, contending that "as individual citizens, migrants should integrate into society, but, as Muslims, they should have the right to set up their own institutions, just as Catholics and Protestants do."[50]

The new leadership considered pillarization part of their rights as Dutch citizens and used it as the political goal of the Platform for Contact between Muslims and Government (Contactorgaan Moslims en Overheid, CMO), founded in February 2004.[51] The Dutch government has stipulated that from 2007 onward, the recruitment of *imams* from migrants' countries of origin will be illegal. The Dutch government seems determined to establish training facilities for *imams*, controlled by the state—a development that many observers consider a serious violation of the constitutional freedom of religion.[52]

On March 6, 2002, the Leeftbaar Rotterdam Viable party obtained 36 percent of the Dutch vote in the first round of municipal elections. The party's leader, Pim Fortuyn, a sociology professor who was openly homosexual, once claimed that he "understood" Moroccans because he had slept with so many Moroccan boys.[53] Fortuyn was assassinated on May 6, 2002. His murder effectively ended eight years of Labor government in The Hague. Fortuyn became the first person in the history of Dutch politics to have publicly expressed anti-Islamic sentiments. He was expelled from the party, Leftbaar Nederland, shortly before the 2002 elections. But he remained the party's candidate at the local level and eventually founded his own party, Lijst Fortuyn, in an attempt to compete in municipal elections. Fortuyn's book, *Against the Islamization of Our Culture: Dutch Identity as Foundation*, warned against the presence of Muslims in the Netherlands as a threat to Dutch society.[54]

In November 2004, Mohammad Bouyeri, a Moroccan immigrant, assassinated the filmmaker and critic of radical Islam, Theo van Gogh, sparking a wave of violence by and against Muslim immigrants. The murder of van Gogh was a consequence of the merging of two trends: the call to fight blasphemy, and the leap of young Westernized Muslims into "international jihadism."[55] This event raised the specter of political assassination as part of the European jihadist arsenal in Europe. Mohmmad Bouyeri, an average second-generation immigrant who graduated from Amsterdam's best high school, was collecting unemployment benefits when he murdered van Gogh.[56] While the Madrid train bombings of March 2004 were committed by Moroccan immigrants, van Gogh's killer and his group were born and raised in Europe.[57] The Dutch General Intelligence and Security Service (AIVD) says that radical Islam has become "an autonomous phenomenon," in that without direct influence or connections from abroad, Dutch youth are now embracing militancy. The same attraction applies to angry young Muslims in Brussels, London, Paris, Madrid, and Milan.[58]

The formation during 1995–96 of two Muslim organizations, the Muslim Youth of Norway (NMU) and the Muslim Student Society (MSS), provides helpful insights into the construction of Muslim identity in Norway. A majority of members of these organizations have immigrant parents and were either born or raised in Norway. Young Muslims have gradually established their authority to speak to the Muslim public in such forums as the Islamic Council of Norway and to the wider public through interfaith dialogue and media debates.[59] Both the NMU and MSS are gender-mixed and their members come mostly from families with higher levels of education than the immigrant Muslim population as a whole.[60] They criticize "popular Islam" and tend to underline a normative vision of true Islam. Islamic authenticity has thus become a central discourse through which second-generation Muslims negotiate and reconstruct identities, norms, and values in their complex and evolving lives.[61]

The discourse of authenticity helps young Muslims to counter the culturalist portrayal of Islam as anti-modern, irrational, and oppressive.[62] In their quest for recognition, these young Muslims base their claims to religious freedom on a delinking of religion and culture. This approach underscores an individualized and universalist attachment to Islam and refuses to locate its roots in particular local cultures. To these young Muslims, religious freedom is better protected by appeal to universal human rights instruments than by emphasizing the right to retain cultural distinctiveness.[63]

In Norway, public discourse often represents Muslims as unwilling or unable to maintain the separation of religion and state. Islamic symbols and practices, such as the *hijab* and the *adhan* (ritual call to prayer) are too often problematized as symbols of an alien religion and culture intrinsically hostile to women. Similarly, the question of *adhan* (saying public prayers) has been treated politically in terms of public health regulations on noise. The provision of *halal* meat has been virtually impossible due to the government's restrictions regarding animal protection and food control. Similar attempts have been made to prohibit the circumcision of boys on medical grounds and to ban headscarves by privileging health and security over religious freedoms.[64]

The Moroccan community is the most sizable Muslim presence in Spain. Controversy regarding wearing the headscarf (*hijab*) first emerged in February 2002 in Spain when a Moroccan girl in a Madrid school insisted on wearing a headscarf in class. The controversy has subsided to some extent. In reality, however, as one study suggests, for many Moroccan female migrants "Muslim" visibility presents an obstacle to establishing new social relations and finding a job. A Moroccan woman working as a housemaid reflected on such public prejudice: "I am confronted with many difficulties because of *hijab*. . . . I still eat *halal* meat, I do my prayers . . . but I never go out with my scarf on, because everybody stares at me and then no-one wants to hire me. What really matters to them is that you should not wear a scarf, not that you can do the job."[65]

The process of identification with religion is particularly pronounced among women, both in the public sphere and in domestic spaces. For many females, their continued adherence to Islam's cultural and religious values has come to define their identity; they do not see such an identity as in conflict with women's development and emancipation.[66] Moroccan women's personal and financial independence coexists with their Islamic identity. To them, "customs and traditions imposed in their homeland (Morocco) are not the same as practicing Islam as a universal religious faith that encompasses all humanity."[67] Religion for these women is increasingly perceived in terms of an essentially individual faith in a personalized God rather than in the fulfillment of religious practices and duties imposed by religious institutions, authorities, or the family. Many young Muslim women in Spain have actually integrated multiple and fluid identities as part of an ongoing process of religious and cultural reconstruction.[68]

Turkish workers resident in Germany, today known as *Ausländer*, were initially brought in under the 1962 agreement between Germany and Turkey as *gastarbeiter* (guest workers). This first generation of Turkish workers was accommodated mainly in factory dormitories; and because they were almost all men, they lacked the social fabric of family life. German companies, however, decided to hold on to existing Turkish workers in order to avert the inefficiencies and costs associated with training new ones. Germany was concerned about the presence of a large foreign minority and the challenge this group could pose to German conceptions of exclusionary, genealogically based citizenship.[69]

As a result of the 1973 Arab oil embargo, unemployment grew noticeably in Germany, and with it antagonism toward Turkish guest workers increased. The German government, under Chancellor Willy Brandt, ended the import of foreign labor. Turkish guest workers were reluctant to return home because of economic difficulties in Turkey. Ironically, the oil embargo altered the composition of the resident Turkish population from initially single men to reconstituted families as the wives and children of these guest workers arrived. Yet Turks were excluded from German society in many ways. Foreigners cannot participate fully in the German political process. Turks in Germany can participate at a local level only by giving recommendations to local government as advisory boards, recommendations that are nonbinding insofar as government policy is concerned. Turks have generally been excluded from the affluence of German society; there is no Turkish middle class. Most have a residency permit—not a right of residency—which can be revoked by the German state.[70]

The largest Turkish neighborhood in Germany is in Berlin Kreuzberg, generally known as "Small Istanbul," one of the country's most economically depressed areas. A German concept of civic exclusion has pushed the Turkish guest workers to concentrate in this area; consequently, they maintain a strong sense of continuity and identity with Turkish society in their homeland. Very few states (North Rhine-Westphalia and Berlin) have actually provided separate funding for Turkish language and Islamic religious education. Most states provide educational programs furnished by the Turkish state. The language of these programs is Turkish, not German, which makes it immensely difficult for Muslim children to become integrated into German society. The German state has been reluctant to grant Islam a legal status similar to that given to Protestantism, Catholicism, and Judaism in terms of state tax privileges, education, and cultural recognition.[71]

Both Germany and Turkey agreed in 1981 that only *imams* (leaders of the congregational prayers in the mosque; also prominent jurists) and religious teachers approved by Turkey's Department of Religious Affairs (Diyanet) would be allowed to work with Turkish Muslims in Germany. The increase in xenophobic attacks against the Turks in the aftermath of the 1989 Germany reunification has intensified the sense of isolation among the Turks in German society. There are more than two million Turks residing in Germany, most of whom are without German citizenship. An important citizenship law was passed in 1999, which further expanded foreigners' citizenship rights by curtailing the required time of residence in Germany from fifteen to eight years, granting automatic citizenship to children born in Germany of foreign parents (who have resided in Germany for more than eight years), and even permitting dual citizenship until the age of eighteen.[72]

An overwhelming majority of Turks (1.6 million of 2.1 million) prefer dual citizenship. There is little evidence to suggest that large numbers of Turks residing in Germany will return to Turkey. This is particularly true of second- and third-generation Turks who have been born and raised in Germany and conspicuously lack a formal memory of the "home" country.

In short, Turks in Germany have constructed an identity that some observers have described as "between states." That is, Turks have discovered identities of their own that, while influenced by both states—Germany and Turkey—are not entirely connected to either. Many Turks in Germany have reconstructed the notion of "Turk" in religious terms, which contradicts the secular basis of the Turkish state.[73]

For a long time, Christopher Caldwell writes, Britain has had a well-grounded reputation as the European country that best integrated its new arrivals. It had rich and poor immigrants. Many Muslims arrived with some capital, hired their fellow exiles, and educated their families. Britain's tradition of local democratic institutions, such as town and city councils, has allowed the growth of a class of political leaders in these immigrant communities. There are now several Muslims in Britain's Parliament and even in the House of Lords. This stands in stark contrast with France, where one in ten residents is Muslim but there are no Muslims among the 577 deputies in the National Assembly.[74] But over the past quarter century, as Caldwell points out, Britain has been a site of a disheartening inclination toward segregation or resegregation. Young newcomers have not found a niche in the service economy as the arrivals of some fifty years ago did in the industrial one. Others, born in Britain, have sought identities other than the British one they were raised with.[75]

This segregation is especially ingrained among Muslims. Some researchers have demonstrated that only 1 percent of British Bangladeshis and Pakistanis have white partners, when compared to 20 percent of Afro-Caribbeans. The percentage of South Asian Britons who return to Bangladesh and Pakistan to find wives or husbands is slightly above 50 percent by some estimates, a figure some European demographers consider "arrestingly high."[76]

The French Model: A Secular Identity for All

In the late fall of 2005, the French government was shaken by a series of riots in the depressed outskirts of Paris that threatened to engulf the entire nation. In a country that is host to more than six million Muslims, riots in these housing projects, where many of the residents are Muslims, were harbingers of a massive social crisis to come. It is wrong to treat these riots as if they were spearheaded by terrorists and criminals. Some French officials, such as then Interior Minister Nicolas Sarkozy, attributed the riots to criminal activities. Such social stigmatization lay at the heart of this brewing crisis.

The riots were touched off on October 27, 2005, when two teenagers were accidentally electrocuted while hiding from the police in the immigrant-heavy, working-class suburbs of Paris. These riots subsequently and swiftly spread to three hundred French towns and cities. It soon became clear from the French political response that the government was helpless against angry youths of Arab and North African descent who felt impotent politically and excluded socially.

Confronted by the most dramatic social uprising since 1968, French policy makers failed to realize that this growing identity crisis has its roots in failed social policies as well as in the futile assimilation model that France has adopted. In France, according to some estimates, unemployment among workers in their twenties exceeded 20 percent, twice the overall national rate. In urban housing projects, where a younger population resides, average unemployment has reached 36 percent, and even higher among the young.

Most of the rioters were second- and third-generation immigrants, the French-born children of immigrants from Arab and African countries. Most of them were Muslim, but they tended to identify themselves as French Muslims. They have faced decades of high unemployment, they are overrepresented in jail, and they have been, both socially and economically, marginalized. Disconnected from their parents' homeland and uncertain about their future in Europe, these youths feel abandoned.

A careful scrutiny demonstrates that France's integration model has failed in all its social, political, and economic dimensions. The French people are fearful of losing their European identity, indicated by their decision to vote against the European Union constitution in the summer of 2005. They have expressed deep reservations about Turkey's possible entry into the EU. France lacks an affirmative action for these immigrants. French officials have justified the lack of such action on the grounds that it averts creating "ghettos" and "minority status" for this class of people. While other European countries have extended citizenship to newcomers and encouraged strong ethnic communities (premised on a multicultural model), France has insisted on maintaining the character of its secular republic by simply ignoring ethnic or religious differences while emphasizing and privileging French identity over others.

The March 2004 law prohibiting the wearing of all religious symbols in public schools is based on a rigid conception of secularism. Under such circumstances, Muslims' demands for the recognition of Islamic norms, wearing the *hijab*, and separation of the sexes are viewed as an attack on the French secular lifestyle and modern human rights.

The idea of citizenship in contemporary France has come increasingly to the fore in current discussions on the Muslim presence there. Competing definitions of citizenship reveal schisms in French politics concerning what constitutes culture, race, and identity. Citizenship is determined not only by nationality laws but also by discursive devices that establish forms of cultural belonging to the national community. These discourses could exclude or include groups of people on the basis of their "culture" irrespective of whether they are legal citizens.[77]

In recent years, the French extreme right political party, the Front National, and the culturalist new right, the Nouvelle Droite, have shaped the debate on nationhood. The left-wing discourse of *la droite à la différence* (the right to difference) has been appropriated by the extreme right, which has demonstrated its power to exclude non-European immigrants who do not partake in the dominant cultural benchmarks on which French citizenship is predicated.[78] It is worth noting that many leftist and liberal political parties, politicians, and intellectuals kept their distance from these riots and felt no obligation to defend Muslim immigrants who belong to socially marginalized, disenfranchised, and disempowered classes.[79]

This marginalization from the dominant culture carries the danger of excluding immigrants from the national community. The discourse of cultural rights today challenges the French extreme right's monopoly of the discursive terrain of culture. If cultural diversity in relation to the establishment of the national community is promoted, immigrants feel empowered to shape the debate over immigration and citizenship. They will therefore play a more constructive role in advancing the overall objectives of EU integration. The idea of citizenship can become a dynamic concept if it is conceptualized through diverse cultural and ideological lenses.[80]

The need for a new identity among Muslim immigrants, especially among those born and raised in the new country, can no longer be overlooked. In the meantime, these youths, who often see little prospect of moving out of their poor economic conditions, have found comfort and familiarity in their religion. Although riots and violence in such communities must not be directly linked to radical Islamism, it is important to realize that, as French scholar on Islam Olivier Roy once noted, "In Western Europe, radical Islamism is homegrown, not an import."[81] Given the scope and gravity of these riots, the radical fringe will surely seek a new base among the local Muslim population there.

Issues of immigration, social justice, and jobs continue to fester, and these riots could be a prelude to difficult times ahead if not dealt with properly. Unless this crisis is confronted at its roots, France is approaching a social explosion that could prove costly for the stability of the republic for years to come. Respect for ethnic, racial, and religious communities must be restored in ways that will not upset the ideals of separating church and state. This means that pluralistic models of socioeconomic and political development must replace the strictly integrative model to which France has adamantly adhered.

Some experts have noted that the growth of the younger generations of Muslims in France has created an opportunity to foster a hybrid Franco-Islamic identity. The development of such an identity, however, is dependent upon the creation of an equitable place for Muslims in mainstream French society, one that is not based on an unmitigated subjugation of religious practice to loyalty to the state.[82] The need to develop a more inclusive sociopolitical model in France to equitably integrate Muslims—particularly those born in France—into mainstream society has never been so urgent. The key for linking pluralism with democracy in France is to maintain a balance between multiculturalism and cultural, ethnic, and religious communities.[83]

Swiss-born professor of Islamic studies and philosophy Tariq Ramadan criticizes a rooted feeling of victimization, emphasizing the need for Arabs and Muslims, living in both the homeland and the Western diasporic communities, to move beyond attitudes of victimization and nonresponsibility and to stop placing all the blame for their political, economic, and social problems on the West. Undoubtedly, Ramadan argues, "the key to the inaction and regression within the Muslim world might be found in the analysis of this attitude."[84] Muslims will not progress toward reform and renewal of their faith unless they escape from such harmful attitudes and logic. Offering a so-called third way of integrating Muslims into European society, Ramadan urges young European Muslims neither to assimilate—and thus lose their cultural identity—nor to separate themselves and reject Europe; rather, he encourages them to remain both true to their faith and loyal to the secular societies in which they live.[85]

The Cartoon Controversy

When the Danish newspaper *Jylland-Posten* published twelve cartoons of the Prophet Muhammad in late September 2005, including one in which he was shown wearing a turban shaped as a bomb with a burning fuse, a strong backlash ensued not only in Denmark but also across the globe, including demonstrations in the Indian-controlled part of Kashmir, death threats against the artists, condemnation from many Muslim countries, and a rebuke from the United Nations. The publication of these cartoons provoked a fierce national debate over whether Denmark's liberal and secular laws on freedom of speech had gone too far.[86] This incident has also tested the patience of Denmark's 200,000 Muslims, many of whom believed that the cartoons reflected an intensifying anti-immigrant climate that was stigmatizing minorities and radicalizing young Muslims.

When these cartoons were reprinted on February 1, 2006, in France, Germany, Italy, the Netherlands, Spain, and Switzerland, the Muslim world's uproar over caricatures of the Prophet Muhammad was on display in the streets of Afghanistan, Egypt, Turkey, Pakistan, Iraq, Iran, Indonesia, Malaysia, Lebanon, and the Palestinian regions. Mocking and depicting the Prophet Muhammad wearing a bomb-shaped turban, these caricatures that reappeared in major European press were viewed as blasphemous by many Muslims, both in the diaspora and in their homelands. To Muslims, these images were offensive because they portrayed the Prophet as a bomb-carrying terrorist.

These deliberate acts of targeting Muslims rekindled the debate over the larger and deeper issues of multiculturalism and liberalism in Europe. Although the EU's economic integration has proceeded somewhat smoothly, its multiculturalism has caused many tensions. European cultural elites, who seem to lack any new ideas for advancing multiculturalism, feel paranoid and threatened by their local Muslim populations and consider upholding higher standards of free speech the key to maintaining the secular nature of their societies. In this uneasy climate, Europeans' claim to moral superiority resurfaced. Muslims argued that it is far from clear that pluralism is equated with such deliberate anti-Muslim acts of provocation.

Arguably, the European press intended to provoke Muslim reactions to test Muslim tolerance of pluralistic norms and also to prove that Muslim immigrants will likely create fissures within Europe's democratic culture. This incident was reminiscent of the 1988 Salman Rushdie affair. Iran's Ayatollah Ruhollah Khomeini declared a death sentence against Rushdie for publishing a novel called *The Satanic Verses*, in which he made a mockery of Muslim traditions, the Prophet, and his lifestyle.

In response to the cartoon prints, some Muslim countries, notably Saudi Arabia and Syria, recalled their ambassadors from Denmark, while the Danish government reciprocated by summoning other foreign envoys in Copenhagen to explain its official position. In some Muslim countries, Danish flags were burned and Danish consulates were torched in widespread protests against the European press. The problem was not that the Danish government could not control the press. Rather, Danish cultural elites, who felt threatened by multiculturalism, decided to fuel the dispute with the Muslims.

One Danish journalist points to Denmark's uneasy relationship with Muslims, noting that a few decades ago, Denmark had no Muslim minority. Today there are more than 200,000 Muslims in Denmark—that is more than 3 percent in a country with a population of 5.4 million. Understandably, "Islam has come to be viewed by many as a threat to the survival of Danish culture."[87] For their part, Muslims should not play into the hands of the European media elite by resorting to violent means of settling this cultural dispute. The cycle of violence would undermine the Muslims' ability to adjust themselves to their changing conditions.

Muslim social elites, who are aware of the power of new ideas, should opt for a better tactic than violence and boycott. For their part, European elites should embrace the notion that freedoms are not absolute and unlimited, but that they entail responsibility and proper judgment.[88] Europe may be a continent of laws and liberties, but its leaders have hardly lived up to their core principle of promoting tolerance and respect toward their Muslim minorities, which they clearly perceive as "the other." Trying to force their Muslim immigrants to choose between European citizenship, on the one hand, and their faith and religious identity, on the other, is flawed and bound to backfire.

Likewise, Muslim leaders should avoid building drama from satire. It is insensitive, although not illegal, to print caricatures as a form of political speech in secular democracies. Judging from the way the European media have graphically and deliberately offended Muslims, it seems safe to conclude that provoking cultural disputes of this sort clearly runs counter to creating social integration in Europe. The American experience, as one scholar notes, suggests that steadfast self-restraint and self-censorship can bring progress in multiethnic societies. That kind of self-censorship has "helped make America one of the most harmonious multiethnic and multireligious societies in the history of the world."[89]

Danish counterterrorism officials argue that more and more young Danish Muslims are being drawn to Hizb ut-Tahrir (the Party of Liberation), a radical Muslim group that seeks the unification of all Muslim countries under one leader and Islamic law (shari'a). This group, which distributes radical literature at mosques and on the Internet, is banned in most Muslim countries as well as in Russia and Germany. And yet it is allowed to operate in Denmark because its main emphasis is the spread of ideology, not violence.[90]

Some Western analysts argue that Hizb ut-Tahrir, though not itself a terrorist organization, can be regarded as a conveyor belt for terrorists. It indoctrinates individual Muslims with radical ideology, preparing them for recruitment by more militant organizations and operations. By combining radical rhetoric and strategy with Wahhabi theology, Hizb ut-Tahrir has become a potent menace that is extremely difficult for liberal societies to counter. The real danger lies in this group's enlarging its social or ideological base by aligning with other extremist movements.[91]

Al-Qaeda has fully exploited the tolerance and freedom of association enshrined in Western liberal democracies. Beyond its ideological penetration of Muslim communities by recruiting *imams* and other mosque officials, Al-Qaeda has created a huge network by establishing, infiltrating, and even trying to gain control of many Islamic NGOs. One-fifth of all Islamic NGOs worldwide, according to the CIA, have been infiltrated by Al-Qaeda and other terrorist support groups. Al-Qaeda and its associates have sought to mobilize the Islamic diaspora.[92] The train bombings in Spain in 2004 and the London bombings of July 7, 2005, have shown the seriousness of radical Muslims' operations on the European continent.

The Identity Debate

Although European Muslims are not a monolithic group, they generally tend to identify first with Islam rather than with either their parents' country of origin or the European country in which they reside. Younger Muslims, who have been born and raised in Europe, have adopted attributes of the European societies, such as language, socialization through schooling, and mostly the secular perspectives pervasive there. They nevertheless lack a sense of belonging to the larger society. Nor do they feel that they have a stake in it.[93]

What is more, even though they may be third-generation citizens, too often they are not seen as fellow citizens by the general public but are still identified as foreigners and immigrants.[94] This perception tends to reinforce the *we/them* perspective and is part of the reason Muslims resist assimilation into Europe, which would lead to the total loss of identity-related indicators of extant differences from European societies. Muslims instead insist on integration—that is, a reconstituted identity that underscores remaining differences. In short, diasporic Muslims aspire for integration but not assimilation. They will most likely find it difficult to adopt Europe's liberal democratic views on gender equality, sexual liberalization, egalitarianism, and identification with the state. These issues challenge both the traditional and individual views of Europe's Muslims, regardless of their Arabic, Turkish, or South Asian heritage.[95]

Increasingly, however, the proportion of Muslims becoming citizens of Europe is on the rise. More than three fifths of Muslims in France and the United Kingdom are citizens of those countries. In Germany, nearly one fifth have citizenship and in Italy nearly 10 percent hold Italian citizenship. The same is true in Scandinavia, where citizenship is normally obtainable after five years of residency.[96] These trends notwithstanding, Europe's Muslims, including the younger generation, fear that assimilation—that is, total absorption into European society—will strip them of their Islamic identity. What accounts for this behavior? Real or perceived discrimination in European societies clearly affects employment, education, housing, and religious practices. Many second- and particularly third-generation Muslims tend to embrace Islam as their badge of identity.[97]

The unemployment rate among Muslims is generally double that of non-Muslims and it is even higher than that of non-Muslim immigrants. Educational achievements are relatively low, participation by Muslim women in the workforce is minimal, opportunities for social mobility are limited, and biases against Muslims are pervasive. These factors have resulted in the isolation and encapsulation of Muslim communities in Europe. Recent studies have shown that Muslim identification with Islam has grown in 2001 compared to what it was in 1994 and 1989.[98] A combination of cultural shock and disaffection and alienation pushes Muslim immigrants toward radicalism and extremism.

The increasing Muslim presence in Europe has spurred debates over Europe's very identity. The rise of right-wing or far-right parties (e.g., Belgium's Flemish Bloc, the British National Party, Denmark's People's Party, Jean-Marie Le Pen's French National Front, Italy's Northern League, and Switzerland's People's Party) has resulted in the upsurge of right-leaning adjustments in the political agendas of mainstream parties. This rightward shift has led to anti-Muslim views and was reflected in recent moves such as those in France and Germany to ban the wearing of the Muslim headscarf in public schools and by the Netherlands to expel up to 26,000 asylum seekers.[99]

In France, those who rejected the EU constitution said they were worried that the EU would impose what is known as Anglo-Saxon economics on all its members, obviously weakening the French welfare state with its emphasis on job preservation and a generous social safety net. For other opponents, the issue was immigration. They argued that EU Muslim minorities are already too large and that the constitution would ultimately open the door to further admission of Muslim immigrants. The possible admission of Turkey to the EU must be seen in this context.[100]

While the EU political leaders bear considerable responsibility for the current state of affairs, European citizens have their share of hypocrisy. As noted above, many Europeans have opposed liberal immigration policies for fear of increased competition in domestic labor markets. At the same time, they have condoned illegal immigration if it has provided them with cheap labor. They have, for example, welcomed cheap builders from East-Central Europe who have renovated their summer homes at much lower costs than would have been possible with native workers.[101] Modern migration policy has embraced Arab-inspired architecture, Jewish or Lebanese trading activity, and the extraordinary vibrancy of classical and early medieval Mediterranean culture. Migration control is needed but not at the cost of closing borders, blocking cultural exchanges, and buttressing xenophobic instincts.

Some experts have offered a contrasting view, noting that Muslim immigrant communities in the West will be the ultimate battlefield where the struggle for the democratization of Islamic societies will be won or lost. It is imperative, Gilles Kepel notes, to work toward full democratic participation for young European Muslims through institutions—especially those of education and culture—that foster upward social mobility and the emergence of new elites. These young men and women will present a new face of Islam—one that is reconciled with modernity and globalization—to the rest of the word.[102]

Rights and Cultural and Religious Diversity

One view is that the increasing presence of Muslim immigrants in the West may accelerate a process similar to the Christian Reformation. Muslims in the West may end up thinking in Western ways, even when they oppose

Western values.[103] A delinking of religion and culture in Islam has transpired on the European continent as European Muslims have sought a new means of building a community as a subset of the *umma*—a globalized Islam through the new transnational identity and networks. This approach has contributed to the sociological Westernization of Muslim immigrants, as many European Muslims seem to have multiple and overlapping identities. One can be both a devout Muslim and a loyal citizen of a European community. Most Muslim communities are strongly adaptationist in style.[104] Today, European Muslims tend to use the concepts of human rights and minority rights to advance their values and consequently express those in a Western manner. Muslim women excluded from schools or jobs wearing the *hijab* go to court demanding antidiscrimination. Islamic revivalism may therefore be experienced according to Western and modern paradigms of social and professional behavior while embracing a way of internalizing such modernity.[105]

The tensions rising from the processes of integrating Muslim immigrants into the society are multiple. Some relate to the relevance and role of religion in public and private domains and others reflect the individual's stance on religion. The headscarf issue, for instance, comes from the age-old sensitivity to the public presence of religion in schools as well as from a European notion that religion properly belongs in the private sphere. Many Europeans have shown social anxieties about the possible links between public expressions of Islamic identity and radical Islamism. In France, for example, this fear is often linked to growing "communalism," Islamism, and sexism. Feminists have mobilized public opinion against the *hijab* by linking communalism and Islamism to the oppression of women—that is, sexism and violence against women—in France and throughout the world.[106] This oppression is also believed to be linked to anti-Semitism and to the long-standing struggle of women for their rights.[107] Critics argue that for those who are called on to integrate into French society, this demand raises important questions about whether *läicité* (secularism) should mask differences or celebrate them. French norms of gender equality and *läicité*, they note, have been defined so narrowly that they fail to take into account legitimate differences in religious institutions and practices.[108]

In most cases dealing with the *hijab*, the European Convention of Human Rights (ECHR) tends to cite the principle of gender equality as a central consideration justifying restrictions on women's freedom of choosing clothing. In the case of *Dahlab v. Switzerland*, for example, a public schoolteacher was asked to remove her headscarf. She evoked both Articles 9 and 14 of the ECHR, citing discrimination on the grounds of sex. The European Court of Human Rights noted that the headscarf "appears to be imposed on women by a precept which is laid down in the Qur'an and which . . . is hard to square with the principle of gender equality."[109]

Similarly, in *Leyla Sahin v. Turkey*, where a university student was prohibited from wearing a headscarf for the first time in 2004, the *hijab* was interpreted as hostile to the constitutionally embedded principles of secularism. Clearly, in this case, the chief consideration underlying the ban on wearing headscarf—or for that matter, any religious symbols—in universities was the principle of secularism. The European Court of Human Rights made a similar judgment, while refraining from giving the principle of gender equality any specific content. The Grand Chamber of the European Court of Human Rights noted, "Those in favor of the headscarf-*hijab* see wearing it as a duty and/or form of expression linked to religious identity."[110] In both cases, the influence of religion on women was perceived to be negative and the relationship between gender equality and cultural diversity was assumed to be conflictive.[111]

Proponents of liberal traditions of tolerance and multiculturalism often proceed from the assumption that Western liberal societies have actually departed from their patriarchal past by prescribing gender equality in the law, whereas non-Western cultures have failed to adopt a set of liberal legal norms. Critics call into question such assumptions, arguing that the principle of gender equality is also embedded in culture. The infallible belief that liberal orders are gender-neutral overlooks the all-too-familiar feminist critique that "exposes liberalism as itself deeply inscribed with hidden but pervasive signs of male dominance."[112]

Another difficulty with liberal secular views is that wearing the headscarf can be seen as part of an individual's expression of cultural or religious identity. In such instances, identity is protected by human rights, which would include rights such as religion, expression, and privacy. Commenting on Article 18 of the International Covenant on Civil and Political Rights (ICCPR), the Human Rights Committee stated: "The observance and practice of religion or belief may include not only ceremonial acts but also such customs as . . . the wearing of distinctive clothing."[113] It is vitally important to recognize that some Muslim girls and women consider wearing the headscarf-*hijab* part of their individual and group identity.[114]

Conclusion

This chapter has argued that Muslims have become a permanent presence in Europe. Nevertheless, they are more inclined to integrate than to assimilate into or accommodate European societies. Whether Muslims could become an integral part of European social and political milieu is an open question. A growing number of Muslim immigrants, especially second- and third-generation Muslims, tend to discover identities of their own, which belong neither to their parents' homeland nor to the country in which they reside—that is, "in-between" identities. For many Muslims, however, religion is an important marker of identity. What Muslim immigrants want is their space, a space in which their identity is recognized within the law as a normal element of European societies.

As explained above, a multitude of factors (terrorism, jobs, and cultural identities) has deepened the social friction in European societies over the politics of immigration, presenting a major setback to the processes of cultural and social integration.[115] Investment and job creation are as significant as the treatment of Muslim immigrants with equal concern and respect. Migration to Europe, as most experts concur, has created a sizable underclass and numbers of jobless youth, many of whom were born and socialized in the Western secular democracies. They tend to reject their minority status and feel utterly dejected.

The enforcement of equal laws and the fair treatment of Muslim minorities could reduce cultural and ethnic tensions. While equality is a constant quest for every Muslim immigrant, assimilation is not. Assimilation is unlikely to work in European multicultural societies. That is an unrealistic expectation. Recognition for the Muslim presence and identity makes it imperative for Europeans to grasp a better understanding of Islam and Muslims' culture. The introduction of such cultural understanding into Europeans' school curricula would be a way forward. Elevating the economic conditions of Muslim migrants is bound to have a moderating impact on their social and political attitudes.

Identities, Interests, and Human Rights

Since the end of the Cold War, there has been an upsurge in identity and cultural politics. In much of the post–Cold War debate about culture, Islam has presented a particular challenge to some aspects of Western modernity.[1] As Islam has come under closer scrutiny in the post-9/11 period, young Muslims have sought to learn more about their religion and strengthen their sense of identity.[2] More specifically, since the March 2003 invasion of Iraq by the United States, the culture of resistance has found its place throughout the Middle East. Hizbollah's victory declaration following the Israeli offensive in southern Lebanon in summer 2006 has also become an important turning point not only for the Shia, but also for the Sunnis in Egypt, where Hizbollah is famous and Nasrallah, the leader of Lebanese Shiites, has become a hero.[3]

Some Middle Eastern politicians see the revival of the identity issue as a result of the democratization process. Abdullah Gul, Turkey's president, argues that "as Muslim societies democratize, you will see greater religious expression everywhere in society. It is a consequence of democracy. People in Muslim countries are devout and socially conservative. You cannot fight against this. You have to understand it and allow some expression of this belief."[4]

Others hold the view that opposition to globalization is reflected in the religious beliefs and practices of Muslims. Significantly, religion has helped humans deal with uncertainty and fear while giving meaning and organization to the behavior of individuals, families, and groups in global society.[5] To fully understand identity politics in the Muslim world, we must place it in both its conceptual and historical contexts. Several factors have led to the formation of a new Islamic identity for Muslims in the past half century. The reawakening of an Islamic consciousness has been facilitated largely by mass education and mass communication. The latter has been greatly facilitated by the revolution in information technology and the Internet. Nonstate actors, market forces, and satellite technology have affected collective identities in the Muslim world.[6]

Additionally, the persistence of authoritarian governments throughout the Muslim world, as well as the unresolved status of the Israeli-Palestinian conflict, helps to explain the resurgent enthusiasm for Islam throughout the Muslim world.[7] The humiliating Arab defeat by the Israelis in the 1967 Six-Day War dealt a severe blow to Arab nationalism/socialism and gave rise to Islamic fundamentalism. More recently, anger and resentment toward the occupation of Iraq, along with the shame caused by the mistreatment of Iraqi prisoners, have incited a new cycle of hatred among Muslims that has only emboldened Islamic extremism. Using Islam as grassroots counter-hegemony, militant Islamic groups have energized an insurgency capable of disrupting Iraq's postwar reconstruction.

To many experts, Islamic radicalism was born as a reaction to the decline of Muslim power.[8] To others, Islamic militancy is a nuanced and subtle backlash against foreign interference, as many in the Muslim world seek to define and forge new identities and paths for their future.[9] To still others, Islamic radicals are bent on promoting the discourse of opposition, which is increasingly antidemocratic, illiberal, and, in social and economic terms, regressive.[10] It was such an Islamic extremist who assassinated former prime minister Benazir Bhutto on December 27, 2007, in an attempt to plunge Pakistan into political chaos, civil war, or an internally led Islamist army coup.[11]

Some observers have favored including moderate Islamists in elections and the political process. The examples of Islamist participation in open elections in Jordan, Kuwait, and Lebanon, they assert, illustrate governments' willingness to play by the rules, at least while these groups are in the minority. More specifically, the process of inclusion promotes pragmatism and moderation. Inclusionary politics tend to reduce militancy.[12] It can also be argued that the political inclusion of Islamist parties may or may not lead to their ideological and political moderation. In Jordan, inclusion has prompted ideological moderation of the Islamist party, but this has not been the case in Yemen. Different experiences in Jordan and Yemen can be attributed to structural changes in public political space, internal group structures, and the creation of new ideas and narratives governing political practice. In Jordan, for instance, the regime could rely on a longer history of participatory politics to strengthen democracy and national unity. In both cases, however, there is also skepticism about the possibility that Islamists can secure a genuine commitment to sustaining a democratic state.[13]

Roots of Islamic Identity

In an important finding, Shibley Telhami showed that Arabs' increasing embrace of Islam as the primary source of their identity did not begin with the U.S. invasion of Iraq in March 2003 or even after the September 11, 2001, terrorist attacks in the United States. This reaction was in part the result of the failed Israeli-Palestinian negotiations in 2000, the subsequent rise of the second Palestinian Intifida (social uprising), and the Israeli response to it. The unresolved status of Jerusalem in the negotiations, along with the need to broaden support for the Palestinian cause among Arabs and Muslims, has increasingly turned the issue into an Islamic one.[14] Today, Telhami continues, Palestine is far more significant in non-Arab states such as Malaysia, Indonesia, and Turkey than it used to be only a few years ago.

The occupation of Iraq and the way the war on terrorism has been perceived in much of the Muslim world have further intensified identification with being a Muslim. Increasingly, Muslims see the war on terrorism as a war on Islam.[15] Muslims all over the world are now searching for a modern Islamic identity as they increasingly rely on Islam to provide structure and meaning to their everyday lives.[16] The *hijab* has become a potent symbol of the Islamic resurgence since the 1970s. Amid the confusion and uncertainty of modern life, Islam has provided Muslims with a familiar sense of stability, direction, and hope.[17] The resentment of the younger generation of Muslims is directed at the West and the failure of its political and social regimes to provide them with basic freedoms and economic and social justice, as well as at orthodox Islamic institutions and elites whose services have failed to match the current evolving demands, interests, and identities of the younger generation.

Some observers have argued that the lack of political willingness to counter the imperial encroachment in Iraq, Palestine, and other areas has invariably created further rifts between Arab governments and their people.[18] On balance, as one observer notes, "the roots of political Islam lie not in a struggle with the West, but rather in a struggle within Muslim-majority countries. In the end, those roots may even prove to be more political than they are Islamic."[19]

The cases reviewed here have shown the extent to which Islam has been divided by Turkish, Indonesian, Iranian, and Arab nationalism. As these cases illustrate, Islamic identity—in both its local and translocal manifestations—has resurfaced in all Muslim countries. Some of these countries (e.g., Iran) have represented the most dramatic revival of Islamic political identity in the region since the 1980s. Throughout the Muslim world, many ordinary Muslims have expressed their desire to have a voice.[20] Although notions such as cultural "reformation," political accountability, and freedom of expression inform the writings of the country's public intellectuals, the evolving discourse is influenced by the pervasiveness of religion at all levels of Iranian life: rural and urban, rich and poor, politically conscious or apathetic.[21]

The countries examined in this book can also be organized along different theoretical claims regarding the relationship between globalization and identity. Although the processes of globalization (economic, cultural, and otherwise) have had transforming impacts on Muslim identities, many actors in the Muslim world (individuals, groups, institutions, and states) have socially constructed globalization. I have engaged both constructivist and rationalist theoretical approaches to deepen our understanding of the conditions under which local cultures and global standards interact and how such interactions will shape Muslims' identities and interests in a globalizing world.

The prevailing pattern in all these cases is the simultaneous formation of Islamic, national, and state identities. In all of these cases (with the exception of Iraq), state identity has been sustained despite the persistence of a deep suspicion toward formal authority structures. The state retains some nationalist legitimacy in large part because it remains the only viable defender of the nation's sovereignty against the persistent machinations of foreign adversaries.[22]

With the exception of the United Arab Emirates, in all these cases, the existence of religious and ethnic minorities and subnational identities (the Copts, the Kurds, the Sunni-Shia divide, and the Indonesian Chinese minority) has posed formidable challenges to national identity. In all these countries, Islamic, national, and Western influences have shaped the way identity has taken on different values. In Iran, state identity (Islamic Republic) and national identity (Iranian) have coexisted uneasily at times, as the divide between the state and society has grown. Under Ahmadinejad, Iranians have seen the reorganization of state identity through populist methods. Only Turkey has allowed international forces to directly shape its domestic priorities. The country's desire to be admitted into the European Union has rendered its state elites tolerant of such domestic consequences while trying to maintain an imperfect but functioning democratic system since 1983.[23]

In Iraq, in contrast, identification with the territorial state has been politically weak and tended to focus on the substate unit—the city, the tribe, and the religious sect—or with the larger Islamic community (the *umma*). Ironically, as one expert notes, "the United States' invasion of Iraq and its subsequent overthrow of the Iraqi state in 2003 appear to have strengthened authoritarian hard-liners throughout the Middle East."[24] In Iran, Egypt, and Turkey, which are societies with substantial peasantries and hence attachment to the land, contemporary states have inherited and manifested distinct features of the nation-state model.[25] These countries can, therefore, be correctly described as nation-states, with historical Egyptian, Turkish, and Iranian identities.

Seeking Identity and Power in a Globalizing World

Since the postcolonial era, Muslims have struggled to define themselves in relation to modernizing and secularizing forces. Today, despite the globalization process, Muslims belong to many cultures and display multiple cultural identities (Islamic, Arabic, Turkish, Indonesian, transnational, and European Muslim). In trying to fathom the complexities of this world, Stanley Hoffmann correctly points out that globalization has not profoundly changed the enduring national nature of citizenship. Although economic life has transpired on a global scale, human identity has remained national.[26]

To revisit the theoretical framework laid out in Chapter 2, in which we examined the degree to which global norms have met resistance or have been accommodated, it is important to remember the diversity of the contemporary Islamic experiences within local, national, regional, and transnational contexts. To reflect this diversity, we return to rival secularist, nationalist, and Islamist conceptions and identities among conservatives, neofundamentalists, reformists, and secularists in a selected number of Muslim countries.

Conservatives

Conservatives throughout the Muslim world have called for a return to original—and at times mainstream—Islamic traditions as a way of invoking shared Islamic symbols. Clerics and *ulama* in Egypt, for example, typify this group, and their pervasive influence is not overlooked by the Egyptian government. To remain part of the power structure, they have sought local alliances with the state, even as this has meant a closer collaboration with or co-optation by state officials. From the state vantage point, the support of the clerics and *ulama* gives the government a veneer of legitimacy (see Table 10). In the case of the United Arab Emirates, conservative clerics' close cooperation with the modernizing/technocratic elite shapes a statist-nationalist identity, one which in a broader framework is referred to as the "ruling bargain," where citizens are pledged economic prosperity in exchange for restrictions on freedoms (see Table 10).

In the cases of Iran and Iraq, such cooperation has transcended state boundaries, as Shia clerics and *ulama* have routinely interacted with each other to bolster their interests and power across national lines. Likewise, in some European countries, conservative clerics have been hired—or even imported—by governments to organize Muslim communities and expand their membership in ways commensurate with adopting European citizenship and assimilation. These conservative clerics have grounded their legitimacy in their exclusive access to sacred texts and their "authority" to interpret them.[27] This monopolistic control by religious elites, however, has been called into question by Muslim translocal/transnational movements and their newly formed identities in Europe (more on that later).

Neofundamentalists

The proponents of a neofundamentalist ideological orientation, in contrast, have generally separated themselves from state identity by emphasizing the moral reconstruction of the individual. They underscore the importance of activism across local communities by relying on grassroots movements. These Islamists, who tend to be young, educated, and professional, have also appealed to the rural peasantry. In Iran since 2005, neofundamentalists and certain traditional Islamic groups have forged a governing alliance that today rules the country (see Table 10). Since its inception, the Islamic Republic has promoted the notion of Islamic nationalism by bridging over ethnicity, class, and ideology in an effort to fill the gaps in a sharply divided community. Class-conscious workers have, for the most part, remained nationalists.[28]

Inspired by the teachings of Sheikh Umar Abd al-Rahman in the early 1990s, one Islamist group successfully reached out to a mix of peasants, seasonal workers, fishermen, drivers, and ordinary workers in rural areas in upper Egypt.[29] The youthfulness of participants in Islamist movements reflects the demographic trends in Egypt, Saudi Arabia, Kuwait, Gaza and the West Bank, Morocco, Indonesia, and Pakistan. These trends illustrate the

Table 10. Competing Identities in Selected Muslim Countries (Secularist, Nationalist, and Islamist Identities)

Competing Groups	Turkey	Iran	Egypt	Indonesia	UAE
Conservatives	Traditional-Islamist identity	Traditional-Islamist-statist identity (governing alliance)†	Traditional-Islamist identity (co-opted by government: statist identity)	Traditional-Islamist identity	Traditional and modern identity, with statist-nationalist identity ("ruling bargain")
Neofundamentalists	*	Islamist-populist-statist identity	Islamist identity (antigovernment dissent)	Islamist identity (opposition)	*
Reformists	Religious-nationalist identity (Muslim democrats in a tacit compact with secularists)†	Religious-nationalist identity (Muslim democrats out of power)	Islamist identity (seeking participation in the political process)	Islamist-nationalist identity (a tacit compact between Islamists and secularists)°	*
Secularists	Statist-secularist-nationalist identity (military-bureaucratic elites)	*	Statist-secularist identity (secularist autocrats pursuing a strategy of simultaneous accommodation and repression of Islamist groups)	Statist-nationalist identity (military-bureaucratic elites)	*

*A group with negligible influence.

†Governing alliance: a network of power relationships based on mutual interests and shared meanings and identities.

massive involvement of unemployed and underclass youth. In the case of Shia members of the Hizb al-Da'wa al-Islamiyya (Islamic Call Party) in Iraq, the majority have come from the urban lower-middle classes and include university students, soldiers, and small businessmen.[30]

The case of student movements in Iran stands in stark contrast with the aforementioned case studies. A general characteristic of student movements prior to the 1979 Islamic Revolution had been their criticism of the status quo. Some student movements under the Islamic Republic have often been critical of conditions detrimental to freedom of thinking, globalization of information/knowledge, and the expansion of civil society. In the first two decades of the revolution, however, student activism became dependent on the political structure of the Islamic Republic. Since the late 1990s, this trend has changed dramatically, as student riots have erupted on several occasions in response to the country's declining standard of living and soaring unemployment, changing gender profiles in the universities, widening alienation and apathy among the people, and continuing repressive policies of the government.[31]

This growing disillusionment culminated in the 1999 and 2003 student protests, both of which were brutally suppressed. The protesters' demands included, among other things, respect for internationally recognized human rights, the rule of law, and democratic processes. These demands/grievances were framed in both secular and culturally Islamic discourses and were addressed to Iranian citizens of various backgrounds, to the Islamic Republic, to the media, and to the global community.[32]

In other Muslim societies, the religious upsurge was less a return of religious orthodoxy than an explosion of neo-orthodoxies.[33] These neo-orthodoxies deployed sophisticated and politically competent organizations, which used the newest technologies to recruit new members, delivered social services, and pressed their agenda in their country's politics. Several organizations or groups in the Muslim world employed such practices: the Muslim Brotherhood in Egypt and Jordan, Hamas in the Palestinian territories, Hizbollah in Lebanon, and the Nahdlatul Ulama in Indonesia.[34]

Many developments in the twentieth century set a broader trend, one in which religious movements helped end colonial rule and further democratization in Latin America, Eastern Europe, sub-Saharan Africa, and Asia. Religion mobilized millions of people to question authoritarian regimes and relieve human suffering. Such trends were consistent with similar developments transpiring in the West, where modernization, democratization, and globalization have simply made belief in God stronger.[35]

It should be noted, however, that a different version of neofundamentalism—mostly radical, violent, and generally known as global jihadism—has resurfaced in global politics; its full treatment is beyond this chapter's scope. Suffice it to say that these groups have their own networks and operations in such countries as Afghanistan, Pakistan, and Iraq since the 2003 U.S.-led invasion. Operating as a transnational movement, these groups seek not simply to effect changes in enemies' actions but to forcibly destroy enemies. Internally, they engage in antigovernment dissent as an act of defiance of the state's authority and legitimacy.

Reformists

From the reformists' standpoint, Islamism is a modern response to contemporary problems. The reformists express the concerns of many disaffected adherents to traditional values who have embraced a political movement that challenges the dominance of secular nationalism.[36] This is the case in both Turkey and Indonesia, where Muslim democrats have reached a tacit compact with secularists (see Table 10). In today's multicultural societies, as Mark Juergensmeyer argues, religion, ethnicity, and traditional culture have stepped in to redefine public communities and have thus become resources for national identification. The decline of the territorial state, as well as disillusionment with the old forms of secular nationalism, has created both the opportunity and the need for new nationalisms. As a result, religious and ethnic nationalism has provided a solution in this emerging climate to the perceived inadequacies of the Western-style secular politics of the global era.[37]

These new ethnoreligious identities, Juergensmeyer continues, are in fact alternative conceptions of modernity with international and supranational components of their own. In this basic sense, identity and control are linked in that the loss of a sense of belonging results in a feeling of impotency. Likewise, a perceived loss of faith in secular nationalism is seen as a loss of agency as well as selfhood. The assertion of traditional forms of religious identities is connected to attempts to reclaim personal and cultural power.[38]

In the Arab Middle East, reformists' influence on shaping local and national identities cannot evade the overlapping Islamic identity and transcendental Arabism. The recent advent of Arab satellite TV has increased cross-border communication and participation in common discourses. Ideas and information circulate widely in the Arab world and people have become interconnected by sharing ideas on a greater scale. Significantly, there has been a widespread feeling of belonging to a distinct Arab world (*al-alam al-arabi*). Increasingly, surveys beginning in the 1980s in the Arab states have demonstrated that Arabs feel they constitute a nation and that the state boundaries dividing them are artificial.[39] The loss of Palestine, the 1967 defeat by Israel, the sanctions against Iraq, and the 2003 U.S. invasion of Iraq are all viewed as shared Arab humiliations while the 1973 war and 1973–74 Arab oil embargo, Israel's evacuation of southern Lebanon under Hizbollah pressure in June 2000, and the Israeli assaults on southern Lebanon in August 2006, which bolstered the popularity of Hizbollah, have been experienced as shared victories in the Arab world.[40] All these events have demonstrated that Islamic identity and Arabism are mutually reinforcing.[41]

In other parts of the Muslim world, by contrast, reformists have adopted pragmatic and nationalistic policies. This is even exemplified by competing nationalisms in non-Arab parts of the Muslim world. Islamic-oriented parties in Bangladesh, Indonesia, Malaysia, Pakistan, and Turkey have taken a pragmatic tack toward political life (see Table 10). Muslim democrats, as they are often called, do not seek to embed Islam in politics, though they make sure to harness its potential to help them win votes.[42] These democratic movements have been spearheaded not by intellectuals but by politicians such as Turkey's Recep Tayyib Erdoğan, Pakistan's Nawaz Sharif, and Malaysia's Anwar Ibrahim and Mahatir bin Mohammed, all of whom were primarily concerned with promoting their countries' economic interests.[43] The success of the Justice and Development Party's (Adalet ve Kalkinma Partisi, or AKP) platform in the 2002 (and 2007) elections in Turkey was less a triumph of religious piety over Kemalist secularism than the victory of an independent bourgeoisie over a centralizing state.[44] The AKP's reelection and impressive victory in the July 2007 national elections demonstrated that Turkey's Islamic-minded party has successfully synthesized Islamic values and the country's economic interests.

Secularists

Muslim secularists, who have supported secularization of Muslim culture through technological and economic modernization, have lost a great deal of public support throughout the Muslim world in the last quarter century. Kemal Atatürk (Turkey), Reza Shah (Iran), and Gamal Abdel Nasser (Egypt) represented Muslim secular leaders who were military men and who sought to build their countries' powers based on strong secular states and modernized armies. These secular leaders were committed not to equality and freedoms but to perpetuating their authoritarian, modernizing regimes. They tried to accomplish modernization programs without broad grassroots support and attempted to monopolize not only power but also political legitimacy.[45] In all these regimes, religious activities outside state control were vehemently suppressed. In the post-Atatürk period, the military-bureaucratic elite excluded Islamic elements from power-sharing in the government. Since the late 1990s, with the collapse of communism and the start of the post–Cold War era, the Turkish army has gradually developed the habit of engaging Islamist groups in a political debate. The upshot has been a decline in the role of the military-bureaucratic elite and the bourgeoisie's rise to the forefront of national politics, as Turkey has tried to bolster its candidacy for full membership in the European Union.[46]

The next generation of secular leaders consisted of a Westernized elite who adhered to the religious neutrality of the state and rejected Islamic ideas as framing the basis of their political legitimacy. These leaders promoted secular nationalism, Kemalism, socialism, pan-Arabism, and Baathism but failed to stem the rising tides of Islamism in the face of their poor economic performance and endemic corruption. While in Iran a mass-based Islamic movement led to the confiscation of political power by the clerics, in Turkey, Islamic groups engaged in political debates and power sharing through a democratic process. In Egypt, as part of a strategy of simultaneous accommodation and repression of its Islamist groups, the Egyptian government has allowed "a creeping Puritanism and censoriousness to pervade the country."[47] Secularist leaders have resorted to co-opting—and even exploiting—Islamic groups for their own political purposes whenever it seemed politically advantageous to do so (see Table 10). The outcome, however, has been quite the opposite: "Muslim secularists have legitimized political Islam as an idiom of anti-government dissent and have strengthened the Islamic revival."[48]

In Indonesia, the country's political stability owes much to an effective mediation by the ruling elites between Islamists and secularists. The intellectual transformation of Islamic political ideas and practices—from formative and legalistic to substantive and ethical—has led to an evolving stance of the state toward Islam. It is important to recognize, however, that although Indonesian secular leaders have generally encouraged bargaining and ideological pluralism, their politics have reinforced sectarian and often authoritarian policies.

In recent times, Muslim secularists have encountered numerous challenges from Islamists of different ideological stripes. Faced with a rising Islamic consciousness and the growing significance of transnational Islamic movements, such as the Tablighi Jama'at, secular governments—both in the Muslim world and in the West—have found it difficult to curb this movement's growth largely because of its avowed apoliticism. Such transnational movements have constructed religious, social, and translocal identities beyond national and territorial nation-states.[49] These transnational Islamic movements, however, have produced concern and unease in several European countries. It is to these movements and the challenges that they pose to European secular systems and cultural traditions that we next turn.

Diaspora Cultures in Europe

The enlargement of the European Union (EU) has infused renewed religious vitality into European political and social life. The increasing prominence of religion in European politics, along with the resurgence of transnational religious communities, has made it difficult to strike a balance between secular and Christian markers of European identity. Catholicism, Orthodoxy, and Islam are all transnational religious traditions: each has its own conception of European identity, European unity, and even of European modernity.[50]

The challenges posed by such transnational religious communities will be amplified in the coming years as the social and political diversity reflected in Europe's competing religious and secular traditions may not be hospitable to the unifying effects of Europeanization.[51] While Catholicism and Orthodoxy offer their definition of European identity and modernity in relation to their own religious traditions and institutional histories, the relationship between Muslim traditions and European unity remains much more problematic.[52]

Significantly, the domestic integration of minority groups has become an issue inseparable from the broader integration process unfolding in the EU. Muslims have become permanent members of European societies ("Eurabia") in large part because of emerging demographic trends. The aging population of Europe poses a clear and present threat to the economic growth of European countries. This explains Europe's growing reliance on the use of foreign labor. Demands for the accommodation of the cultural and religious needs of migrants will surely increase and require prompt adjustment by European politicians at the local, regional, and national levels.[53] Muslim migrants, as some experts suggest, are unlikely to assimilate in the same way as previous waves of migration. Islam has now become a European religion.[54]

Many jobless and disillusioned young Muslims in Europe suffer from social polarization, marginalization, and stigmatization. They are largely excluded from the social benefits that normal citizens enjoy. Alienation from the government and the demand for legal recognition are among the perennial reasons Muslim migrants in Europe have returned to Islam. Cyberspace has contributed to the construction of new identities among Muslim migrants. Perceptions, symbols, values, and theological frameworks depicted on the Internet are designed to influence ideologies compatible with an Islamic agenda. To understand the complexity of identity politics in Europe and the Muslim world, it is necessary to take seriously the Internet and its function in promoting Islamist groups' agenda. The Internet has played an important role in creating cohesive identities in cyberspace for the Islamic agendas of diverse actors. By spreading information, ideas, and cultural values around the globe, the Internet has led to virtual interconnections among Muslims.

As noted throughout the book, radical Islam does not come out of traditional Muslim societies but is a manifestation of modern identity politics—a side effect of the modernization process itself. Islamic militancy arises largely in response to casting about for identity.[55] Francis Fukuyama points out that modern identity politics revolve around demands for legal recognition of group identities—a recognition that is premised on the rights of ethnic, racial, religious, or cultural groups.[56] Multiculturalism in Europe, Fukuyama insists, has only served as a framework for the coexistence of separate cultures or groups rather than as "transitional mechanism for integrating newcomers into the dominant culture."[57]

The failure to fully integrate Muslims into European societies or to create communities that rest on harmony between social groups is likely to cause more instability for the EU enlargement project in the near future. Granting European Muslims equal treatment under the law and allowing them the choice of whether to assimilate or not is the key to their integration in the EU. Many analysts emphasize the need to foster interfaith cooperation in order to ensure domestic stability in the European contexts.[58] The consequences of excluding Muslims, as manifested in violent outbursts such as the 2005 riots in France, will only become graver in the long run. By incrementally changing popular perceptions of an evolving community of European states to reflect the continent's religious diversity—Catholic and Protestant in the West, Muslim in the South, and Orthodox in the East—the EU can forge more constructive interfaith interaction among member states.[59]

In a survey by the Pew Global Attitudes Project for 2006, Muslims from Jordan, Turkey, Egypt, Indonesia, and Pakistan, including the large Muslim populations in Britain, France, Germany and Spain, broadly blamed the West for the poor relations between the Muslim world and the West, while Westerners tended to blame Muslims. Muslims in the Middle East and Asia described Westerners as immoral and selfish while Westerners portrayed Muslims as fanatical.[60] Muslims surveyed in Europe were less inclined to view a "clash of civilizations" than were general publics in Europe or Muslims elsewhere.[61]

When faced with the banning of religious symbols (such as the *hijab*, the headscarf or veil) from public schools, European Muslims have decided to preserve their identity in a society dominated by non-Muslims and within a societal context of social and economic exclusion. Under such circumstances, for some Muslim women the headscarf can be an empowering statement of individual and collective Islamic identity. For those Muslim migrants who have a lower social status in a class-divided society such as France, Islamic revival provides a point of opposition. Some studies demonstrate that young French women perceive the headscarf "as an autonomous expression of their identity and not as a form of domination."[62] Even those who do not wear a headscarf believe that women should be able to choose. Identity, they argue, is an aspect of individual human dignity, autonomy, and self-determination. It is an aspect of religious freedom, expression, and privacy that "allows individuals to function freely and to enjoy the possibility of self-definition and self-determination."[63]

Despite the diversity of approaches across European states, most European countries have rejected the concept of group rights, even as they have promoted policies of liberalism and multiculturalism.[64] For French Muslims, the mere equality of French law is not enough. It disregards the quest for recognition of group identity. Muslims are not seeking merely equality of treatment but rather equality of respect.[65]

The European Court of Human Rights (ECHR) has frequently stated that the principles of secularism, religious neutrality, and gender equality must be considered central to national decisions of the member states of the European Union. In *Dahlab v. Switzerland*, the applicant was a schoolteacher in charge of a class of small children. In 1996, she was prohibited from wearing a headscarf when teaching. That decision was upheld by the

Geneva cantonal government on the grounds that teachers must fulfill the obligation of denominational neutrality. The Islamic dress code in this case, according to the government, conveyed a religious message in a manner that could have repercussions for the state school system.[66] The European Court supported Switzerland's decision, stating that it appeared difficult to reconcile wearing an Islamic headscarf with the message of tolerance, respect for others, equality, and nondiscrimination that all teachers in a democratic society must convey to their students.[67]

National identity, some observers argue, can be understood as part of "political status" as well as an aspect of "social and cultural development."[68] France equates national identity with homogeneity of the nation. It downplays the idea of cultural difference. As such, France's prohibition of the headscarf could thus be viewed as part of its cultural policy. A central part of French national identity is premised on the idea that it is a secular state.[69]

In the West, big majorities—up to 83 percent in Spain, 80 percent in Germany, and 77 percent in France—saw Muslims as not respectful of women.[70] Pew, which interviewed Muslims in Europe as a group for the first time in 2006, concluded that their views represented "a bridge" between the greatly diverse views of other Europeans and those of Muslims in Asia and the Middle East. Andrew Kohut, director of the Pew Research Center, pointed out that on balance, "even though [Muslim-Western] relations are not good, there hasn't been a spike in outright hostility between the two groups over the past year."[71] Nevertheless, majorities in every country surveyed (except Pakistan) expressed skepticism regarding these relations, with Germans having the most strongly unfavorable view (70 percent), followed by France (66 percent), Turkey (64 percent), Spain and Britain (61 percent), and Egypt (58 percent).[72]

Some analysts question the fears of some Western commentators that Muslims as a unified Islamic movement—or as a bloc—will influence the domestic and foreign policy of various European states. They argue that because Islam is a highly decentralized religion, it is structurally biased against facilitating large-scale collective action by its adherents. Divided by ethnicity and religious belief, Muslims in Europe as a group will be unable to impose their goals on European foreign and domestic policy.[73] Even as Europe appears to provide Muslims with an opportunity to create an Islam detached from cultural forces, ethnic ties, and state influences, that possibility is undermined by the multiple meanings, practices, and claims to spiritual leadership that the decentralized structure of Islam permits.[74]

In France, so-called French Islam (Islam Français) is diverse in terms of origin, aspiration, and socioeconomic success. Only a minority of French Muslims describe themselves as practicing Muslims, and the vast majority can be classified as moderates. It is more accurate to describe them as Muslims in a cultural rather than a strictly religious sense.[75] Olivier Roy has suggested that the concept of a Muslim vote in France is untenable because French Muslims are too varied and too "Gallic" to form a monolithic community.[76] But one crucial consequence of this impotent political representation is that it facilitates the development of militant groups who tend to react to their sense of exclusion in other ways.[77]

Women's Voices and Identity Formation

The study of women in Islamic societies views cultural politics—a process of conflict over cultural norms and symbols—as inseparable from sexual politics—women's struggle for power and authority at domestic, community, national, and international levels. Modernizing Muslim women have challenged the patriarchal structures of the Muslim world by demanding civil, political, and social rights. Consistent with these local demands, transnational pressures, through the activities of NGOs and international organizations, have also unleashed a process of norm internalization within the Muslim world. A major difficulty facing women's rights activists there, according to one expert, is the tension between a national identity based on Islamic civilization and culture and the call for civil and political rights typically seen as improperly inspired by Western societies and traditions.[78] In the context of equal citizenship rights for women, nationalism and Islamism remain the discursive frameworks that both shape and constrain the idea of human rights. Women's organizations need to develop a framework for recognizing identities and laying down the foundations for equal rights for all in a way that draws on history, cultural understandings, and global standards.[79]

Reformist Islamic movements have given Muslim women new tools of empowerment and prominence in all the cases studied here, with the exception of the United Arab Emirates. Reformists' emphasis on the task of textual reinterpretation or a rereading of Islamic theology, though critical to challenging religious fundamentalism, has proven insufficient by itself. Reform in the political economy and legal empowerment of women are imperative. Socioeconomic development and women's collective action are the most effective tools for reforming archaic laws and traditions. Given the fact that cultural influences are contested, political in nature, and inherently dynamic and fluid, women's collective actions appear inevitable.

The best protection for the human rights of Muslim women may come not from outside the Muslim world but rather from active, informed Muslim citizens. This accounts for the growing efficacy of local nongovernmental organizations. National and local feminists have been successful in bringing about change in the gender approach and policies of the Islamic Republic of Iran (increasing marriage age, child custody, payment for domestic services of women in divorce cases). Women's NGOs are sometimes showcased by the state to international audiences although they are not accorded much substantive weight locally. The common problem faced by most women's NGOs is their inability to draw in rural and lower class women. This may also be related to problems with needs assessments done by donor agencies and the government. Such assessments at times have been culturally and contextually insensitive.

Paradoxically, women groups continue to grow in their reliance on both local and transnational NGOs, despite these predicaments. Some domestic activists have framed their grievances in a universal human rights language. A major success for Muslim women's rights activists in recent years has been the growth of transnational networks, such as Women Living under Muslim Laws and Sisters in Islam. Taking advantage of the Internet and information technology, these networks advocate legal reform and organize resistance to archaic Islamic laws. Others have relied solely on a domestic culture of resistance—not transnational influences and activism. For them, social and political change has come largely through an expansion of individual and organizational activism as well as by mass public protests and resistance.[80]

The development of Islamic feminism, some observers note, is emblematic of a "discursive, forward-looking movement generated by women to rationalize their activism and employment outside the home—not as a product of changing economic opportunities or emulation of Western cultural models, but as the product of a true indigenous Islamic heritage."[81] The convergence between Islamic and secular feminists on matters relating to gender-specific violence against women, negotiating culture, and protecting women's rights has gained more public appeal than focusing on distinct or profound differences among such groups. Put another way, the gap between the secular and religious identity of feminists has noticeably narrowed. Although Islamic and secular feminists fall into opposite camps, they have found room for collaboration. Such cooperation and links with women's NGOs across borders has persisted, albeit not effectively. Additionally, grassroots movements stand a decent chance to initiate reform via the activities and ideas of nonconformist dissidents. They represent an internal, legitimate force capable of confronting the status quo.

The Prospects

As we illustrated through case studies, change is a constant that shapes, influences, and alters identities. Islamic identity is deeply embedded in the beliefs and daily practices of Muslim societies.[82] Muslim identities are multiple, fluid, and contentious, and the construction of identity is influenced by the various and complex ways in which local cultures and globalization interact. Further analysis of these interactions demonstrates that globalization compels groups and societies to "identify" themselves.[83] There is little agreement today on what the study of identity should be about. This volume has focused on the transformative power that ideas and communication networks have on emerging identities and global norms. More specifically, we have attempted to reveal the fault lines that sharply divide Islamic societies. While secular thinkers defend replacing arcane and obsolete traditions with rational ideas and universal norms, Islamists see in the defense of local culture a foundation for safeguarding authentic identity.[84]

Increasingly, Islamic movements, heirs to failed secular nationalists, have incorporated modern human rights concepts into their political campaigns. Normative ideas, such as democracy, rationalism, and human rights, are gaining a central place in Islamist and reform-oriented discourses. This possibility is likely to allow space where cultural change and continuity can coexist with possible global advances, including the desire to protect and promote universal human rights.[85]

Some scholars have argued that Islam is neither the source of human rights nor the cause of human rights violations. Rather, political structures explain most human rights violations in the Muslim world, and political and religious pathologies there are largely perpetrated through the acts of their leaders.[86] It is nonetheless essential to recognize that these leaders have been the least faithful to Islam's own normative and ethical foundations. It is equally important to underscore the fact that Islamic grassroots organizations have created wide-ranging social welfare networks that address the socioeconomic needs of the masses in the face of governments' failure to do so.

Globalization poses two central challenges to the issue of authenticity in the Muslim world. First, Muslims have to balance old cultural traditions with modern standards and practices in order to exercise their power and enhance their values in global contexts. It is not possible to specify precisely how this ought to be done because social change affects various Muslim societies differently, and there is no consensus on how change must be absorbed without losing one's national identity. It should be noted, however, that reformist Islam with its long tradition of original *ijtihad* (autonomous reasoning), which is deeply rooted in Islamic thought and history, is capable of striking this balance. In its current manifestation, as some scholars suggest, reformist Islam is part of a broader discourse of universal human rights.[87]

Second, given that human rights embody the fundamental values of human civilizations, the lingering question is determining whose conception or understanding of human rights should prevail in the Muslim world.[88] In Islamic societies, Abdullahi An-Na'im writes, the balance of the "competing demands of the Islamic identity of the community" and "the requirement of constitutionalism, pluralism, stability, and development" may change at different times, but the crucial issue is always whether the negotiation process is fair, open, and fully inclusive of all segments of the population. How that balance is maintained and sustained over time is the function of a contextual negotiation within each society.[89]

The lack of open political space, sectarian strife, poverty, and outside pressures, such as the U.S. occupation of Iraq or U.S. support for the political regime in Egypt, have combined to shape a culture of resistance as well as to perpetuate and even aggravate the issue of identity construction in the countries studied in this book. The U.S. invasion of Iraq has exacerbated the sense of impotence, humiliation, and rage among Muslims.[90] That sense, along with the presence of corrupt, incompetent, and repressive secular regimes in the Muslim world, has broadened the appeal of an Islamic identity.

Significantly, political struggles in Muslim societies are not only about tensions between traditional and modern forces but also about whether or how the desire to concurrently accept globalization and preserve authenticity can be articulated through this ongoing dialectic. To the extent that Muslims' demands relate to basic freedoms, their leaders have yet to solve the issue of what is properly "universal" and what is properly "cultural."

Cultural interactions with the non-Muslim world as well as transnational ties and interests are likely to empower Muslims and alter the way they form images of the "self" and the "other." Together with the acceptance of new ideas and norms, such cultural dialogues and exchanges could potentially influence the social context within which identities and interests are constructed.

For many Muslims, the pivotal questions are these: How could Muslims best preserve their national/Islamic identity in the face of the sea changes caused by globalization? Will Europeans recognize the fact of differences as far as their Muslim minorities are concerned and work toward pursuing common goals? Or will Muslims' role in defining multiple conceptions of modernity and varied narratives of world politics be recognized? The answers to these questions depend partly on how Muslims themselves define power, interests, identity, and human rights and partly on how the Western world regards the stakes involved in determining the global agenda alone. Reconstructing an agenda trusted by all participants and reconciling methods by which all political, cultural, and social communities can define their own interests, identities, and rights in conjunction with the rest is a major challenge facing the international community in the coming years.

Notes

Chapter 1

1. Simon W. Murden, *Islam, the Middle East, and the New Global Hegemony* (Boulder, Colo.: Lynne Rienner, 2002), p. 40.

2. James H. Mittelman, *The Globalization Syndrome: Transformation and Resistance* (Princeton, N.J.: Princeton University Press, 2000), p. 4.

3. Peter Mandaville, *Transnational Muslim Politics: Reimagining the Umma* (New York: Routledge, 2004), p. 112.

4. Murden, *Islam*, p. 24.

5. Nader Entessar, *Kurdish Ethnonationalism* (Boulder, Colo.: Lynne Rienner, 1992), pp. 6–9.

6. Ibid., p. 10.

7. Michael M. Gunter, *Historical Dictionary of the Kurds* (Lanham, Md.: Scarecrow Press, 2004), p. 174.

8. Robert Olson, *The Goat and the Butcher: Nationalism and State Formation in Kurdistan-Iraq since the Iraqi War* (Costa Mesa, Calif.: Mazda, 2005), p. 37.

9. Ibid., pp. 244–45.

10. The divide between adherents of Shi'ism and Sunnism can be traced back to their major differences over the succession to Prophet Mohammad, interpretation of the Qur'an and the Prophet's Hadith (Sayings), Islamic jurisprudence, liturgical prayers, religious tradition, and clerical establishment, among other things. Despite a number of similarities, such as believing in the indivisibility of God and the story of creation, Islam's foundational principles, Islamic law, the sanctity of life, jihad, and the Messianic Savior, the two sects parted ways early in Muslim history, each viewing itself as the original orthodoxy. For more information on this subject, see Mir Zohair Husain, *Islam and the Muslim World* (Dubuque, Ia.: McGraw-Hill/Contemporary Learning Series, 2006), pp. 17–21.

11. Vali Nasr, *The Shia Revival: How Conflict within Islam Will Shape the Future* (New York: W. W. Norton, 2006).

12. Ibid.

13. See, for example, Benedict Anderson, *Imagined Communities*, 2nd ed. (London: Verson, 1991), and R. B. J. Walker, *Inside/Outside: International Relations as Political Theory* (Cambridge: Cambridge University Press, 1993).

14. Nicholas Onuf, "Constructivism: A User's Manual," in Vendulka Kubalkova, Nicholas Onuf, and Paul Kowert, eds., *International Relations in a Constructed World* (Armonk, N.Y.: M. E. Sharpe, 1998), pp. 58–78, esp. p. 65.

15. Nicholas Onuf, "Identity: Theories of the Self," available at http://www

.bridgewater.edu/~jfrueh/WPolitics/Identityreading.doc, last visited on March 24, 2005.

16. Thomas Risse and Kathryn Sikkink, "The Socialization of International Human Rights Norms into Domestic Practices: Introduction," in Thomas Risse, Stephen C. Ropp, and Kathryn Sikkink, eds., *The Power of Human Rights: International Norms and Domestic Change* (Cambridge: Cambridge University Press, 1999), pp. 1–38, esp. p. 9.

17. Ronald L. Jepperson, Alexander Wendt, and Peter J. Katzenstein, "Norms, Identity, and Culture in National Security," in Peter J. Katzenstein, ed., *The Culture of National Security: Norms and Identity in World Politics* (New York: Columbia University Press, 1996), pp. 33–75, esp. p. 41.

18. Ibid., p. 52.

19. Nicholas Onuf, "Worlds of Our Making: The Strange Career of Constructivism in International Relations," in Donald P. Puchala, ed., *Visions of International Relations: Assessing an Academic Field* (Columbia: University of South Carolina Press, 2002), pp. 119–41, esp. p. 126.

20. Patrick Imbert, "Globalization and Differences: Displacement, Culture, and Homeland," *Globalization* 1, no. 2 (December 2004): 194–204, esp. 196.

21. This assumption is borrowed from Patricia M. Goff and Kevin C. Dunn, eds., *Identity and Global Politics: Theoretical and Empirical Elaborations* (New York: Palgrave Macmillan, 2004), p. 6.

22. Dale F. Eickelman, "The Coming Transformation of the Muslim World," available at http://www.comw.org/pda/muslim799.html, last visited on February 3, 2005.

23. Dominic McGoldrick, *Human Rights and Religion: The Islamic Headscarf Debate in Europe* (Portland, Ore.: Hart, 2006), p. 61.

24. S. V. R. Nasr, "European Colonialism and the Emergence of Modern Muslim States," in John E. Esposito, ed., *The Oxford History of Islam* (Oxford: Oxford University Press, 1999), pp. 549–99, esp. pp. 550–51.

25. Bergedorf Round Table/Isfahan, Iran, *The Middle East and Western Values: A Dialogue with Iran* (Berlin, Germany: Bergedorfer Gesprachskreis, October 25–26, 2003), p. 82, esp. comments by Homayra Moshirzadeh.

26. Francois Burgat, *Face to Face with Political Islam* (New York: I. B. Tauris, 2003), p. 50.

27. Murden, *Islam*, p. 23.

28. Imbert, "Globalization and Difference," p. 194.

29. Mahmood Monshipouri, *Islamism, Secularism, and Human Rights in the Middle East* (Boulder, Colo.: Lynne Rienner, 1998), p. 11.

30. John L. Esposito, *The Islamic Threat: Myth or Reality*, 3rd ed. (New York: Oxford University Press, 1999), pp. 7–9.

31. Murden, *Islam*, p. 135.

32. Ibid., p. 137.

33. Ibid., p. 150.

34. Mustapha Kamal Pasha, "Predatory Globalization and Democracy in the Islamic World," *Annals of the American Academy of Political and Social Science* 581 (May 2002): 121–32, esp. 130.

35. Murden, *Islam,* p. 204.

36. Ibid., p. 151.

37. Anthony Giddens, *Modernity and Self-Identity: Self and Society in the Late Modern Age* (London: Polity Press, 1991), pp. 21–23.

38. Roger Hardy, "Islam and the West," August 12, 2002, available at http://news.bbc.co.uk/2/hi/in_indepth/world/2002/islamic_world/2188307.stm, last visited on February 2, 2005.

39. Mustapha Kamal Pasha and Ahmed I. Samatar, "The Resurgence of Islam," in James H. Mittelman, ed., *Globalization: Critical Reflections* (Boulder, Colo.: Lynne Rienner, 1996), pp. 187–201, esp. p. 191.

40. Ibid., p. 197.

41. Jan Aart Scholte, *Globalization: A Critical Introduction* (New York: St. Martin's Press, 2000), p. 177.

42. Ibid., p. 188.

43. Pasha and Samatar, "The Resurgence of Islam," p. 200.

44. James H. Mittelman, "How Does Globalization Really Work?" in James H. Mittelman, ed., *Globalization: Critical Reflections* (Boulder, Colo.: Lynne Rienner, 1996), pp. 229–41, esp. p. 240.

45. Roger Hardy, "Islam and the West."

46. Kenneth Cragg, "Muslim Encounters with the West," in Robert Wuthnow, *Encyclopedia of Politics and Religion*, vol. 2 (Washington, D.C.: Congressional Quarterly, 1998), pp. 538–43.

47. Ibid.

48. Burgat, *Face to Face,* p. 49.

49. Roger Owen, *State, Power and Politics in the Making of the Modern Middle East*, 2nd ed. (New York: Routledge, 2000), p. 173.

50. John E. Esposito, "Contemporary Islam: Reformation or Revolution," in John E. Esposito, ed., *The Oxford History of Islam* (Oxford: Oxford University Press, 1999), pp. 643–90, esp. p. 656.

51. Beverley Milton-Edwards, *Islam and Politics in the Contemporary World* (Malden, Mass.: Polity Press, 2004), p. 209.

52. Graham E. Fuller, "The Future of Political Islam," available at http://www.cceia.org/viewMedia.php/prm TemplateID/8/prmID/934, last visited on October 20, 2004.

53. Graham E. Fuller, *The Future of Political Islam* (New York: Palgrave Macmillan, 2003).

54. Burgat, *Face to Face*, p. 22.

55. Ibid.

56. John L. Esposito and John O. Voll, *Islam and Democracy* (Oxford: Oxford University Press, 1996), pp. 177–78.

57. Mahmood Mamdani, "American and Political Islam," *Global Agenda Magazine,* available at http://www.globalagendamagazine.com/2005/mahmood mamdani.asp, last visited on February 2, 2005.

58. "Islam after 9/11," Islamic Societies: Conversation with Ira Lapidus, available at http//:globetrotter.berkeley.edu/people3/lapidus/lapidus-cono.html, last visited on February 23, 2005.

59. Peter Mandaville, *Transnational Muslim Politics: Reimagining the Umma* (New York: Routledge, 2004), pp. 115 and 132.

60. Ibid., pp. 151 and 190.

61. Peter Mandaville, "Reimagining Islam in Diaspora: The Politics of Mediated Community," *Gazette* 63, nos. 2–3 (2001): 169–86.

62. Amaney Jamal, "Religious Identity, Discrimination and 9–11: The Determinants of Arab American Levels of Political Confidence in Mainstream and Ethnic Institutions," a paper presented at the conference Middle Eastern Diasporas: (In)-visible Minorities, March 18–19, 2005, Yale Center for International Studies and Area Studies, New Haven, Conn.

63. Iqbal Jhazbhav, "An Emerging Muslim Identity in the Global Village: The South African Presentation at the International Conference '*Azmat Al-Hawiyya*,'" *Journal of Muslim Minority Affairs* 20, no. 2 (October 2000): 369–72.

64. Olivier Roy, *Globalized Islam: The Search for a New Ummah* (New York: Columbia University Press, 2004), p. 15.

65. Gilles Kepel, *The War for Muslim Minds: Islam and the West* (Cambridge: Belknap Press of Harvard University Press, 2004), p. 6.

66. Roy, *Globalized Islam*, p. 18.

67. Ibid., pp. 25 and 39.

68. Ibid., p. 89.

69. Ibid., p. 99.

70. Ibid., p. 330.

71. Sayres S. Rudy, "Subjectivity, Political Evaluation, and Islamist Trajectories," in Birgit Schaeber and Leif Stenberg, eds., *Globalization and the Muslim World: Culture, Religion, and Modernity* (Syracuse, N.Y.: Syracuse University Press, 2004), pp. 39–79, esp. p. 68.

72. Roy, *Globalized Islam*, p. 102.

73. Ibid., p. 103.

74. Ibid., p. 201.

75. Ibid., p. 331.

76. Dalia Abdel-Hady, "Public Engagement of Lebanese Immigrants in Three World Cities," paper presented at the conference Middle Eastern Diasporas: (In)visible Minorities, March 18–19, 2005, Yale Center for International Studies and Area Studies, New Haven, Conn.

77. Paul Kowert and Jeffrey Legro, "Norms, Identity, and Their Limits: A Theoretical Reprise," in Peter J. Katzenstein, ed., *The Culture of National Security: Norms and Identity in World Politics* (New York: Columbia University Press, 1996), pp. 451–97, esp. p. 474.

78. G. John Ikenberry, quoted in Michael Cox, "Empire by Denial: The Strange Case of the United States," *International Affairs* 81, no. 1 (January 2005): 15–30, esp. p. 19.

79. Patrick Thaddeus Jackson, "Whose Identity? Rhetorical Commonplaces in 'American' Wartime Foreign Policy," in Patricia M. Goff and Kevin C. Dunn, eds., *Identity and Global Politics: Theoretical and Empirical Elaborations* (New York: Palgrave Macmillan, 2004), pp. 169–89, esp. p. 175.

80. For a critique of Samuel Huntington, "The Clash of Civilizations?" see

Mahmood Monshipouri and Gina Petonito, "Constructing the Enemy in the Post–Cold War Era: The Flaws of the 'Islamic Conspiracy' Theory," *Journal of Church and State* 37, no. 4 (Autumn 1995): 773–92.

81. Quoted in Jackson, "Whose Identity?" p. 185.

82. Ibid.

83. Roy, *Globalized Islam*, p. 332.

84. Bergedorf Round Table/Isfahan, Iran, *The Middle East and Western Values*, p. 34.

85. Gustav Neibuhr, "All Need Toleration: Some Observations about Recent Differences in the Experiences of Religious Minorities in the United States and Western Europe," *Annals of the American Academy of Political and Social Science* 612 (July 2007): 172–86.

86. Ibid., p. 173.

87. Fuller, "The Future of Political Islam."

88. See Adrian Karatnycky's comments in Kenneth Jost and Benton Ives-Halperin, "Democracy in the Arab World," in CQ Researcher, *Global Issues* (Washington, D.C.: CQ Press, 2005), pp. 181–206, esp. p. 199.

89. Pasha, "Predatory Globalization and Democracy," pp. 121–32, esp. p. 129.

90. Jeremy Jones, *Negotiating Change: The New Politics of the Middle East* (London: I. B. Tauris, 2007), pp. 9–10.

91. Darren C. Zook, "Decolonizing Law: Identity Politics, Human Rights, and the United Nations," *Harvard Human Rights Journal* 19 (2006): 95–122, esp. 121.

Chapter 2

1. Richard A. Falk, *Human Rights Horizons: The Pursuit of Justice in a Globalizing World* (New York: Routledge, 2000).

2. Michael Ignatieff, *Human Rights as Politics and Idolatry* (Princeton, N.J.: Princeton University Press, 2001).

3. Jan Aart Scholte, *Globalization: A Critical Introduction* (New York: St. Martin's Press, 2000).

4. Amin Maalouf, *In the Name of Identity: Violence and the Need to Belong* (New York: Arcade Publishing, 2000), p. 93.

5. Ibid., p. 96.

6. S. R. Ameli, "Cultural Globalization and Muslim Identity," in M. S. Bahmanpour and H. Bashir, eds., *Muslim Identity in the 21st Century: Challenges and Modernity* (London: Institute of Islamic Studies, 2000), pp. 151–70; see p. 160.

7. Ibid.

8. Mahmoud M. Ayoub, "Islam and the Challenge of Religious Pluralism," *Global Dialogue* 2, no. 1 (Winter 2000): 53–64, esp. 63.

9. Ibid., p. 62.

10. Mustafa Malik, "Islam's Missing Link to the West," *Middle East Policy* 10, no. 1 (Spring 2003): 121–34, esp. 133.

11. Ali Mohammadi, "The Culture and Politics of Human Rights in the Context of Islam," in Ali Mohammadi, ed., *Islam Encountering Globalization* (New York: RoutledgeCurzon, 2002), pp. 111–30, esp. p. 118.

12. Maimul Ahsan Khan, *Human Rights in the Muslim World: Fundamentalism, Constitutionalism, and International Politics* (Durham, N.C.: Carolina Academic Press, 2003), p. 97.

13. Abdullahi Ahmed An-Na'im, *Toward an Islamic Reformation: Civil Liberties, Human Rights and International Law* (Syracuse: Syracuse University Press, 1990).

14. Fatima Mernissi, *Islam and Democracy: Fear of the Modern World* (London: Virago, 1992).

15. Louay Safi, "Human Rights and Islamic Legal Reform," http://home.att.net/~1.safi/articles/.

16. The classification of this group is based on the study by Mir Zohair Husain, *Global Islamic Politics*, 2nd ed. (New York: Longman, 2003). This section is also drawn from my recent essay "The Politics and Practice of Human Rights in the Muslim World," *Global Dialogue* 6, no. 1 (Winter–Spring 2004): 67–78.

17. I have borrowed these categories from James H. Mittelman and Christine B. N. Chin, "Conceptualizing Resistance to Globalization," in James H. Mittelman, ed., *The Globalization Syndrome: Transformation and Resistance* (Princeton, N.J.: Princeton University Press, 2000), pp. 165–78, esp. pp. 176–78.

18. John L. Esposito, *Islam: The Straight Path* (New York: Oxford University Press, 1988), pp. 179–80.

19. Mir Zohair Husain, *Global Islamic Politics*, 2nd ed. (New York: Longman, 2003), pp. 129–30.

20. Salafists are those who closely emulate the pious companions of Prophet Mohammad. Salafists wish to return Islam to its purest roots. Their reference point is the teachings of Imam Ahmad bin Hanbal and Abu Haneefah, as well as other scholars who adhered to the methodology of the salaf.

21. Guilain Denoeux, "The Forgotten Swamp: Navigating Political Islam," *Middle East Policy* 9, no. 2 (June 2002): 56–81, esp. 60.

22. Ibid., pp. 66–67.

23. Husain, *Global Islamic Politics*, pp. 125–30.

24. Ibid., p. 93.

25. Denoeux, "The Forgotten Swamp," p. 67.

26. Husain, *Global Islamic Politics*, p. 128.

27. Ibid., p. 237.

28. Ibid, pp. 270–71.

29. Ali Mohammadi, "The Culture and Politics of Human Rights in the Context of Islam," in Ali Mohammadi, ed., *Islam Encountering Globalization* (New York: RoutledgeCurzon, 2002), pp. 111–30, esp. p. 114.

30. Gilles Kepel, *The War for Muslim Minds: Islam and the West* (Cambridge: Harvard University Press, 2004), p. 253.

31. Ali Paya, "Muslim Identity and Civil Society: Whose Islam? Which Society?" in M. S. Bahmanpour and H. Bashir, eds., *Muslim Identity in the 21st Century:*

Challenges and Modernity (London: Institute of Islamic Studies, 2000), pp. 105–24, esp. pp. 119–20.

32. Abdulaziz A. Sachedina, "Freedom of Conscience and Religion in the Qur'an," in David Little, John Kelsay, and Abdulaziz A. Sachedina, eds., *Human Rights and the Conflict of Cultures: Western and Islamic Perspectives on Religious Liberty* (Columbia: University of South Carolina Press, 1988), pp. 53–90, esp. p. 57.

33. Beverley Milton-Edwards, *Islam and Politics in the Contemporary World* (Malden, Mass.: Polity Press, 2004), p. 139.

34. For a broader view of this topic, see Daphne Grace, *The Woman in the Muslim Mask: Veiling and Identity in Postcolonial Literature* (London: Pluto Press, 2004), p. 206.

35. Milton-Edwards, *Islam and Politics,* p. 138.

36. Salwa Ismail, *Rethinking Islamist Politics: Culture, the State and Islamism* (London: I. B. Tauris, 2003), pp. 175–76.

37. Quoted in Ismail, *Rethinking Islamist Politics,* p. 176.

38. Ibid.

39. Muqtedar Khan, "Reason and Individual Reasoning," in John J. Donohue and John L. Esposito, eds., *Islam in Transition: Muslim Perspectives,* 2nd ed. (New York: Oxford University Press, 2007), pp. 501–6, esp. p. 506.

40. Ibid.

41. See a summary of remarks by Abdolkarim Soroush and Charles Butterworth at the Middle East Institute, November 21, 2000, "Islamic Democracy and Islamic Governance," available at http://www.mideasti.org/html/b-soroush.html.

42. Forough Jahanbaksh, "Abdolkarim Soroush: New Revival of Religious Sciences," available at http://www.isim.nl/newsletter/8/jahanbaksh.htm.

43. Mahmoud Sadri and Ahmad Sadri, eds., *Reason, Freedom, and Democracy in Islam: Essential Writings of Abdolkarim Soroush* (New York: Oxford University Press, 2000), p. 128.

44. Ibid., p. 129.

45. Abdou Filali-Ansary, "Islam and Liberal Democracy: The Challenge of Secularization," *Journal of Democracy* 7, no. 2 (1996): 76–80, esp. 78.

46. Husain, *Global Islamic Politics,* p. 129.

47. Mir Zohair Husain, *Islam and the Muslim World* (Dubuque, Iowa: McGraw-Hill/Contemporary Learning Series, 2006), pp. 28–31.

48. Ibid., p. 31.

49. Mehranguiz Kar, "Women's Strategies in Iran from the 1979 Revolution to 1999," in Jane H. Bayes and Nayereh Tohidi, eds., *Globalization, Gender, and Religion: The Politics of Women's Rights in Catholic and Muslim Contexts* (New York: Palgrave, 2001), pp. 177–201, esp. pp. 198–99.

50. Nayereh Tohidi, "The Global-Local Intersection of Feminism in Muslim Societies: The Cases of Iran and Azerbaijan," *Social Research* 69, no. 3 (Fall 2003): 851–87, esp. 860.

51. Ibid., p. 862.

52. Afsaneh Najmabadi, "Feminism in an Islamic Republic: Years of Hardship, Years of Growth," in Yvonne Yazbeck Haddad and John L. Esposito, eds.,

Islam, Gender, and Social Change (New York: Oxford University Press, 1998), pp. 59–84, esp. p. 60.

53. Valentine M. Moghadam, *Modernizing Women: Gender and Social Change in the Middle East*, 2nd ed. (Boulder, Colo.: Lynne Rienner, 2003), p. 218.

54. Quoted in *International Iran Times*, October 17, 2003, pp. 1 and 3.

55. For further discussion on this subject, see Mahmood Monshipouri, "The Road to Globalization Runs through Women's Struggle: Iran and the Impact of the Nobel Peace Prize," *World Affairs* 167, no. 1 (Summer 2004): 3–14, esp. 6.

56. Ghada Hashem Talhami, "European, Muslim and Female," *Middle East Policy* 11, no. 2 (Summer 2004): 152–68, esp. 154.

57. Sami Al-Khazendar, "The Political Obstacles Encountering the Euro-Muslim Coexistence," *Alternatives: Turkish Journal of International Relations* 3, nos. 2 and 3 (Summer and Fall 2004): 67–97, esp. 81.

58. Talhami, "European, Muslim and Female," p. 163.

59. Ibid., pp. 163–67.

60. Homelands of Muslim immigrants in various European countries are as follows: Austria (Turkey, 50 percent), Belgium (Morocco, 55 percent), Denmark (Turkey, 27 percent), Finland (Somalia, 23 percent), France (Algeria, 30 percent), Germany (Turkey, 68 percent), Greece (Turkey, 50 percent), Italy (Morocco, 34 percent), Luxembourg (Montenegro, 25 percent), Netherlands (Turkey, 40 percent), Portugal (Mozambique, N/A), Spain (Morocco, N/A), Sweden (former Yugoslavia, 25 percent), UK (Pakistan, 45 percent). See Ross Douthat, "A Muslim Europe?" *Atlantic Monthly* 295, no. 1 (January–February 2005): 58–59, esp. 58.

61. Ibid.

62. Ibid.

63. Ibid.

64. Ibid.

65. Abdullahi An-Na'im, "Human Rights and Islamic Identity in France and Uzbekistan: Mediation of the Local and Global," Occasional Paper, Claus M. Halle Institute for Global Learning, Emory Law School, Atlanta, Ga., pp. 3–44, esp. p. 15.

66. Kristen Hill Maher, "Who Has a Right to Rights? Citizenship's Exclusion in an Age of Migration," in Alison Brysk, ed., *Globalization and Human Rights* (Berkeley: University of California Press, 2002), pp. 19–43, esp. p. 25.

67. Ibid., pp. 37–38.

68. Graham E. Fuller and Ian O. Lesser, *A Sense of Siege: The Geopolitics of Islam and the West* (Boulder, Colo.: Westview Press, 1995), pp. 88–95.

69. Mahmood Monshipouri, "The West's Modern Encounter with Islam: From Discourse to Reality," *Journal of Church and State* 40, no. 1 (Winter 1998): 25–56, esp. 38.

70. Dale F. Eickelman and James Piscatori, *Muslim Politics* (Princeton, N.J.: Princeton University Press, 1996).

71. Frederick M. Denny, "Islam and the Muslim Community," in H. Byron Earhart, ed., *Religious Traditions of the World: A Journey through Africa, Mesoamerica, North America, Judaism, Christianity, Islam, Hinduism, Buddhism, China, and Japan* (New York: HarperCollins, 1993), pp. 603–712, esp. p. 703.

72. Gilles Kepel, *The War for Muslim Minds: Islam and the West* (Cambridge: Harvard University Press, 2004), p. 8.

73. Ali A. Mazrui, "Pretender to Universalism: Western Culture in a Globalizing Age," *Global Dialogue* 3, no. 1 (Winter 2001): 33–45, esp. 38.

74. John Obert Voll, *Islam: Continuity and Change in the Muslim World* (Syracuse, N.Y.: Syracuse University Press, 1994), p. 366.

75. Ibid.

76. Jocelyne Cesari, "Islam in the West," in Birgit Schaebler and Leif Stenberg, eds., *Globalization and the Muslim World: Culture, Religion, and Modernity* (Syracuse, N.Y.: Syracuse University Press, 2004), pp. 80–92, esp. p. 83.

77. Valerie Amiraux, "Restructuring Political Islam: Transnational Belonging and Muslims in France and Germany," in Azza Karam, ed., *Transnational Political Islam: Religion, Ideology and Power* (London: Pluto Press, 2004), pp. 28–58, esp. p. 49.

78. Mustafa Malik, "Muslims Pluralize the West, Resist Assimilation," *Middle East Policy* 11, no. 1 (Spring 2004): 70–83, esp. 72.

79. Ibid., pp. 79–81.

80. Khurshid Ahmad, "Islam and the West: Confrontation or Cooperation?" *Muslim World* 85, nos. 1–2 (January–April 1995): 63–81, esp. 74–81.

81. Bert F. Breiner and Christen W. Troll, "Christianity and Islam," in John L. Esposito, ed., *The Oxford Encyclopedia of the Modern Islamic World* (Oxford: Oxford University Press, 1995), vol. 1, pp. 280–86.

82. Olivier Roy, *Globalized Islam: A Search for a New Ummah* (New York: Columbia University Press, 2004).

83. Bahman Baktiar, "Cybermuslim and the Internet: Searching for Spiritual Harmony in the Digital World," in M. S. Bahmanpour and H. Bashir, eds., *Muslim Identity in the 21st Century: Challenges and Modernity* (London: Institute of Islamic Studies, 2000), pp. 219–31, esp. p. 221.

84. Ibid.

85. Ibid., p. 225.

86. Susan Waltz, "Universal Human Rights: The Contribution of Muslim States," *Human Rights Quarterly* 26, no. 4 (November 2004): 799–844, esp. 814–19.

87. Ann Elizabeth Mayer, *Islam and Human Rights: Tradition and Politics*, 4th ed. (Boulder, Colo.: Westview Press, 2007), p. 15.

88. Waltz, "Universal Human Rights," p. 807.

89. Ibid., p. 808.

90. Quoted in Waltz, "Universal Human Rights," p. 839.

91. Steven D. Krasner, "International Political Economy: Abiding Discord," *Review of International Political Economy* 1, no. 1 (1994): 13–19.

92. Mayer, *Islam and Human Rights*, p. 18. Mayer attributes this argument to Karen Engle's analysis, "Culture and Human Rights: The Asian Values Debate in Context," *New York University Journal of International Law and Politics* 32 (2000): 291–332.

93. Mayer, *Islam and Human Rights*, pp. 178–92.

94. Neil MacFarquhar, "Muslim Scholars Increasingly Debate Unholy War," *New York Times*, December 10, 2004, pp. A1 and A12.

95. James Piscatori, "The Turmoil Within: The Struggle for the Future of the Islamic World," *Foreign Affairs* 81, no. 3 (May–June 2002): 145–50, esp. 150.

96. The Organization of Islamic Conference includes Afghanistan, Albania, Algeria, Azerbaijan, Bahrain, Bangladesh, Benin, Brunei-Darusalaam, Burkina Faso, Cameroon, Chad, Comoros, Côte d'Ivoire, Djibouti, Egypt, Gabon, Gambia, Guinea, Guinea-Bissau, Guyana, Indonesia, Iran, Iraq, Jordan, Kazakhstan, Kuwait, Kyrgyzstan, Lebanon, Libya, Malaysia, Maldives, Mali, Mauritania, Morocco, Mozambique, Niger, Nigeria, Oman, Pakistan, Palestine, Qatar, Saudi Arabia, Senegal, Sierra Leone, Somalia, Sudan, Surinam, Syria, Tajikistan, Togo, Tunisia, Turkey, Turkmenistan, Uganda, United Arab Emirates, Uzbekistan, and Yemen. Of these the following countries have yet to ratify the Convention on the Elimination of All Forms of Discrimination against Women (CEDAW) Afghanistan, Bahrain, Iran, Mauritania, Qatar, Saudi Arabia, Somalia, Sudan, Syria, United Arab Emirates, and Palestine. For more details, see UNDP, *Human Development Report 2000* (New York: Oxford University Press, 2000), pp. 48–51.

97. Falk, *Human Rights Horizons,* pp. 152–63.

98. Jürgen Habermas, "On Legitimation through Human Rights," in Pablo De Greiff and Ciaran Cronin, eds., *Global Justice and Transnational Politics: Essays on the Moral and Political Challenges of Globalization* (Cambridge: MIT Press, 2002), pp. 197–214, esp. p. 205.

99. Ibid.

100. Ibid., p. 211.

101. Falk, *Human Rights Horizons,* p. 149.

102. Lynda S. Bell, Andrew J. Nathan, and Ilan Peleg, "Culture and Human Rights," in Lynda S. Bell, Andrew J. Nathan, and Ilan Peleg, *Negotiating Culture and Human Rights* (New York: Columbia University Press, 2001), pp. 3–20, esp. p. 12.

103. Ibid., p. 19

104. Khan, *Human Rights in the Muslim World,* p. 117.

105. An-Na'im, "Human Rights and Islamic Identity," pp. 3–44, esp. pp. 6–7.

106. Charles Kurzman, "The Globalization of Rights in Islamic Discourse," in Ali Mohammadi, ed., *Islam Encountering Globalization* (New York: Routledge-Curzon, 2002), pp. 131–55.

107. Bhikhu Parekh, "Non-Ethnocentric Universalism," in Tim Dunne and Nicholas J. Wheeler, *Human Rights in Global Politics* (Cambridge: Cambridge University Press, 1999), pp. 128–59, esp. p. 158.

108. R. Dean Peterson, Delores F. Wunder, and Harlan L. Mueller, *Social Problems: Globalization in the Twenty-First Century* (Upper Saddle River, N.J.: Prentice Hall, 1999), p. 69.

109. Abdullahi An-Na'im, "Area Expressions and the Universality of Human Rights: Mediating a Contingent Relationship," in David P. Forsythe and Patrice C. McMahon, eds., *Human Rights and Diversity: Area Studies Revisited* (Lincoln: University of Nebraska Press, 2003), pp. 1–21, esp. pp. 6–7.

110. An-Nai'm, "Human Rights and Islamic Identity," p. 37.

111. John O. Voll, "For Scholars of Islam, Interpretation Need Not Be Advocacy," *Chronicle of Higher Education,* March 22, 1989, p. 48.

Chapter 3

1. Dale F. Eickelman, "Inside the Islamic Reformation," in Barry Rubin, ed., *Revolutionaries and Reformers: Contemporary Islamist Movements in the Middle East* (Albany: State University of New York Press, 2003), pp. 203–6, esp. p. 206.

2. Elsewhere I have elaborated on "The Muslim World, Globalization, and Women's Rights," *International Studies Journal* 1, no. 1 (Summer 2004): 27–49.

3. Jane H. Bayes and Nayereh Tohidi, eds., *Globalization, Gender, and Religion: The Politics of Women's Rights in Catholic and Muslim Contexts* (New York: Palgrave, 2001).

4. John L. Esposito, "Women in Islam and Muslim Societies," in Yvonne Yazbeck Haddad and John L. Esposito, eds., *Islam, Gender, and Social Change* (Oxford: Oxford University Press, 1998), pp. ix–xxvii, esp. p. xxvii.

5. Deniz Kandiyoti, "Women, Islam and the State, *Middle East Report* (November–December 1991): 9–13, esp. 10.

6. Ibid., p. 12.

7. Ibid.

8. Mounira M. Charrad, *States and Women's Rights: The Making of Postcolonial Tunisia, Algeria, and Morocco* (Berkeley: University of California Press, 2001), pp. 218–19.

9. Ibid., p. 219.

10. See Jaafar Alj Hakim, "Moroccan Family Code Enhances Women's Rights," available at http://web.lexis-nexis.com/universe/document?_m + e583d 68139ae7c0d83fb657448 b34dc9, last accessed on March 8, 2004.

11. See "Legal Reforms for Moroccan Women," *Weekend All Things Considered*, March 6, 2004, Saturday, available at http://web.lexis-nexis.com/universal/ document?_m = 9c7e8114692f4fc2babf3f12f360bf99&_, last accessed on March 8, 2004.

12. Ashraf Khalil, "Iraq's Women See Victory in Constitution," *Middle East Online*, available at www.middle-east-online.com/english/?id + 9089, last accessed on March 10, 2004.

13. Bevereley Milton-Edwards, *Islam and Politics in the Contemporary World* (Malden, Mass.: Polity Press, 2004), p. 128.

14. Esposito, "Women in Islam and Muslim Societies," pp. ix–xxvii, esp. p. xiii.

15. Jan Jindy Pettman, "Gender Issues," in John Baylis and Steve Smith, eds., *The Globalization of World Politics: An Introduction to International Relations* (Oxford: Oxford University Press, 2001), pp. 582–98, esp. p. 592.

16. Farhat Haq, "Jihad over Human Rights, Human Rights as Jihad: Clash of Universals," in Lynda S. Bell, Andrew J. Nathan, and Ilan Peleg, eds., *Negotiating Culture and Human Rights* (New York: Columbia University Press, 2001), pp. 242–57, esp. p. 251.

17. Ibid., p. 256.

18. Afsaneh Najmabadi, "Feminism in an Islamic Republic: Years of Hardship, Years of Growth," in Yvonne Yazbeck Haddad and John L. Esposito, eds.,

Islam, Gender, and Social Change (Oxford: Oxford University Press, 1998), pp. 59–84, esp. pp. 65–67.

19. Mehranguiz Kar, "Women's Strategies in Iran from the 1979 Revolution to 1999," in Jane H. Bayes and Nayereh Tohidi, eds., *Globalization, Gender, and Religion: The Politics of Women's Rights in Catholic and Muslim Contexts* (New York: Palgrave, 2001), pp. 177–201. For a thoughtful and provocative discussion on this subject, see also Valentine Moghadam, "Islamic Feminism and Its Discontents: Notes on a Debate," available at http://www.iran-bulletin.org/islamic_feminism .htm, last accessed November 1, 2002.

20. Kar, "Women's Strategies," p. 189.

21. Nayereh Tohidi and Jane H. Bayes, "Women Redefining Modernity and Religion in the Globalized Context," in Jane H. Bayes and Nayereh Tohidi, eds., *Globalization, Gender, and Religion: The Politics of Women's Rights in Catholic and Muslim Contexts* (New York: Palgrave, 2001), pp. 17–60, esp. pp. 43–48.

22. Shadi Mokhtari, "A Constructivist Analysis of the Impact of International Human Rights Norms: The Case of Women's Rights under Islamic Law in Iran" (LLM thesis, York University, Toronto, 2004).

23. Mahmood Monshipouri, "The Politics of Culture and Human Rights in Iran: Globalizing and Localizing Dynamics," in Mahmood Monshipouri, Neil Englehart, Andrew J. Nathan, and Kavita Philip, eds., *Constructing Human Rights in the Age of Globalization* (Armonk, N.Y.: M. E. Sharpe, 2003), pp. 113–44, esp. p. 135.

24. Mokhtari, "A Constructivist Analysis."

25. Shirin Ebadi and Hadi Ghaemi, "The Human Rights Case against Attacking Iran," *New York Times*, February 8, 2005, p. A25.

26. See Women's Aid Organization, "Women's Equality in Malaysia: Status Report," March 2001, available at http://www.wao.org.my/news/20010301status port.html, last accessed November 27, 2002.

27. See "Women's Rights," available at http://www.malaysia.net/aliran./hr/ js6.html, last accessed November 27, 2002.

28. Norani Othman, "Grounding Human Rights Arguments in Non-Western Culture: Shari'a and the Citizenship Rights of Women in a Modern Islamic State," in Joanne R. Bauer and Daniel A Bell, eds., *The East Asian Challenge for Human Rights*, (New York: Cambridge University Press, 1999), pp. 169–192, esp. p. 178.

29. Jack Donnelly, "Human Rights, Globalizing Flows, and State Power," in Alison Brysk, ed., *Globalization and Human Rights* (Berkeley: University of California Press, 2002), pp. 226–41, esp. p. 239.

30. Jan Jindy Pettman, "Gender Issues," in John Baylis and Steve Smith, eds., *The Globalization of World Politics: An Introduction to International Relations* (Oxford: Oxford University Press, 2001), pp. 582–98, esp. p. 586.

31. An-Na'im Abdullahi, "The Dichotomy between Religious and Secular Discourse in Islamic Societies," in Mahnaz Afkhami, ed., *Faith and Freedom: Women's Human Rights in the Muslim World* (Syracuse, N.Y.: Syracuse University Press, 1995), pp. 51–60.

32. Ann Elizabeth Mayer, "Rhetorical Strategies and Official Policies on Women's Rights: The Merits and Drawbacks of the New World Hypocrisy," in

Mahnaz Afkhami, ed., *Faith and Freedom: Women's Human Rights in the Muslim World* (Syracuse, N.Y.: Syracuse University Press, 1995), pp. 104–32.

33. Ibid., pp. 126–29.

34. Mahnaz Afkhami, "Introduction," in Mahnaz Afkhami, ed., *Faith and Freedom: Women's Human Rights in the Muslim World* (Syracuse, N.Y.: Syracuse University Press, 1995), pp. 1–15, esp. p. 4.

35. Valentine M. Moghadam, "Global Feminism, the State, and Women's Citizenship in the Muslim World: The Cases of Iran, Algeria, Afghanistan," a paper presented at the conference Citizenship, Borders, and Gender: Mobility and Immobility, Yale University, March 8–10, 2004.

36. Quoted in Caryle Murphy, "In the Throes of a Quiet Revolution: Muslims Reexamine the Meaning of Islam and Rethink Its Place in Modern Life," *Washington Post*, October 12, 2002, p. B9.

37. A. M. Weiss, "Challenges for Muslim Women in a Postmodern World," in Akbar S. Ahmed and Hastings Donnan, eds., *Islam, Globalization and Postmodernism* (New York: Routledge, 1994), pp. 127–40.

38. Mahmood Monshipouri, "Islam and Human Rights in the Age of Globalization," in Ali Mohammadi, ed., *Islam Encountering Globalization* (New York: RoutledgeCurzon, 2002), pp. 91–110, esp. p. 104.

39. Kathryn M. Young, "Discourses on Women, Gender, and Health in Muslim Societies: An Historical Perspective," in Suad Joseph, ed., *Encyclopedia of Women and Islamic Cultures* (Leiden: Brill Academic, 2004).

40. Cathy Benton, "Many Contradictions: Women and Islamists in Turkey," *Muslim World* 86, no. 2 (April 1996): 106–27.

41. Ayse Gunes-Ayata, "The Politics of Implementing Women's Rights in Turkey," in Jane H. Bayes and Nayereh Tohidi, eds., *Globalization, Gender, and Religion: The Politics of Women's Rights in Catholic and Muslim Contexts* (New York: Palgrave, 2001), pp. 157–75, esp. p. 159.

42. Ibid., p. 161.

43. Ibid., p. 173.

44. Ali Akbar Mahdi, "Iranian Women: Between Islamicization and Globalization," in Ali Mohammadi, ed., *Iran Encountering Globalization: Problems and Prospects* (London: RoutledgeCurzon, 2003), pp. 47–72, esp. p. 54.

45. Hammed Shahidian, *Women in Iran: Gender Politics in the Islamic Republic* (Westport, Conn.: Greenwood Press, 2002), p. 270.

46. Jill Carrol, "Young Muslims in Cairo Transform the *Hijab*," *Christian Science Monitor*, May 16, 2007, p. 12.

47. Mehranguiz Kar, "Women's Strategies in Iran from the 1979 Revolution to 1999," in Jane H. Bayes and Nayereh Tohidi, eds., *Globalization, Gender, and Religion: The Politics of Women's Rights in Catholic and Muslim Contexts* (New York: Palgrave, 2001), pp. 177–201, esp. pp. 198–99.

48. Afsaneh Najmabadi, "Feminism in an Islamic Republic: Years of Hardship, Years of Growth," in Yvonne Yazbeck Haddad and John L. Esposito, eds., *Islam, Gender, and Social Change* (New York: Oxford University Press, 1998), pp. 59–84, esp. p. 60.

49. Valentine M. Moghadam, *Modernizing Women: Gender and Social Change in the Middle East*, 2nd ed. (Boulder, Colo.: Lynne Rienner, 2003), p. 218.

50. Mahboobeh Abbasgolizadeh as quoted in Azadeh Kian, "Women and Politics in Post-Islamist Iran: The Gender Conscious Drive to Change," in *Dossier 21: Women Living under Muslim Laws* (Paris: Grabels Cedex, September 1998), pp. 32–55, esp. p. 50.

51. Mahdi, "Iranian Women," p. 64.

52. Ibid., p. 67.

53. Heba Raouf Ezzat, "The Silent Ayesha: An Egyptian Narrative," in Jane H. Bayes and Nayereh Tohidi, eds., *Globalization, Gender, and Religion: The Politics of Women's Rights in Catholic and Muslim Contexts* (New York: Palgrave, 2001), pp. 231–57, esp. p. 239.

54. Ibid., p. 250.

55. Ibid., p. 253.

56. Farhat Haq, "Women, Islam and the State in Pakistan," *Muslim World* 86, no. 2 (April 1996): 158–75, esp. 158.

57. Ibid., p. 162.

58. Ibid., p. 166.

59. Ibid., pp. 172–75.

60. Mahmood Monshipouri, *Islamism, Secularism and Human Rights in the Middle East* (Boulder, Colo.: Lynne Rienner, 1998), p. 168.

61. For more information on this account, see Farhat Haq, "Jihad over Human Rights, Human Rights as Jihad: Clash of Universals," in Lynda S. Bell, Andrew J. Nathan, and Ilan Peleg, eds., *Negotiating Culture and Human Rights* (New York: Columbia University Press, 2001), pp. 242–57, esp. p. 255.

62. Jane H. Bayes and Nayereh Tohid, eds., *Globalization, Gender, and Religion: The Politics of Women's Rights in Catholic and Muslim Contexts* (New York: Palgrave, 2001), p. 27.

63. Sondra Hale, "The New Muslim Woman: Sudan's National Islamic Front and the Invention of Identity," *Muslim World* 86, no. 2 (April 1996): 176–99, esp. 184.

64. Ibid., p. 197.

65. Jack Donnelly, "Human Rights, Globalizing Flows, and State Power," in Alison Brysk, ed., *Globalization and Human Rights* (Berkeley: University of California Press, 2002), pp. 226–41, esp. p. 239.

66. Laurie A. Brand, "Jordan: Women and the Struggle for Political Opening," in Eleanor Abdella Doumato and Marsha Pripstein Posusney, eds., *Women and Globalization in the Arab Middle East: Gender, Economy, and Society* (Boulder, Colo.: Lynne Rienner, 2003), pp. 143–68, esp. p. 161.

67. Ibid., pp. 162–65.

68. Emma C. Murphy, "Women in Tunisia: Between State Feminism and Economic Reform," in Eleanor Abdella Doumato and Marsha Pripstein Posusney, eds., *Women and Globalization in the Arab Middle East: Gender, Economy, and Society* (Boulder, Colo.: Lynne Rienner, 2003), pp. 169–93, esp. p. 171.

69. Ibid., p. 191.

70. Ibid., p. 181.

71. Ibid., p. 185.

72. Ibid., p. 192.

73. Sondra Hale, "Sudanese Women in National Service, Militias, and the Home," in Eleanor Abdella Doumato and Marsha Pripstein Posusney, eds., *Women and Globalization in the Arab Middle East: Gender, Economy, and Society* (Boulder, Colo.: Lynne Rienner, 2003), pp. 195–213, esp. p. 195.

74. Ibid., p. 196.

75. Ibid., p. 206.

76. Eleanor Abdella Doumato, "Education in Saudi Arabia: Gender, Jobs, and the Price of Religion," in Eleanor Abdella Doumato and Marsha Pripstein Posusney, eds., *Women and Globalization in the Arab Middle East: Gender, Economy, and Society* (Boulder, Colo.: Lynne Rienner, 2003), pp. 239–57, esp. p. 254.

77. Moghadam, *Modernizing Women*, p. 118.

78. Ibid., p. 123.

79. Ibid., pp. 127–30.

80. UNDP, Arab Fund for Economic and Social Development, *Arab Human Development Report 2002: Creating Opportunities for Future Generations* (New York: UNDP, 2002), p. 27. The seven world regions are North America, Oceana, Europe, Latin America and the Caribbean, South and East Asia, sub-Saharan Africa, and Arab countries.

81. For gender empowerment measures, see UNDP, *Human Development Report 2002: Deepening Democracy in a Fragmented World* (New York: Oxford University Press, 2002), pp. 226–29.

82. Ibid., pp. 28 and 52.

83. Ibid., p. 29.

84. Ibid.

85. William Spencer, *Global Studies: The Middle East* (Dubuque, Iowa: McGraw-Hill/Contemporary Learning Services, 2005), p. 18.

86. Ibid.

87. See Nicolas Pelham, "Arab Women Demand Quotas," *Christian Science Monitor*, November 6, 2002, p. 7. The first Arab Women's Summit convened in Cairo in November 2001. More information on the first Arab Women's Summit is available at http://www.jordanembassyus.org/11122001002.htm, last accessed on November 29, 2002.

88. Ibid.

89. "On the Situation of Afghan Women," Revolutionary Association of Women in Afghanistan, April 27, 2002, available at http://rawa.fancymarketing.net/wom-view.htm.

90. Diana Ayton-Shenker, ed., *A Global Agenda: Issues before the 57th General Assembly of the United Nations* (New York: Rowman and Littlefield, 2002), p. 197.

91. See comments by Hojjat al-Eslam Sa'idzadeh in Ziba Mir Hossieni, "Hojjat al-Eslam Sa'idzadeh—Iran," in *Dossier 21: Women Living under Muslim Law* (Paris: Grabels Cedex, September 1998), pp. 56–59, esp. p. 57

92. Moghadam, *Modernizing Women*, p. 219.

93. Ibid., pp. 136–39.

94. Ibid., p. 136.

95. Ibid., p. 138.

96. Najma Chowdhury, "The Politics of Implementing Women's Rights in Bangladesh," in Jane H. Bayes and Nayereh Tohidi, eds., *Globalization, Gender, and Religion: The Politics of Women's Rights in Catholic and Muslim Contexts* (New York: Palgrave, 2001), pp. 203–80, esp. p. 210.

97. Ibid.

98. Ibid., p. 211.

99. Abdullah Hadi, "The NGO Intervention and Women's Empowerment: The Bangladesh Experience," available at http://www.qweb.kvinnofroum.se/papers/Hadi.htm.

100. The Grameen Bank was founded by Dr. Mohammad Yunus in 1976 to provide micro-loans to the poor excluded by the conventional banking system—which believes, mistakenly, that poor people are bad credit risks. Women, in particular, have been rejected by bankers who still see them as "only housewives," downplaying their immense value to the country's labor force. For further information, see http://www.oneworld.org/guides/women/yunus.html, last accessed on November 26, 2002.

101. W. R. Duncan, Barbara Jancar-Webster, and Bob Switky, *World Politics in the 21st Century* (New York: Longman, 2002), p. 473.

102. Ibid., p. 471.

103. Mehran Kamrava, ed., *The New Voices of Islam: Rethinking Politics and Modernity: A Reader* (Berkeley: University of California Press, 2006), p. 14.

104. Ziba Mir-Hosseini, *Islam and Gender: The Religious Debate in Contemporary Iran* (Princeton: Princeton University Press, 1999), p. 272.

105. See the most recent collections of such contributions in M. A. Muqtedar Khan, ed., *Islamic Democratic Discourse: Theory, Debates, and Philosophical Perspectives* (Lanham, Md.: Lexington Books, 2006), and also Kamrava, *The New Voices of Islam.*

106. Diane Singerman, "Rewriting Divorce in Egypt: Reclaiming Islam, Legal Activism, and Coalition Politics," in Robert W. Hefner, ed., *Remaking Muslim Politics: Pluralism, Contestation, Democratization* (Princeton, N.J.: Princeton University Press, 2005), pp. 161–88, esp. pp. 162–63.

107. Ibid.

108. Ibid., p. 163.

109. Ibid., p. 165.

110. See the fourth Arab Development Report—UNDP, "Toward the Rise of Women in the Arab World," available at http://www.google.com/intl/en/help/features.html, last accessed on September 26, 2007.

111. Minoo Moallem, *Between Warrior Brother and Veiled Sister: Islamic Fundamentalism and the Politics of Patriarchy in Iran* (Berkeley: University of California Press, 2005), pp. 130–31.

112. Richard Tapper, "Screening Iran: The Cinema as National Forum," *Global Dialogue* 3, no. 2–3 (Spring–Summer 2001): 120–31, esp. 127–28.

113. Ibid., p. 131.

114. Gwendolyn Beetham, "Globalization," in Leslie L. Heywood, ed., *The*

Women's Movement Today: An Encyclopedia of Third Wave Feminism (Westport, Conn.: Greenwood, 2006), pp. 163–66, esp. p. 164.

115. Marsha Pripstein Posusney and Eleanor Abdella Doumato, "Introduction: The Mixed Blessing of Globalization," in Eleanor Abdella Doumato and Marsha Pripstein Posusney, eds., *Women and Globalization in the Arab Middle East: Gender, Economy, and Society* (Boulder, Colo.: Lynne Rienner, 2003), pp. 1–22, esp. p. 14.

116. Emma C. Murphy, "Women in Tunisia: Between State Feminism and Economic Reform," in Eleanor Abdella Doumato and Marsha Pripstein Posusney, eds., *Women and Globalization in the Arab Middle East: Gender, Economy, and Society* (Boulder, Colo.: Lynne Rienner, 2003), pp. 169–93, esp. p. 191.

117. Golnar Mehran, "Islam and Women's Roles," in Nelly P. Stromquist, ed., *Women in the Third World: An Encyclopedia of Contemporary Issues* (New York: Garland, 1998), pp. 115–24, esp. p. 119.

118. Susan Waltz as quoted in Emma C. Murphy, "Women in Tunisia: Between State Feminism and Economic Reform," in Eleanor Abdella Doumato and Marsha Pripstein Posusney, eds., *Women and Globalization in the Arab Middle East: Gender, Economy, and Society* (Boulder, Colo.: Lynne Rienner, 2003), pp. 169–93, esp. p. 191.

119. Murphy, "Women in Tunisia," p. 191.

120. Valentine Moghadam, *Modernizing Women*, p. 139.

121. Mir Zohair Husain, *Global Islamic Politics*, 2nd ed. (New York: Addison-Wesley Educational, 2003), p. 106.

122. Ibid., p. 107.

123. Doumato, "Education in Saudi Arabia," p. 248.

124. Ibid.

125. Asma M. Abdel Halim, "Reconciling the Opposites: Equal but Subordinate," in Courtney W. Howland, ed., *Religious Fundamentalisms and the Human Rights of the Women* (New York: Palgrave, 2001), pp. 203–13, esp. p. 204.

126. Ibid., p. 210.

Chapter 4

1. Richard F. Nyrop, ed., *Egypt: A Country Study* (Washington, D.C.: Government Printing Office, 1983), p. 53.

2. Ibid., p. 54.

3. Ali E. Hillal, "Egypt," in Philip Mattar, ed., *Encyclopedia of the Modern Middle East and North Africa*, 2nd ed. (New York: Thomson Gale, 2004), pp. 763–69, esp. p. 763.

4. Ibid.

5. Ibid., p. 767.

6. James L. Gelvin, *The Modern Middle East* (New York: Oxford University Press, 2005), pp. 245–46.

7. James A. Bill and Robert Sprinborg, *Politics in the Middle East*, 5th ed. (New York: Longman, 2000), pp. 164–65.

8. Hillal, "Egypt," p. 768.

9. Arthur Goldschmidt Jr., "Egypt under Mubarak," in Karl Yambert, ed., *The Contemporary Middle East* (Boulder, Colo.: Westview Press, 2006), pp. 211–20, esp. pp. 219–20.

10. Nicholas S. Hopkins and Reem Saad, "Egypt," in Melvin Ember and Carol R. Ember, eds., *Countries and Cultures: Denmark to Kyrgszstan*, vol. 2 (New York: Macmillan Reference USA, 2001), pp. 673–90, esp. p. 677.

11. Tareq Y. Ismael, *Middle East Politics Today: Government and Civil Society* (Gainesville: University Press of Florida, 2001), pp. 420–21.

12. Ibid., p. 421.

13. Ibid., p. 425.

14. Mehran Kamrava, *The Modern Middle East* (Berkeley: University of California Press, 2005), p. 89.

15. William L. Cleveland, *A History of the Modern Middle East*, 3rd ed. (Boulder, Colo.: Westview Press, 2004), p. 321.

16. Ibid., p. 344.

17. See review by Arthur Goldschmidt Jr. of Joseph P. Lorenz, *Egypt and the Arabs: Foreign Policy and the Search for National Identity* (Boulder, Colo.: Westview Press, 1990), *International Journal of Middle East Studies* 24, no. 3 (August 1992): 523–24, esp. p. 523.

18. Ibid.

19. Robert Sprinborg, "Identity in Crisis: Egyptian Political Identity in the Face of Globalization," *Harvard International Review* 25, no. 3 (Fall 2003), available at http://hir.harvard.edu/articles/1140/1/, last accessed on January 12, 2006.

20. Saidis are the inhabitants of an area in Upper Egypt from Cairo to Aswan. They are more conservative than the delta people but are ethnically similar to Lower Egyptians. In some areas, women still do not appear in public without a veil. For more on this ethnic group, see *Encyclopedia of Britannica online*.

21. Robert Sprinborg, "Identity in Crisis."

22. Kirk H. Sowell, *The Arab World: An Illustrated History* (New York: Hippocrene Books, 2004), p. 225.

23. Gregory Starrett, "Islam after Empire: Turkey and the Arab Middle East," in R. Michael Feener, ed., *Islam in World Cultures: Comparative Perspectives* (Santa Barbara, Calif.: ABC-CLIO, 2004), pp. 41–71, esp. pp. 52–53.

24. Denis J. Sullivan, "Muslim Brotherhood in Egypt," in John L. Esposito, ed., *Oxford Encyclopedia of the Modern Islamic World* (New York: Oxford University Press, 1995), pp. 187–91.

25. Ibid., p. 189.

26. Maysam J. Al Faruqi, "Muslim Brotherhood," in Philip Mattar, ed., *Encyclopedia of the Modern Middle East and North Africa*, 2nd ed. (New York: Macmillan Reference USA, 2004), pp. 1620–22.

27. Starrett, "Islam after Empire," pp. 55–56.

28. Geneive Abdo, *No God but God: Egypt and the Triumph of Islam* (New York: Oxford University Press, 2000), p. 5.

29. Sprinborg, "Identity in Crisis."

30. Ibid.

31. Ibid.

32. Roger Hardy, "Egypt: Crisis of Identity," BBC News, July 16, 2002, available at http://news.bbc.co.uk/1/hi/in_depth/world/2002/islamic_world/ 213, last accessed on June 23, 2006.

33. A. Saad Eddin Ibrahim, "Egypt's Muslim Militants," in Marvin E. Gettleman and Stuart Schaar, eds., *The Middle East and Islamic World Reader* (New York: Grove Press, 2003), pp. 307–13, esp. p. 308.

34. Abdo, *No God but God,* p. 8.

35. Ibid., p. 11.

36. Farha Ghannam, *Remaking the Modern: Space, Relocation, and the Politics of Identity in a Global Cairo* (Berkeley: University of California Press, 2002).

37. Abdo, *No God but God,* pp. 5–6.

38. Ibid., p. 6.

39. Salwa Ismail, *Rethinking Islamist Politics: Culture, the State, and Islamism* (London: I. B. Tauris, 2003), pp. 80–81.

40. Carrie Rosefsky Wickham, "Interests, Ideas, and Islamist Outreach in Egypt," in Quintan Wiktorowicz, ed., *Islamic Activism: A Social Movement Theory Approach* (Bloomington: Indiana University Press, 2004), pp. 231–49, esp. p. 232.

41. Ibid., p. 233.

42. Ibid., p. 237.

43. Ibid., p. 236.

44. Ibid., p. 247.

45. Salwa Ismail, "Confronting the Other: Identity, Culture, Politics, and Conservative Islamism in Egypt," *International Journal of Middle East Studies* 30, no. 2 (May 1998): 199–225, esp. 200.

46. Ibid.

47. Ibid., p. 202.

48. Ibid., p. 212.

49. Ibid., p. 199.

50. Ibid., p. 204.

51. Kathryn M. Yount, "Symbolic Gender Politics, Religious Group Identity, and the Decline in Female Genital Cutting in Minya, Egypt," *Social Forces* 82, no. 3 (March 2004): 1063–90, esp. 1068.

52. Ismail, "Confronting the Other," p. 206.

53. Ibid., p. 207.

54. Ibid., p. 210.

55. Ibid., p. 215.

56. Abdo, *No God but God*, p. 18.

57. Raymond William Baker, *Islam without Fear: Egypt and the New Islam*ists (Cambridge, Mass.: Harvard University Press, 2003), p. 3.

58. Ibid., p. 13.

59. Ibid., p. 24.

60. Ibid., p. 276.

61. Azzam Tamimi, "The Origins of Arab Secularism," in Azzam Tamimi and John L. Esposito, eds., *Islam and Secularism in the Middle East* (New York: New York University Press, 2000), pp. 13–28, esp. p. 27.

62. Ibid.

63. Ibid., p. 28.

64. Jeremy Jones, *Negotiating Change: The New Politics of the Middle East* (London: I. B. Tauris, 2007), p. 260.

65. Dan Murphy, "As Egypt Cracks Down, Charges of Wide Abuse," *Christian Science Monitor*, October 10, 2007, pp. 1 and 11.

66. Dan Murphy, "Egypt Extends Crackdown to Press," *Christian Science Monitor*, September 18, 2007, p. 6.

67. Ibid.

68. Nadje Al-Ali, *Secularism, Gender and the State in the Middle East: The Egyptian Women's Movement* (New York: Cambridge University Press, 2000), p. 135.

69. Ibid., p. 137.

70. Ibid., p. 129.

71. Ibid., p. 130.

72. Ibid., p. 139.

73. Ibid., p. 148.

74. Ibid., p. 215.

75. For more information on the Arabic Network for Human Rights Information, see http://www.anhri.net/en/about/, last accessed on September 4, 2008.

76. Mervat F. Hatem, "Secularist and Islamist Discourses on Modernity in Egypt and the Evolution of the Post-colonial Nation-State," in Yvonne Yazbeck Haddad and John L. Esposito, eds., *Islam, Gender, and Social Change* (New York: Oxford University Press, 1998), pp. 85–99, esp. p. 87.

77. Ibid., p. 88.

78. Ibid., pp. 89–90.

79. Ibid., p. 92.

80. Ibid., pp. 96–97.

81. Yount, "Symbolic Gender Politics," p. 1068

82. Ibid.

83. Ibid., pp. 1070 and 1085.

84. Jill Carroll, "Young Muslims in Cairo Transform the *Hijab*," *Christian Science Monitor*, May 16, 2007, p. 12.

85. Interview with Dr. Mona El Baradei at Cairo University on May 24, 2007.

86. Dr. Mona El Baradei made this point abundantly clear in my interview with her at Cairo University on May 24, 2007.

87. Arthur Goldschmidt Jr., "Egypt under Mubarak," in Karl Yambert, ed., *The Contemporary Middle East* (Boulder, Colo.: Westview Press, 2006), pp. 211–20, esp. p. 211.

88. Ibid.

89. Ibid., p. 212.

90. Mark Huband, "Egypt: The Community of Muslims," in Karl Yambert, ed., *The Contemporary Middle East* (Boulder, Colo.: Westview Press, 2006), pp. 221–29, esp. p. 221.

91. Ibid., p. 222.

92. Ibid., p. 224.

93. Ibid., p. 226.

94. Huband, "Egypt: The Community of Muslims," p. 228.

95. Hesham Al-Awadi, "Mubarak and the Islamists: Why Did the 'Honeymoon' End?" *Middle East Journal* 59, no. 1 (Winter 2005): 62–80, esp. 62.

96. Ibid.

97. Mohammed M. Hafez and Quintan Wiktorowics, "Violence as Contention in the Egyptian Islamic Movement," in Quintan Wiktorowicz, ed., *Islamic Activism: A Social Movement Approach* (Bloomington: Indiana University Press, 2004), pp. 61–88, esp. p. 78.

98. Ibid., pp. 79–80.

99. Joel Beinin, "Political Islam and the New Global Economy: The Political Economy of an Egyptian Social Movement," *New Centennial Review* 5, no. 1 (Spring 2005): 111–39, esp. 125.

100. Al-Awadi, "Mubarak and the Islamists," p. 65.

101. Beinin, "Political Islam and the New Global Economy," p. 135.

102. Maye Kassem, *Egyptian Politics: The Dynamics of Authoritarian Rule* (Boulder, Colo.: Lynne Rienner, 2004), pp. 147–55.

103. Ibid., p. 155.

104. Ibid., p. 157.

105. Ibid., p. 73.

106. Ibid., p. 75.

107. Ibid., p. 77.

108. Ibid., p. 80.

109. Yasmine Saleh, "Muslim Brotherhood Prevented from Shura Council Elections in Menufiya," *Daily Star*," May 22, 2007, p. 1.

110. Jamal Essam El-Din, "Opposition Slams Political Rights Law," *Al-Ahram Weekly*, May 10–16, 2007, p. 4.

111. Ibid.

112. *Egyptian Mail*, "A Democratic Imperative," *Weekly Edition of the Egyptian Gazette*, May 22, 2007, p. 3.

113. Gamal Essam El-Din, "Grandstanding or Boycott?" *Al-Ahram Weekly*, May 10–16, 2007, p. 1.

114. Amr Hamzawy and Nathan J. Brown, "Can Egypt's Troubled Elections Produce a More Democratic Future?" *Policy Outlook: Democracy and Rule of Law*, Carnegie Endowment for International Peace, December 2005, pp. 1–10, esp. p. 4.

115. Ibid.

116. Michele Dunne, "Evaluating Egyptian Reform," *Carnegie Papers on Democracy and Rule of Law Project*, Carnegie Endowment for International Peace, no. 66 (January 2006): 1–18, esp. 6.

117. Bassma Kodmani, "The Dangers of Political Exclusion: Egypt's Islamist Problem," *Carnegie Papers on Democracy and Rule of Law Project*, Carnegie Endowment for International Peace, no. 63 (October 2005): 1–23, esp. 4.

118. Ibid., pp. 14–15.

119. Magdi Khalil, "Egypt's Muslim Brotherhood and Political Power: Would Democracy Survive?" *Middle East Review of International Affairs* 10, no. 1 (March 2006), available at http://meria.idc.ac.il/journal/2006/issue1/jv10no1a3.html, last accessed on June 23, 2006.

120. Interview with Professor Dan Tschirgi at the American University in Cairo on May 25, 2007.

121. Galal Nassar, "More than an Identity Crisis," *Al-Ahram Weekly*, May 17–23, 2007, p. 12.

122. Timothy C. Lim, *Doing Comparative Politics: An Introduction to Approaches and Issues* (Boulder, Colo.: Lynne Rienner, 2006), p. 88.

123. Interview with Professor Tarek Selim at the American University in Cairo on May 25, 2007.

124. Khaled Ahmed, a young and brilliant Egyptian student in the field of international business at the Sadat Academy for Management Sciences in Cairo, was my guide during my stay in Cairo. I had several fruitful conservations with him.

125. Interview with Professor Mostafa Elwi Saif, chair of the Department of Political Science at Cairo University on May 24, 2007.

126. Caryle Murphy, *Passion for Islam: Shaping the Modern Middle East: The Egyptian Experience* (New York: Scribner, 2002).

127. Jon B. Alterman, "Islam in Egyptian Politics: From Activism to Alienation," Review Article, *Middle East Journal* 57, no. 2 (Spring 2003): 319–23, esp. 322. Here Alterman makes a reference to Carrie Rosefsky Wickham's book *Mobilizing Islam: Religion, Activism and Political Change in Egypt* (New York: Columbia University Press, 2002).

128. Raymond William Baker, "Egypt in the Time and Space of Globalism," *Arab Studies Quarterly* 21, no. 3 (Summer 1999): 1–11, esp. 7.

129. Ibid., p. 8.

Chapter 5

1. Christina Chinloy, "Iraqi Reconstruction: Not Easy, but Doable," *Yale Herald* 30, no. 12 (April 18, 2004), available at http://www.yaleherald.com/article.php?Article=2093, last accessed on April 6, 2005.

2. See Noah Feldman, "What We Owe Iraq: An Interview with Noah Feldman," *Mother Jones*, available at http://www.motherjones.com/news/qa/2005/01/feldman.html, last accessed on April 6, 2005.

3. Vali Nasr, *The Shia Revival: How Conflicts within Islam Will Shape the Future* (New York: W. W. Norton, 2006), pp. 26–27.

4. Sam Dagher, "As Troops Exit an Iraqi City, a Glimpse of What Follows," *Christian Science Monitor*, September 17, 2007, pp. 1 and 11–13.

5. Nasr, *The Shia Revival*, p. 28.

6. Marina Ottaway and Judith Yaphe, "Political Reconstruction in Iraq: A Reality Check," Carnegie Endowment for International Peace, March 27, 2003, available at http://www.ceip.org/files/pdf/IraqBrief.Ottaway.pdf, last accessed on April 6, 2005.

7. Graham E. Fuller, "Islamist Politics in Iraq after Saddam Hussein," *United States Institute of Peace: Special Report* no. 108 (August 2003): 1–15, esp. 1.

8. Ibid.

9. Marc Lynch, *Voices of the New Arab Public: Iraq, Al-Jazeera, and Middle East Politics Today* (New York: Columbia University Press, 2006), p. 11.

10. Augustus Richard Norton, "The United States in the Middle East: Grand Plans, Grand Ayatollahs, and Dark Alleys," in Louis J. Cantori and Augustus Richard Norton, "Evaluating the Bush Menu for Change in the Middle East," *Middle East Policy* 12, no. 1 (Spring 2005): 97–121, esp. 98.

11. Michael C. Hudson, "Can Middle East Political Reform Survive the American Embrace," *Middle East Policy* 12, no. 1 (Spring 2005): 110–14, esp. 112.

12. Raymond Hinnebusch, *The International Politics of the Middle East* (Manchester: Manchester University Press, 2003), p. 59.

13. Thomas E. Ricks, *Fiasco: The American Military Adventure in Iraq* (New York: Penguin Group, 2007), p. 163.

14. John Gee, "From Sanctions to Occupation: The US Impact on Iraq," in Rick Fawn and Raymond Hinnebush, eds., *The Iraq War: Causes and Consequences* (Boulder, Colo.: Lynne Rienner, 2006), pp. 225–34, esp. p. 229.

15. Ricks, *Fiasco*, p. 165.

16. Ibid., p. 166.

17. Gee, "From Sanctions to Occupation," p. 232.

18. Ibid.

19. Henry Munson, "Islamic Militancy," in Rick Fawn and Raymond Hinnebush, eds., *The Iraq War: Causes and Consequences* (Boulder, Colo.: Lynne Rienner, 2006), pp. 235–46, esp. pp. 240–41.

20. Gareth Stansfield, "The Transition to Democracy in Iraq: Historical Legacies, Resurgent Identities and Reactionary Tendencies," in Alex Danchev and John MacMillan, eds., *The Iraq War and Democratic Politics* (New York: Routledge, 2005), pp. 134–59, esp. p. 138.

21. Ibid., p. 141.

22. Munson, "Islamic Militancy," p. 242.

23. Ricks, *Fiasco*, p. 291.

24. Bob Herbert, "Torture, American Style," *New York Times*, February 11, 2005, p. A25.

25. Liam Anderson and Gareth Stansfield, *The Future of Iraq: Dictatorship, Democracy, or Division?* (New York: Palgrave, 2004), p. 112.

26. Islam al-Khafaji, "War as a Vehicle for the Rise and Demise of a State-Controlled Society: The Case of Ba'thist Iraq," in Steven Heydemann, ed., *War, Institutions, and Social Change in the Middle East* (Berkeley: University of California Press, 2000), pp. 258–91, esp. p. 282.

27. Ibid., p. 274.

28. Anderson and Stansfield, *The Future of Iraq*, p. 113.

29. Toby Dodge, *Inventing Iraq: The Failure of Nation Building and a History Denied* (New York: Columbia University Press, 2003), p. 169.

30. Gilles Kepel, *The War for Muslim Minds: Islam and the West* (Cambridge: Harvard University Press, 2004), p. 209.

31. Ibid., p. 291.

32. *New York Times*, February 12, 2005, pp. A1 and A8.

33. "Mugged by Reality," *Economist*, March 24, 2007, pp. 29–31, esp. p. 30.

34. Ibid.

35. Noah Feldman, *What We Owe Iraq: War and the Ethics of Nation Building* (Princeton, N.J.: Princeton University Press, 2004), pp. 96–97 and 130.

36. Ronald Bruce St. John, "Nation-building vs. State-building in Iraq," *Global Beat Syndicate*, August 4, 2003, available at http://www.nyu.edu/globalbeat/syndicate/stjohn-2-080403.html, last accessed on April 6, 2005.

37. Peter Grier and Gordon Lubold, "Private Security in Iraq: Whose Rules?" *Christian Science Monitor*, September 20, 2007, pp. 1 and 10.

38. P. W. Singer, "Outsourcing War," *Foreign Affairs* 84, no. 2 (March–April 2005): 119–32, esp. 124.

39. Ibid., p. 125.

40. Ibid., p. 127.

41. Anderson and Stansfield, *The Future of Iraq*, p. 119.

42. Vali Nasr, "When the Shiites Rise," *Foreign Affairs* 85, no. 4 (July–August 2006): 58–74, esp. 58–59.

43. Mir Zohair Husain, *Islam and the Muslim World* (Dubuque, Iowa: McGraw-Hill/Contemporary Learning Series, 2006), p. 15.

44. Anderson and Stansfield, *The Future of Iraq*, p. 119.

45. Juan Cole, "A 'Shiite Crescent'? The Regional Impact of the Iraq War," *Current History* 105, no. 686 (January 2006): 20–26, esp. 20.

46. Anderson and Stansfield, *The Future of Iraq*, p. 118.

47. Nasr, "When the Shiites Rise," p. 61.

48. Anderson and Stansfield, *The Future of Iraq*, p. 117.

49. Ibid., p. 123.

50. Ibid., pp. 118–19.

51. Ibid., p. 123.

52. Nasr, *The Shia Revival*, p. 183.

53. Ibid., pp. 171–72

54. Ibid., pp. 177–80

55. San Dagher, "Oil under Basra Fuels Fight to Control Iraq's Economic Might," *Christian Science Monitor*, September 19, 2007, pp. 12–13, esp. p. 12.

56. Sam Dagher, "'Shiite Taliban' Rises as British Depart Basra," *Christian Science Monitor*, September 18, 2007, p. 11–12, esp. p. 11

57. Ibid., p. 12.

58. Nasr, *The Shia Revival*, p. 184.

59. Ibid.

60. Fuller, "Islamist Politics in Iraq," p. 3.

61. Maximilian Terhalle, "Are the Shia Rising?" *Middle East Policy* 14, no. 2 (Summer 2007): 69–83, esp. 74–79.

62. Ibid., p. 80.

63. Anderson and Stansfield, *The Future of Iraq*, p. 140.

64. Ibid., p. 142.

65. Ibid., p. 146.

66. Ibid., p. 152.

67. Nasr, *The Shia Revival*, p. 250.

68. Ibid., p. 231.

69. Cole, "A 'Shiite Crescent'?" p. 24.

70. Ibid., p. 26.

71. Ahmad H. Hashim, "Iraq's Civil War," *Current History* 106, no. 696 (January 2007): 3–10, esp. 8.

72. Howard LaFranchi, "As Mideast Realigns, US Tilts Sunni," *Christian Science Monitor*, October 9, 2007, pp. 1 and 11, esp. p. 11.

73. Hashim, "Iraq's Civil War," pp. 8–9.

74. Andrew F. Krepinevich,, Jr., "How to Win in Iraq," *Foreign Affairs* 84, no. 5 (September–October 2005): 88–89.

75. Stephen M. Walt, "Taming American Power," *Foreign Affairs* 84, no. 5 (September–October 2005): 105–20, esp. 117.

76. Peter W. Galbraith, "As Iraqis Celebrate, the Kurds Hesitate," *New York Times*, February 1, 2005, p. A19. See also Nir Rosen, "In the Balance," *New York Times Magazine*, February 20, 2005, pp. 30–37, 50, 56, and esp. 58.

77. Rosen, "In the Balance," p. 58.

78. Galbraith, "As Iraqis Celebrate," p. A19.

79. Kepel, *The War for Muslim Minds,* p. 212.

80. Sandra Mackey, "The Coming Clash over Kirkuk," *New York Times*, February 9, 2005, p. A23.

81. Ibid.

82. James Dobbins, John G. McGinn, Keith Crane, Seth G. Jones, Rollie Lal, Andrew Rathmell, Rachel Swanger, and Anga Timilsina, *America's Role in Nation-Building: From Germany to Iraq* (Santa Monica, Calif.: RAND, 2003), p. 190.

83. Anderson and Stanfield, *The Future of Iraq,* p. 115.

84. Carrie Rosefsky Wickham, "The Problem with Coercive Democratization," *Middle East Policy* 12, no. 1 (Spring 2005): 104–8, esp. 105.

85. Nicholas Blanford, "Is Iran Driving New Saudi Diplomacy?" *Christian Science Monitor*, January 16, 2007, p. 6.

86. John Montgomery and Dennis Rondinelli, "A Path to Reconstruction: Proverbs of Nation-building," *Harvard International Review* 26, no. 2 (Summer 2004): 26–29, esp. 26.

87. Joe Stephens and David B. Ottaway, "Postwar Reconstruction Efforts Have Had Dicey History," *Washington Post*, April 28, 2003, p. A13.

88. Montgomery and Rondinelli, "A Path to Reconstruction," p. 27.

89. Mahmood Mamdani, "American and Political Islam," *Global Agenda Magazine*, available at http://www.globalagendamagazine.com/2005/mahmood mamdani.asp, last accessed on February 2, 2005.

90. Judith S. Yaphe, "War and Occupation in Iraq: What Went Right? What Could Go Wrong?" *Middle East Journal* 57, no. 3 (Summer 2003): 381–99, esp. 390.

91. Husain Haqqani, "U.S. Risks a Wave of Extremism," available at http://www.ceip.org/files/publications/Haqqani040103.asp, last accessed on April 4, 2005.

92. Eva Bellin, "The Iraqi Intervention and Democracy in Comparative Historical Perspective," *Political Science Quarterly* 119, no. 4 (Winter 2004–5): 595–608, esp. 595.

93. Ibid., p. 599.

94. Ibid., pp. 601–3.

95. Ibid., p. 605.

96. Ahmed S. Hashim, "Iraq: From Insurgency to Civil War?" *Current History* 104, no. 678 (January 2005): 10–18.

97. Augustus Richard Norton and Farhad Kazemi, "The Limits of Shock and Awe: America in the Middle East," *Current History* 104, no. 678 (January 2005): 3–9, esp. 5.

98. Ibid.

99. Charles W. Kegley Jr. and Gregory A. Raymond, *The Global Future: A Brief Introduction to World Politics*, 2nd ed. (Belmont, Calif.: Thomson/Wadsworth, 2007), p. 213.

100. Dobbins et al., *America's Role in Nation-Building*, p. 169.

101. Ibid., pp. 181–82.

102. "Iraqi Refugees," *Religion and Ethics Newsweekly*, Episode no. 1039, May 25, 2007, available at http://www.pbs.org/wnet/religionandethics/week1039/cover .html, last accessed September 27, 2007.

103. LaFranchi, "As Mideast Realigns, US Tilts Sunni," pp. 1 and 11.

104. Marina Ottaway, "Arab Dictators," *Foreign Policy* 159 (March–April 2007): 46–47.

105. Nasr, *The Shia Revival*, p. 243.

106. Dodge, *Inventing Iraq*, p. 158.

107. Fuller, "Islamist Politics in Iraq," p. 13.

Chapter 6

1. Frauke Heard-Bey, "The United Arab Emirates: Statehood and Nation-building in a Traditional Society," *Middle East Journal* 59, no. 3 (Summer 2005): 357–75, esp. 371.

2. Sean Foley, "What Wealth Cannot Buy: UAE Security at the Turn of the Twenty-first Century," in Barry Rubin, ed., *Crises in the Contemporary Persian Gulf* (London: Frank Cass, 2002), pp. 33–74, esp. pp. 35–36.

3. Ibid., p. 36.

4. Ibid.

5. Philip Mattar, ed., *Encyclopedia of the Modern Middle East and North Africa*, vol. 4 (Detroit: Macmillian Reference USA, 2004), p. 2270.

6. Christopher Hurndall, *The Colours of Fujairah* (Lake City, Fla.: Zodiac, 2002), p. 14.

7. National Bank of Dubai, *Dubai: The Arabian Dream* (London: Transglobal, 2003), p. 26.

8. Ibid., pp. 26–29.

9. Hurndall, *The Colours of Fujairah*, p. 15.

10. Hassan M. Al-Naboodah, "From a Traditional Society to a Modern State," in Joseph A. Kechichian, ed., *A Century in Thirty Years: Shaykh Zayed and the United Arab Emirates* (Washington, D.C.: Middle East Policy Council, 2000), pp. 9–30, esp. p. 12.

11. Ibid., pp. 13–14.

12. National Bank of Dubai, *Dubai: The Arabian Dream*, p. 34.

13. Ibid., p. 15.

14. Hurndall, *The Colours of Fujairah*, p. 15.

15. Foley, "What Wealth Cannot Buy," pp. 33–74, esp. p. 35.

16. Ali Mohammed Khalifa, *The United Arab Emirates: Unity in Fragmentation* (Boulder, Colo.: Westview Press, 1979), p. 178.

17. Shafi'is are those who follow the teachings of Muhammad ibn Idris ash-Shafi'i (767–820 C.E.), who attempted to reconcile the Maliki and Hanafi schools of Islamic jurisprudence. Shafi'i decreed that the Qur'an and the Sunnah (the Prophet's tradition), *Ijma'* (consensus of the Prophet's companions), and *Qiyas* (laws derived from analogical deduction based on the Qur'an and the Sunnah) are the sources of Islamic epistemology.

18. Al-Naboodah, "From a Traditional Society," p. 22.

19. Ibid.

20. Ibid., pp. 24–26.

21. Heard-Bey, "The United Arab Emirates," p. 361.

22. Khalifa, *The United Arab Emirates*, pp. 130–31.

23. Ibid., p. 131.

24. Ibid., p. 132.

25. Symposium: Sheikh Zayed and the UAE, "A Century in Thirty Years: Sheikh Zayed and the United Arab Emirates," *Middle East Policy* 6, no. 4 (June 1999): 1–33, esp. comments by Mary Ann Tetreault, p. 4.

26. Ahmed K. A. Al-Mansoori, *The Distinctive Arab Heritage: A Study of Society, Culture and Sport in UAE* (Abu Dhabi: Emirates Heritage Club, 2004), pp. 128–29 and 156.

27. Christopher M. Davidson, *The United Arab Emirates: A Study in Survival* (Boulder, Colo.: Lynne Rienner, 2005), p. 298.

28. Al-Mansoori, *The Distinctive Arab Heritage*, pp. 141–44.

29. Ibid., p. 157.

30. Ibid., p. 158.

31. *Encyclopedia of the Modern Middle East and North Africa*, p. 2272.

32. Ibid.

33. Foley, "What Wealth Cannot Buy," pp. 33–74; see p. 39.

34. Ibid., p. 41.

35. Ibid., p. 37.

36. Davidson, *The United Arab Emirates*, p. 238.

37. Ibid.

38. Foley, "What Wealth Cannot Buy," p. 37.

39. Symposium: Sheikh Zayed and the UAE, "A Century in Thirty Years," p. 16.

40. Foley, "What Wealth Cannot Buy," pp. 33–74, esp. p. 65.

41. *Encyclopedia of the Modern Middle East and North Africa*, p. 2270.

42. This point was made by Ahmed A. Elewa, business editor of the daily *Khaleej Times*, Dubai, UAE, on April 28, 2005.

43. Foley, "What Wealth Cannot Buy," pp. 33–74, esp. p. 60.

44. See http://www.uaeinteract.com/news/default.asp?cntDisplay=10&ID=134, last visited on July 29, 2005.

45. Carolyn I. Wright, "United Arab Emirates," in Bahira Sherif-Trask, ed., *The Greenwood Encyclopedia of Women's Issues Worldwide: The Middle East and North Africa*, vol. 4 (Westport, Conn.: Greenwood Press, 2003), pp. 411–35, esp. p. 411.

46. Fatma Al Sayegh, "Post-9/11 Changes in the Gulf: The Case of the UAE," *Middle East Policy* 11, no. 2 (Summer 2004): 107–24, esp. 116.

47. Karen Pfeifer and Marsha Pripstein Posusney, "Arab Economies and Globalization: An Overview," in Eleanor Abdella Doumato and Marsha Pripstein Posusney, eds., *Women and Globalization in the Arab Middle East: Gender, Economy, and Society* (Boulder, Colo.: Lynne Rienner, 2003), pp. 25–54, esp. pp. 51–52.

48. Foley, "What Wealth Cannot Buy," p. 60.

49. Ibid.

50. Ibid.

51. Ibid., p. 63.

52. Ibid., p. 95.

53. Ibid.

54. Ibid., p. 96.

55. Ibid., p. 98.

56. Davidson, *The United Arab Emirates*, p. 2.

57. Ibid., p. 51.

58. Interview with Ahmed Al-Shareif, country manager of Thuraya Satellite Telecommunications Company, Abu Dhabi, on April 25, 2005.

59. Symposium: Sheikh Zayed and the UAE, "A Century in Thirty Years," pp. 1–33, esp. comments by Mary Ann Tetreault, p. 7.

60. Judith Caesar and Fatima Badry, "The United Arab Emirates," in Ali Akbar Mahdi, ed., *Teen Life in the Middle East* (Westport, Conn.: Greenwood Press, 2003), pp. 229–46, esp. p. 230.

61. Ibid., p. 232.

62. Ibid., p. 233.

63. Ibid., p. 234.

64. Ibid., p. 236.

65. Ibid., p. 239.

66. Ibid., p. 241.

67. Ibid., p. 244.

68. Ibid.

69. William A. Rugh, *Arab Mass Media: Newspapers, Radio, and Television in Arab Politics* (Westport, Conn.: Praeger, 2004), chapter 4: "The Loyalist Press: Saudi Arabia, Bahrain, Qatar, Oman, the United Arab Emirates, and Palestine," pp. 59–85, esp. pp. 60–61.

70. Ibid., p. 64.

71. Ibid., p. 65.

72. Ibid., p. 68.

73. Ibid.

74. Ibid., p. 73.

75. Ibid., p. 79.

76. Ibid., p. 74.

77. United Nations Development Programme, *Human Development Report 2004: Cultural Liberty in Today's Diverse World* (New York: UNDP, 2004), p. 217.

78. Peter Lienhardt and Ahmed Al-Shahi, eds., *Shaikhdoms of Eastern Arabia* (New York: Palgrave, 2001), p. xvii.

79. United Nations Development Programme, *Human Development Report 2004*, p. 221.

80. Ibid., p. 238.

81. Wright, "United Arab Emirates," vol. 4, pp. 411–35, esp. p. 413.

82. Heard-Bey, "The United Arab Emirates," p. 366.

83. Wright, "United Arab Emirates," vol. 4, p. 413.

84. Ibid., pp. 414–15.

85. Ibid., pp. 416–17.

86. Ibid., pp. 422–23

87. Ibid., pp. 423–24.

88. Interview with P. V. Vivekanand, editor of the daily *Gulf Today*, April 26, 2005, in Sharjah, UAE.

89. *Encyclopedia of the Modern Middle East and North Africa*, p. 2270.

90. National Bank of Dubai, *Dubai: The Arabian Dream*, p. 51.

91. This point was emphasized by Dr. Mustafa Alani, program director of the Gulf Research Center, Dubai, UAE, interviewed on April 25, 2005.

92. Daniel L. Byman and Jerrold D. Green, "The Enigma of Political Stability in the Persian Gulf Monarchies," in Barry Rubin, ed., *Crises in the Contemporary Persian Gulf* (London: Frank Cass, 2002), pp. 75–103, esp. p. 83.

93. Ibid., p. 88.

94. Davidson, *The United Arab Emirates*, p. 263.

95. Ibid.

96. Sally Findlow is cited as the conductor of the survey in Davidson, *The United Arab Emirates*, p. 264.

97. Al-Mansoori, *The Distinctive Arab Heritage*, p. 251.

98. Davidson, *The United Arab Emirates*, pp. 82–84.

99. Al Sayegh, "Post-9/11 Changes in the Gulf," p. 107.

100. Ibid., p. 108.

101. Ibid., pp. 110–12.

102. Ibid., pp. 113–14.

103. Ibid., p. 120.

104. Ibid., pp. 122–23.

105. P. R. Kumaraswamy, "Who Am I? The Identity Crisis in the Middle East," *Middle East Review of International Affairs* 10, no. 1 (March 2006): 63–73, esp. 66–68.

106. See comments by Charles W. Freeman Jr., president, Middle East Policy Council, in Joseph A. Kechichian, ed., *A Century in Thirty Years: Shaykh Zayed and the United Arab Emirates* (Washington, D.C.: Middle East Policy Council, 2000), p. vi.

107. Heard-Bey, "The United Arab Emirates," p. 375.

108. Davidson, *The United Arab Emirates,* pp. 269 and 286.

Chapter 7

1. John L. Esposito, ed., *The Oxford Dictionary of Islam* (New York: Oxford University Press, 2003), p. 323.

2. For further analysis on this point, see Mahmood Monshipouri, "Modern Islam and Secularism in Turkey: Prospects for Democracy and Human Rights," in *Islamism, Secularism, and Human Rights in the Middle East* (Boulder, Colo.: Lynne Rienner, 1998), pp. 105–37

3. Ayse Kadioglu, "The Paradox of Turkish Nationalism and the Construction of Official Identity," *Middle Eastern Studies* 32, no. 2 (April 1996): 177–93, esp. 188.

4. Ibid.

5. Ibid., p. 190.

6. Ibid.

7. Robert D. Kaplan, "At the Gates of Brussels," *Atlantic Monthly* 294, no. 5 (December 2004): 44–45, esp. 44.

8. Ibid.

9. Binnaz Toprak, "A Secular Democracy in the Muslim World: The Turkish Model," in Shireen Hunter and Huma Malik, eds., *Modernization, Democracy, and Islam* (Westport, Conn.: Praeger, 2005), pp. 277–92, esp. pp. 279–80; see also Donald Quataert, "Ottoman Empire," in Philip Mattar, ed., *Encyclopedia of the Modern Middle East and North Africa*, vol. 3 (New York: Thomson Gale, 2004), pp. 1728–34, esp. p. 1732.

10. Stanford J. Shaw, "Ottoman Empire," in John L. Esposito, ed., *The Oxford Encyclopedia of the Modern Islamic World* (New York: Oxford University Press, 1995), pp. 269–76, esp. p. 275.

11. Ibid., p. 276.

12. Toprak, "A Secular Democracy in the Muslim World," p. 283.

13. Mahmood Monshipouri, *Islamism, Secularism, and Human Rights in the Middle East* (Boulder, Colo.: Lynne Rienner, 1998), p. 107.

14. Ibid., p. 109.

15. Helen Chaplin Metz, *Turkey: A Country Study* (Washington, D.C.: Library of Congress, 1995), p. 118.

16. Ibid., pp. 119–20.

17. M. Hakan Yavuz, *Islamic Political Identity in Turkey* (Oxford: Oxford University Press, 2003), p. 3.

18. Noah Feldman, *After Jihad: America and the Struggle for Islamic Democracy* (New York: Farrar, Straus and Giroux, 2003), p. 109.

19. This point has been emphasized by several NGOs in Turkey. I interviewed both the former president of the Organization of Human Rights and Solidarity for Oppressed People, Yilmaz Ensaroglu, and its current president, Ayhan Bilgen, in Ankara, Turkey, on May 5, 2005. They made a similar argument.

20. Yildiz Atasoy, *Turkey, Islamists and Democracy: Transition and Globalization in a Muslim State* (London: I. B. Tauris, 2005), p. 71.

21. Ibid., p. 72.

22. Ibid., p. 73.

23. Ibid.

24. Ibid.

25. Sefa Şimşek, "New Social Movements in Turkey since 1980," *Turkish Studies* 5, no. 2 (Summer 2004): 111–39, esp. 121.

26. Ibid.

27. Fethullah Gülen is a Turkish writer, former Islamic preacher, and the leader of the Gülen movement, which is one of the largest Islamic movements in Turkey. Advocating tolerance, peace, and dialogue, Gülen sees the solution to many of the world's problems in a return to religious faith. He also argues that in true Islam, terrorism is murder and is strictly forbidden. His followers have formed more than five hundred educational institutions in over ninety countries around the world.

28. Umit Sayin and Aykut Kence, "Islamic Scientific Creationism: A New Challenge in Turkey," available at http://www.ncseweb.org/resources/mcse_content/vol19/8300_isla mic_scienti fic_creationism_12–30_1899.asp, last accessed on November 27, 2007.

29. Şimşek, "New Social Movements in Turkey," p. 123.

30. M. Hakan Yavuz, *Islamic Political Identity in Turkey* (Oxford: Oxford University Press, 2003), p. 196.

31. Ibid., pp. 197–98.

32. Ibid., p. 266

33. Ibid., p. 204.

34. Ibid., p. 4.

35. Ibid., p. 5.

36. Ibid.

37. Jenny B. White, *Islamist Mobilization in Turkey: A Study in Vernacular Politics* (Seattle: University of Washington Press, 2002), p. 27.

38. Ibid., p. 28.

39. Yavuz, *Islamic Political Identity in Turkey*, p. 267.

40. Feroz Ahmad, *Turkey: The Quest for Identity* (Oxford: Oneworld Publications, 2003), pp. 172–73.

41. Ibid., p. 173.

42. Toprak, "A Secular Democracy in the Muslim World," p. 288.

43. Jenny B. White, "The Ebbing Power of Turkey's Secularist Elite," *Current History* 106, no. 704 (December 2007): 427–33, esp. 430.

44. John K. Cooley, "Islam on the Ballot: Turkey's Test," *Christian Science Monitor*, May 7, 2007, available at http://fe28.new.sp1.yahoo.com/s/csm/20070507/cm_csm/ycooley, last accessed on June 5, 2007.

45. Quoted in Fareed Zakaria, "A Quiet Prayer for Democracy," *Newsweek*, May 14, 2007, p. 45.

46. Ibid.

47. Ely Karmon, "Radical Islamic Political Groups in Turkey," *Middle East*

Review of International Affairs 1, no. 4 (December 1997), available at http://www .biu.ac.il/Besa/meria/journal/jv1v4a2.html, last accessed on November 27, 2007.

48. Bulent Aras and Sule Toktas, "Al-Qaeda, 'War on Terror' and Turkey," *Third World Quarterly* 28, no. 5 (2007): 1033–50, esp. 1045.

49. Ibid., p. 1046.

50. Ibid., p. 1048.

51. Karmon, "Radical Islamic Political Groups in Turkey."

52. "A Battle for the Future," *Economist*, July 21–27, 2007, pp. 25–28, esp. p. 26.

53. Ibid., p. 26.

54. Scott Peterson, "Economy Trumps Religion in Turkey," *Christian Science Monitor*, July 24, 2007, p. 6.

55. Ihsan Dagi, "Understanding Turkish Islam and Turkish Politics," *Today's Zaman*, October 5, 2007, available at http://www.todayszaman.com/tz-web/yazar Detay.do?haberno = 126285. See also Ihsandagi.blogspot.com, last accessed on October 10, 2007.

56. Ibid.

57. Cooley, "Islam on the Ballot."

58. Amberin Zaman, "Turkey Elects Islamist President Abdullah Gul," *Telegraph Co. UK*, available at http://www.telegraph.co.uk/news/main.jhtml?xml = / news/2007/08/29/wturkey129.x ml, last accessed on November 24, 2007.

59. Scott Peterson, "New Turkish Mandate Bolsters Gul," *Christian Science Monitor*, August 20, 2007, p. 6.

60. Ayse Kadioglu, "Women's Subordination in Turkey: Is Islam Really the Villain?" *Middle East Journal* 48, no. 4 (Autumn 1994): 645–60, esp. 651.

61. Ibid.

62. Human Rights Watch, "Turkey: Constitutional Court Ruling Upholds Headscarf Ban," available at http://www.hrw.org/english/docs/2008/06/06/Turkey 19050htm, last accessed on July 12, 2008.

63. Ihsan Dagi, "AK Party Survives Closure Case: What Is Next?" *SETA PolicyBrief* 19 (August 2008): 1–10, esp. 5.

64. Ibid., pp. 6–9.

65. *Capital City Women's Platform*, Ankara, Turkey. This is an Islamic feminist NGO in Ankara. I had an extended interview with its members.

66. Kadioglu, "Women's Subordination in Turkey," p. 651.

67. I met a group of Islamic feminists in an NGO called Baskent Kadin Platformu (Capital City Women's Platform) in Ankara, Turkey, on May 5, 2005. This point was underscored by several members of this NGO.

68. W. Shadid and P. S. Van Koningsveld, "Muslim Dress in Europe: Debates on the Headscarf," *Journal of Islamic Studies* 16, no. 1 (2005): 35–61, esp. 48.

69. Ibid., p. 38.

70. Gunter, *The Historical Dictionary of the Kurds*, p. 5.

71. I interviewed Cevat Dargin, an Alevi student from Bogazici University, Istanbul, Turkey, on May 3, 2005.

72. Gunter, *The Historical Dictionary of the Kurds*, p. 5.

73. I had a fruitful discussion with Mr. Dogan Bermek in Istanbul, Turkey, on May 8, 2005.

74. Ihsan D. Dagi, "Rethinking Human Rights, Democracy, and the West: Post-Islamist Intellectuals in Turkey," *Critique: Critical Middle Eastern Studies* 13, no. 2 (Summer 2004): 135–51, esp. 149.

75. Ibid., p. 150.

76. Noah Feldman, *After Jihad: America and the Struggle for Islamic Democracy* (New York: Farrar, Straus and Giroux, 2003), p. 112.

77. Michael M. Gunter, *Historical Dictionary for the Kurds* (Lanham, Md.: Scarecrow Press, 2004), p. 202.

78. Martin Irvine, "Global Cyberculture Reconsidered: Cyberspace, Identity, and the Global Information City," available at http://www.georgetown.edu/irvinemj/articles/globalculture.html, last accessed on April 12, 2005.

79. Gunter, *Historical Dictionary,* p. 202.

80. Martin van Bruinessen, "Kurdistan Workers Party (PKK)," in Philip Mattar, ed., *Encyclopedia of the Modern Middle East and North Africa*, vol. 2 (New York: Thompson Gale, 2004), pp. 1342–44, esp. p. 1343.

81. Ibid., p. 1344.

82. Henri J. Barkey and Graham E. Fuller, *Turkey's Kurdish Question* (New York: Carnegie Corporation of New York, 1998), p. 61.

83. Ibid., p. 62.

84. Karen Parker, "The Kurdish Insurgency in Turkey in Light of International Humanitarian Law," in Mohammed M. A. Ahmed and Michael M. Gunter, eds., *The Kurdish Question and International Law: An Analysis of the Legal Rights of the Kurdish People* (Oakton, Va.: Ahmed Foundation for Kurdish Studies, 1999), pp. 47–74, esp. p. 57.

85. Şimşek, "New Social Movements in Turkey," p. 134.

86. Ihsan D. Dagi, "What Does the Security Establishment Really Want?" *Today's Zaman*, June 5, 2007, available at http://www.todayszaman.com/tz-web/yazar Ad.do?kn = 73, last accessed on June 5, 2007.

87. Scott Peterson and Sam Dagher, "Turkish Raids Unsettle Iraq," *Christian Science Monitor*, December 19, 2007, pp. 1 and 11.

88. Ibid., p. 11.

89. Recep Tayyib Erdoğan, "Turkey, Islam and the West," *Global Agenda*, available at http:www.globalagendamagazine.com/2004/receptayyiperdogan.asp, last accessed on April 12, 2005.

90. Ihsan D. Dagi, "Transformation of Islamic Political Identity in Turkey: Rethinking the West and Westernization," *Turkish Studies* 6, no. 1 (March 2005): 21–37, esp. 26.

91. Birol A. Yesilada, "Turkey's Candidacy for EU Membership," *Middle East Journal* 56, no. 1 (Winter 2002): 94–111, esp. 95.

92. Ibid., p. 100.

93. Atasoy, *Turkey, Islamists and Democracy,* p. 189.

94. Ibid., p. 100.

95. Robert D. Kaplan, "At the Gates of Brussels," *Atlantic Monthly* 294, no. 5 (December 2004): 44–45, esp. 45.

96. Yesilada, "Turkey's Candidacy for EU Membership," p. 102.

97. Kaplan, "At the Gates of Brussels," p. 45.

98. Yesilad, "Turkey's Candidacy for EU Membership," p. 107.

99. Ahmet Turan Ayhan, opinion editor of *Zaman Daily News*, stressed this point in an interview with me on May 2, 2005 in Istanbul, Turkey.

100. Abdullah Gul, "Why Turkey?" *Zaman Online*, December 16, 2004, available at http:///www.zaman.com, last accessed on April 12, 2005.

101. Ibid.

102. Recep Tayyip Erdoğan, "Why the EU Needs Turkey," *Insight Turkey* 6, no. 3 (July-September 2004): 7–15, esp. 8.

103. Ibid, pp. 10–11.

104. Bulent Aras, "Terror, the International System and Turkey," *Insight Turkey* 6, no. 1 (January–March 2004): 129–34, esp. 132.

105. Michael Emerson and Nathalie Tocci, "Integrating EU and Turkish Foreign Policy," *Insight Turkey* 6, no. 3 (July–September 2004): 16–26, esp. 22.

106. Heather Grabbe, "From Drift to Strategy: Why the EU Should Start Accession Talks with Turkey," *Insight Turkey* 6, no. 3 (July–September 2004): 27–37, esp. 29–30.

107. Erdoğan, "Why the EU Needs Turkey," p. 11.

108. Arthur Bonner, "Turkey, the European Union and Paradigm Shifts," *Middle East Policy* 12, no. 1 (Spring 2005): 44–71, esp. 46.

109. Ibid.

110. Ibid., p. 109.

111. Dagi, "Rethinking Human Rights," p. 135; see also Dagi, "Transformation of Islamic Political Identity in Turkey," p. 30.

112. Dagi, "Transformation of Islamic Political Identity in Turkey," p. 31.

113. Bonner, "Turkey, the European Union and Paradigm Shifts," p. 53.

114. Dagi, "Rethinking Human Rights," p. 136.

115. Ibid., p. 139.

116. Ibid., p. 143.

117. Dagi, "Transformation of Islamic Political Identity in Turkey," p. 31.

118. Ibid., p. 28

119. Ihsan D. Dagi, "The Justice and Development Party: Identity, Politics, and Human Rights Discourse in the Search for Security and Legitimacy," in M. Hakan Yavuz, ed., *The Emergence of a New Turkey: Democracy and the AK Parti* (Salt Lake City: University of Utah Press, 2006), pp. 88–106, esp. p. 103.

120. Dagi, "Rethinking Human Rights," p. 145.

121. Etyen Mahçupyan, domestic policy director of the Turkish Economic and Social Studies Foundation, Istanbul, Turkey, underscored this point during an interview on May 3, 2005.

122. Kadioglu, "The Paradox of Turkish Nationalism," p. 192.

123. I interviewed Av. Mustafa Ercan, President of a human rights NGO, *Insan Haklari ve Mazlumder Inçin Dayanisma Derneği*, and Lutfi Sunar, the editor of *Insan Haklari* (Human Rights Review) in Istanbul branch of Mazlumder, on May 7, 2005. They both eloquently made this point.

124. Daniel C. Peterson, "Muslim Identity," in Richard C. Martin, ed., *Ency-*

clopedia of Islam and the Muslim World (New York: Thomson Gale, 2004), pp. 339–44, esp. p. 339.

125. Musa Agacik, from *Star Gazetesi*, a daily in Istanbul, made this comment during an interview on May 8, 2005.

126. Professor M. Hayri Kirbasoglu, Aknara Üniversitesi Ilahiyat Fakültesi, emphasized this point during an interview on May 6, 2005, in Ankara, Turkey.

127. Mehmet Fatih Seyhanoglu, a journalist who works for *Zaman Daily News*, offered a similar explanation during an interview on May 8, 2005, Istanbul, Turkey.

128. Emma Ross-Thomas, "Turkish Women Gain Voice in Fight to Stay Secular," available at http://p227.news.mud.yahoo.com/s/nm/20070604/If_nm/turkey _wom en.dc, last accessed on June 5, 2007.

Chapter 8

1. Daniel C. Peterson, "Muslim Identity," in Richard C. Martin, ed., *Encyclopedia of Islam and the Muslim World*, vol. A–L (New York: Macmillan Reference USA, 2004), pp. 339–44, esp. p. 343.

2. John L. Esposito, "Contemporary Islam: Reformation or Revolution?" in John L. Esposito, ed., *The Oxford History of Islam* (New York: Oxford University Press, 1999), pp. 643–90, esp. p. 661.

3. Struan Hellier, "What Were the Main Factors behind the Ayatollah's Revolution in Iran in 1979?" available at http://www.shellier.co.uk/iranrevolution.htm, last accessed on July 22, 2005.

4. Esposito, "Contemporary Islam," p. 663.

5. Nikki Keddie, "Iran: Understanding the Enigma: A Historian's View," *Middle East Review of International Affairs* 2, no. 3 (September 1998): 1–10.

6. John L. Esposito and John O. Vall, *Islam and Democracy* (New York: Oxford University Press, 1996), p. 53.

7. Ibid.

8. For an illuminating account of this social breakdown, see Nikki Keddie, *Roots of the Revolution: An Interpretive History of Modern Iran* (New Haven, Conn.: Yale University Press, 1993).

9. Hellier, "What Were the Main Factors."

10. Ervand Abrahamian, "The Making of the Modern Iranian State," in Mark Kesselman, Joel Krieger, and William A. Joseph, eds., *Introduction to Comparative Politics: Political Challenges and Changing Agenda* (New York: Houghton Mifflin, 2000), pp. 607–54, esp. p. 647.

11. Robin Wright, "Dateline Tehran: A Revolution Implodes," *Foreign Policy* 103 (2000): 161–74, esp. 163–64.

12. Mahmood Monshipouri, *Islamism, Secularism, and Human Rights in the Middle East* (Boulder, Colo.: Lynn Rienner, 1998), p. 191.

13. More information is available at http://www.electionworld.org/election/ iran.htm.

14. Under the Iranian constitution, the ultimate authority rests with the supreme leader, Ayatollah Sayyed Ali Khamenei, who currently controls many powerful institutions, including the military, the Ministry of Intelligence, the *basij* paramilitary forces, the national police, the Ministry of Information and Intelligence, and the Revolutionary Guards. Moreover, he maintains control of the judiciary and national broadcasting—that is, state radio and television—and names the key members of the Council of Guardians (*showray-e neghahban*), which serves as a watchdog body capable of blocking any legislation that it sees as unfit according to Islamic ideals.

15. Mark J. Gasiorowski, "Iran under Khatami: Deadlock or Change?" *Global Dialogue* 3, nos. 2–3 (Spring–Summer 2001): 9–18, esp. 15–16.

16. Esposito, "Contemporary Islam," p. 665.

17. Mahmood Monshipouri, "The Politics of Culture and Human Rights in Iran: Globalizing and Localizing Dynamics," in Mahmood Monshipouri, Neil Englehart, Andrew J. Nathan, and Kavita Philip, eds., *Constructing Human Rights in the Age of Globalization* (New York: M. E. Sharpe, 2003), pp. 113–44, esp. p. 119.

18. Farhad Khosrokhavar, "The New Conservatives Take a Turn," *Middle East Report* 34, no. 4 (Winter 2004): 24–27, esp. 24.

19. Olivier Roy, *Globalized Islam: The Search for a New Ummah* (New York: Columbia University Press, 2004).

20. Ali Akbar Mahdi, "The Iranian Women's Movement: A Century Long Struggle," *Muslim World* 91, no. 4 (October 2004): 427–48, esp. 443.

21. Ibid., pp. 441–43.

22. CBC News Online, "Iran: Facing a Demographic Revolution," June 15, 2005, available at http://www.cbc.ca/news/background/iran, last accessed on July 19, 2005.

23. Eric Rouleau, "Islam Confronts Islam in Iran," *Le Monde diplomatique*, June 1999, available at http://mondediplo.com/1999/06/02iran, last assessed on July 22, 2005.

24. Ibid.

25. Special Report: Women in Iran, "Shorn of Dignity and Equality," *Economist*, October 18, 2003, pp. 23–25, esp. p. 23.

26. For more on this topic, see Mahmood Monshipouri, "The Road to Globalization Runs through Women's Struggle: Iran and the Impact of the Nobel Peace Prize," *World Affairs* 167, no. 1 (Summer 2004): 3–14, esp. 8.

27. Tahmineh Milani, activist-filmmaker, *Adventure Divas*, available at http://www.pbs.org/adventuredivas/iran/divas/milani.html, last accessed on July 22, 2005.

28. Mahboobeh Abassgholizadeh, "Iranian Women's Movement Is without Head," *Zanan* 102 (September 2003), available at http://www.zanan.co.ir/culture/000153.html, last accessed on November 11, 2003.

29. Interview with Elaheh Koolaee, a parliament deputy of the Islamic Republic of Iran, July 19, 2003, Tehran.

30. Interview with Mostafa Tajzadeh, ex-deputy to Iranian President Mohammad Khatami, July 23, 2003, Tehran.

31. Mahboobeh Abbasgholizadeh, "The Experience of Islamic Feminism in Iran," *Farzaneh* 15, no. 10 (Winter 2000): 7–14.

32. This third generation of feminists includes Shahla Sherkat, Maryam Behrouzi, Monireh Gorji, Zahra Rahnavard, Mahboobeh Abassgholizadeh, Faezeh Hashemi, Fatimeh Haqiqatjoo, Zahra Eshraqi, and Jamileh Kadivar.

33. For further details on Shirin Ebadi's thoughts and contributions, see Monshipouri, "The Road to Globalization."

34. Nayereh Tohidi, "Islamic Feminism: Perils and Promises," *Middle East Women's Studies Review* 16, nos. 3–4 (Winter 2002), available at http://www.amews.org/review/reviewarticles/tohidi.htm, last accessed on October 25, 2003.

35. Ibid.

36. Valentine Moghadam, "Islamic Feminism and Its Discontents: Notes on a Debate," available at http://www.Iran-bulletin.org/islamic_feminism.htm, last accessed on October 25, 2003.

37. Ibid.

38. Mehranghiz Karr, *Eliminating Discrimination against Women: A Comparison of the Convention on Elimination of All Forms of Discrimination against Women with Iran's Domestic Laws* (Tehran: Parvin, 1999), p. 334.

39. *Twenty-Four Human Rights Documents* (New York: Center for Human Rights Study, Columbia University, 1992), 181.

40. For more on this issue, see Monshipouri, "The Politics of Culture," p. 133.

41. Haideh Moghissi, "Public Life and Women's Resistance," in Saeed Rahnema and Sohrab Behdad, eds., *Iran after the Revolution: Crisis of an Islamic State* (London: I. B. Tauris, 1995), pp. 251–67, esp. pp. 253–54.

42. Ibid., pp. 261–62.

43. Brian Murphy, "Iran's Election: Human Rights vs. Prosperity," June 25, 2005, available at http://www.perspectives.com/forums/forum71/48429.html, last accessed on July 19, 2005.

44. Sami Moubayed, "A Victory for the Youth and Poor," *Gulf News*, June 27, 2005, available at http://web.lexis-nexis.com/universe/document?, last accessed on July 27, 2005.

45. Ibid.

46. See comments made by Vahid Pourostad in Murphy, "Iran's Election."

47. Murphy, "Iran's Election."

48. This way of thinking is reflected in an article by Erika, "Change in Iran," *Peace Magazine*, January–March 2002, available at http://www.peacemagazine.org/archive/v18n1p15.htm, last accessed on July 23, 2005.

49. See the status of the major international human rights instruments, UNDP, *Human Development Report 2004: Cultural Liberty in Today's Diverse World* (New York: United Nations Development Programme, 2004), pp. 238–41.

50. Scott Peterson, "Regime-change Fears Drive Iran's Vice Crackdown," *Christian Science Monitor*, December 20, 2007, pp. 1 and 10, esp. 10.

51. More on the Amnesty International Report on Iran is available at http://www.amnestyusa.org/news/document.do?id = ENGMDE131482008, last accessed on December 21, 2007.

52. Reza Afshari, *Human Rights in Iran: The Abuse of Cultural Relativism* (Philadelphia: Pennsylvania University Press, 2001), p. 195.

53. Ibid., p. 199.

54. Vali Nasr and Ray Takeykh, "How Iran's President Is Being Undercut," *Christian Science Monitor*, December 14, 2007, p. 9.

55. Michael Slackman, "For the Poor in Oil-Rich Iran, the Voting for President Was About Making Ends Meet," *New York Times*, July 3, 2005, p. N9.

56. Siavosh Ghazi, "Iran's Ahmadinejad Faces Tough Wish-List from Poor Supporters," *Agence France Presse*, June 29, 2005, available at http://web.lexis-nexis.com/universal/document?, last accessed on July 27, 2005.

57. Mark Gasiorowski, "The Causes and Consequences of Iran's June 2005 Presidential Election," submitted to *Strategic Insights*.

58. Ibid.

59. Michael Slackman, "No Candidate Wins Majority in Iranian Presidential Election, Forcing a Second Round," *New York Times*, June 18, 2005, p. A7.

60. *The World Factbook*, July 14, 2005, available at http://www.cia.gov/cia/publications/factbook/geos/ir.html, last accessed on July 19, 2005.

61. Kamran M. Dadkhah, "Iran and the Global Finance Markets," in Ali Mohammadi, ed., *Iran Encountering Globalization: Problems and Prospects* (New York: RoutledgeCurzon, 2003), pp. 86–106, esp. pp. 92–93.

62. *Agence France Presse*, "Ahmadinejad Moves to Calm Worried Investors," June 26, 2005, available at http://web.lexis-nexis.com/universe/document?, last accessed on July 27, 2005.

63. Hashem Dezhbakhsh, "Privatization in Iran: Past, Present, and Prospects," *Journal of Iranian Research and Analysis* 20, no. 2 (November 2004): 23–38, esp. 32–33.

64. Kamran M. Dadkhah, "Iran and the Global Finance Markets," in Ali Mohammadi, ed., *Iran Encountering Globalization: Problems and Prospects* (New York: RoutledgeCurzon, 2003), pp. 86–106, esp. p. 105.

65. Murphy, "Iran's Election."

66. Ibid.

67. Moubayed, "A Victory for the Youth and Poor."

68. Christopher de Bellaigue, "Iran," *Foreign Policy* 148 (May–June 2005): 18–24, esp. 20.

69. Eliyahu Kanovsky, "Iran's Sick Economy: Prospects for Change under Khatami," in Patrick Clawson, Michael Eisenstadt, Eliyahu Kanovsky, and David Menashri, *Iran under Khatami: A Political, Economic, and Military Assessment* (Washington, D.C.: Washington Institute for Near East Policy, 1998), pp. 53–70, esp. p. 60.

70. Ibid.

71. Kanovsky, "Iran's Sick Economy," p. 53.

72. Michael Rubin, *National Review Online*, July 26, 2002, "Watershed: The Will of the Iranian People Should Not Be Ignored This Time Around," available at http://www.washingtoninstitute.org/templateC06.php?CID = 606, last accessed on July 19, 2005. Also Michael Rubin, "What Are Iran's Domestic Priorities?" *Middle East Review of International Affairs* 6, no. 2 (June 2002): 25–39, esp. 31.

73. Ibid.

74. Ibid.

75. Kanovsky, "Iran's Sick Economy," p. 67.

76. Hamid Zangeneh, "The Iranian Economy and the Globalization Process," in Ali Mohammadi, ed., *Iran Encountering Globalization: Problems and Prospects* (New York: RoutledgeCurzon, 2003), pp. 107–33, esp. p. 127.

77. Ibid.

78. Hamid Zangeneh, "Socioeconomic Trends in Iran: Successes and Failures," *Muslim World* 94, no. 4 (October 2004): 481–93, esp. 493.

79. Zangeneh, "The Iranian Economy," p. 120.

80. Ibid.

81. See Gary Sick, "Bush of the US and Ahmadinejad of Iran," available at http://www.freerepublic.com/focus/f-news/1434143/posts, last accessed on July 21, 2005.

82. Zangeneh, "The Iranian Economy," p. 129.

83. Ibid., p. 130.

84. Michael Ignatieff, "Iranian Lessons," *New York Times Magazine*, July 17, 2005, pp. 46–51, esp. p. 51.

85. Ibid.

86. Robin Wright, "Tehran Jails American Scholar after Long House Arrest," *Washington Post*, May 9, 2007, p. A12.

87. Radio Fee Europe, "Nobel Laureate Condemns Arrest of Iranian-American Scholar," available at http://www.rferl.org/featuresarticle/2007/05/9ebe0299-f7b3-42d-b3 7a-5311a0f565 15.html, last accessed on May 31, 2007.

88. Ignatieff, "Iranian Lessons," p. 49.

89. Kayhan Barzegar, "Understanding the Roots of Iranian Foreign Policy in the New Iraq," *Middle East Policy* 12, no. 2 (Summer 2005): 49–57, esp. 50.

90. Ibid., p. 51.

91. Ibid., p. 52.

92. Scott Peterson, "Populists: Shiite Leaders Craft Message for Masses," *Christian Science Monitor*, June 7, 2007, p. 1 and pp. 12–14, esp. p. 12.

93. Dan Bilefsky, "Europe Approves More Sanctions against Iran," *New York Times*, April 24, 2007, available at http://www.nytimes.com/2007/04/24/world /europe/24nukes.html, last accessed on May 28, 2007.

94. Shirin Ebadi and Muhammed Sahimi, "Link the Nuclear Program to Human Rights," *International Herald Tribune*, January 19, 2006, available at http:// www.iht.com/articles/2006/09/19/opinion/edebadi, last accesssed on May 28, 2007.

95. Ibid.

96. Philip Grant, "After the Revolution," available at http://www.thefriday times.com/page16.shtml, last accessed on July 22, 2005.

97. Ibid.

98. Azadeh Kian-Thiebaut, "From Islamization to the Individualization of Women in Post-revolutionary Iran," in Sarah Ansari and Vanessa Martin, eds., *Women, Religion and Culture in Iran* (London: Curzon Press, 2002), pp. 127–42, esp. p. 141.

99. Ibid.

Chapter 9

1. William H. Frederick and Robert L. Worden, eds., *Indonesia: A Country Study* (Washington, D.C.: Library of Congress, 1993), p. 3.

2. Barbara Crossette, "A Challenge to Asia's Own Style of Islam," *New York Times*, December 30, 2001, sec. 4, p. 3.

3. Frederick and Worden, *Indonesia*, p. 5.

4. For a collection of essays on this, see Freek Colombijn and J. Thomas Lindblad, eds., *Roots of Violence in Indonesia: Contemporary Violence in Historical Perspective* (Seattle: University of Washington Press, 2002).

5. Jean-Marc F. Blanchard, "East Asia's Slow Recovery from Financial Crisis," *Current History* 102, no. 663 (April 2003): 180–85, esp. 183.

6. Daniel Brumberg, "Dissonant Politics in Iran and Indonesia," *Political Science Quarterly* 116, no. 3 (Fall 2001): 381–411, esp. 395.

7. David Rohde, "Indonesia Unraveling?" *Foreign Affairs* 8, no. 4 (July–August 2001): 110–24, esp. 123.

8. Timothy Samuel Shah and Monica Duffy Toft, "Why God Is Winning," *Foreign Policy* 155 (July–August 2006): 38–43, esp. 41

9. Ibid., p. 42.

10. Rohde, "Indonesia Unraveling?" p. 48.

11. Ibid., p. 114.

12. Ibid.

13. Michael R. J. Vatikiotis, *Indonesian Politics under Suharto: Order, Development and Pressure for Change* (New York: Routledge, 1993), p. xix.

14. Ibid., p. 219.

15. George Hicks and J. A. C. Mackie, "A Question of Identity," *Far Eastern Economic Review*, July 14, 1994, pp. 46–48, esp. p. 47.

16. Minxin Pei, "Will China Become Another Indonesia?" *Foreign Policy* 116 (Fall 1999): 94–109, esp. 94.

17. Ibid., p. 107.

18. Dewi Fortuna Anwar, "The Fall of Suharto: Understanding the Politics of the Global," in Francis Loh Kok Wah and Joakim Ojendal, eds., *Southeast Asian Responses to Globalization: Restructuring Governance and Deepening Democracy* (Copenhagen, Denmark: Nordic Institute for Asian Studies, 2005), pp. 201–29, esp. p. 219.

19. Ibid., p. 221.

20. Rohde, "Indonesia Unraveling?" p. 114.

21. Lex Reiffel, "Indonesia's Quiet Revolution," *Foreign Affairs* 83, no. 5 (September–October 2004): 98–110, esp. 106.

22. Ibid., p. 108.

23. Anna Gade and R. Michael Feener, "Muslim Thought and Practice in Contemporary Indonesia," in R. Michael Feener, ed., *Islam in World Cultures: Comparative Perspectives* (Santa Barbara, Calif.: ABC-CLIO, 2004), pp. 183–215, esp. p. 213.

24. Frederick and Worden, *Indonesia*, p. 12.

25. Bahtiar Effendy, *Islam and the State in Indonesia* (Singapore: Institute of Southeast Asian Studies, 2003), p. 15.

26. Clifford Geertz, *Islam Observed: Religious Development in Morocco and Indonesia* (New Haven, Conn.: Yale University Press, 1968).

27. Gade and Feener, "Muslim Thought and Practice in Contemporary Indonesia," p. 183.

28. Fred R. von der Mehden, "Indonesia," in John L. Esposito, ed., *The Oxford Encyclopedia of the Modern Islamic World*, vol. 2 (New York: Oxford University Press, 1995), pp. 196–203, esp. p. 197.

29. Gade and Feener, "Muslim Thought and Practice in Contemporary Indonesia," p. 185.

30. Ibid., p. 186.

31. Von der Mehden, "Indonesia," p. 197.

32. Gade and Feener, "Muslim Thought and Practice in Contemporary Indonesia," p. 187.

33. Ibid., p. 192.

34. Ibid., p. 195.

35. Effendy, *Islam and the State in Indonesia*, pp. 19–20.

36. Ibid., p. 21.

37. Gade and Feener, "Muslim Thought and Practice in Contemporary Indonesia," p. 197.

38. Jean Gelman Taylor, *Indonesia: Peoples and Histories* (New Haven, Conn.: Yale University Press, 2003), p. 358.

39. Ibid., p. 359.

40. Ibid., p. 300.

41. Ibid., p. 301.

42. Gade and Feener, "Muslim Thought and Practice in Contemporary Indonesia," p. 203.

43. Von der Mehden, "Indonesia," p. 198.

44. Gade and Feener, "Muslim Thought and Practice in Contemporary Indonesia," p. 205.

45. Von der Mehden, "Indonesia," p. 199.

46. Ibid.

47. Justus M. van der Kroef, "The Role of Islam in Indonesian Nationalism and Politics," *Western Political Quarterly* 11, no. 1 (March 1958): 33–54, esp. 50.

48. Ibid., pp. 51–52.

49. Von der Mehden, "Indonesia," p. 200.

50. Ibid.

51. See Philip J. Eldrige, *The Politics of Human Rights in Southeast Asia* (New York: Routledge, 2002), pp. 118–19; see also Von der Mehden, "Indonesia," p. 201.

52. Effendy, *Islam and the State in Indonesia*, p. 150.

53. Ibid.

54. Ibid., p. 139.

55. Ibid., pp. 139–40.

56. Karim Raslan, "Indonesia's Moderate Islamists," *Foreign Policy* 131 (July–August 2002): 77–79, esp. 77.

57. Ibid., p. 78.

58. Brumberg, "Dissonant Politics in Iran and Indonesia," p. 396.

59. Saiful Mujani and R. William Liddle, "Indonesia's Approaching Elections: Politics, Islam, and Public Opinion," *Journal of Democracy* 15, no. 1 (January 2004): 109–23, esp. 112.

60. Ibid.

61. Ibid.

62. Ibid., p. 114.

63. Ibid., pp. 115–16.

64. Birgit Bräuchler, "Islamic Radicalism Online: The Moluccan Mission of the Laskar Jihad in Cyberspace," *Australian Journal of Anthropology* 15, no. 3 (2004): 267–85, esp. 268.

65. Ibid., p. 269.

66. Birgit Bräuchler, "Cyberidentities at War: Religion, Identity, and the Internet in the Moluccan Conflict, *Indonesia* 75 (April 2003): 123–51, esp. 134.

67. Ibid., p. 150.

68. Bräuchler, "Islamic Radicalism Online," pp. 271–76.

69. Ibid., pp. 277–78.

70. Gerald Tan, *The Asian Currency Crisis* (Singapore: Times Media Private, 2000), p. 1

71. Ibid., pp. 116–17.

72. George Hicks and J. A. C. Mackie, "A Question of Identity," *Far Eastern Economic Review*, July 14, 1994, pp. 46–48.

73. Zakaria Haji Ahmad and Baladas Ghoshal, "The Political Future of ASEAN after the Asian Crisis," *International Affairs* 75, no. 4 (October 1999): 759–78, esp. 763.

74. Ahmad and Ghoshal, "The Political Future of ASEAN," p. 767.

75. Tan, *The Asian Currency Crisis*, p. 114.

76. Ibid., p. 115.

77. Ibid., p. 171.

78. Ibid., p. 172.

79. Dwight Y. King, "Corruption in Indonesia: A Curable Cancer?" *Journal of International Affairs* 53, no. 2 (Spring 2000): 603–24, esp. 604.

80. Carlyle A. Thayer, "Southeast Asia's Marred Miracle," *Current History* 103, no. 672 (April 2004): 177–82, esp. 177.

81. Linda Connor and Adrian Vickers, "Crisis, Citizenship, and Cosmopolitanism: Living in a Local and Global Risk Society in Bali," *Indonesia* 75 (April 2003): 153–80, esp. 160–61.

82. Tan, *The Asian Currency Crisis*, p. 122.

83. Eldrige, *The Politics of Human Rights in Southeast Asia*, p. 132.

84. King, "Corruption in Indonesia," p. 604.

85. Ahmad and Ghoshal, "The Political Future of ASEAN," p. 774.

86. Jusuf Wanandi, "Indonesia: A Failed State?" *Washington Quarterly* 25, no. 33 (Summer 2002): 135–46, esp. 137.

87. Ibid.

88. Eldrige, *The Politics of Human Rights in Southeast Asia*, p. 125.

89. Mark R. Woodward, "Indonesia, Islam, and the Prospect for Democracy," *SAIS Review* 21, no. 2 (Summer–Fall 2001): 29–37, esp. 32.

90. Ibid., p. 33.

91. Francis Fukuyama, Björn Dressel, and Boo-Seung Chang, "Facing the Perils of Presidentialism?" *Journal of Democracy*, 16, no. 2 (April 2005): 102–16, esp. 106–7.

92. Muhammad Qodari, "Challenge and Change in East Asia: Indonesia's Quest for Accountable Governance," *Journal of Democracy* 16, no. 2 (April 2005): 73–87, esp. 81.

93. Ibid., p. 87

94. Edward Aspinall, "Indonesia after the Tsunami," *Current History* 104, no. 680 (March 2005): 105–9, esp. 106–9.

95. Fareed Zakaria, *The Future of Freedom: Illiberal Democracy at Home and Abroad* (New York: W. W. Norton, 2003), p. 117.

96. Ibid., p. 118.

97. Ibid.

98. Susan Blackburn, "Women and the Nation," *Inside Indonesia*, April–June 2001, available at http://www.serve.com/inside/edit66/susan1.htm, last accessed on June 10, 2007.

99. Ibid.

100. Saskia E. Wieringa, "Sexual Politics in Indonesia: From Soekarno's Old Order to Soeharto's New Order," in Sheila Rowbotham and Stephanie Linkogle, eds., *Women Resist Globalization: Mobilizing for Livelihood and Rights* (London: Zed Books, 2001), pp. 134–52, esp. p. 147.

101. Blackburn, "Women and the Nation."

102. Melani Budianta, "The Blessed Tragedy: The Making of Women's Activism during the *Reformasi* Years," in Ariel Heryanto and Sumit K. Mandal, eds., *Challenging Authoritarianism in Southeast Asia: Comparing Indonesia and Malaysia* (New York: RoutledgeCurzon, 2003), pp. 145–77, esp. p. 153.

103. Ibid., pp. 147–48.

104. Blackburn, "Women and the Nation."

105. Krishna Sen, "The Human Rights of Gendered Citizens: Notes from Indonesia," in Anne-Marie Hilsdon, Martha Macintyre, Vera Mackie, and Maila Stivens, eds., *Human Rights and Gender Politics: Asia-Pacific Perspectives* (London: Routledge, 2000), pp. 107–23, esp. pp. 117–18.

106. Ibid., p. 120.

107. Julia Suryakusuma, "Indonesia: Megawati Hasn't Helped Her Countrywomen," *International Herald Tribune*, January 18, 2003, available at http://www.iht.com/articles/2003/01/18/edjulia_ed3, last accessed on June 10, 2007.

108. Eldrige, *The Politics of Human Rights in Southeast Asia*, p. 150 and esp. chapter 5.

109. Suryakusuma, "Indonesia."

110. Susan Blackburn, *Women and the State in Modern Indonesia* (New York: Cambridge University Press, 2004), pp. 225–30.

111. Ibid., p. 225.

112. Ibid., p. 228.

113. Ibid., p. 224.

114. Rebecca Elmhirst, "Negotiating Land and Livelihood: Agency and Identities in Indonesia's Transmigration Programme," in Brenda S.A. Yeoh, Peggy Teo, and Shirlena Huang, eds., *Gender Politics in the Asia-Pacific Region* (London: Routledge, 2002), pp. 79–98, esp. p. 95.

115. Blackburn, "Women and the Nation."

116. Woodward, "Indonesia, Islam, and the Prospect for Democracy," p. 31.

117. Ibid., pp. 32–33.

118. K. H. Abdurrahman Wahid, "Indonesia's Mild Secularism," *SAIS Review* 21, no. 2 (Summer–Fall 2001): 25–28, esp. 27.

119. Ibid.

120. Woodward, "Indonesia, Islam, and the Prospect for Democracy," p. 34.

121. Ibid., p. 35.

122. Ibid., pp. 35–36

123. Robert W. Hefner, *Civil Islam: Muslims and Democratization in Indonesia* (Princeton, N.J.: Princeton University Press, 2000), p. 128.

124. Ibid., p. 127.

125. Daniel Brumberg, "Islamists and the Politics of Consensus," *Journal of Democracy* 13, no. 3 (July 2002): 109–15, esp. 114.

126. Effendy, *Islam and the State in Indonesia,* p. 224.

127. Ibid.

128. Mujani and Liddle, "Indonesia's Approaching Elections," p. 122.

129. Wanandi, "Indonesia: A Failed State?" p. 145.

130. Blackburn, *Women and the State in Modern Indonesia*, p. 31.

131. Effendy, *Islam and the State in Indonesia*, pp. 151 and 224.

132. Brumberg, "Dissonant Politics in Iran and Indonesia," p. 410.

133. Gade and Feener, "Muslim Thought and Practice in Contemporary Indonesia," p. 213.

134. Mujani and Liddle, "Indonesia's Approaching Elections," p. 110.

Chapter 10

1. Valerie Amiraux, "Discrimination and Claims for Equal Rights amongst Muslims in Europe," in Jocelyne Cesari and Sean McLoughlin, eds., *European Muslims and the Secular State* (Burlington, Vt.: Ashgate, 2005), pp. 25–38, esp. p. 29.

2. Jocelyne Cesari, "Islam, Secularism and Multiculturalism after 9/11: A Transatlantic Comparison," in Jocelyne Cesari and Sean McLoughlin, eds., *European Muslims and the Secular State* (Burlington, Vt.: Ashgate, 2005), pp. 39–51, esp. pp. 43–44.

3. Amiraux, "Discrimination and Claims for Equal Rights," p. 33.

4. Ibid., p. 31.

5. Peter Ford, "Europe's Rising Class of Believers: Muslims," *Christian Science Monitor*, February 24, 2005, p.10.

6. Timothy M. Savage, "Europe and Islam: Crescent Waxing, Cultures Clashing," *Washington Quarterly* 27, no. 3 (Summer 2005): 25–50, esp. 44.

7. Theodore Karasik and Cheryl Benard, "Muslim Diasporas and Networks," in Angel M. Rabasa, Cheryl Benard, Peter Chalk, Christine Fair, Theodore Karasik, Rolle Lal, Ian Lesser, and David Thaler, eds., *The Muslim World after 9/11* (Santa Monica, Calif.: RAND, 2004), pp. 433–90, esp. p. 442.

8. Ibid.

9. Ibid.

10. Ibid.

11. Ibid.

12. Ibid., p. 444.

13. Robert S. Leiken, "Europe's Angry Muslims," *Foreign Affairs* 84, no. 4 (July–August 2005): 120–35, esp. 122. Other experts, such as Ross Douthat, have projected that Europe's Muslim population will double by 2015. See "A Muslim Europe," *Atlantic Monthly* 295, no. 1 (January–February 2005): 58–59, esp. p. 58.

14. Douhat, "A Muslim Europe," p. 58.

15. Leiken, "Europe's Angry Muslims," p. 123.

16. Savage, "Europe and Islam," p. 26.

17. Ibid., p. 27.

18. Ibid., p. 28.

19. Ibid.

20. Ibid.

21. Ibid., p. 29.

22. Douthat, "A Muslim Europe," p. 59

23. Karasik and Benard, "Muslim Diasporas and Networks," p. 482.

24. Ibid.

25. Douthat, "A Muslim Europe," p. 59.

26. Karasik and Benard, "Muslim Diasporas and Networks," p. 483.

27. Ibid.

28. James Helicke, "Turks in Germany: Muslim Identity 'Between' States," in Yvonne Yzabeck Haddad and Jane I. Smith, eds., *Muslim Minorities in the West: Visible and Invisible* (New York: Altamira Press, 2002), pp. 175–91, esp. p. 179.

29. Douthat, "A Muslim Europe," p. 59.

30. Karasik and Benard, "Muslim Diasporas and Networks," p. 436.

31. Ibid.

32. Ibid., p. 434.

33. Peter Mandaville, *Transnational Muslim Politics: Reimaging the Umma* (New York: Routledge, 2004), p. 151.

34. Ibid., p. 134.

35. Ibid., p. 135.

36. Ibid., p. 147.

37. Nadia Fadil, "Individualizing Faith, Individualizing Identity: Islam and Young Muslim Women in Belgium," in Jocelyne Cesari and Sean McLoughlin, eds., *European Muslims and the Secular State* (Burlington, Vt.: Ashgate, 2005), pp. 143–54, esp. p. 152.

38. Ibid.

39. BBC News, "Muslim Hardship under Spotlight," May 14, 2006, available at http://news.bbc.co.uk/2/hi/uk_news/4771233.stm, last accessed on June 5, 2006.

40. Olivier Roy, "EuroIslam: The Jihad Within," *National Interest* 71 (Spring 2003): 63–73, esp. 65–68.

41. Ibid., p. 71.

42. Christine Jacobsen, "The Quest for Authenticity: Islamization among Muslim Youth in Norway," in Jocelyne Cesari and Sean McLoughlin, eds., *European Muslims and the Secular State* (Burlington, Vt.: Ashgate, 2005), pp. 155–68, esp. pp. 155–56.

43. Ibid., p. 156.

44. Christopher Caldwell, "Islam on the Outskirts of the Welfare State," *New York Times Magazine*, February 5, 2006, pp. 54–59, esp. p 56.

45. Ibid., pp. 58–59.

46. Ibid., p. 59.

47. Jane Kramer, "The Dutch Model," *New Yorker*, April 3, 2006, pp. 60–67, esp. p. 63.

48. Ibid., p. 66.

49. Cesari, "Islam, Secularism and Multiculturalism," p. 49.

50. Thijil Sunier, "Interests, Identities, and the Public Sphere: Representing Islam in the Netherlands since the 1980s," in Jocelyne Cesari and Sean McLoughlin, eds., *European Muslims and the Secular State* (Burlington, Vt.: Ashgate, 2005), pp.85–97, esp. p. 87.

51. Ibid.

52. Ibid., p. 92.

53. Kramer, "The Dutch Model," p. 66.

54. Cesari, "Islam, Secularism and Multiculturalism," p. 48.

55. Olivier Roy, "A Clash of Cultures or a Debate on Europe's Values?" *ISIM Review* 15 (Spring 2005): 6–7, esp. 6.

56. Leiken, "Europe's Angry Muslims," pp. 124–25.

57. Ibid., p. 125.

58. Ibid., p. 126.

59. Jacobsen, "The Quest for Authenticity," p. 157.

60. Ibid.

61. Ibid., p. 158.

62. Ibid., p. 160.

63. Ibid., p. 165.

64. Ibid., p. 164.

65. Gema Martin-Munoz and Ana Lopez-Sala, "Migration and Religiosity of Muslim Women in Spain," in Jocelyne Cesari and Sean McLoughlin, eds., *European Muslims and the Secular State* (Burlington, Vt.: Ashgate, 2005), pp. 129–42, esp. p. 139.

66. Ibid., p. 136.

67. Ibid., p. 137.

68. Ibid., p. 139.

69. Helicke, "Turks in Germany," p. 180.

70. Ibid., pp. 180–81.

71. Ibid., pp. 182–83.

72. Ibid., pp. 186–87.

73. Ibid., pp. 188–89.

74. Christopher Caldwell, "After Londonistan," *New York Times Magazine*, June 25, 2006, pp. 40–47, 62, and 74–75, esp. p. 47.

75. Ibid.

76. Ibid.

77. Katrina Gorjanicyn, "Citizenship and Culture in Contemporary France: Extreme Rights Interventions," in Andrew Vangenberg, ed., *Citizenship and Democracy in a Global Era* (New York: St. Martin's Press, 2000), pp. 138–55, esp. p. 139.

78. Ibid., p. 152.

79. Hossein Daheshiar, "Unrests in France: Roots and Internal and International Implications," *Political and Economic Ettela'at* (Tehran, Iran) 217–18 (January–February 2006): 4–15, esp. 10.

80. Gorjanicyn, "Citizenship and Culture in Contemporary France," p. 153.

81. Olivier Roy, "Europe's Response to Radical Islam," *Current History* 104, no. 685 (November 2005): 360–64, esp. 362.

82. Robert J. Pauly Jr., *Islam in Europe: Integration or Marginalization?* (Burlington, Vt.: Ashgate, 2004), p. 44.

83. Ibid., p. 47.

84. Tariq Ramadan, "The Arab World and the Muslims Faced with Their Contradictions," in John J. Donohue and John L. Esposito, eds., *Islam in Transition: Muslim Perspectives*, 2nd ed. (New York: Oxford University Press, 2007), pp. 474–79, esp. p. 475.

85. Sarah Wildman, "Third Way Speaks to Europe's Young," *Christian Science Monitor*, May 19, 2003, available at http://www.csmonitor.com/2003/0519/p07s02-woeu.htm; see also Peter Ford, "A Radical Idea: How Muslims Can Be European, Too," *Christian Science Monitor*, October 31, 2006, available at http://www.cs monitor.com/2006/1031/p01s04-woeu.html, last accessed on June 14, 2007.

86. Dan Bilefsky, "Denmark Is Unlikely Front in Islam-West Culture War," *New York Times*, January 8, 2006, p. A3.

87. Martin Burcharth, "Capture the Flag," *New York Times*, February 12, 2006, p. WK 15.

88. Joel Brinkley and Ian Fisher, "U.S. Says It Also Finds Cartoons of Muhammad Offensive," *New York Times*, February 4, 2006, p. A3.

89. Robert Wright, "The Silent Treatment," *New York Times*, February 17, 2006, p. A23.

90. Bilefsky, "Denmark Is Unlikely Front," p. A3.

91. Zeyno Baran, "Fighting the War of Ideas," *Foreign Affairs* 84, no. 6 (November–December 2005): 68–78, esp. 68.

92. Rohan Gunaratna, *Inside Al Qaeda: Global Network of Terror* (New York: Columbia University Press, 2002), p. 6.

93. Savage, "Europe and Islam," p. 30.

94. Ibid.

95. Ibid., pp. 44–45.

96. Ibid., pp. 30–31.

97. Ibid., p. 31.

98. Ibid.

99. Ibid., pp. 35–36.

100. Roy, "Europe's Response to Radical Islam," p. 362.

101. Jochen Lorentzen, "Keep Out, Protectionism, Migration Control, and Globalization," in Ronald Tiersky, ed., *Europe Today: National Politics, European Integration, and European Security*, 2nd ed. (Lanham, Md.: Rowman and Littlefield, 2004), pp. 145–75, esp. p. 171.

102. Gilles Kepel, *The War for Muslim Minds: Islam and the West* (Cambridge: Belknap Press of Harvard University Press, 2004), p. 295.

103. Olivier Roy, *Globalized Islam: The Search for a New Umma* (New York: Columbia University Press, 2004), p. 201.

104. Mahmood Monshipouri, "The West's Modern Encounter with Islam: From Discourse to Reality," *Journal of Church and State* 40, no. 1 (Winter 1998): 25–56, esp. 39.

105. Roy, *Globalized Islam*, pp. 218–19.

106. John R. Bowen, *Why the French Don't Like Headscarves: Islam, the State, and Public Space* (Princeton, N.J.: Princeton University Press, 2007), p. 156.

107. Ibid., p. 240.

108. Ibid., p. 247.

109. Anastasia Vakulenko, "Islamic Dress in Human Rights Jurisprudence: A Critique of Current Trends," *Human Rights Law Review* (September 2007): 1–23, esp. 14.

110. Dominic McGoldrick, *Human Rights and Religion: The Islamic Headscarf Debate in Europe* (Portland, Ore.: Hart, 2006), p. 242.

111. Vakulenko, "Islamic Dress," p. 16.

112. Ibid., p. 17.

113. McGoldrick, *Human Rights and Religion*, p. 242.

114. Ibid.

115. "Immigration Paradox," *Scotsman*, February 21, 2005, available at http:news.scotsman.com/archive.cfm?id = 601692004, last accessed on January 10, 2006.

Conclusion

1. Simon Murden, "Culture in World Affairs," in John Baylis and Steve Smith, eds., *The Globalization of World Politics: An Introduction to International Relations*, 3rd ed. (Oxford: Oxford University Press, 2005), pp. 539–53, esp. p. 546.

2. Jane Lampman, "In Many Ways, U.S. Muslims Are in Mainstream America," *Christian Science Monitor*, May 24, 2007, p. 2.

3. Scott Peterson, "Islam's Minority Reaches New Prominence," *Christian Science Monitor*, June 6, 2007, pp. 13–16, esp. p. 16.

4. Quoted in Fareed Zakaria, "A Quiet Prayer for Democracy," *Newsweek*, May 14, 2007, p. 45.

5. Murden, "Culture in World Affairs," p. 544.

6. Shibley Telhami and Michael Barnett, "Identity and Foreign Policy in the

Middle East," in Shibley Telhami and Michael Barnett, eds., *Identity and Foreign Policy in the Middle East* (Ithaca, N.Y.: Cornell University Press, 2002), pp. 1–25, esp. pp. 19–25.

7. Caryle Murphy, *Passion for Islam: Shaping the Modern Middle East: The Egyptian Experience* (New York: Scribner, 2002).

8. Vali Nasr, *The Shia Revival: How Conflicts within Islam Will Shape the Future* (New York: W. W. Norton, 2006), p. 93.

9. John L. Esposito, *The Islamic Threat: Myth or Reality* (New York: Oxford University Press, 1995), p. 253.

10. Fred Halliday, *The Middle East in International Relations: Power, Politics, and Ideology* (New York: Cambridge University Press, 2005), p. 161.

11. Mansoor Ijaz, "The Benazir Bhutto I Knew," *Christian Science Monitor*, December 28, 2007, p. 9.

12. Augustus Richard Norton, "The Quest for Inclusion in the Middle East," *Current History* 94, no. 588 (January 1995): 1–6.

13. Jillian Schwedler, *Faith in Moderation: Islamist Parties in Jordan and Yemen* (Cambridge: Cambridge University Press, 2006).

14. Shibley Telhami, "Middle East; A Growing Muslim Identity; Increasingly, Arabs Define Themselves in Terms of Islam," *Los Angeles Times*, July 11, 2004, p. M1.

15. Ibid.

16. Jon B. Alterman, "Islam in Egyptian Politics: From Activism to Alienation," *Middle East Journal* 57, no. 2 (Spring 2003): 319–23, esp. 321.

17. Mir Zohair Husain, *Global Studies: Islam and the Muslim World* (Dubuque, Ia.: McGraw-Hill/Contemporary Learning Series, 2006), p. 32.

18. Ramzy Baroud, "Arabs and Globalization," *Al-Ahram Weekly Online*, December 23–29, 2004, opinion page, available at http://weekly.ahram.org.eg/2004/722/op12.htm, last accessed on June 2, 2007.

19. Alterman, "Islam in Egyptian Politics," p. 323.

20. Mahmood Monshipouri, "The Bush Doctrine and Democracy Promotion in the Middle East," in David P. Forsythe, Patrice C. McMahon, and Andrew Wedeman, eds., *American Foreign Policy in a Globalized World* (New York: Routledge, 2006), pp. 313–34.

21. Mehran Kamrava, *The Modern Middle East: A Political History since the First World War* (Berkeley: University of California Press, 2005), p. 355.

22. Ibid., p. 343.

23. Ibid., p. 357.

24. Ibid.

25. Raymond Hinnebusch, "The Politics of Identity in Middle East International Relations," in Louise Fawcett, ed., *International Relations of the Middle East* (New York: Oxford University Press, 2005), pp. 151–71, esp. p. 153.

26. Stanley Hoffmann, "Clash of Globalization," *Foreign Affairs* 81, no. 4 (July–August 2002): 104–15.

27. Dale F. Eickelman and James Piscatori, *Muslim Politics* (Princeton, N.J.: Princeton University Press, 1996), p. 111.

28. Asef Bayat, "Does Class Ever Opt Out of the Nation? Nationalist Modernization and Labour in Iran," in Willem van Schendel and Erik J. Zürcher, eds., *Iden-*

tity Politics in Central Asia and the Muslim World (London: I. B. Tauris, 2001), pp. 189–207, esp. p. 204.

29. Eickelman and Piscatori, *Muslim Politics,* p. 111.

30. Ibid., pp. 110–11.

31. Ali Akbar Mahdi, "The Student Movement in the Islamic Republic of Iran," *Journal of Iranian Research and Analysis* 15, no. 2 (November 1999): 5–32, esp. 12.

32. Valentine Moghadam, "The Student Protests and the Social Movement for Reform in Iran: Sociologoical Reflections," *Journal of Iranian Research and Analysis* 15, no. 2 (November 1999): 97–105, esp. 103.

33. Timothy Samuel Shah and Monica Duffy Toft, "Why God Is Winning," *Foreign Policy* 155 (July–August 2006): 38–43.

34. Ibid., p. 42.

35. Ibid., p. 43.

36. Saiful Mujani and R. William Liddle, "Indonesia's Approaching Elections: Politics, Islam, and Public Opinion," *Journal of Democracy* 15, no. 1 (January 2004): 109–23, esp. 117.

37. Mark Juergensmeyer, "Holy Orders: Religious Opposition to Modern States," *Harvard International Review* 25, no. 4 (Winter 2004): 34–38, esp. 37–38.

38. Ibid., p. 38.

39. Hinnebusch, "The Politics of Identity," p. 155.

40. Ibid.

41. Ibid., p. 156.

42. Vali Nasr, "The Rise of Muslim Democracy," *Journal of Democracy* 16, no. 2 (April 2005): 13–27, esp. 14.

43. Ibid., p. 16.

44. Ibid., p. 18.

45. Erik J. Zürcher, "Fundamentalism as an Exclusionary Device in Kemalist Turkish Nationalism," in Willem van Schendel and Erik J. Zürcher, eds., *Identity Politics in Central Asia and the Muslim World* (London: I. B. Tauris, 2001), pp. 209–22, esp. pp. 213–14.

46. This conclusion is consistent with some of the arguments offered by Feroz Ahmad and Jacob M. Landau, "Conclusion: Opting Out of the Nation," in Willem van Schendel and Erik J. Zürcher, eds., *Identity Politics in Central Asia and the Muslim World* (London: I. B. Tauris, 2001), pp. 223–35, esp. p. 235.

47. Jeremy Jones, *Negotiating Change: The New Politics of the Middle East* (London: I. B. Tauris, 2007), p. 260.

48. Husain, *Global Studies: Islam and the Muslim World,* p. 31.

49. Eickelman and Piscatori, *Muslim Politics,* p. 149.

50. Peter J. Katzenstein and Timothy A. Byrnes, "Transnational Religion in an Expanding Europe," *Perspective on Politics* 4, no. 4 (December 2006): 679–94, esp. 679.

51. Ibid., p. 690.

52. Ibid., p. 687.

53. Robert J. Pauly Jr., *Islam in Europe: Integration and Marginalization?* (Burlington, Vt.: Ashgate, 2004), p. 120.

54. Nezar AlSayyad, "Muslim Europe or Euro-Islam: On the Discourses of Identity and Culture," in Nezar AlSayyad and Manuel Castells, eds., *Muslim Europe or Euro-Islam: Politics, Culture, and Citizenship in the Age of Globalization* (Lanham, Md.: Lexington Books, 2002), pp. 9–29, esp. p. 10.

55. Olivier Roy, *Globalized Islam: The Search for a New Ummah* (New York: Columbia University Press, 2004); see also Francis Fukuyama, "Identity, Immigration, and Liberal Democracy," *Journal of Democracy* 17, no. 2 (April 2006): 5–20, esp. 6–10.

56. Fukuyama, "Identity," p. 9.

57. Ibid., p. 14.

58. Pauly, *Islam in Europe*, p. 27.

59. Ibid., p. 153.

60. Meg Bortin, "Poll Finds Discord between the Muslim and Western Worlds," *New York Times*, June 23, 2006, p. A3. Pew surveyed 14,030 people from March 31 to May 14, 2006, in Britain, Egypt, France, Germany, India, Indonesia, Jordan, Nigeria, Pakistan, Russia, Spain, Turkey, and the United States. The margin of sampling error was plus or minus two to four percentage points, except in Britain and Germany, where it was six points.

61. Ibid.

62. Dominic McGoldrick, *Human Rights and Religion: The Islamic Headscarf Debate in Europe* (Portland, Ore.: Hart, 2006), p. 61.

63. Ibid., p. 242.

64. Ibid., p. 204.

65. Ibid., p. 244.

66. Ibid., p. 121.

67. Ibid., p. 131.

68. Ibid., p. 290.

69. Ibid., pp. 290–91.

70. Bortin, "Poll Finds Discord," p. A3.

71. Ibid.

72. Ibid.

73. Carolyn M. Warner and Manfred W. Wenner, "Religion and the Political Organization of Muslims in Europe," *Perspectives on Politics* 4, no. 3 (September 2006): 457–79.

74. Ibid., p. 472.

75. McGoldrick, *Human Rights and Religion*, p. 54.

76. Quoted in Stephanie Giry, "France and Its Muslims," *Foreign Affairs* 85, no. 5 (September–October 2006): 87–104, esp. 97.

77. Warner and Wenner, "Religion and the Political Organization of Muslims," pp. 472–73.

78. Valentine Moghadam, "Women, Citizenship, and Civil Society in the Arab World," in Anthony Chase and Amr Hamzawy, eds., *Human Rights in the Arab World: Independent Voices* (Philadelphia: University of Pennsylvania Press, 2006), pp. 89–104, esp. p. 104.

79. Ibid.

80. Robert M. Press, *Peaceful Resistance: Advancing Human Rights and Demo-*

cratic Freedoms (Aldershot, UK: Ashgate, 2006); see also Sidney Tarrow, *The New Transnational Activism* (Cambridge: Cambridge University Press, 2005).

81. Marsha Pripstein Posusney and Eleanor Abdella Doumato, "Introduction: The Mixed Blessing of Globalization," in Eleanor Abdella Doumato and Marsha Pripstein Posusney, eds., *Women and Globalization in the Arab Middle East: Gender, Economy, and Society* (Boulder, Colo.: Lynne Rienner, 2003), p. 9.

82. For further information on this, see Hinnebusch, "The Politics of Identity."

83. Timothy C. Lim, *Doing Comparing Politics: An Introduction to Approaches and Issues* (Boulder, Colo.: Lynne Rienner, 2006), pp. 285–86.

84. Amr Hamzawy, "Globalization and Human Rights: On a Current Debate among Arab Intellectuals," in Anthony Chase and Amr Hamzawy, eds., *Human Rights in the Arab World: Independent Voices* (Philadelphia: University of Pennsylvania Press, 2006), pp. 51–63.

85. Ibid., p. 63.

86. Anthony Chase and Amr Hamzawy, eds., *Human Rights in the Arab World: Independent Voices* (Philadelphia: University of Pennsylvania Press, 2006).

87. Mehran Kamrava, "Introduction: Reformist Islam in Comparative Perspective," in Mehran Kamrava, ed., *The New Voices of Islam: Rethinking Politics and Modernity* (Berkeley: University of California Press, 2006), pp. 1–27, esp. p. 24.

88. Shirin Ebadi, "Human Rights Embody the Fundamental Values of Human Civilizations," in UNDP, *Human Development Report 2004: Cultural Liberty in Today's Diverse World* (New York: UNDP, 2004), p. 23.

89. Quoted in Salbiah Ahmad, "Islam in Malaysia: Constitutional and Human Rights Perspectives," in Mashood Baderin, Mahmood Monshipouri, Lynn Welchman, and Shadi Mokhtari, eds., *Islam and Human Rights: Advocacy for Social Change in Local Contexts* (New Delhi: Global Media Publications, 2006), pp. 179–225, esp. p. 205.

90. Henry Munson, "Lifting the Veil: Understanding the Roots of Islamic Militancy," in Mir Zohair Husain, *Global Studies: Islam and the Muslim World* (Dubuque, Iowa: McGraw-Hill/Contemporary Learning Series, 2006), pp. 323–25.

Glossary

Ahl-ak-Kitab: People of the Book.

Ahmadis: An offshoot of Sunni Islam that was founded by Mirza Ghulam Ahmad (1837–1908), who was born in a village in the Indian Punjab called Qadian. While they enjoy the right of self-identification and other freedoms in India, Ahmadis in Pakistan are denied such rights.

Alawite: An offshoot of the Twelver Shiite sect that glorifies Ali ibn Abu Talib by considering him an incarnation of divinity.

Allah: The Arabic/Islamic term for God.

Ansar: Plural of *naseer*, which means helper or supporter.

Asharite: Follower of the Iraqi-born *alim* Abul Hassan al-Ashari (873–935), who spearheaded a traditional Islamic movement. Abbasid rulers (833–942) used al-Ashari's theological arguments to marginalize the liberal rationalism of the Mutazilites and safeguard the authenticity of Islamic movements and dynamics.

ayatollah: A revered Shiite theologian and jurist who studies and interprets God's directives embodied in the Qur'an. The term literally means the "sign of Allah."

Bahais: Followers of the Bahai faith, a religion founded by Baha'ulllah in nineteenth-century Persia, emphasizing the spiritual unity of all humankind. There are an estimated five to six million Bahais around the world in more than two hundred countries and territories.

Baath: The term literally means "rebirth or renaissance." In Iraq and Syria, it refers to an ideology that emphasizes secular nationalism, pan-Arabism, Arab socialism, and anti-Western imperialism.

basiji: Literally, "mobilization." In Iran, "basiji" refers to the Islamic Revolutionary Guards.

bay'a: A pledge, pact, or social contract between the rulers and the ruled.

bazaar: Market or marketplace. The term "bazzaris" typically refers to the merchants and craftsman who work in a bazaar.

burqa: A head-to-toe covering worn by Muslim women. It has a mesh grid over the eyes. This form of veil is prevalent in such conservative Muslim societies as Afghanistan.

caliphate: Both the rule by a khalifah (caliph) under Islamic rule and the office or jurisdiction of a caliph. The last caliphate was held by Ottoman Turkish sultans until it was abolished by Kemal Atatürk in 1924.

dhimmis: Non-Muslims (mostly Christians and Jews) living in Muslim countries who were granted freedom of worship and government protection. Dhimmis paid no *zakat* (Islamic tax), but paid *jizya* (poll tax) for state protection.

Faqih: An expert in Islamic jurisprudence.

Fiqh: Islamic jurisprudence covering all aspects of religious, socioeconomic, and political life.

fitna: Civil disorder within the Muslim community or between Muslims.

hadd: Punishment prescribed by the shari'a (Islamic law) for crimes.

Hadith: Prophet Mohammad's recorded sayings and statements that were memorized or written down by members of his family and close companions.

hajj: Literally, "pilgrimage." Adult Muslims are required to engage in the formal ritual of pilgrimage to Mecca, Islam's holiest city.

Hanafis: Sunni Muslims who follow the teachings of the Iraqi-born imam Abu Hanifa al-Nu'man inb-Thabit (699–769). The Hanafi sect was promoted by a number of Abbasid and Ottoman rulers and is widely prevalent in Turkey, Afghanistan, Egypt, Central Asia, China, and South Asia.

Hanbalis: Sunni Muslims who follow the teachings of the Iraqi-born theologian and jurist Ahmad ibn-Hanbal (780–855). Hanbalis are concentrated in Saudi Arabia and Qatar.

hijab: The veil (proper Islamic dress) or headscarf worn by Muslim women when they are in public.

Hizbollah: Literally, "Party of Allah." The term refers to Shiite groups or factions, especially in Iran and Lebanon.

ijma: The consensus reached by Islamic jurists and scholars inside and outside the Muslim community.

ijtihad: Independent reasoning and judgment, implying independent interpretation or reinterpretation of Islamic laws.

Ikwan al-Muslimun: The Muslim Brotherhood. Hassan al-Banna founded an Islamic political party called the Muslim Brotherhood in Egypt in 1928. Over the years, the Islamic party has spread and won over many supporters throughout the Muslim world.

Infitah: Literally, "opening up." Market and economic liberalization associated with Egypt's President Muhammad Anwar al-Sadat, who attempted an open-door policy and adoption of a free-enterprise economy during the 1970s.

Intifada: A social uprising in the occupied territories. Specifically, it refers to the revolt by young Palestinians against the occupying Israeli forces on December 9, 1987, and later on September 28, 2000. Intifada has become the symbol of internal Palestinian uprisings against Israeli soldiers.

Islam: Literally, "submission" or "surrender."

Islamism: The phenomenon of Islamic revivalism transpiring across the Muslim world and beyond.

jihad: Struggle. The term basically refers to efforts by individuals to reform bad habits or shortcomings in the practice of the faith, either within themselves or in the larger Islamic community. On a broader level, it refers to war waged in the defense of Islam.

Kemalists: Supporters of the secular principles of Kemal Atatürk, the founder of modern Turkey. His reforms represented a political revolution, a change from the multinational Ottoman Empire to the establishment of the nation-state of Turkey and the realization of national identity for modern Turkey. Kemalists believe that it is the republican regime that can best represent the wishes of the people. In recent years, the relations between Kemalists and Islamists in Turkey have become contentious, as the Islamist Justice and Development Party (AKP) has gained the support of the majority of the Turkish people.

Malikis: Sunni Muslims who follow the Islamic legal interpretation of the jurist Abu Allah Malik ibn-Anas (716–95). The Maliki sect spread in Muslim Spain and Africa.

millet: A religious community under the Ottoman Empire (1820–1923), usually used for the *dhimmis* (non-Muslims), who enjoyed some measure of autonomy under the Ottomans.

mujahideen: Muslims who fight in a jihad. Generically the term refers to "freedom fighters." With logistical, financial, and ideological support from both Muslim countries and the Western world, mujahideen were instrumental in driving Russian troops out of Afghanistan in the late 1980s.

Mutazilites: Followers of a school of Islamic theologians and jurists advocating rationalism and free will. The Mutazilites, who influenced the intellectual setting of the eighth and ninth centuries, tended to be a minority intellectual force of their time.

Orientalism: A system of representations framed by political forces that brought the Orient into Western learning, Western consciousness, and Western empire. The Orient exists for the West and is constructed by and in relation to the West. It is based on the image of what is inferior and alien ("other") to the West. Orientalism is a manner of regularized writing, vision, and study, dominated by ideological biases and perspectives particularly suited to the Orient. It is the image of the Orient expressed as an entire system of thought and scholarship. Edward Said's assessment and critique of the set of beliefs known as Orientalism form an important background for postcolonial studies. His work (*Orientalism*, 1978) highlights the inaccuracies of a multitude of assumptions as it questions various paradigms of thought that are accepted on individual, academic, and political levels.

qiyas: Literally, "analogical reasoning." This reasoning is used by Islamic jurists to arrive at an Islamic solution in situations that are covered in the Qur'an and the *Sunnah*.

Qur'an: Muslims' holy book.

Ramadan: The holy month in which God revealed the Qur'an to Prophet Mohammad through the agency of Archangel Gabriel. It is observed with fasting.

Salafis: Those who closely emulate the pious companions of Prophet Mohammad. Two Egyptian modernist Islamic intellectuals, Muhammad Abduh (1849–1905) and Muhammad Rashid Rida (1865–1935), called their mission to reform Islam "the Salafiyyah movement."

Saidis: Members of an ethnic group who inhabit what is termed the middle Nile Valley—roughly the area from Cairo to Aswan. Though the Saidis as a group tend to be more culturally conservative than other Egyptian groups, they are ethnically similar to lower Egyptians.

Shafi'is: Those who follow the teachings of Muhammad ibn Idris ash-Shafi'i (767–820), who tried to reconcile the Maliki and Hanbali schools of Islamic jurisprudence.

shari'a: Islamic law that governs the individual and the community of Muslims.

Shiites: Literally, "followers" or "partisans" of Imam Ali. They believe that only the heirs of the fourth caliph, Ali ibn-i-Abu Talib, are the legitimate successors of Mohammad. Shiite Muslims are concentrated in Iran, Iraq, and Lebanon and believe that they suffered the loss of divinely guided political leadership at the time of the Twelfth Imam's disappearance. It is believed that the Twelfth Imam disappeared in 874. His followers, who have adopted the name Twelvers, believe that God rescued him, that he went in occultation soon after, and that he will return as a messiah to restore peace and justice in the world. Not until the ascendancy of Ayatollah Ruhollah Khomeini in 1978 did they believe that they had once again begun to live under the authority of a legitimate religious figure. They, like the Sunnis, believe in the fundamentals of Islam.

shura: Literally, "consultation." It generally refers to a group, assembly, or council of knowledgeable and pious Muslims who are consulted by leaders.

Sufis: Early Muslim ascetics and pious mystics who wore simple clothes made out of *suf* (coarse wool). Sufis devoted their lives to mediation and proselytization. They emphasize the spirit—not the literal interpretation—of the Qur'an and the *Sunnah* and a search for eternal truth and goodness.

sultanate: The office of and territory ruled by a sultan under the Ottoman Empire.

Sunni: Refers to the majority Islamic sect, whose members follow the *Sunnah,* or "the way, the path, or the road shown by Prophet Mohammad."

Taliban: Generally, students or graduates of a *madrasah* (religious school). Specifically, the Revolutionary Islamic Afghan regime (made up of Pashtuns) that ruled Afghanistan from 1996 to the end of 2001, when they were toppled by the U.S. invasion of Afghanistan—an invasion that was precipitated by the attacks on the United States on September 11, 2001.

umma: The community of Muslims at the local, national, regional, and even global levels. Some historians argue that the most powerful competing alternative to the notion of a secular Arab nation was the concept of a united Muslim community. Islam was a broader entity than pan-Arabism because it did not differentiate between Arab and non-Arabs. The Muslim *umma* was a unity in which ethnicity played no part.

Velayat-i-Faqih: "Government of the Islamic jurist." In Iran, this term refers to the position of the Supreme Leader, who is the guardian of the Islamic state.

Wahhabis: Followers of Muhammad inb Abd al-Wahhab (1703–92). Today, Wahhabis are known as revolutionary Islamists who revert to the Qur'an and *Sunnah* to establish an Islamic state based on the shari'a and classical Islamic principles. Wahhabis are known to be engaged in a perpetual personal jihad to improve their genuine faith and internal representation and struggles.

zakat: Alms for the poor. Muslims are enjoined by their faith to donate 2.5 percent of their wealth to the poor or to charitable institutions.

Index

Abbassgholizadeh, Mahboobeh, 57, 175
Abdul, Muhammad, 85
Abdul Hadi, Sayyid Shaykh, 198
Abdullah, King, 10; secular leaders, 35
Abshar-Abdallah, Ulil, 201
Abu Ghraib, 21, 102, 104, 119
Abulbari, Qayamud-Din, 29
Abu Zeid, Hikmat, 89
adat, 53
adhan (ritual call to prayer), 228
Al-Afghani, Sayyid Jamal al-Din, 33, 85
Afnan, Bedia, 41
Ahmadinejad, Mahmoud, 178–91, 182–86, 188–91, 246
Ahmed, Begum Aziz, 41
Aleviler, 153–55
allochtonen (immigrants in the Netherlands), 226
Amara, Mohamed, 86
Amin, Hussein Ahmad, 68
apostasy, 29
Arabic Network for Human Rights Information (ANHRI), 88
Arab identity, 101
Arab-Israeli war, 12
Arkoun, Mohammed, 68
Al-Ashmawi, Muhammed Said, 87
Asian currency crisis, 203, 205, 210, 214
Ausländer, 229
Atatürk, Mustafa Kemal, 141, 252, 253
Ayoub, Mahmoud M., 27
Azimal, Parnaz, 187

Al-Banna, Hasan, 30; Egyptian politics, 77, 85, 92, 198
Barelvi, Ahmad Raza Khan, 29
Baroody, Jamil, 41
Barzani, Massoud, 113, 157
Basma, Princess, 60
baya, 32

Bâyar, Celal, 142
Bedouins, 125
Bermek, Dogan, 154
Bhutto, Ali Zulifkar, 10; gender rights, 58; human rights, 35
Bhutto, Benazir, 244
Bin Zayid, Sheik Abdullah, 132
Al Bishry, Tareq, 85
Blackwater, 106
bonyads, 184
Bourguiba, Habib, 49
Brandt, Willy, 229
Bulac, Ali, 142, 161
Bush, George W.: democracy promotion, ix; Iranian politics, 182–87; Iraqi politics, 100–105

Caldwell, Christopher, 231
cartoon controversy, 234–37
Chackchouk, Mohammed, 41
Çiler, Tansu, 143
Convention against Torture and Other Cruel, Inhuman or Degrading Treatment or Punishment, Iranian politics, 179
Convention on the Elimination of All Forms of Discrimination against Women (CEDAW), 69
Convention on the Rights of the Child, 42
cultural politics, 55; and cultural identity, 69; and Iranian politics, 179

Dagi, Ihsan, 150, 161
Dahlab v. Switzerland, 240, 256
Dahlan, Ahmad, 197
de-Baathification, 102
democratic transition, 114–18; democratization and human rights in Turkey, 159
dhimmis, 27
diasporic Muslims, 224
diyah (blood money), 58, 175, 177

Al-e-Ahmad, Jalal, 167
Ebadi, Shirin, 34–35, 176, 187, 299
El-Erian, Abdullah, 41
Emiratis, 136–38
Emiratization, 127, 129
Enlightenment, 26, 44
Erbakan, Necmettin, 10; Turkish politics, 143, 148, 150, 163
Erdoğan, Recept Tayyip, 148, 150, 157–63, 252
Al-Eryan, Essam, 96
Esfandiari, Haleh, 187
Esposito, John L., 48, 167
European Convention of Human Rights (ECHR), 240–41, 256
European Union, 19; EU-Turkey relations, 157–60
expatriates, 127, 129, 135, 138

Faddallah, Sayyed Mohammed Hussein, 30
Falk, Richard, 25
Family Protection Law of 1967 in Iran, 56
Fansuri, Hamzah, 197
Farhat, Muhammad Nur, 87
fitra, 31
Foda, Farag, 87, 93
Fortuyn, Pim, 277
French Islam (Islam Français), 258
Fukuyama, Francis, 255
Fuller, Graham E., 101

Gasparo, Balbi, 122
gastarbeiter, 221, 229; Turkish guest workers in Germany, 229
Al-Ghannouchi, Sheikh Rashid, 33
Al-Ghazaly, Zeinab, 89
Al-Ghazzaly, Muhammad, 85
Golkar, 201
Gul, Abdullah, 148, 151–52, 159
Gülen, Fethullah, 145

Habermas, Jürgen, 43
Habibie, Dr. B. J., 195, 204–5, 209
Haji Ali, Wan Mustapha bin, 41
halal, 228
Hamas, 14, 39
Al-Hasan, Mahmud, 29
Hashemi Rafsanjani, Ali Akbar, 168
Hassan, Ahmad, 197
Hassan, Prince, 60
Hassan, Rifat, 58
Hendraningrat, Abdul Latif, 41

hijab (headscarf), 6, 35, 36, 56, 133, 228–29, 245, 256–57; in Europe, 228–29, 233, 240–41; gender, identity, and negotiating rights, 47; the headscarf issue in Turkey, 151–53; Hizb al-Da'wa al-Islamiyya, 109, 250; in Indonesia, 201; in Iran, 174; in Malaysia, 53; in Saudi Arabia, 62
Hizbollah, 39, 149
Hizb ut-Tahrir, 236–37
Hussein, Adel, 86
Hussein, Ali, 107
Hussein, King, 10
Hussein, Magdi, 86
Hussein, Saddam, 103–5, 111, 114, 117–19; secular leader, 35
Huwaidy, Fahmy, 85
hybridized political identity, 222

Ibrahim, Anwar, 252
identity politics, 180, 202–3, 212, 214, 243, 255
Ignatieff, Michael, 25, 186, 188
ijma, 32
ijtihad, 29, 32, 67, 261
Ikatan Cendekiawan Muslim Se-Indonesia (ICMI; the Indonesian Association of Muslim Intellectuals), 214
Ikramullah, Shaista, 41
Imdadullah, Haji, 29
Indonesian Association of Muslim Intellectuals (ICMI), 213–14
Indonesian Women's Congress, 208
Inönü, Ismet, 141
International Covenant on Civil and Political Rights (ICCPR), 42, 241
International Covenant on Economic and Social Rights (ICESR), 42
interstitial identity ("third-space"), 222
Intifidah, 14, 245
Iqbal, Muhammad, 198
Islamic conservatives, 28–29, 247–48
Islamic feminism, 47, 50, 51, 56, 259; in Egypt, 90; in Iran, 176–77; Iranian politics, 179; in Turkey, 153
Islamic identity, 139, 147, 165–66, 170, 217, 225, 229, 238, 240, 243, 245–47, 260–61; and Arabism, 252; French politics, 234; national/Islamic identity, 262
Islamic neoconservatives, 29–31
Islamic reformists, 31–33, 180–81

Islamism, 20
Islamophobia, 217, 225

Jahangir, Asma, 59
Al-Jama'a al-Islamiyya, 82
Jemmah Islamiyah, 212–13
jihadi *madrasas*, 15
jihadis, 22
Justice and Development Party (Adalet ve Kalkinma Partisi; AKP), 143–63, 252; Morocco's Party of Justice and Development, 50
Jylland-Posten, 234

Kadivar, Mohsen, 68
Kar, Mehrangis, 56
Karim Amrullah, Haji Abdul Malik (Hamka), 198
Kavakc, Merve, 153
Kayaly, Abdul, 41
Kebangsaan Muslim, 198
Kemalism, 139, 253
Kepel, Gilles, 106, 239
Khamenei, Ayatollah Sayyed Ali, 170, 298
Khan, Ayub, 58
Khan, M. A. Muqtedar, 32, 68
Khatami, Mohammad, xiii; gender rights, 52; Iranian politics, 169–71, 173–75, 179, 183–85, 189–90; Islamic philosophy, 33
Khomeini, Ayatollah Ruhollah, 15; Iranian politics, 165, 168, 183, 235
Kiran, Abdeilela bin, 50
Kohut, Andrew, 257
Koolae, Elahe, 175
Kurdish identity, 155–56
Kurdish Workers Party (PKK), 155
Kurds, 3, 100–120; Kurdish minority, 101; the Kurdish problem, 155–57, 163; revival of ethnonationalism, 113–14
Kutan, Recai, 148, 162

Lakar Jihad, 201, 202, 212
Luxor Massacre, 93

Madjid, Nurcholish, 198
Magd, Kamal Abu, 85
Maghreb, xiii
Mahdi Army, 110
Majles, in Iran, 168, 181–82
Al-Maktoum, Sheikh Mohammad bin Rashid, 130, 134, 137

Malek, Anwar Adel, 86
Al-Maliki, Nouri, 106, 112
Mandaville, Peter, 1, 222, 224
Masjumi Party, 199
Mawdudi, Sayyid Abu al Ala, 77, 198
Menderes, Adnan, 150
Mernissi, Fatima, 28
Milani, Tahmineh, 175
Millet System, 27, 141
Miltan-Edwards, Beverley, 13
Mir-Hosseini, Ziba, 32
Moghadam, Valentine, 63, 299
Mohammed, Mahatir bin, 252
Mohammed VI, King, 50
Moussavian, Hossuein, 187
Mubarak, Husni, 74, 86, 92, 93
Mufti, Jawaat, 41
Muhammadiyah, 201, 212–13, 215
mujahideen, 15, 115
multiculturalism, 218, 235, 241, 255–56; threatened by multiculturalism, 236
Musharraf, Pervez, 10, 35
Muslim Brotherhood (Ikhwan), 39, 57, 64, 74, 77, 80, 82–99, 111, 250; dissolved by government, 92; earthquake in Egypt, 93–94; the most formidable challenge to the Waft, 91; political alliance between the Sadat regime and the Muslim Brotherhood, 89; Sayyid Qutb, 78
Muslim secularist, 33–35
Muslim Student Society (MSS), 228; the construction of Muslim identity in Norway, 228
Muslim Youth of Norway (NMU), 228
Muzaffar, Chandra, 33, 68

Nahdlatul Ulama (NU), 193, 201, 206, 211–13, 215, 250
Al-Nahyan, Sheikh Zayid, 126
An-Na'im, Abdullahi Ahmed, 261
Nasr, Vali, 100, 108, 110
Nasrallah, Hassan, 243
Nasser, Gamal Abdel, 74, 252
Nathan, Andrew J., 44
National Awakening Party (PKB), 201
National Mandate Party (PAN), 201, 212
Natsir, Mohammad, 197
neofundamentalists, Iranian politics, 180–81, 248–51
neopatrimonial government, 126, 138

New Order, 200, 204, 208
NGOs, 55, 64; empowering Bangladeshi women, 66
Nursi, Said, 145

Ocalan, Abdullah, 155–56
Oktar, Sheikh Adnan, 145
Omar, Mullah, 15
Organization of the Islamic Conference (OIC), 42
Oslo accords, 14
Özal, Turgut, 142, 144
Ozdenoren, Rasim, 142

Pahlavi, Mohammad Reza Shah, 165–68, 174, 178; conclusion, 252; Pahlavi dynasty, 56
Palestine, 245; Palestinian Liberation Organization, 14
pan-Arabism, 104–5, 253
Pancasila, 200, 206, 209, 213–16
Partai Nasional Indonesia (PNI; Indonesian National Party), 197
Partai Persatuan Pembangunan (PPP), 200
Paya, Ali, 31
Pazhwak, Abdul Rahman, 41
People's Consultative Assembly, 212
Personal Status Law (PSL), 68
populism, 165–66, 178, 186, 191; and Islamism, social justice, and equality, 179
private security companies, 106; Blackwater, 106; private military firms, 106
Prophet Mohammad, 11; cartoon controversy, 235; Indonesian politics, 212; Iraqi politics, 107

Qaddafi, Moammar, 10
Al-Qaeda, 15, 18, 30, 203; European politics, 237; Iraqi politics, 100–107, 111, 115, 118; Islamic philosophy, 31; Turkish politics, 159
qalb, 31
Al-Qaradawy, Yusuf, 85
Qazim, Safinaz, 86
qisas (retribution), 58
Qutb, Sayyid, 77, 84, 198

Al-Rahman, Sheik Uma Abd, 248
Rais, Amieu, 212
Ramadan, Tariq, 234
reformists, Iranian politics, 180–81, 251–52
rentier state, 182–83
Rida, Muhammad Rashida, 33

Risse, Thomas, 4
Rouleau, Eric, 174
Roy, Olivier, 172, 225, 233, 258
Rushdie, Salman, 168; European politics, 235

Sachedina, Abdulaziz A., 31, 68
Al-Sadat, Muhammad Anwar, 10; Egyptian politics, 74, 80, 91, 99; human rights, 35
Al-Sadr, Ayatollah Muhammad Baqir, 109
al-Sadr, Muqtada, 106, 109
Al-Said, Karim, 89
Salafism, 29; human rights, 29; Iraqi politics, 111; Islamic philosophy, 31; Salafis, 17
Sarekat Islam (SI), 197
Sarkozy, Nicolas, 231
The Satanic Verses, 235; Salman Rushdie affair, 235
secular feminism, 47, 51, 259; in Turkey, 56
secularization, 8–10, 13; defending modernization by secular nationalists, 58; Muslim secularists, 253; secular governments, 254; and secularism, 8–10, 87, 140, 142, 147, 240–41; secularists, 252–54; secular nationalism, 253; in Turkey, 154; Turkish secularism and nationalism, 155, 161
September 11, 2001, 2, 10
sexual politics, 55
Shahin, Abd Al-Sabur, Egyptian politics, 82
Sharawi, Shaykh, 82, 89
shari'a, 27–28, 30, 31, 32 , 34, 85–86, 129, 135, 201, 211–16; in Indonesia, 210, 216; in Pakistan, 58; in post-Saddam Iraq, 50; pro-shari'a parties, 201; secular-oriented women's movements and shari'a, 87; Sudanese women, 59; target of attacks by the secularists, 85; in Turkey, 141, 153
Shariati, Ali, 33, 167, 198; Iranian politics, 178
Shariatmadari, Sayyid Kazem, 29
Sharif, Nawaz, 252
Sharon, Ariel, 14
Shiites, 100–120; identities and networks, 108; political resurgence, 107–10; sectarian tensions, 100; Shiism and nationalism, 110; Shiite Islam, 167; Shiite religious identity, 167; Shiite-Sunni divide, 101; Twelver Shiism, 167
shura, 32
Sikkink, Kathryn, 4
al-Sistani, Grand Ayatollah ali al-Husayni, 109

socialization, 4
Soroush, Abdolkarim, 33; fundamentalist interpretation of, 71; male jurists in Iran, 65, 67
state feminism, 53, 60–63, 208
Sufism, 197; Sufi mysticism and Sufi orders, 197
Suharto, 193–94, 205–9, 214, 216
Sukarno, 192–94, 204–8
Sukarnoputri, Megawati, 196, 205–6, 209, 211, 214
Sunnis, 100–120; Sunni Arab minority, 103; Sunni-Shia divide, 107–13, 246
Supreme Council for Islamic Revolution in Iraq (SCIRI), 109

Tablighis Jama'at, 16, 254
Al-Tahtawi, Rifa'ah, 33
Tajzadeh, Mostapha, 175–76
Taliban, 15, 18; gender rights, 64; human rights, 30; Talibanization of politics, 23
Tamini, Azzam, 86
taqlid, 29
Tholib, Al-Ustaz, 212
Al-Tilimsani, Umar, Egyptian politics, 77
Tohidi, Nayereh, 176
torture, 104; outsourcing, 104
translocality, 222, 248; identities, 254; Western translocalities, 224
transnational feminist networks (TFNs), 54
transnational identity, 240; ties, interests, and identities, 262
transnational Islam, 222
trans-state identities, 102
tsunami disaster, 206–7
Tunisian Code of Personal Status (CPS), 49–50
Turabi, Bashir, 18
Al-Turabi, Hassan, 30
Turco-Islamic synthesis, 144

ulama, 30, 107, 137, 180, 247–48
ul-Haq, General Zia, 10, 49
umma, 39, 218, 225, 240
Universal Declaration of Human Rights (UDHR), 29, 31; social construction of, 40–42
Universal Islamic Declaration of Human Rights (UIDHR; *also called* Cairo Islamic Human Rights Declaration), 31, 42, 177

van Gogh, Theo, 227; the call to fight blasphemy, 227
velvet revolution, 187
Voll, John O., 46

Al-Wa, Selim, 85
Wahhabism, 29; human rights, 29; Iraqi politics, 111; Wahhabi Salafism, 202; Wahhabist, 10, 17
Wahid, Abdurahman, 195, 198, 205–6, 209, 211, 214
Waltz, Susan, 40
Warzazi, Halima Embarek, 41
Wassat Party (Wassateyya), 84–85
Westoxification, 167
Women Living under Muslim Law (WLUML), 54, 259
women's rights, 55, 57, 65, 71, 206, 258–60; and gender identity, 55; in Iran, 169, 174

Yavuz, M. Hakan, 147
Yudhoyono, Susilo Bambang, 206, 209–10, 214

Zakaria, Fareed, 207
Zakariya, Fuad, 87
Al-Zarqawi, Abu Musab, Iraqi politics, 111

Acknowledgments

Many individuals and offices have assisted in the research and writing of this book. Mr. Raouf Mashayekh and Mrs. Taraneh Larijani were generous with their time and ideas in Dubai, arranging several meetings and interviews for me in the United Arab Emirates. Professor Zehra Arat, of SUNY-Purchase, helped me enormously in my trip to Turkey by setting up several interviews and contacts with scholars in the field of international relations and several NGOs in Istanbul and Ankara. I benefited immensely from interviews with Professor Ihsan Dagi, of the Middle Eastern Technical University in Ankara, Turkey, who also made it possible for me to contact human rights NGOs in Ankara. Professor Mohammad Elahee, visiting professor at the Sadat Academy for Management Sciences in Cairo, Egypt, helped me immensely in my travel to Egypt.

I benefited from interviews with Professors Mona El Baradei and Mostafa Elwi Saif at Cairo University and Professors Dan Tschirgi and Tarek Selim at the American University in Cairo. In Iran, I profited from discussions with Professors Mehdi Zakerian, Hossein Daheshiar, and Mahmoud Sariulghalam at the Center for Scientific Research and Middle East Strategic Studies, Tehran. Contacts with Mr. Alireza Taheri, the director of the Organization for Defending Victims of Violence (ODVV), a reputable and active NGO, were enormously helpful. My research assistant, Mr. Ahmad Taghizadeh, proved to be a great asset to me during my stay in Tehran.

I am especially grateful to Professor Sean Duffy, of Quinnipiac University, whose insights into the identity perspective were valuable to me and whose comments on the draft manuscript in its entirety were immensely helpful. I would also like to gratefully acknowledge comments made by Ms. Erin Goldin and Professor Dreama G. Moon of California State University–San Marcos; Professor Chris Bettinger and Professor Margaret Leahy from the College of Behavioral and Social Science at San Francisco State University; and Suzanne Levi-Sanchez of Rutgers University. I would like to express my deep gratitude to Dr. Burnet Davis, who kindly read the entire manuscript and offered valuable suggestions. Mr. Tomá Furmánek, of Behavioral and Social Science Computing at San Francisco State University, graciously assisted me in reviewing the copyedited computer files and making the needed revisions.

Finally, the generous financial support given to me by Quinnipiac University in recognition of having been selected the school's outstanding faculty scholar of the year in 2004 made it possible for me to travel to Iran, the United Arab Emirates, and Turkey during the spring of 2005. In preparing my short glossary, I was largely informed by Professor Mir Zohair Husain, *Global Islamic Politics,* 2nd ed. (New York: Longman, 2003). The ultimate responsibility for the accuracy and academic merit of this manuscript remains mine.